ACCA

CORPORATE AND BUSINESS LAW (LW) (ENG)

STUDY TEXT

FOR EXAMS FROM 1 SEPTEMBER 2018 TO 31 AUGUST 2019

BPP LEARNING MEDIA

First edition 2007
Eleventh edition January 2018

ISBN 9781 5097 1675 3
(Previous ISBN 9781 5097 0850 5)

e-ISBN 9781 5097 1705 7
(Previous e-ISBN 9781 5097 0980 9)

British Library Cataloguing-in-Publication Data

A catalogue record for this book is available from the British Library

Published by

BPP Learning Media Ltd
BPP House, Aldine Place
142–144 Uxbridge Road
London W12 8AA

www.bpp.com/learningmedia

Printed in the United Kingdom

Your learning materials, published by BPP Learning Media Ltd, are printed on paper obtained from traceable sustainable sources.

We are grateful to the Association of Chartered Certified Accountants for permission to reproduce past examination questions. The suggested solutions in the practice answer bank have been prepared by BPP Learning Media, unless otherwise stated.

A note about copyright

Dear Customer

What does the little © mean and why does it matter?

Your market-leading BPP books, course materials and e-learning materials do not write and update themselves. People write them on their own behalf or as employees of an organisation that invests in this activity. Copyright law protects their livelihoods. It does so by creating rights over the use of the content.

Breach of copyright is a form of theft – as well as being a criminal offence in some jurisdictions, it is potentially a serious breach of professional ethics.

With current technology, things might seem a bit hazy but, basically, without the express permission of BPP Learning Media:

- Photocopying our materials is a breach of copyright

- Scanning, ripcasting or conversion of our digital materials into different file formats, uploading them to facebook or emailing them to your friends is a breach of copyright

You can, of course, sell your books, in the form in which you have bought them – once you have finished with them. (Is this fair to your fellow students? We update for a reason.) Please note the e-products are sold on a single user licence basis: we do not supply 'unlock' codes to people who have bought them secondhand.

And what about outside the UK? BPP Learning Media strives to make our materials available at prices students can afford by local printing arrangements, pricing policies and partnerships which are clearly listed on our website. A tiny minority ignore this and indulge in criminal activity by illegally photocopying our material or supporting organisations that do. If they act illegally and unethically in one area, can you really trust them?

BPP
LEARNING MEDIA

Contents

Page

Introduction

Helping you to pass   v
Studying Corporate and Business Law (LW)   vii
The exam   x

Part A Essential elements of the legal system

1   Law and the legal system   3
2   Sources of law   17

Part B The law of obligations

3   Formation of contract I   37
4   Formation of contract II   55
5   Content of contracts   73
6   Breach of contract and remedies   89
7   The law of torts and professional negligence   105

Part C Employment law

8   Contract of employment   125
9   Dismissal and redundancy   143

Part D The formation and constitution of business organisations

10   Agency law   161
11   Partnerships   171
12   Corporations and legal personality   181
13   Company formation   201
14   Constitution of a company   217

Part E Capital and the financing of companies

15   Share capital   235
16   Loan capital   251
17   Capital maintenance and dividend law   265

Part F Management, administration and the regulation of companies

18   Company directors   277
19   Other company officers   303
20   Company meetings and resolutions   313

Part G Insolvency law

21   Insolvency and administration   331

Part H Corporate fraudulent and criminal behaviour

22   Fraudulent and criminal behaviour   351

Practice question bank   369

Practice answer bank   383

Bibliography   393

Case bibliography   397

List of cases and index   405

Review form

Helping you to pass

BPP Learning Media – ACCA Approved Content Provider

As an ACCA **Approved Content Provider**, BPP Learning Media gives you the **opportunity** to use study materials reviewed by the ACCA examining team. By incorporating the examining team's comments and suggestions regarding the depth and breadth of syllabus coverage, the BPP Learning Media Study Text provides excellent, **ACCA-approved** support for your studies.

These materials are reviewed by the ACCA examining team. The objective of the review is to ensure that the material properly covers the syllabus and study guide outcomes, used by the examining team in setting the exams, in the appropriate breadth and depth. The review does not ensure that every eventuality, combination or application of examinable topics is addressed by the ACCA Approved Content. Nor does the review comprise a detailed technical check of the content as the Approved Content Provider has its own quality assurance processes in place in this respect.

The PER alert!

Before you can qualify as an ACCA member, you not only have to pass all your exams but also fulfil a three year **practical experience requirement** (PER). To help you to recognise areas of the syllabus that you might be able to apply in the workplace to achieve different performance objectives, we have introduced the '**PER alert**' feature. You will find this feature throughout the Study Text to remind you that what you are **learning to pass** your ACCA exams is **equally useful to the fulfilment of the PER requirement**.

Your achievement of the PER should be recorded in your online *My Experience* record.

Tackling studying

Studying can be a daunting prospect, particularly when you have lots of other commitments. The **different features** of the Study Text, the **purposes** of which are explained fully on the **Chapter features** page, will help you whilst studying and improve your chances of **exam success**.

Developing exam awareness

Our Study Texts are completely **focused** on helping you pass your exam.

Our advice on **Studying LW** outlines the **content** of the exam and the **necessary skills** you are expected to be able to demonstrate and any **brought forward knowledge** you are expected to have.

Exam focus points are included within the chapters to highlight when and how specific topics were examined, or how they might be examined in the future.

Testing what you can do

Testing yourself helps you develop the skills you need to pass the exam and also confirms that you can recall what you have learnt.

We include **Questions** – lots of them – both within chapters and in the **Practice Question Bank**, as well as **Quick Quizzes** at the end of each chapter to test your knowledge of the chapter content.

Chapter features

Each chapter contains a number of helpful features to guide you through each topic.

Topic list

Topic list	Syllabus reference

What you will be studying in this chapter and the relevant section numbers, together with ACCA syllabus references.

Introduction

Puts the chapter content in the context of the syllabus as a whole.

Study Guide

Links the chapter content with ACCA guidance.

Exam Guide

Highlights how examinable the chapter content is likely to be and the ways in which it could be examined.

FAST FORWARD

Summarises the content of main chapter headings, allowing you to preview and review each section easily.

Examples

Demonstrate how to apply key knowledge and techniques.

Key terms

Definitions of important concepts that can often earn you easy marks in exams.

Exam focus points

When and how specific topics were examined, or how they may be examined in the future.

Formula to learn

Formulae that are not given in the exam but which have to be learnt.

Gives you a useful indication of syllabus areas that closely relate to performance objectives in your Practical Experience Requirement (PER).

Question

Gives you essential practice of techniques covered in the chapter.

Chapter Roundup

A full list of the Fast Forwards included in the chapter, providing an easy source of review.

Quick Quiz

A quick test of your knowledge of the main topics in the chapter.

Practice Question Bank

Found at the back of the Study Text with more comprehensive chapter questions. Cross referenced for easy navigation.

Studying LW

The Corporate and Business Law (LW) exam examines a basic understanding of legal principles and their application. You may find the material a little different from what you are used to because there are virtually no numbers involved. All students should attempt as many exam standard questions as they can.

1 What LW is about

The main aims of the LW exam are:

- To develop knowledge and skills in the understanding of the general legal framework and of specific legal areas relating to business, but

- To recognise the need to seek further specialist legal advice where necessary

The exam is not designed to turn you into a legal expert. Instead you will be a well-informed professional accountant who appreciates the legal issues of doing business but who recognises the boundaries of their legal knowledge and therefore the point at which professional legal expertise must be sought. The sequence of the syllabus and study guide takes you through the main areas of what you need to know.

Essential elements of the legal system

In this part of the syllabus you are covering areas that underlie all the other areas, namely: what is law and how the UK legal system creates and administers it. The distinctions between criminal law and civil law, between common law and civil law and between public law and private law, are very important. Most of the exam is concerned with civil law, namely the law that sets out the rights and duties of persons in relation to each other. There are elements of criminal law in relation to companies, insolvency, insider dealing and money laundering, in addition to the topical area of human rights legislation.

Law of obligations

The syllabus clearly distinguishes two important types of obligation that individuals and businesses have.

Contract

When individuals or businesses make agreements, a legally binding contract may be formed. This exam focuses on the requirements that must be met for a contract to be binding on the parties, what valid contracts must contain, under which circumstances the contractual terms are breached and what remedies are available for the affected party.

Tort

All members of society have a duty not to harm others and this principle forms the basis of tort. The tort of negligence is highly topical and has an impact on individuals, businesses and professionals (such as accountants). It is important for you to understand how such a duty is formed, the circumstances that will cause a breach of that duty and if there are any defences to a breach that the perpetrator can call on.

Employment law

Employees and employers are bound to each other by an employment contact. It is important that you have a good understanding of the contents of such a contract. Both employers and their employees owe duties to each other and breach of these duties can result in legal action being taken.

Termination of employment can be fraught with danger for employers if it is not handled correctly. The terms of 'wrongful' and 'unfair' dismissal are used commonly in the media, but the causes and remedies are distinct and it is important for you to understand the difference.

Formation and constitution of business organisations

The syllabus is very concerned with the various legal forms through which business transactions may be conducted. It is important to distinguish initially between natural persons (human beings) and legal persons (including natural persons, but extending to some forms of partnership and, most significantly, companies). The law of agency underlies a substantial part of our study of business forms, since partners and directors can and sometimes do act as agents.

Capital and the financing of companies

Most trading companies are financed by a mix of share capital (provided by their owners) and loan capital (provided by third party lenders). Share capital may take a variety of forms, with each class of share having different rights within the company. However, the primary responsibility of the shareholder is to contribute funds to the company in accordance with the terms of the company's constitution and the shares which they own. The return of these funds to shareholders is restricted since they are seen as the 'creditors' buffer', that is the funds which are available to settle creditors' outstanding debts in preference to amounts due to shareholders. Hence there are detailed laws on 'capital maintenance'. These extend to how far companies may distribute accumulated retained earnings to their shareholders in the form of dividends or buyback of shares.

Loan capital is usually provided by lenders only if they can be assured of its repayment to them. If lenders supply funds in return for debentures in the company, they usually require security for their loan: the debenture is secured by means of a registered charge on particular or general assets of the company, which can (within limitations) be realised so that the loan is repaid.

Management, administration and regulation of companies

As an artificial legal person a company cannot manage itself. This is the role primarily of the company's directors, who owe duties to the company to manage it for the benefit of the company and thereby for the benefit of its owners, the shareholders. There are a great many legal rules which regulate the appointment, remuneration, disqualification, powers and duties of directors. These have grown up largely because of problems that frequently occur. Most of these can be said to arise from conflicts between directors' personal interests and their duties to act in the company's interest. Directors are termed officers of the company along with the company secretary. Many companies also have to have an auditor.

Directors come into immediate contact with shareholders via company meetings, and the resolutions that are passed at these meetings. There are, therefore, a plethora of legal rules on meetings and resolutions, designed to ensure that the company is taking decisions properly and in accordance with the legitimate interests of shareholders as a body.

Insolvency law

Not everything goes according to plan and frequently companies will encounter financial or other difficulties, or will even reach crisis point and find themselves insolvent. At this point all parties – shareholders, directors, lenders, customers, suppliers and employees – are in danger of losing out. There are procedures designed to protect struggling companies to give them a 'breathing space' while they resolve their issues. There are also rules for how a company which cannot be saved should be 'wound up', depending on whether or not the company has any funds left.

Corporate fraudulent and criminal behaviour

Finally the syllabus covers the situations where activities of directors and others have strayed into criminal behaviour. This often arises in the context of companies running out of money, but the law is also concerned with company insiders with superior knowledge benefiting from insider dealing, and crime in the form of money laundering.

2 What skills are required?

To pass the LW exam you will need to bring different professional attributes to bear.

First you need **technical knowledge**. There is a huge amount of technical content in the syllabus: case law, conventions, codes of practice and legislation. You need to learn this and be able to identify which parts of the knowledge you have are being called for in a particular question.

Second, you need to be able to **apply knowledge** to the scenarios that are presented in the last five questions on the exam. You are aiming to solve practical problems here.

3 How to improve your chances of passing

- There is no choice in this exam – all questions have to be answered. You must, therefore, study the **entire syllabus**; there are no short-cuts

- The first section of the exam consists of **45 Multiple Choice Questions** (MCQs) worth either one or two marks each. The total marks on offer in this section is 70. These will inevitably cover a wide range of the syllabus

- The second section of the exam consists of **5 Multiple Task Questions** (MTQs) worth 6 marks each. Each MTQ will be broken down into sub-questions. The total marks on offer in this section is 30. Each MTQ question will be based on a scenario and will require some application of your knowledge

- Practising questions under timed conditions is essential. BPP's **Practice & Revision Kit** contains questions on all areas of the syllabus

- Keep an eye out for **articles** as the **examining team** will use *Student Accountant* to communicate with students

- **Read journals** etc to pick up on ways in which real organisations apply the law and think about your own organisation if that is relevant

The exam

Format of the exam

The exam lasts two hours and is divided into two sections.

Section A consists of 45 MCQs, a mixture of one or two marks each. One mark MCQs will require you to choose one correct option from three, and two mark MCQs will require you to choose one correct option from four.

Section B consists of 5 MTQs containing a total of 6 marks each.

All questions are compulsory.

The exam will cover as much of the syllabus as possible.

Syllabus and Study Guide

The complete LW syllabus and study guide can be found by visiting the exam resource finder on the ACCA website: www.accaglobal.com/uk/en/student/exam-support-resources.html

P
A
R
T

A

Essential elements of the legal system

Law and the legal system

Topic list	Syllabus reference
1 What is law?	A1(a)
2 Types of law	A1(a)
3 The system of courts	A1(b)

Introduction

Welcome to your study of **corporate and business law**. In this chapter we set the scene and framework of the English legal system.

We start by **defining** what law is and why it is important to society. Our study continues by considering the **different types of law** that we have in the UK and how they have developed over time.

The chapter concludes with an analysis of the **criminal and civil court systems**.

Study guide

		Intellectual level
A	**Essential elements of the legal system**	
1	**Law and the legal system**	
(a)	Define law and distinguish types of law	1
(b)	Explain the structure and operation of the courts	1

Exam guide

The nature of law and the operation of the legal system form a basis for your later studies but will also be examined as a topic all by itself.

1 What is law?

Law is the enforceable body of rules that govern any society.

Human society has developed over thousands of years from a primitive culture where the very survival of the species was at stake to the complex, diverse and dominating species that humans are today.

Much of the success of this development can be attributable to **rules** and **regulations** laid down by society. With a little further study the need for such rules becomes clear. In the early days of human existence, **survival** was achieved by working as a group. There was a fine line between **life** and **death**, for example the **stealing** of food from another group member could eventually result in starvation or death of the victim.

Social order, created by rules, is at the foundation of the society that we see today. The framework that was created influences how **individuals interact** and how **businesses** operate. In other words, it provides social control.

The framework of social control can be viewed as having two aspects:

* **Formal** control mechanisms
* **Informal** control mechanisms

Law is a formal control mechanism. It provides a **structure** for dealing with and resolving disputes that may arise, as well as providing some **deterrent** to those wishing to disrupt social order.

Informal mechanisms include **ethical** and **moral guidance**. These are 'norms' or behavioural expectations that society has developed over time through its culture. Such mechanisms have **little formal structure** to organise, control or to punish – such matters are dealt with informally by pressure from other individuals or groups.

PO1 requires you to 'act diligently and honestly, following codes of conduct, giving due regard to, and keeping up to date with, relevant legislation'.

The contents of this Study Text should help you identify legal and regulatory compliance requirements to help achieve this.

2 Types of law

The English legal system distinguishes several different types of law.

* **Common** law and **equity**
* **Statute** law
* **Private** law and **public** law
* **Criminal** law and **civil** law

2.1 Common law and equity

The earliest element of the English legal system is **common law**, a system of rigid rules laid down by **royal courts** following the Norman conquest. Application of law was by **judges** who travelled around the country to keep the King's peace and judgements often resulted in harsh **consequences**.

The judges actually made the law by **amalgamating** local customary laws into one 'law of the land'. **Remedies** under common law are **monetary**, and are known as **damages**.

However, there are times when money is not a **suitable remedy**. For example, you have agreed to buy a unique painting from an art dealer. Should the dealer at the last minute sell the painting to someone else, damages are unlikely to be acceptable, after all you wanted **that** painting.

Equity was developed two or three hundred years after common law as a system to resolve disputes where damages are not a suitable remedy and to introduce **fairness** into the legal system.

2.2 Statute law

Whilst the judiciary is responsible for the creation of common law, **Parliament** is responsible for **statute law**. Statute law is usually made in areas so **complicated** or **unique** that suitable common law alternatives are unlikely, or would take an unacceptable length of time, to develop – company law is one example of this.

2.3 Private law and public law

Most of the law that you will be studying is **private law**. That is law which deals with **relationships** and **interactions** between businesses, and **private individuals**, **groups** or **organisations**.

The **state** provides a **framework** for dealing with **disputes** and for **enforcing decisions**, but it is for individuals to handle matters between themselves. For example, the Consumer Rights Act 2015 regulates the sale of goods. It provides **rules** that must be adhered to when making a sale. Should any dispute arise that is covered by the Act, it is up to **the parties** to resolve the matter **themselves** using rules laid down by the legislation, the **state** does not get involved.

Public law is mainly concerned with **government** and the **operation** and **functions** of **public organisations** such as councils and local authorities. It will not be of great interest to you in your studies of corporate law, however examples of public law can be found in **planning rules** that must be adhered to when building or expanding offices.

A key **distinction** between **public** and **private** law is who takes up the case when a wrong is committed. The **state** prosecutes the alleged perpetrator under **public** law, whereas, under **private** law it is for the **individual** concerned to take action.

Criminal law is a part of **public** law and deals with behaviour that the **state** considers unwelcome and wishes to prevent. Criminal law also decides how those guilty of committing unlawful behaviour should be **punished**. You will notice the names of criminal cases are reported as *R v Jones* or *Regina v Jones*. This indicates that the state takes action on behalf of the crown (*Regina* is Latin for Queen).

2.4 Criminal and civil law

FAST FORWARD

The distinction between **criminal liability** and **civil liability** is central to the English legal system.

It is often the **criminal law** about which the general public has a clearer perception and keener interest. Some of the high profile criminal cases at **London's Old Bailey** are deemed extremely newsworthy. **Civil law**, on the other hand, receives less overt media coverage. However, every time you buy or sell goods, or start or finish an employment contract, your actions, and those of the other party, are governed by civil law.

The **distinction** between criminal and civil liability is central to the English legal system and to the way the court system is structured.

2.4.1 Criminal law

FAST FORWARD

In criminal cases, the **state** prosecutes the wrongdoer.

Key term

A **crime** is conduct prohibited by the law.

In a criminal case the State is the prosecutor because it is the community as a whole which suffers as a result of the law being broken. Persons guilty of crime may be punished by **fines** payable to the State, **imprisonment**, or a community-based punishment.

Generally, the **police** take the initial decision to prosecute, but this is then reviewed by the Crown Prosecution Service. Some prosecutions are started by the Director of Public Prosecutions, who is the head of the Crown Prosecution Service.

In a criminal trial, the **burden of proof** to convict the **accused** rests with the **prosecution**. The prosecution must meet the **standard of proof**, which means proving its case **beyond reasonable doubt**.

2.4.2 Civil law

FAST FORWARD

Civil law exists to regulate disputes over the rights and obligations of persons dealing with each other and seeks to compensate injured parties.

Civil law is a form of **private law**. In civil proceedings, the **standard of proof** means that the claimant must prove their case on the **balance of probability**. The claimant must convince the court that it is more probable than not that their assertions are true.

There is no concept of **punishment**, and **compensation** is paid to the wronged person. Both parties may choose to **settle** the dispute **out of court** should they wish.

Terminology in civil cases is different to that of criminal cases. A **claimant** sues a **defendant**. A civil case would therefore be referred to as, for example, *Smith v Megacorp plc*.

One of the most important areas of civil liability for business, and accountants in particular, is **contract law**.

2.4.3 Distinction between criminal and civil cases

It is not an act or event which creates the distinction, but the **legal consequences**. A single event might give rise to criminal and civil proceedings.

Illustration

A broken leg caused to a pedestrian by a drunken driver is a single event which may give rise to:

- **Criminal case** (prosecution by the State for the offence of driving with excess alcohol), and
- **Civil case** (the pedestrian sues for compensation for pain and suffering).

The two types of proceedings can be easily distinguished because **three vital factors** are different:

- The **courts** where the case is heard
- The **procedures**
- The **terminology**

3 The system of courts

The **courts** have to be organised to facilitate the working of the legal system. There are four main functional aspects of the court system which underlie its structure.

(a)   **Civil and criminal law** differ so much in substance and procedure that they are best administered in separate courts.

(b)   **Local courts** allow the vast bulk of small legal proceedings to be decentralised. But important civil cases begin in the High Court in London.

(c)   Although the courts form a single system, and many courts have a general civil jurisdiction, there is some **specialisation** both within the High Court and in other courts with separate functions.

(d)   There is a system of review by **appeals** to higher courts.

3.1 The civil court structure

FAST FORWARD

The **civil court structure** comprises the following.

- **Magistrates' Courts** mostly deal with small domestic matters.

- **County Courts** hear claims in contract and tort, equitable matters and land and probate disputes among others.

- The **Crown Court** hears appeals from Magistrates' Courts.

- The **High Court** is divided into three specialist divisions; Queen's Bench, Family and Chancery.

- The **Court of Appeal** hears appeals from the County Court, the High Court, the Restrictive Practices Court and the Employment Appeal Tribunal.

- The **Supreme Court** hears appeals from the Court of Appeal and the High Court.

The diagram below sets out the English **civil** court structure.

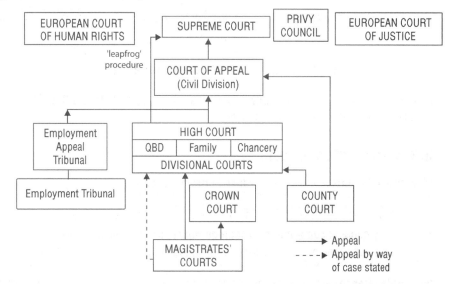

In appropriate cases it is possible to refer a case to either the **European Court of Human Rights** or the **European Court of Justice**, although they are not strictly within the English court structure.

3.2 The criminal court structure

FAST FORWARD

The **criminal court structure** comprises the following.

- **Magistrates' Courts** hear summary offences and committal proceedings for indictable offences.

- The **Crown Court** tries serious criminal (indictable) offences and hears appeals from Magistrates' Courts.

- The **Divisional Court of QBD** hears appeals by way of case stated from Magistrates' Courts and the Crown Court.

- The **Court of Appeal** hears appeals from the Crown Court.

- The **Supreme Court** hears appeals from the Court of Appeal or a Divisional Court of QBD.

The diagram below sets out the English **criminal** court structure.

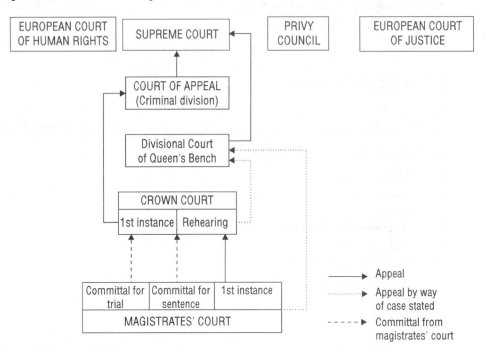

A limited number of **Commonwealth** countries allow appeal to the **Privy Council** in London, which is mostly staffed by Supreme Court judges.

3.3 Magistrates' Courts

Magistrates' Courts are the **lowest ranked criminal courts**.

- They try **summarily** (without a jury) all minor offences.

- They conduct **committal proceedings**, which are preliminary investigations of the prosecution case, when the offence is **triable** only on indictment (by a Crown Court).

Key terms

Indictable offences are more serious offences that can only be heard in a Crown Court.

Summary offences are minor crimes, only triable summarily in Magistrates' Courts.

Some offences are **'triable either way'**, meaning the accused has the choice of court that is used.

Magistrates also have **some civil jurisdiction** which includes the following:

- **Family proceedings** (financial provision for parties to a marriage and children, the custody or supervision of children and guardianship, and adoption orders).

- Enforcement of **local authority** charges and rates.

3.3.1 Appeals

A decision in a criminal case in a Magistrates' Court may be re-heard by a Crown Court. A **'case stated' appeal on a point of law** to a Divisional Court of the High Court is based on the idea that Magistrates or the Crown Court have **wrongly interpreted the law**. If they have, then the case may be sent back to the lower court with instructions as to how it should be decided.

On **family matters**, appeals are to the Crown Court with a further (or alternative) appeal on a point of law to a divisional court of the **Family Division of the High Court**. On other civil matters appeal on a point of law is to a Divisional Court of the Queen's Bench Division (QBD).

3.3.2 Personnel

The key personnel in the Magistrates' Court are the **Magistrates** who hear the cases. These fall into two categories:

- **Magistrates**, who are lay persons (Justices of the Peace) selected by the **Lord Chancellor**
- **District Judges** (professional paid magistrates)

The Magistrates' Courts are also staffed by **clerks**, who can provide legal advice for lay Magistrates.

3.4 The County Court

County Courts have **civil jurisdiction only** but deal with almost every kind of civil case. The practical importance of the County Courts is that they deal with **the majority of the UK's civil litigation**.

The County Court is involved in the following matters.

- **Contract and tort** (except defamation of character) claims
- **Equitable matters** concerning trusts, mortgages and partnership dissolution
- Disputes concerning **land**
- **Undefended matrimonial** cases
- **Probate matters**
- **Miscellaneous matters**, such as those under consumer law
- Some **bankruptcy**, company winding-up and admiralty cases

3.4.1 Appeals

From the **County Court** there is a right of appeal direct to the **Civil Division of the Court of Appeal** for some cases. In most other cases an appeal goes to the relevant Division of the **High Court**.

3.4.2 Personnel

The personnel in the **County Court** consist of:

- **Circuit judges**, assisted by
- **District judges**

3.5 Civil Procedure Rules Act 1998

The **Civil Procedure Rules Act 1998** (TSO, 1998) encourages parties to consider **alternative methods** of dispute resolution and to avoid **expensive litigation**, resolving cases **quickly and without unnecessary confrontation**. Early settlement of disputes is encouraged during proceedings. The court has the power to control every aspect of the **litigation process**, shifting responsibility away from the litigants and their advisers. The court is intended to be a place of **last, rather than first, resort**. There are two principal areas in which the **civil procedure rules** are relevant, these are **tracking** and **case management**.

3.5.1 Tracking

After a defence has been filed, the **case will be allocated** to one of three tracks.

(a) The **small claims track**, deals with low value claims (typically less than £10,000). These are cases that are to be dealt with quickly and informally, often without the need for legal representation or for a full hearing.

(b) The **fast track** is for medium value claims (typically £10,000 to £25,000) where the trial is to last no longer than one day and there is limited need for experts in court. These are subject to a simplified court procedure and a fixed timetable designed to enable the claim to be determined within 30 weeks.

(c) The **multi-track** is for high value or complex claims (typically over £25,000) which are to be managed by the courts.

Broadly speaking, **small** and **fast track** claims are heard by the **County Courts**; the more complex **multi-track** cases are heard by the **High Court**.

3.5.2 Case management

After allocation, the court will give directions setting out the procedures to be followed in bringing **multi-track cases** to trial. These will be an initial **'case management conference'** to encourage parties to settle the dispute or to consider alternative dispute resolutions (such as mediation or arbitration). Features of the procedures include the following.

(a) Published **pre-action protocols** for particular types of claim, such as personal injury and professional negligence claims, which entail setting out the claim to the defendant in an attempt to negotiate a settlement. The emphasis is placed on co-operation to identify the main issues. Failure to co-operate may lead to cost penalties, regardless of the eventual outcome of the case.

(b) A strict **timetable** for exchange of evidence is set by the court, including witness statements and relevant documents.

(c) Cost **penalties** for failing to meet any deadline or date set by the court.

3.6 The Crown Court

The **Crown Court** is a single court but it sits in 92 different towns and cities and also at the **Central Criminal Court** (the Old Bailey) in London. It deals with the following matters:

- **Indictable offences** with a jury
- **Appeals** from Magistrates' Courts
- **Committals for sentencing** from Magistrates' Courts

The Crown Court deals with a few types of **civil case**, for example **appeals** from the Magistrates' Court on matters of affiliation, betting, gaming and licencing.

3.6.1 Appeals

From the **Crown Court** there is a right of appeal on criminal matters to the **Criminal Division of the Court of Appeal**. An appeal by way of 'case stated' on a point of law may also be made to the **Divisional Court of the Queen's Bench Division**, in the High Court.

3.6.2 Personnel

The **Crown Court** has the following personnel:

- **High Court judges** (for serious offences)
- **Circuit judges**
- **Recorders**

3.7 The High Court

The **High Court** is organised into three Divisions, each of which hears particular types of case:

- **Queen's Bench Division (QBD)**
- **Chancery Division**
- **Family Division**

Rather confusingly, each Division of the High Court has a **Divisional Court**. The role of a Divisional Court is to hear appeals, as we have already seen, from:

- The Magistrates' Courts (on a point of law to Divisional Courts of the Family Division or QBD as relevant)

- The County Court (to one of the three Divisional Courts as relevant)

- The Crown Court (on a point of law to the Divisional Court of QBD)

3.7.1 Queen's Bench Division

The Queen's Bench Division deals mainly with common law matters, such as:

- Actions based on **contract** or **tort**
- Some appeals from the **County Court**
- Appeals by way of case stated from **Magistrates' Courts**
- Some appeals from the **Crown Court**

It also has a **supervisory role** over inferior courts. It is the largest of the three divisions, having 73 judges of which the Principal Judge is the Lord Chief Justice. It includes a separate Admiralty Court to deal with shipping matters, and a Commercial Court which specialises in commercial cases. The QBD sits in London and a small number of large cities in England and Wales. It may issue a writ of *habeas corpus*, which is an order for the release of a person **wrongfully detained**, and also prerogative orders against inferior courts, tribunals and other bodies such as local authorities.

There are three types of **prerogative order**.

- A **mandatory order** requiring the court or other body to carry out a public duty

- A **prohibitory order** preventing a court or tribunal from exceeding its jurisdiction

- A **quashing order** ordering a court or tribunal which has taken action to submit the record of its proceedings to the High Court for review

3.7.2 Chancery Division

This division, headed by the **Lord Chancellor**, deals with traditional equity matters.

- **Trusts** and **mortgages**
- **Revenue** matters
- **Bankruptcy** (though outside London this is a County Court subject)
- Disputed **wills** and administration of estates of deceased persons
- **Partnership** and company **matters**

There is a separate **Companies Court** within the division which deals with liquidations and other company proceedings, and a Patents Court established under the Patents Act 1977.

3.7.3 Family Division

This division deals with:

- **Matrimonial** cases
- **Family property** cases
- **Proceedings relating to children** (wardship, guardianship, adoption, legitimacy)
- **Appeals** from Magistrates' Courts on family matters
- **Appeals** from County Courts on family matters

3.7.4 Appeals

Civil appeals from the High Court may be made to the **Court of Appeal (Civil Division)** or to the **Supreme Court**, under what is known as the **'leapfrog'** procedure. This procedure is rarely used.

Criminal appeals are made direct to the Supreme Court where the case has reached the High Court on appeal from a Magistrates' Court or from the Crown Court.

3.7.5 Personnel

The High Court is staffed by **High Court (puisne) judges**. The chief judges in each division are as follows:

- Queen's Bench Division: Lord Chief Justice
- Family Division: President
- Chancery Division: Lord Chancellor (nominally), in practice the Vice Chancellor

3.8 The Court of Appeal

Key terms

> A **court of first instance** is the court where the case is originally heard in full. The **appeal court** is the court to which an appeal is made against the ruling or the sentence.

If the appeal court finds in favour of the appellant the original decision is **reversed**, ie the result is changed, but the law is not. This is different from **overruling**, which happens when a higher court finds a lower court's decision to be wrong in law and in future the law is changed.

3.8.1 Civil Division

The **Civil Division of the Court of Appeal** hears appeals from the **High Court, County Courts** and certain **other courts** and **special tribunals**. It may uphold or reverse the earlier decision or order a new trial.

3.8.2 Criminal Division

The **Criminal Division of the Court of Appeal** hears appeals from the **Crown Court**. It may also be asked to review criminal cases by the **Government** or consider points of law at the request of the **Attorney General**.

3.8.3 Appeals

Appeals lie to the **Supreme Court**.

3.8.4 Personnel

The Court of Appeal is staffed by the **Lord Justices of Appeal**. The chief judges in each division are as follows:

- Civil division: Master of the Rolls
- Criminal division: Lord Chief Justice

3.9 The Supreme Court

The **Supreme Court** was established by the Constitutional Reform Act 2005 (TSO, 2005) and opened for business in October 2009 when it replaced the judicial function of the House of Lords. Its personnel consists of **12 judges** known as '**Justices of the Supreme Court**' and include a **President** and a **Deputy President**.

The role of the Supreme Court is to act as the **final appeal court** in civil cases in the UK, hearing appeals on points of law that have **public** or **constitutional importance**. It is also the highest court of appeal in criminal cases for England, Wales and Northern Ireland (the highest criminal appeal court for Scotland is the Scottish High Court of Justiciary). The Supreme Court may in some instances be called to **interpret EU law** and the **European Convention on Human Rights** as they relate to UK law.

BPP LEARNING MEDIA

Cases are typically heard by panels of **five**, **seven** or **nine Justices** who give their verdicts collectively rather than as individual decisions. This is to **encourage discussion** among those at the top of the legal profession, which should result in **robust**, **clear decisions** that the rest of the judicial system can rely on.

Exam focus point

An article titled 'The Supreme Court' was included in an edition of *Student Accountant* and is available on the ACCA website.

3.10 The European Court of Human Rights (ECHR)

The European Court of Human Rights is the **supreme court** of those European states which have signed up to the **European Convention of Human Rights**. Any individual who alleges that their human rights have been violated can bring an action against those responsible.

Since the **Human Rights Act 1998** (TSO, 1998) the UK has incorporated the European Convention of Human Rights into UK law, enabling enforcement to be exercised by UK courts.

3.11 The European Court of Justice (ECJ)

The **European Court of Justice** has the role of **interpreting** European Treaty law and ensuring it is **observed**. European laws are enacted in the UK and are therefore directly applicable to **individuals** and **businesses** within the UK. Cases are usually between nation states or European institutions; however, individuals **can appeal** to the ECJ if they are affected personally.

In the *Factortame* case, the ECJ ruled that the domestic courts of each EU state must ignore any national laws that are contrary to European Union law. As a consequence, the Supreme Court became effectively bound by the decisions of the ECJ in relation to EU law.

3.12 The Privy Council

The **Judicial Committee of the Privy Council** is the final Court of Appeal for certain Commonwealth countries. Their decisions are also important to cases heard in the UK as they have **persuasive influence** over hearings concerning points of law applicable under the UK's jurisdiction.

Chapter Roundup

- **Law** is the enforceable body of rules that govern any society.

- The distinction between **criminal liability** and **civil liability** is central to the English legal system.

- In criminal cases, the **state** prosecutes the wrongdoer.

- **Civil law** exists to regulate disputes over the rights and obligations of persons dealing with each other and seeks to compensate injured parties.

- The **civil court structure** comprises the following.

  - **Magistrates' Courts** mostly deal with small domestic matters.

  - **County Courts** hear claims in contract and tort, equitable matters and land and probate disputes among others.

  - The **Crown Court** hears appeals from Magistrates' Courts.

  - The **High Court** is divided into three specialist divisions; Queen's Bench, Family and Chancery.

  - The **Court of Appeal** hears appeals from the County Court, the High Court, the Restrictive Practices Court and the Employment Appeal Tribunal.

  - The **Supreme Court** hears appeals from the Court of Appeal and the High Court.

- The **criminal court structure** comprises the following.

  - **Magistrates' Courts** hear summary offences and committal proceedings for indictable offences.

  - The **Crown Court** tries serious criminal (indictable) offences and hears appeals from Magistrates' Courts.

  - The **Divisional Court of QBD** hears appeals by way of case stated from Magistrates' Courts and the Crown Court.

  - The **Court of Appeal** hears appeals from the Crown Court.

  - The **Supreme Court** hears appeals from the Court of Appeal or a Divisional Court of QBD.

BPP
LEARNING MEDIA

Quick Quiz

1   **Fill in the blanks** in the statements below.

    The distinction between (1) ……………….. and (2) ……………….. liability is central to the English legal system.

2   What is the standard of proof in civil proceedings?

3   The Employment Appeal Tribunal (EAT) is a court of equal status with the High Court.

    True   ☐

    False   ☐

4   All the following statements relate to criminal and civil law. Which one of the statements is correct?

    A   A criminal case may subsequently give rise to a civil case, but a civil case cannot subsequently give rise to a criminal case.

    B   The main purpose of civil law is to compensate the injured party and to punish the injuring party.

    C   A custodial sentence can be passed on the defendant in a civil case, providing the defendant is a natural person and not an incorporated body.

    D   The main purpose of civil law is to enforce the claimant's rights rather than to punish the defendant.

5   What are the three tracks in the tracking system that allocates civil court cases?

Answers to Quick Quiz

1   (1) criminal (2) civil

2   The case must be proved on the balance of probability.

3   True. The EAT is of equal status with the High Court.

4   D. Punishment is not an objective of civil law. A civil case may subsequently give rise to a criminal case.

5   (1) small claims track (2) fast track (3) multi-track

Now try the questions below from the Practice Question Bank

Number
1, 2, 3

Sources of law

Topic list	Syllabus reference
1 Case law and precedent	A2(a)
2 Legislation	A2(b)
3 Statutory interpretation	A2(c)
4 The European Convention on Human Rights	A2(d)
5 The Human Rights Act 1998 (HRA)	A2(d)
6 The Impact of the Act	A2(d)

Introduction

Continuing with our study of the English legal system, we now look at **sources of law** and how law is **interpreted** by the courts.

You will discover that the main law-making bodies are the **Courts** (who develop the 'common law') and **Parliament** (which produces statutes and delegated legislation).

EU law is another source of law for the UK. Its detail is outside the scope of your syllabus but you must be aware of it as a source of law.

The rules on **statutory interpretation** are used by judges when deciding cases that involve statutes which are open to different meanings.

Study guide

		Intellectual level
A	**Essential elements of the legal system**	
2	**Sources of law**	
(a)	Explain what is meant by case law and precedent	1
(b)	Explain legislation and evaluate delegated legislation	1
(c)	Illustrate the rules and presumptions used by the courts in interpreting statutes	1
(d)	Identify the concept and impact of human rights law	1

Exam guide

Questions could be set on the operation of case law and precedent or may focus on how legislation is passed by government and interpreted by the courts.

1 Case law and precedent

FAST FORWARD

The first legal source of law, consisting of decisions made in the courts, is **case law**, which is judge-made law based on the underlying principle of consistency. Once a legal principle is decided by an appropriate court it is a **judicial precedent**.

1.1 Common law and equity

The earliest element of the legal system to develop was the **common law**, a system incorporating rigid rules applied by royal courts, often with harsh consequences. **Equity** was developed, two or three hundred years later, as a system of law applied by the Lord Chancellor in situations where justice did not appear to be done under common law principles.

Key terms

Common law is the body of legal rules common to the whole country which is embodied in judicial decisions.

Equity is a term which applies to a specific set of legal principles which were developed by the Court of Chancery to supplement (but not replace) the common law. It is based on fair dealings between the parties. It added to and improved on the common law by introducing the concept of fairness.

The **interaction** of **equity** and **common law** produced three major changes.

(a) **New rights**. Equity recognised and protected rights for which the common law gave no safeguards.

(b) **Better procedure**. Equity may be more effective than common law in resolving a disputed matter.

(c) **Better remedies**. The standard common law remedy for the successful claimant was the award of damages for their loss. The Lord Chancellor developed remedies not available in other courts. Equity was able to make the following orders.

    (i) That the defendant must do what they had agreed to do (**specific performance**)
    (ii) That the defendant must abstain from wrongdoing (**injunction**)
    (iii) Alteration of a document to reflect the parties' true intentions (**rectification**)
    (iv) Restoration of the pre-contract status quo (**rescission**)

Where equitable rules **conflict** with common law rules then **equitable rules** will **prevail**.

Case law incorporates decisions made by judges under both historic legal systems and the expression 'common law' is often used to describe all case law whatever its historic origin.

A court's decision is expected to be **consistent with previous decisions** and to provide an opinion which can be used to direct future relationships. This is the basis of the system of **judicial precedent**.

1.2 Doctrine of judicial precedent

The system of judicial precedent is based on a fundamental feature of English law which is that **principles of English law do not become inoperative through the lapse of time**.

> The doctrine of consistency, following precedent, is expressed in the maxim **stare decisis** which means 'to stand by a decision'. In any later case to which a legal principle is relevant the same principle should (subject to certain exceptions) be applied.
>
> A **precedent** is a previous court decision which another court is bound to follow by deciding a subsequent case in the same way.

The doctrine of **judicial precedent** means that a judge is bound to apply a decision from an earlier case to the facts of the case before him, provided, among other conditions, that there is no material difference between the cases and the previous case created a 'binding' precedent.

Judicial precedent is based on three elements.

- **Reports.** There must be adequate and reliable reports of earlier decisions.

- **Rules.** There must be rules for extracting a legal principle from a previous set of facts and applying it to current facts.

- **Classification.** Precedents must be classified into those that are **binding** and those which are merely **persuasive**.

1.3 Law reports

There are several major series of **law reports** bound as annual volumes. In addition, there are several electronic databases which include cases reported in the paper reports and other cases.

Every case has a title, usually (in a civil case) in the form *Carlill v Carbolic Smoke Ball Co.* This denotes Carlill (claimant) versus Carbolic Smoke Ball Co (defendant). In the event of an appeal, the **claimant's** name is still shown first, whether they are the **appellant** or the **respondent**. All judgements of the superior courts are given a 'uniform citation' to facilitate publication on the internet.

Some cases are cited by reference to the **subject matter**. Thus case names have included *Re Barrow Haematite Steel Co* (a company case), *Re Adams and Kensington Vestry* (a trust case) and in shipping cases the name of the ship, for example, *The Wagon Mound*.

Some older cases may be referred to by a **single name**, for example *Pinnel's case*. In a full citation the title of the case is followed by abbreviated particulars of the volume of the law reports in which the case is reported, for example, *Best v Samuel Fox & Co Ltd 1952* 2 All ER 394 (the report is at p 394 of Vol. 2 of the All England Reports for 1952).

As regards content a **full law report** includes details of the following.

- Names of the parties
- Court in which the case was decided
- Judge or judges
- Date of the hearing
- Points of law established
- Earlier cases cited
- Previous history of the litigation

- Facts
- Names of counsel and their arguments
- Verbatim text of the judgement
- Order of the court
- Whether leave to appeal was granted
- Solicitors
- Reporting barrister

It is only decisions of the **higher courts** in important cases (the High Court, the Court of Appeal and the Supreme Court) which are included in the general law reports.

The doctrine of **judicial precedent** is designed to provide **consistency** in the law. Four things must be considered when examining a precedent before it can be applied to a case.

(a) A decision must be based on a **proposition of law** before it can be considered as a precedent. It may **not** be a decision on a **question of fact**.

(b) It must form part of the **ratio decidendi** of the case.

(c) The **material facts** of each case must be the same or comparable.

(d) The preceding court must have had a **superior (or in some cases, equal) status** to the later court, such that its decisions are binding on the later court.

1.4 Ratio decidendi

FAST FORWARD

Statements made by judges can be classified as **ratio decidendi** or **obiter dicta**.

A judgement will start with a description of the facts of the case and probably a review of earlier precedents. The judge will then make **statements of law applicable to the legal problems** raised by the material facts which, **if used as the basis for the decision**, are **known as the ratio decidendi** of the case. This is the **vital element that binds future judges**.

Key term

The **ratio decidendi** of a case is the principle that a judge followed when coming to their decision. In other words it is the reason for their decision.

Statements made by a judge are either classed as **ratio decidendi** or **obiter dicta**. There are two types of obiter dicta (which means something said 'by the way').

- A judge's statements of **legal principle** that do not form the basis of the decision.
- A judge's statements that are not based on the material facts, but on **hypothetical facts**.

Key term

Obiter dicta are words in a judgement which are said 'by the way'.
They **do not** form part of the **ratio decidendi** and are not binding on future cases but merely persuasive.

It is not always easy to identify the **ratio decidendi**. In decisions of appeal courts, where there are three or even five separate judgements, the members of the court may reach the same conclusion but give different reasons. Many judges indicate in their speeches which comments are 'ratio' and which are 'obiter'.

1.5 Distinguishing the facts

Although there may arguably be a finite number of **legal principles** to consider when deciding a case, there is an infinite variety of facts which may be presented.

It is necessary to consider how far the facts of the previous and the latest case are similar. If the differences appear significant the court may **distinguish the earlier case on the facts** and thereby **avoid following it as a precedent**.

1.6 Status of the court

Not every decision made in every court is binding as a judicial precedent. The **court's status** has a significant effect on whether its decisions are binding, persuasive or disregarded.

Court	Bound by	Decisions binding on
Magistrates' Court	• High Court • The Court of Appeal • Supreme Court • European Court of Justice	• No one • Not even itself
County Court	• High Court • The Court of Appeal • Supreme Court • European Court of Justice	• No one • Not even itself
Crown Court	• High Court (QBD) • The Court of Appeal • Supreme Court • European Court of Justice	• No one • However, its decisions are reported more widely and are more authoritative

The High Court
consists of divisions:
• **Queen's Bench**
• **Chancery**
• **Family**
	• Judge sitting alone
	  – The Divisional Court
	  – The Court of Appeal
	  – Supreme Court
	  – European Court of Justice
		• Judge sitting alone
		  – Magistrates' Court
		  – County Court
		  – Crown Court

The Court of Appeal	• Own decisions • Supreme Court (subject to an exception below) • European Court of Justice	• All inferior English courts • Itself (subject to the exception)
Supreme Court	• Itself (except in exceptional cases) • European Court of Justice	• All English Courts • Itself (except in exceptional cases)
The European Court of Justice	• No one • Not even itself	• All English Courts

1.7 Court of Appeal exception

In *Young v Bristol Aeroplane Co 1944,* it was decided that the **civil division** of the Court of Appeal is usually bound by its own decisions and those of what was the House of Lords, and which is now the Supreme Court, unless:

- Two of its previous decisions conflict, when it must decide which to follow
- The previous decision conflicts with a subsequent Supreme Court decision
- The previous decision was made with a lack of care in relation to either a relevant precedent or statute (*per incuriam*)

Exam focus point

> It is important to learn the operation of the court hierarchy and how courts are bound.

1.8 Persuasive precedents

Apart from binding precedents, reported conclusions of any court may be treated as **persuasive precedents**. Persuasive precedents may be, but need not be, followed in a later case.

A court of higher status is not only free to disregard the verdict of a court of lower status, it may also deprive it of authority and expressly **overrule** it. Remember that this **does not reverse** the previous decision. Overruling a judgement does not affect its outcome.

Where an earlier decision was made by a lower court, the judges can **overrule** the ratio of that earlier case if they disagree with the lower court's statement of the law. **The outcome of the earlier judgement remains the same, but will not be followed in future.**

If the decision of a lower court is appealed to a higher one, the higher court may **reverse** the result if they feel the lower court has wrongly interpreted the law. **When a decision is reversed through appeal, the higher court is usually also overruling the lower court's statement of the law.**

If, in a case before the Supreme Court, there is a **dispute about a point of European Union law** it must be referred to the European Court of Justice for a ruling. The ECJ does not create or follow precedents as such, and the provisions of EU directives should not be used to interpret UK legislation.

1.9 Avoidance of a binding precedent

Even if a precedent appears to be binding, there are **a number of grounds on which a court may decline to follow it**.

(a)   It may be able to **distinguish the facts**.

(b)   It may **declare the ratio decidendi obscure**, particularly when a Court of Appeal decision by three or five judges gives as many reasons for the decision.

(c)   It may **declare the previous decision made per incuriam**: without taking account of some essential point of law, such as an important precedent.

(d)   It may **declare it to be in conflict with a fundamental principle of law**; for example where a court has failed to apply the doctrine of privity of contract: *Beswick v Beswick 1968*.

(e)   It may **declare an earlier precedent to be too wide**. For example, the duty of care to third parties, created by *Donoghue v Stevenson 1932,* has since been considerably refined.

1.10 The advantages and disadvantages of precedent

Many of the strengths of judicial precedent as the cornerstone of English law also indicate some of its weaknesses.

Factor	Advantage	Disadvantage
Certainty	The law is decided fairly and predictably. Guidance given to judges and risk of mistake reduced.	Judges may sometimes be forced to make illogical distinctions to avoid an unfair result.
Clarity	Following the reasoning of ratio decidendi should lead to statements of general legal principles.	Sometimes, judgements may appear to be inconsistent with each other or legal principles followed.
Flexibility	The system is able to change with changing circumstances.	The system can limit judges' discretion.
Detail	Precedent states how the law applies to facts and should be flexible enough to allow for details to be different.	The detail produces a vast body of reports to take into account. Judges often distinguish on the facts to avoid a precedent.
Practicality	Case law is based on experience of actual cases brought before the courts. This is an advantage over legislation which can be found wanting when tested.	Unfair precedents may be created that allow wrongdoing to be perpetrated.

2 Legislation

FAST FORWARD

The second major source of law is **legislation**. This is also known as statute law and may take the form of **Acts of Parliament** or **delegated legislation** under the Acts.

Statute law is made by **Parliament** (or in exercise of law-making powers delegated by Parliament). Until the United Kingdom entered the European Community (now the EU) in 1973, the UK Parliament was completely **sovereign**.

In recent years however, UK membership of the European Union has restricted the previously unfettered power of Parliament. There is an **obligation**, imposed by the Treaty of Rome, **to bring UK law into line with the Treaty itself and with directives**. Regulations, having the force of law in every member state, may be made under provisions of the Treaty of Rome.

One example of an activity that fulfils PO1 is to continually review legislation and regulation that affects your working environment. Therefore you should maintain your awareness of any legislation identified in the Study Text which affects your role.

2.1 Parliamentary sovereignty

Parliamentary sovereignty gives rise to a number of consequences. Parliament may

- **Repeal** earlier statutes
- **Overrule** or modify case law developed in the courts
- **Make new law** on subjects which have not been regulated by law before

In practice, Parliament usually follows certain **conventions** which limit its freedom.

- No Parliament can legislate so as to **prevent** a future Parliament changing the law.

- Judges have to **interpret** statute law and they may find a meaning in it which those who promoted the statute did not intend.

- The **validity** of an Act of Parliament cannot be questioned. However, judges may declare an Act to be '**incompatible**' with the European Convention on Human Rights.

2.2 Types of legislation

In addition to making new law and altering existing law, Parliament may make the law clearer by passing a **codifying** statute putting case law on a statutory basis (such as the Consumer Rights Act 2015). It may also pass **consolidating** statutes that incorporate an original statute and its successive amendments into a single piece of legislation (such as the Employment Rights Act 1996 or the Companies Act 2006).

Legislation can also be **categorised** in the following ways:

- **Public Acts**: legislation that affects the **general public**

- **Private Acts**: legislation that affects **specific individuals and groups**

- **Enabling legislation that empowers a specific individual or body** to produce the detail required by a parent Act

2.3 Parliamentary procedure

A proposal for legislation can be brought by the Government, a backbench MP, or a peer. A government bill may be aired in public in a **Government Green** or **White Paper**. A government bill may be introduced into either the House of Commons or the House of Lords. When it has passed through one House it must then go through the same stages in the other House.

In each House the successive stages of dealing with the Bill are as follows.

Stage 1   **First reading.** Publication and introduction into the agenda. No debate.

Stage 2   **Second reading.** Debate on the general merits of the Bill. No amendments at this stage.

Stage 3   **Committee stage.** The Bill is examined by a Standing Committee of about 20 members, representing the main parties and including some members at least who specialise in the relevant subject. If the Bill is very important, all or part of the Committee Stage may be taken by the House as a whole sitting as a committee.

Stage 4   **Report stage.** The Bill as amended in committee is reported to the full House for approval.

Stage 5   **Third reading.** This is the final approval stage.

When it has passed through both Houses it is submitted for the **Royal Assent** which is given on the Queen's behalf by a committee of the Lord Chancellor and two other peers. It then becomes an Act of Parliament (statute) but it does not come into operation until a commencement date is notified by statutory instrument.

2.4 Advantages and disadvantages of statute law

Statute law has the following advantages and disadvantages:

(a) **Advantages**

    (i) The House of Commons is elected at intervals of not more than five years. Hence the law making process is theoretically **responsive** to public opinion.

    (ii) Statute law can, in theory, deal with **any** problem.

    (iii) Statutes are **carefully constructed** codes of law.

    (iv) A **new problem** in society or some **unwelcome development** in case law can be dealt with by passing an Act of Parliament.

(b) **Disadvantages**

    (i) Statutes are **bulky**.

    (ii) **Parliament** often **lacks time** to consider draft legislation in **sufficient detail**.

    (iii) A substantial statute can take up a lot of **Parliamentary time**.

    (iv) Statute law is a statement of general rules. **Those who draft it cannot anticipate every individual case** which may arise.

2.5 Delegated legislation

To save time in Parliament, Acts usually contain a section by which power is given to a minister, or public body such as a local authority, to make **subordinate or delegated legislation**.

Key term

> **Delegated legislation** means rules of law, often of a detailed nature, made by subordinate bodies to whom the power to do so has been given by statute.

Delegated legislation appears in various forms.

- Ministerial powers are exercised by **statutory instruments**. Statutory instruments are the most common form of delegated legislation.

- **Local authorities** are given statutory powers to make **bye-laws**.

- **Rules of Court** may be made by the judiciary to control court procedure.

- **Professional Regulations** concerning certain occupations (such as law) can be delegated to authorised bodies (such as the Law Society).

- **Orders in council.** In certain circumstances, the Government may resort to introducing legislation through the Privy Council as it circumvents the need to go through the full Parliamentary process.

2.5.1 Control over delegated legislation

Parliament exercises some **control** over delegated legislation by keeping the production of new delegated legislation under review.

- Some statutory instruments do not take effect until approved by **affirmative resolution** of Parliament.

- Other statutory instruments must be **laid** before Parliament for 40 days before they take effect.

There are standing **Scrutiny Committees** of both Houses whose duty it is to examine statutory instruments from a technical point of view and may raise objections if necessary. However, they have no authority to object to an instrument's nature or content.

A statutory instrument may be **challenged** in the courts on the grounds that Parliament exceeded its authority to delegate and has acted *ultra vires* or that the legislation has been made without due compliance with the correct procedure. The **Human Rights Act 1998** (TSO, 1998) (HRA) does not give courts power to strike out primary legislation which is contrary to the HRA. However, as **secondary legislation**, delegated legislation is not affected and courts **are permitted** to **strike out** any delegated legislation that runs contrary to the HRA.

Both statutes and delegated legislation made under it are expressed in **general terms**. It is not possible to provide in the Act for each eventuality which falls within its remit. It therefore often falls to judges to interpret Acts.

2.5.2 Advantages and disadvantages

Delegated legislation has the following **advantages**:

- It **saves time** as Parliament does not have to examine matters of detail.

- Much of the content of delegated legislation is **technical** and is better worked out in consultation with professional, commercial or industrial groups outside Parliament.

- If new or altered regulations are required later, they can be **issued without referring** back to Parliament.

- The system allows the law to be enacted **quickly**.

The **disadvantages** of the system are as follows.

- There are concerns over the **accountability** of Parliament. Individual MPs and their civil service staff effectively become the source of law rather than Parliament, the actions of which are open to questioning and public scrutiny.

- The system is **unrepresentative** in that some power is given to civil servants who are not democratically elected.

- Because delegated legislation can be produced in large **volumes**, ordinary MPs and the public find it difficult to keep up to date with developments.

- The different sorts of delegated legislation which may be produced by virtue of one statute can greatly **confuse** users.

Exam focus point

Saving Parliamentary time and the use of experts are key benefits of delegated legislation.

3 Statutory interpretation

> Legislation must be **interpreted correctly** before judges can **apply it fairly**. The **literal**, **golden** and **mischief rules** of interpretation developed over time. Nowadays a **purposive approach** is taken.

Judges are faced with task of **applying** legislation to the particular case heard before them. To apply the legislation they must first **interpret** and **understand** it. Problems occur when the judge has difficulty interpreting the statute. There are a number of **situations** which might lead to a need for **interpretation**.

(a) **Ambiguity** might be caused by an error in drafting or words may have a dual meaning.

(b) **Uncertainty** may arise where the words of a statute are intended to apply to a range of factual situations and the courts must decide whether the case before them falls into any of these situations.

(c) There may be **unforeseeable developments**.

(d) The draft may use a **broad term**. Thus, the word 'vehicle' may need to be considered in relation to the use of skateboards or bicycles.

There are a number of **different sources of assistance** for a judge in their task of statutory interpretation.

- **Rules**
- **Presumptions**
- **Other aids** (intrinsic or extrinsic)

3.1 Rules of statutory interpretation

In **interpreting the words of a statute**, courts have developed a number of well-established general rules.

3.1.1 The literal rule and golden rule

Key terms

> The **literal rule** means that words in the Act should be given their literal and grammatical meaning rather than what the judge thinks they mean. It is extended by the **golden rule** which states that words should be given their plain, ordinary or literal meaning unless this would give rise to manifest absurdity or inconsistency with the rest of the statute.

Normally a word should be construed in the **same literal sense** wherever it appears in the statute. In *Whitely v Chappel 1868* a statute aimed at preventing electoral malpractice made it an offence to impersonate 'any person entitled to vote' at an election. The accused was acquitted because he impersonated a dead person, who was clearly not entitled to vote. The case of *Re Sigsworth 1935* saw a son murder his mother. Applying the literal rule to the Administration of Justice Act 1925 would mean that the son would inherit his murdered mother's estate. The court applied the golden rule, stating that a murderer should not benefit from their crime and therefore the law would not be interpreted literally in this case.

3.1.2 The mischief rule

Key term

> Under the **mischief rule** a judge considers what mischief the Act was intended to prevent. Where a statute is designed to remedy a weakness in the law, the correct interpretation is the one which achieves it.

In *Corkery v Carpenter 1950* the court held that a bicycle was a 'carriage' for the purpose of the Licensing Act 1872 where a defendant was charged with cycling whilst intoxicated. The purpose of the Act was to prevent people who are in a state of intoxication from operating any form of transport on public roads.

The case of *DPP v Bull 1995* saw the defendant (a man) charged with prostitution under the Street Offences Act 1959. However, the Magistrate upheld his defence that the Act in question applied only to females and therefore the mischief could not be committed by a male. Thankfully, this offensive interpretation has since been consigned to history when new laws replaced the Street Offences Act.

The 'golden' and 'mischief' rules were used until relatively recently. The **Law Commissioners** recommended that judges interpret statute using the general purposes behind it and the intentions of Parliament. This is known as **purposive interpretation**.

3.1.3 The purposive approach

Key term

> Under the **purposive approach** to statutory interpretation, the words of a statute are interpreted not only in their **ordinary**, **literal** and **grammatical** sense, but also with reference to the **context** and **purpose** of the legislation, ie what is the legislation trying to achieve?

> *Gardiner v Sevenoaks RDC 1950*
>
> *The facts:* The purpose of an Act was to provide for the safe storage of film wherever it might be stored on 'premises'. The claimant argued that 'premises' did not include a cave and so the Act had no application to his case.
>
> *Decision:* The purpose of the Act was to protect the safety of persons working in all places where film was stored. If film was stored in a cave, the word 'premises' included the cave.

The key to the purposive approach is that the judge construes the statute in such a way as to **be consistent with the purpose of the statute** as they understand it, even if the wording of the statute could be applied literally without leading to manifest absurdity.

3.1.4 The contextual rule

Key term

> The **contextual rule** means that a word should be construed in its context: it is permissible to look at the statute as a whole to discover the meaning of a word in it.

A more **purposive approach** is also being taken because so many international and EU regulations come to be interpreted by the courts.

3.2 General rules of interpretation

The following **general rules of interpretation** have also been developed by the courts.

3.2.1 The ejusdem generis rule

Statutes often list a number of **specific things** and end the list with more general words. In that case the general words are to be limited in their meaning to other things of the same kind as the specific items which precede them. In *Powell v Kempton Park Racecourse 1899* it was held that a clause referring to a 'house, office, room or other place' excluded a ring at a racecourse.

3.2.2 Expressio unius est exclusio alterius

To express one thing is by implication to **exclude anything else**.

3.2.3 Noscitur a sociis

It is presumed that words draw meaning from the **other words around them**. If a statute mentioned 'children's books, children's toys and clothes', it would be reasonable to assume that 'clothes' meant children's clothes.

3.2.4 In pari materia

If the statute forms part of a series which deals with **similar** subject matter, the court may look to the interpretation of previous statutes on the assumption that Parliament intended the same thing.

3.3 Presumptions of statutory interpretation

Unless the statute contains express words to the contrary it is assumed that the following **presumptions** of statutory interpretation apply, each of which may be rebutted by contrary evidence.

- **A statute does not alter the existing common law**. If a statute is capable of two interpretations, one involving alteration of the common law and the other one not, the latter interpretation is to be preferred.

- **If a statute deprives a person of property**, say by nationalisation, they are to be compensated for its value.

- **A statute is not intended to deprive a person of liberty**. If it does so, clear words must be used. This is relevant in legislation covering, for example, mental health and immigration.

- **A statute does not have retrospective effect** to a date earlier than its becoming law.

- **A statute does not bind the Crown**. In certain areas, the Crown's potential liability is great and this is therefore an extremely important presumption.

- **A statute generally has effect only in the UK**. However a statute does not run counter to international law and should be interpreted so as to give effect to international obligations.

- **A statute cannot impose criminal liability** without proof of guilty intention. Many modern statutes rebut this presumption by imposing strict liability, say for dangerous driving under the Road Traffic Act.

- **A statute does not repeal other statutes**. Any point on which the statute leaves a gap or omission is outside the scope of the statute.

3.4 Other assistance in interpretation

Key terms

> **Intrinsic aids** are those words contained in the Queen's Printer's copy of the statute. **Extrinsic aids** are those found elsewhere.

3.4.1 The Interpretation Act 1978

The **Interpretation Act 1978** (HMSO, 1978) defines certain terms frequently found in legislation. The Act also states that, unless a specific intention to the contrary exists, the use in a statute of masculine gender terminology also includes the feminine, and vice versa. Similarly, words in the singular include plurals, and vice versa.

3.4.2 Intrinsic aids

Intrinsic aids to statutory interpretation consist of the following.

- The **long title** of an Act, which may give guidance as to the Act's general objective.

- The **preamble** of an Act often directs the judge as to its intentions and objects.

- **Interpretation sections** to Acts. Particularly long, complicated and wide-ranging Acts often contain self-explanations.

- **Side notes**. Statutes often have summary notes in the margin.

3.4.3 Extrinsic aids

Extrinsic aids include the following.

(a)   **Reports** of the **Law Commission**, **Royal Commissions**, the **Law Reform Committee** and other **official committees**.

(b)   **Hansard**, the official journal of UK Parliamentary debates. This follows a decision of the House of Lords in *Pepper v Hart 1992* where it was decided that it is acceptable to look at the original speech which first introduced a bill to ascertain its meaning, but only if the statute is ambiguous or obscure or its literal meaning would lead to absurdity.

4 The European Convention on Human Rights

FAST FORWARD

The **Human Rights Act 1998** is a key example of the influence of international law in the UK.

The **Human Rights Act 1998** (TSO, 1998) incorporates the **'European Convention for the Protection of Human Rights and Fundamental Freedoms'** (more commonly referred to as the 'European Convention on Human Rights') into UK domestic law.

The **European Convention on Human Rights** is an agreement on basic human rights, put together by major powers in the wake of the human rights abuses that occurred during World War Two and signed by those powers, including the UK, in 1951.

During the second half of the **20th century**, the European Convention on Human Rights was used as a **guideline** in the English courts. It was widely believed that UK political and legal institutions were well suited to the protection of **fundamental human rights** and that incorporation of the Convention into English law was not necessary. However, any individual who felt their rights had been violated could take a case to the **European Court of Human Rights (ECHR)** in Strasbourg.

Towards the end of the 1990s, it became clear that the **British Government** was of the opinion that it was **not sufficient** to rely on existing law to ensure protection of human rights. The **Human Rights Act** was developed as a means of ensuring that these fundamental rights were enshrined in the English legal system. English courts now have a statutory duty to ensure that English laws are interpreted 'as far as possible' in a manner which is compatible with the **Convention Rights** incorporated by the Human Rights Act.

Therefore an individual can ask the UK courts to consider their **Convention Rights**, instead of taking their case to Strasbourg. However the ECHR remains the final **appeal court** for human rights issues.

5 The Human Rights Act 1998 (HRA)

FAST FORWARD

The **Human Rights Act 1998** incorporates the European Convention on Human Rights (the Convention) into UK domestic law. The impact of the legislation is **pervasive** in many areas of UK law.

Exam focus point

> The HRA has the **potential** to affect many different areas of law. You should be aware of its provisions so that you can see the potential impacts throughout the Corporate and Business Law syllabus.
>
> You should also ensure that your knowledge of the **Convention** is sufficient that you can understand the **impacts** which are pointed out, and identify further impacts if required.

The **Human Rights Act 1998** (TSO, 1998) binds **public authorities** (defined as bodies undertaking functions of a public nature). These include government departments, local authorities, courts and schools. These public authorities must not breach (or derogate) an **individual's rights**. In the case of proceedings against a public authority, there is a limitation period of one year from the date on which the act complained of is alleged to have occurred.

The **rights** can be relied upon by any **individual** or **non-government organisation** including **companies**. However, where rights have been derogated, the public authority can mitigate its actions by demonstrating a **legitimate** need to derogate and that the derogation was **proportionate** to the need.

6 The impact of the Act

FAST FORWARD

The Act has had an impact on **new legislation**, **statutory interpretation** and the **common law**.

There are many areas where the **Human Rights Act** (TSO, 1998) has **potential impact** on English law. Some ideas of where the legislation has an effect are summarised here.

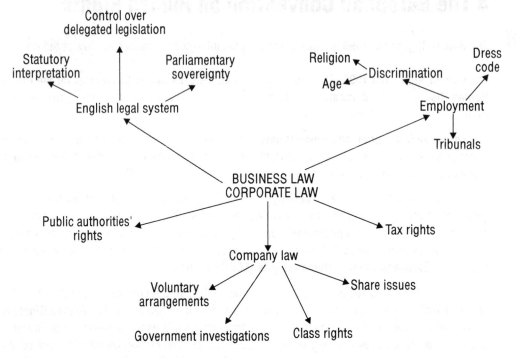

The impact of the Act can be considered in the following areas:

- Impact on **new legislation**
- Impact on **statutory interpretation**
- Impact on the **common law**

6.1 Impact on new legislation

The HRA requires the person **responsible** for a Bill to make a **statement of compatibility** with the Convention before the Bill's second reading. Where a Bill is **incompatible** with the Convention, a statement to that effect can be made should the Government wish to continue with the Bill anyway.

The Act may affect primary and secondary legislation through the courts – for example courts can **strike out secondary legislation** that is contrary to the act. However, courts **do not** have this power where primary legislation is concerned, but they can issue a declaration of incompatibility should they desire.

6.2 Impact on statutory interpretation

Under the HRA **UK courts are required to interpret UK law in a way compatible with the Convention** so far as it is possible to do so. **Existing legislation** must therefore be **interpreted** in a way which is **compatible** with **Convention Rights**. This means that courts must take into account **decisions** and **judgements** of the European Court of Human Rights when hearing a case.

Where legislation can be interpreted in two ways, one **compatible** with the Convention and one that is **incompatible**, courts must follow the interpretation that is compatible. However, if a court feels that legislation is incompatible with the Convention and that it cannot interpret it in such a way to make it compatible, it may make a **declaration of incompatibility**. You should note that such a declaration **does not** make the legislation invalid; however, it is up to the legislator to **remedy** the situation.

Bellinger v Bellinger 2003

The facts: The court had to consider whether or not a male to female transsexual could be treated as a female under the Matrimonial Causes Act 1973.

Decision: The court was unable to interpret the act to allow the transsexual to be considered female. It did however issue a declaration of incompatibility.

6.3 Impact on the common law

UK courts must take into account the **judgements** and **decisions** of the ECHR when interpreting UK law. The Act also requires UK courts to take into account the **case law** of the European Court of Justice when making judgements. To some extent this affects the **doctrine of precedent** as it permits the **overruling** of English law where it **conflicts** with the Convention. However, it has only been applied in exceptional circumstances.

Chapter Roundup

- The first legal source of law, consisting of decisions made in the courts, is **case law**, which is judge-made law based on the underlying principle of consistency. Once a legal principle is decided by an appropriate court it is a **judicial precedent**.

- Statements made by judges can be classified as **ratio decidendi** or **obiter dicta**.

- The second major source of law is **legislation**. This is also known as statute law and may take the form of **Acts of Parliament** or **delegated legislation** under the Acts.

- Legislation must be **interpreted correctly** before judges can **apply it fairly**. The **literal**, **golden** and **mischief rules** of interpretation developed over time. Nowadays a **purposive approach** is taken.

- The **Human Rights Act 1998** is a key example of the influence of International law in the UK.

- The **Human Rights Act 1998** incorporates the European Convention on Human Rights (the Convention) into UK domestic law. The impact of the legislation is **pervasive** in many areas of UK law.

- The Act has had an impact **on new legislation**, **statutory interpretation** and the **common law**.

Quick Quiz

1   Obiter dicta form part of the ratio decidendi.

   True ☐

   False ☐

2   Which of these decisions bind the Crown Court?

   Decisions of the County Court   ☐

   Decisions of the High Court   ☐

   Decisions of the Court of Appeal   ☐

   Decisions of the Supreme Court   ☐

3   In 2010, Mr Justice Jeffries, a High Court judge sitting alone, is deciding a case which has similar material facts to one decided by the Court of Appeal in 1910. He can decline to be bound by this decision by showing that
   A   The status of the previous court cannot bind him
   B   The decision was taken too long ago to be of any relevance
   C   The decision does not accord with the rules of a statute passed in 1975
   D   The obiter dicta are obscure

4   Overruling a decision of a lower court affects the outcome of that earlier decision.

   True ☐

   False ☐

5   UK Courts must interpret legislation in a way that is compatible with the Convention on Human Rights.

   True ☐

   False ☐

Answers to Quick Quiz

1   False. Obiter dicta do not form part of the ratio decidendi.

2   Decisions of the High Court, Court of Appeal and Supreme Court.

3   C. A High Court judge is bound by decisions of the Court of Appeal. However, he can decline to be bound if it conflicts with a principle of law. In this case the 1975 statute has effectively overruled the previous decision.

4   False. The decision in that case will stand.

5   True. UK courts must interpret legislation in a way that is compatible with the Convention and where there are two possible interpretations, and one is incompatible, they must choose the one that is compatible with the Convention.

Now try the questions below from the Practice Question Bank

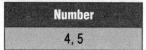

Number
4, 5

The law of obligations

Formation of contract I

3

Topic list	Syllabus reference
1 Definition of contract	B1(a)
2 Factors affecting the modern contract	B1(a)
3 The essentials of a contract	B1(a)
4 Form of a contract	B1(a)
5 Offer	B1(b)
6 Termination of offer	B1(c)
7 Acceptance	B1(d)
8 Communication of acceptance	B1(d)
9 Collateral contracts	B1(c), B1(d)

Introduction

We begin our study of **the law of obligations** by considering contract law.

Individuals and businesses form contracts all the time. Despite what many people believe, contracts **do not** all need to be written and signed documents; indeed, many valid contracts involve no written or spoken communication at all – for example, where a person buys something from a shop.

This chapter **describes** what a contract is, **the essential elements** that make up a contract and the various forms contracts may take.

It continues by analysing the first requirement for a valid contract – **agreement**, which consists of an **offer** and **acceptance** of the offer.

You must be able to **distinguish offers** from **invitations to treat** and to explain what the consequences of acceptance are. The rules concerning when offers can be **terminated** and how acceptance should be communicated are vital knowledge since exam questions may require you to use them to determine whether or not a valid contract exists.

Study guide

		Intellectual level
B	The law of obligations	
1	Formation of contract	
(a)	Analyse the nature of a simple contract	2
(b)	Explain the meaning of an offer and distinguish it from an invitation to treat	2
(c)	Explain the termination of an offer	2
(d)	Explain the meaning and consequence of acceptance	2

Exam guide

Questions may require you to identify whether a valid contract exists, so it is important to understand the circumstances where valid offers are made and where acceptance is communicated acceptably.

1 Definition of contract

FAST FORWARD

A **valid contract is a legally binding agreement**, formed by the mutual consent of two parties.

Key term

A **contract** may be defined as an **agreement which legally binds the parties.** The underlying theory is that a contract is the outcome of 'consenting minds'. However, parties are judged by what they have said, written or done, rather than by what they were actually thinking.

Exam focus point

Almost every sitting will have a scenario-based contract law question requiring you to analyse the situation and provide simple advice.

2 Factors affecting the modern contract

FAST FORWARD

The law seeks to protect the idea of 'freedom of contract', although **contractual terms** may be regulated by **statute**, particularly where the parties are of unequal bargaining strength.

2.1 Inequality of bargaining power

Freedom of contract means that in principle parties are entitled to enter into agreements as they see fit and without restriction. However, where two parties make an agreement, they invariably have differing levels of **bargaining power**. Many contracts are made between experts and ordinary consumers. The law will intervene **only** where the former takes unfair advantage of their position and not simply because one party was in an inferior bargaining position.'

2.2 The standard form contract

Mass production and consumerism have led to the **standard form contract**.

Key term

The **standard form contract** is a document prepared by many large organisations setting out the terms on which they contract with their customers. The individual must usually take it or leave it. For example, a customer has to accept their supply of electricity on the electricity board's terms – they are not likely to succeed in negotiating special terms, unless they represent a large consumer such as a factory.

2.3 Consumer protection

The development of a **mass market** for complex goods in the last century meant that the consumer can no longer rely on their own judgement when buying sophisticated goods or services. **Consumer interests** are now served by two main areas.

(a)   **Consumer protection agencies**, which include organisations such as the Financial Conduct Authority

(b)   **Legislation**

Public policy sometimes requires that the freedom of contract should be modified. For example, the **Unfair Contract Terms Act 1977** and the **Consumer Rights Act 2015** both regulate the extent to which contracts can contain certain terms.

2.4 Battle of the forms

Disputes sometimes arise in commercial agreements because each party is accustomed to doing business on its own **standard terms** and argues that they apply to the contract, rather than the other party's terms. Great care should be taken during the negotiation stage to clarify which standard (or other) terms will apply. Where it is not clear, the contract must be considered objectively, but taking into account what has actually happened (the 'factual matrix').

GHSP Inc v A B Electronic Ltd 2010

The facts: The claimant, a manufacturer of control systems for motor vehicles, purchased pedal sensors from the defendant which were defective and caused substantial losses. Both parties argued that their standard terms applied to the contract. The defendant's standard terms excluded liability for consequential loss or damage and limited liability to carrying out works of repair.

Decision: The contract was not governed by either set of standard terms, as it was clear that neither party had accepted the other party's terms. The court held that the contract was governed by the terms implied by the Sale of Goods Act 1979.

2.5 The electronic contract

English law has been concerned with formulating the rules for oral and written contracts for centuries, and cases decided in the 1800s continue to be valid today. As you will see, there are a number of **important rules** which deal with the timing of the sending and receipt of letters by post. With the advent of **telex** and **fax machines**, the law has had to be applied to new situations. Now the development of the internet for commercial purposes has brought new challenges as new ways of doing business come into being.

3 The essentials of a contract

FAST FORWARD

The **three essential elements** of a contract are **offer and acceptance**, **consideration** and **intention to enter into legal relations**.

The courts will usually look for evidence of **three essential elements** in any contract.

- There must be an **agreement** usually made by **offer and acceptance**.

- There must be a bargain by which the obligations assumed by one party are supported by **consideration** (value) given by the other.

- The parties must have an **intention to create legal relations** between themselves.

3.1 Validity factors

Even if these **essential elements** can be shown, a contract may not necessarily be valid or may only be partially valid. The validity of a contract may also be affected by any of the following factors.

(a) **Capacity**. Some persons have restricted capacity to enter into contracts.

   Minors cannot enter into contracts for goods other than necessities, nor do they have the capacity to contract for loans.

   Those who lack **mental capacity** or who were **intoxicated** can avoid contracts if they can show they did not understand the nature of their actions and the other party ought to have known about their disability. They still must pay a reasonable price for the goods received.

(b) **Form**. Some contracts must be made in a particular form.

(c) **Content**. In general the parties may enter into a contract on whatever terms they choose. Some terms which the parties do not express may be **implied**, and some terms which the parties do express are **overridden** by statutory rules.

(d) **Genuine consent**. A mistake or misrepresentation made by one party may affect the validity of a contract. Parties may be induced to enter into a contract by **undue influence** or **duress**.

(e) **Legality**. The courts will not enforce a contract which is deemed to be illegal or contrary to public policy.

A contract which does not satisfy the relevant tests may be either **void, voidable** or **unenforceable**.

Key terms

> A **void contract** is not a contract at all. The parties are not bound by it and if they transfer property under it they can sometimes recover their goods even from a third party.
>
> A **voidable contract** is a contract which one party may set aside. Property transferred before avoidance is usually irrecoverable from a third party.
>
> An **unenforceable contract** is a valid contract and property transferred under it cannot be recovered even from the other party to the contract. But if either party refuses to perform or to complete their part of the performance of the contract, the other party cannot compel them to do so. A contract is usually unenforceable when the required evidence of its terms, for example, written evidence of a contract relating to land, is not available.

4 Form of a contract

FAST FORWARD

> As a general rule, **a contract may be made in any form.**

Contracts do not usually have to be in writing except in the following circumstances.

- Some contracts must be by **deed**
- Some contracts must be in **writing**
- Some contracts must be **evidenced in writing**

4.1 Contracts by deed

A contract by deed must be in **writing** and it must be **signed**. Delivery must take place. Delivery is conduct indicating that the person executing the deed intends to be bound by it.

These contracts **must** be by deed.

- **Leases** for three years or more

- A **conveyance** or transfer of a legal estate in land (including a mortgage)

- A promise **not** supported by **consideration** (such as a **covenant**, for example a promise to pay a regular sum to a charity)

A **contract by deed** is sometimes referred to as a specialty contract. Any other type of contract may be referred to as a simple contract.

4.2 Contracts which must be in writing

The following contracts must be in **writing and signed** by at least one of the parties.

- A **transfer of shares** in a limited company
- The sale or disposition of an **interest in land**
- **Bills of exchange** and **cheques**
- **Consumer credit** contracts

In the case of **consumer credit transactions**, the effect of failure to make the agreement in the prescribed form is to make the agreement unenforceable against the debtor unless the creditor obtains a court order.

4.3 Contracts which must be evidenced in writing

Certain contracts may be made orally, but are not enforceable in a court of law unless there is written **evidence** of their terms. The most important contract of this type is the **contract of guarantee**.

5 Offer

The first essential element in the formation of a binding contract is **agreement**. This is usually evidenced by **offer and acceptance**. An offer is a definite promise to be bound on specific terms, and must be distinguished from the mere **supply of information** and from an **invitation to treat**.

An **offer** is a **definite promise to be bound on specific terms**.

A **definite offer does not have to be made to a particular person**. It may be made to a class of persons or to the world at large. However, it must be distinguished from a statement which supplies information, from a statement of intention and from an invitation to treat.

Carlill v Carbolic Smoke Ball Co 1893

The facts: The manufacturers of a patent medicine published an advertisement by which they undertook to pay '£100 reward ... to any person who contracts ... influenza ... after having used the smoke ball three times daily for two weeks'. The advertisement added that £1,000 had been deposited at a bank 'showing our sincerity in this matter'. The claimant read the advertisement, purchased the smoke ball and used it as directed. She contracted influenza and claimed her £100 reward. In their defence the manufacturers argued against this, saying:

(a) The offer was so vague that it could not form the basis of a contract, as no time limit was specified.
(b) It was not an offer which could be accepted since it was offered to the whole world.

Decision: The court disagreed.

(a) The smoke ball must protect the user during the period of use – the offer was not vague.
(b) Such an offer was possible, as it could be compared to reward cases.

You should note that **Carlill is an unusual case** in that advertisements are not usually regarded as offers. **A statement which is vague** cannot be an offer but an apparently vague offer can be made certain by reference to previous dealing or customs.

Gunthing v Lynn 1831

The facts: The offeror offered to pay a further sum for a horse if it was 'lucky'.

Decision: The offer was too vague and no contract could be formed.

5.1 Supply of information

Only an offer in the proper sense may be accepted so as to form a binding contract. A statement which sets out **possible terms** of a contract is not an offer unless this is clearly indicated.

Harvey v Facey 1893

The facts: The claimant telegraphed to the defendant 'Will you sell us Bumper Hall Pen? Telegraph lowest cash price'. The defendant telegraphed in reply 'Lowest price for Bumper Hall Pen, £900'. The claimant telegraphed to accept what he regarded as an offer; the defendant made no further reply.

Decision: The defendant's telegram was merely a statement of his minimum price if a sale were to be agreed. It was not an offer which the claimant could accept.

If in the course of **negotiations for a sale**, the vendor states the price at which they will sell, that statement may be an offer which can be accepted.

Bigg v Boyd Gibbons 1971

The facts: In the course of correspondence the defendant rejected an offer of £20,000 by the claimant and added 'for a quick sale I would accept £26,000 ... if you are not interested in this price would you please let me know immediately'. The claimant accepted this price of £26,000 and the defendant acknowledged his acceptance.

Decision: In this context the defendant must be treated as making an offer which the claimant had accepted.

Reference to a more **detailed document** will not necessarily prevent a statement from being an offer – for example, where a consumer is directed to a booklet of terms and conditions.

5.2 A statement of intention

Advertising that an event such as an auction will take place is not an offer to sell. Potential buyers may not sue the auctioneer if the auction does not take place. This is an example of a **statement of intention** which is not actionable.

5.3 An invitation to treat

Where a party is initiating negotiations they are said to have made an invitation to treat. An **invitation to treat** cannot be accepted to form a binding contract. Examples of invitations to treat include.

- **Auction** sales
- **Advertisements** (for example, price lists or newspaper advertisements)
- **Exhibition** of goods for sale
- An **invitation** for tenders

Key term

An **invitation to treat** occurs where a party indicates that they are open to offers for entering into a contract.

5.3.1 Auction sales

The **bid itself is the offer**, which the auctioneer is free to accept or reject. An auction is defined as a contract for the sale of property under which offers are made by bidders stating the price at which they are prepared to buy and **acceptance takes place by the fall of the auctioneer's hammer**. Where an auction is stated to be 'without reserve' the auctioneer is offering goods for sale and the bid is the acceptance. A reserve is a specified minimum price.

5.3.2 Advertisements

An **advertisement** of goods for sale is usually an **attempt to induce offers**.

Partridge v Crittenden 1968

The facts: Mr Partridge placed an advertisement for 'Bramblefinch cocks, bramblefinch hens, 25s each'. The RSPCA brought a prosecution against him for offering for sale a brambling in contravention of the Protection of Birds Act 1954. The justices convicted Partridge and he appealed.

Decision: The conviction was quashed. Although there had been a sale in contravention of the Act, the prosecution could not rely on the offence of 'offering for sale', as the advertisement only constituted an invitation to treat.

The **circulation of a price list** is also an invitation to treat.

5.3.3 Exhibition of goods for sale

Displaying goods in a shop window, or on the open shelves of a self-service shop, or advertising goods for sale, are normally invitations to treat.

Fisher v Bell 1961

The facts: A shopkeeper was prosecuted for offering for sale an offensive weapon by exhibiting a flick knife in his shop window.

Decision: The display of an article with a price on it in a shop window is merely an invitation to treat.

Pharmaceutical Society of Great Britain v Boots Cash Chemists (Southern) 1952

The facts: Certain drugs could only be sold under the supervision of a registered pharmacist. The claimant claimed this rule had been broken by Boots who displayed these drugs in a self-service shop. Boots contended that there was no sale until a customer brought the goods to the cash desk and offered to buy them. A registered pharmacist was stationed at this point.

Decision: The court found for Boots and commented that if it were true that a customer accepted an offer to sell by removing goods from the shelf, he could not then change his mind and put them back as this would constitute breach of contract.

5.3.4 Invitation for tenders

A **tender** is an offer to supply specified goods or services at a stated cost or rate, submitted in response to a prior invitation for tenders by the purchaser. When a supplier tenders for a contract they are making an offer to the purchaser who has advertised a contract as being available.

The **effect of an invitation to tender** depends on the wording used.

- If the invitation states that the purchaser **will** require the successful supplier to supply them, usually for a large 'one-off' supply, then acceptance of the tender by the purchaser will form a binding contract.

- If the invitation states that the purchaser **may** require the successful supplier to supply him, then acceptance by the purchaser of the supplier's offer creates a **standing offer**.

A **standing offer** means that the purchaser does not have to buy any goods from the supplier, but may not purchase goods from another supplier. Any purchase orders that the purchaser makes are separate acceptances that form separate contracts, and delivery must be made within the time stated in the standing offer. Unless there is a binding obligation to keep it open for a certain period of time the supplier may revoke a standing offer at any time, but must fulfil any orders placed, since these created contractual obligations.

6 Termination of offer

FAST FORWARD

An offer may only be accepted while it is still open. In the absence of an acceptance, an offer may be **terminated** in any of the following ways.

- Rejection
- Counter-offer
- Lapse of time

- Revocation by the offeror
- Failure of a condition to which the offer was subject
- Death of one of the parties

6.1 Rejection

As noted earlier, **outright rejection terminates an offer**. A counter-offer, when the person to whom the offer was made proposes new or amended terms, also terminates the original offer.

Hyde v Wrench 1840

The facts: The defendant offered to sell property to the claimant for £1,000 on 6 June. Two days later, the claimant made a counter-offer of £950 which the defendant rejected on 27 June. The claimant then informed the defendant on 29 June that he accepted the original offer of £1,000.

Decision: The original offer of £1,000 had been terminated by the counter-offer of £950.

6.2 Counter-offer

Acceptance must be **unqualified agreement to the terms of the offer**. A purported acceptance which introduces any new terms is a counter-offer, which has the effect of terminating the original offer.

Key term

A **counter-offer** is a final rejection of the original offer. If a counter-offer is made, the original offeror may accept it, but if they reject it, their original offer is no longer available for acceptance.

A **counter-offer** may, of course, be accepted by the original offeror.

Butler Machine Tool Co v Ex-cell-O Corp (England) 1979

The facts: The claimant offered to sell tools to the defendant. Their quotation included details of their standard terms. The defendant 'accepted' the offer, enclosing their own standard terms. The claimant acknowledged acceptance by returning a tear-off slip from the order form.

Decision: The defendant's order was really a counter-offer. The claimant had accepted this by returning the tear-off slip.

6.2.1 Request for information

It is possible to respond to an offer by making a **request for information**. Such a request may be a request as to whether or not other terms would be acceptable – it is not a counter-offer.

Stevenson v McLean 1880

The facts: The defendant offered to sell iron at '40s net cash per ton, open till Monday'. The claimant enquired whether he would agree to delivery spread over two months. The defendant did not reply and (within the stated time limit), the claimant accepted the original offer. Meanwhile the defendant had sold the iron to a third party.

Decision: There was a contract since the claimant had merely enquired as to a variation of terms.

6.3 Lapse of time

An offer may be expressed to last for a **specified time**. If, however, there is no express time limit set, it expires after a **reasonable time**.

> *Ramsgate Victoria Hotel Co v Montefiore 1866*
>
> *The facts:* The defendant applied to the company in June for shares and paid a deposit. At the end of November the company sent him an acceptance by issue of a letter of allotment and requested payment of the balance due. The defendant contended that his offer had expired and could no longer be accepted.
>
> *Decision:* The offer was valid for a reasonable time only and five months was too long.

6.4 Revocation of an offer

The offeror may **revoke** their offer at any time before acceptance. If they undertake that their offer shall remain open for acceptance for a specified time they may still revoke it within that time, unless by a separate contract they agreed to keep it open. This is known as an **option contract**.

> *Routledge v Grant 1828*
>
> *The facts:* The defendant offered to buy the claimant's house for a fixed sum, requiring acceptance within six weeks. Within the six weeks specified, he withdrew his offer.
>
> *Decision:* The defendant could revoke his offer at any time before acceptance, even though the time limit had not expired.

Revocation may be an **express statement** or may be an **act** of the offeror. The offeror's revocation does not take effect until the revocation is communicated to the offeree. This raises two important points.

(a) The first point is that **posting** a letter of revocation is not a sufficient act of revocation.

> *Byrne v Van Tienhoven 1880*
>
> *The facts:* The defendants were in Cardiff; the claimants in New York. The sequence of events was as follows.
>
> | | |
> |---|---|
> | 1 October | Letter posted in Cardiff, offering to sell 1,000 boxes of tinplates. |
> | 8 October | Letter of revocation of offer posted in Cardiff. |
> | 11 October | Letter of offer received in New York and telegram of acceptance sent. |
> | 15 October | Letter confirming acceptance posted in New York. |
> | 20 October | Letter of revocation received in New York. The offeree had meanwhile resold the contract goods. |
>
> *Decision:* The letter of revocation could not take effect until received (20 October); it could not revoke the contract made by the telegram acceptance of the offer on 11 October.

(b) The second point is that **revocation of offer may be communicated by any third party who is a sufficiently reliable informant**.

> *Dickinson v Dodds 1876*
>
> *The facts:* The defendant, on 10 June, wrote to the claimant to offer property for sale at £800, adding 'this offer to be left open until Friday 12 June, 9.00 am.' On 11 June the defendant sold the property to A, another buyer. B, who had been an intermediary between Dickinson and Dodds, informed Dickinson that the defendant had sold to someone else. On Friday 12 June, before 9.00 am, the claimant handed to the defendant a formal letter of acceptance.
>
> *Decision:* The defendant was free to revoke his offer and had done so by sale to a third party; the claimant could not accept the offer after he had learnt from a reliable informant of the revocation of the offer to him.

However, this case should be treated with **caution** and it may be that only an agent can revoke an offer.

6.5 Failure of a condition

An **offer may be conditional** in that it is dependent on some event occurring or there being a change of circumstances. If the condition is not satisfied, the offer is not capable of acceptance.

Financings Ltd v Stimson 1962

The facts: The defendant wished to purchase a car, and on 16 March signed a hire-purchase form. The form, issued by the claimants, stated that the agreement would be binding only upon signature by them. On 20 March the defendant, not satisfied with the car, returned it. On 24 March the car was stolen from the premises of the dealer, and was recovered badly damaged. On 25 March the claimants signed the form. They sued the defendant for breach of contract.

Decision: The defendant was not bound to take the car. His signing of the agreement was actually an offer to contract with the claimant. There was an implied condition in this offer that the car would be in a reasonable condition.

6.6 Termination by death

The **death** of the offeree terminates the offer. The offeror's death terminates the offer, unless the offeree accepts the offer in ignorance of the death, and the offer is not of a personal nature.

Bradbury v Morgan 1862

The facts: X offered to guarantee payment by Y in respect of goods to be supplied by the claimant. X died and the claimant, in ignorance of his death, continued to supply goods to Y. The claimant then sued X's executors on the guarantee.

Decision: X's offer was a continuing commercial offer which the claimant had accepted by supply of goods after X's death. The guarantee stood.

---

7 Acceptance

Acceptance must be an unqualified agreement to all the terms of the offer. **Acceptance** is generally not effective until **communicated** to the offeror, except where the **'postal rule'** applies, in which case acceptance is complete and effective as soon as it is posted.

Key term

Acceptance is a positive act by an offeree which brings a contract into effect.

The contract comes into **effect** once the offeree has **accepted** the terms presented to them. This is the point of no return; after acceptance, the offeror **cannot withdraw** their offer and both parties will be **bound** by the terms that they have agreed.

Acceptance may be by **express words**, by **action** or **inferred from conduct**.

Brogden v Metropolitan Railway Co 1877

The facts: For many years the claimant supplied coal to the defendant. He suggested that they should enter into a written agreement and the defendant's agent sent a draft to him for consideration. The parties applied to their dealings the terms of the draft agreement, but they never signed a final version. The claimant later denied that there was any agreement between him and the defendant.

Decision: The conduct of the parties was only explicable on the assumption that they both agreed to the terms of the draft.

BPP
LEARNING MEDIA

7.1 Silence

There must be some **act** on the part of the offeree to indicate their acceptance.

Felthouse v Bindley 1862

The facts: The claimant wrote to his nephew offering to buy the nephew's horse, adding 'If I hear no more about him, I consider the horse mine'. The nephew intended to accept his uncle's offer but did not reply. He instructed the defendant, an auctioneer, not to sell the horse. Owing to a misunderstanding the horse was sold to someone else. The uncle sued the auctioneer.

Decision: The action failed. The claimant had no title to the horse.

Goods which are sent or services which are rendered to a person who did not request them are not 'accepted' merely because they are not returned to the sender: **Unsolicited Goods and Services Act 1971** (HMSO 1971). The recipient may treat them as an unsolicited gift.

7.2 Acceptance 'subject to contract'

Acceptance **'subject to contract'** means that the offeree is agreeable to the terms of the offer but proposes that the parties should negotiate a formal contract. Neither party is bound until the formal contract is signed. Agreements for the sale of land in England are usually made 'subject to contract'.

Acceptance 'subject to contract' must be distinguished from outright acceptance made on the understanding that the parties wish to replace the **preliminary contract** with another at a later stage. Even if the immediate contract is described as 'provisional', it takes effect at once.

Branca v Cobarro 1947

The facts: A vendor agreed to sell a mushroom farm under a contract which was declared to be 'a provisional agreement until a fully legalised agreement is signed'.

Decision: By the use of the word 'provisional', the parties had intended their agreement to be binding until, by mutual agreement, they made another to replace it.

7.3 Letters of intent

Key term

Letters of intent are an indication by one party to another that they may place a contract with them.

Thus a building contractor tendering for a large **construction contract** may need to subcontract certain (specialist) aspects of the work. The subcontractor will be asked to provide an estimate so that the main contractor can finalise their own tender.

Usually, a **letter of intent** is worded so as not to create any legal obligation. However, in some cases it may be phrased so that it includes an invitation to commence preliminary work. In such circumstances, it creates an obligation to pay for that work.

British Steel Corpn v Cleveland Bridge and Engineering Co Ltd 1984

The facts: The defendants asked the claimants to supply nodes for a complex steel lattice-work frame, and sent the claimants a letter of intent, stating their intention to place an order on their standard terms. The claimants stated that they were unwilling to contract on such terms, but started work, and eventually completed and delivered all the nodes. They sued for the value of the nodes and the defendants counter-claimed for damages for late delivery.

Decision: Since the parties had not reached agreement over such matters as late delivery, there was no contract, and so there could be no question of damages for late delivery. However, since the claimants had undertaken work at the request of the defendants and the defendants had accepted this work, the claimants were entitled to a reasonable remuneration for services rendered.

7.4 Acceptance of a tender

As we saw earlier, an **invitation for tenders** is an invitation to treat. There are two distinct types of tender.

(a) A **tender to perform one task**, such as building a new hospital, is an offer which can be accepted.

(b) A **tender to supply or perform a series of things**, such as the supply of vegetables daily to a restaurant, is not accepted until an order is placed. It is a standing offer. Each order placed by the offeree is an individual act of acceptance creating a separate contract. Until orders are placed there is no contract and the tenderer can terminate their standing offer.

> *Great Northern Railways v Witham 1873*
>
> *The facts:* The defendant tendered successfully for the supply of stores to the claimant over a period of one year. In his tender he undertook 'to supply ... such quantities as the company may order from time to time'. After making some deliveries he refused to fulfil an order which the claimant had given.
>
> *Decision:* He was in breach of contract in refusing to fulfil the order given but might revoke his tender and need not then fulfil any future orders within the remainder of the 12-month period.

7.5 Counter-offers and requests for information

A **counter-offer does not constitute acceptance**; it is the making of a new offer which may, in turn, be accepted or rejected. Nor is a request for further information an acceptance. In *Neale v Merrett 1930* an offer to sell land at £280 was accepted, but payment consisted of £80 and an undertaking to pay the balance by instalments. 'Acceptance' amounted to a counter-offer since it varied the method of payment.

8 Communication of acceptance

FAST FORWARD

> The general rule is that acceptance **must be communicated** to the offeror and that it is not effective (and hence there is no contract) until this has been done. However, this rule does not apply in all cases.

8.1 Waiver of communication

The offeror may **dispense** with the need for communication of acceptance. Such a waiver may be express or may be inferred from the circumstances. In *Carlill v Carbolic Smoke Ball Co 1893*, it was held that it was sufficient for the claimant to act on the offer without notifying her acceptance of it. This was an example of a **unilateral contract**, where the offer takes the form of a promise to pay money in return for an act.

8.2 Prescribed mode of communication

The offeror may call for communication of acceptance by **specified means**. Communication of acceptance by some other means **equally expeditious** generally constitutes a valid acceptance unless specified otherwise. This would probably apply also to acceptance by fax machine or email. The offeror would have to use very precise wording if a specified means of communication is to be treated as mandatory.

> *Yates Building Co v R J Pulleyn & Sons (York) 1975*
>
> *The facts:* The offer called for acceptance by registered or recorded delivery letter. The offeree sent an ordinary letter which arrived without delay.
>
> *Decision:* The offeror had suffered no disadvantage and had not stipulated that acceptance must be made in this way only. The acceptance was valid.

8.3 No mode of communication prescribed

The offeree can use any method but must ensure that their **acceptance is understood** if they choose an **instantaneous method of communication**.

> *Entores v Miles Far Eastern Corporation 1955*
>
> *The facts:* The claimants sent an offer by telex to the defendants' agent in Amsterdam and the latter sent an acceptance by telex. The claimants alleged breach of contract and wished to serve a writ.
>
> *Decision:* The acceptance took effect (and the contract was made) when the telex message was printed out on the claimants' terminal in London. A writ could therefore be issued.

8.4 The postal rule

The offeror may **expressly** or by **implication** indicate that they expect acceptance by means of a letter sent through the post.

Key term

> The **postal rule** states that, where the use of the post is within the contemplation of both the parties, the acceptance is complete and effective as soon as a letter is posted, even though it may be delayed or even lost altogether in the post.

> *Adams v Lindsell 1818*
>
> *The facts:* The defendants made an offer by letter to the claimant on 2 September 1817 requiring an answer 'in course of post'. It reached the claimants on 5 September; they immediately posted a letter of acceptance, which reached the defendants on 9 September. The defendants could have expected a reply by 7 September, and they assumed that the absence of a reply within the expected period indicated non-acceptance and sold the goods to another buyer on 8 September.
>
> *Decision:* The acceptance was made 'in course of post' (no time limit was imposed) and was effective when posted on 5 September.

The **intention** to use the post for communication of acceptance may be deduced from the **circumstances**.

> *Household Fire and Carriage Accident Insurance Co v Grant 1879*
>
> *The facts:* The defendant handed a letter of application for shares to the claimant company's agent in Swansea for posting to the company in London. The company posted an acceptance which never arrived. The defendant was called upon to pay the amount outstanding on his shares.
>
> *Decision:* The defendant had to pay. The contract had been formed when the acceptance was posted, regardless of the fact that it was lost.

Under the postal rule, the **offeror may be unaware** that a contract has been made. If that possibility is clearly inconsistent with the nature of the transaction the letter of acceptance takes effect only when received. In particular, if the offer stipulates a particular mode of communication, the postal rule may not apply.

> *Holwell Securities v Hughes 1974*
>
> *The facts:* Hughes granted to the claimant an option to purchase land to be exercised 'by notice in writing'. A letter giving notice of the exercise of the option was lost in the post.
>
> *Decision:* The words 'notice in writing' must mean notice actually received by the vendor; hence notice had not been given to accept the offer.

Acceptance of an offer may **only** be made **by a person authorised** to do so. This will usually be the offeree or their authorised agents.

Exam focus point

> A good article titled 'Key aspects of the law of contract and the tort of negligence' appeared in *Student Accountant* and is available on the ACCA website.

8.5 Cross-offers

If two offers, identical in terms, **cross in the post**, there is no contract. For example, if A offers to sell their car to B for £1,000 and B offers to buy A's car for £1,000, there is no contract, because there is no acceptance.

8.6 Unilateral contracts

The question arises as to whether contractual obligations arise if a party, in ignorance of an offer, performs an act which fulfils the terms of the offer. If A offers a **reward** to anyone who finds and returns their lost property and B, in ignorance of the offer, does in fact return it, is B entitled to the promised reward? There is agreement by conduct, but B is not accepting A's offer since they are unaware of it.

> **R v Clarke 1927**
>
> *The facts:* A reward was offered for information leading to the arrest and conviction of a murderer. If the information was provided by an accomplice, he would receive a free pardon. C claimed the reward, admitting that he had acted to save his own skin and that all thought of the reward had passed out his mind.
>
> *Decision:* There could not be acceptance without knowledge of the offer.

However, acceptance may still be **valid** even if the offer was not the sole reason for the action.

> **Williams v Carwardine 1833**
>
> *The facts:* A reward was offered to bring criminals to book. The claimant, an accomplice in the crime, supplied the information, with knowledge of the reward.
>
> *Decision:* As the information was given with knowledge, the acceptance was related to the offer.

The case of *Carlill v Carbolic Smoke Ball Company 1893* includes one example of a **unilateral contract**. Here the defendants advertised that they would pay £100 to anyone who caught influenza while using their product. This was held to be an offer to the world at large capable of being accepted by anyone fulfilling the necessary conditions. However, it was not necessary that anyone fulfilled the conditions, but as soon as Carlill began to **use** the product, the defendants were bound by their offer.

An ordinary offer can be revoked at any time before complete acceptance and, once revoked, can no longer be accepted. However, in the case of a **unilateral contract**, the courts have held that an **offer cannot be revoked once the offeree has begun to perform** whatever act is necessary.

9 Collateral contracts

FAST FORWARD

In certain circumstances, the courts may infer the existence of a contract without the formalities of offer and acceptance. This type of contract is a **collateral contract**.

Key term

A **collateral contract** is a contract where consideration is provided by the making of another contract. For example, if there are two separate contracts, one between A and B and one between A and C, on terms which involve some concerted action between B and C, there may be a contract between B and C.

There is a contract between B and C despite the **absence of direct communication** between them.

Shanklin Pier Ltd v Detel Products Ltd 1951

The facts: The defendants gave assurances to the claimants that their paint would be satisfactory and durable if used to repaint the claimant's pier. The claimants in their contract with X for the repainting of the pier specified that X should use this paint. The paint proved very unsatisfactory. The claimants sued the defendants for breach of undertaking. The defendants argued that there was no contract between the claimants and themselves.

Decision: The contract between the claimants and X requiring the use of the defendant's paint was the consideration for a contract between the claimants and the defendant.

Chapter Roundup

- A **valid contract is a legally binding agreement**, formed by the mutual consent of two parties.

- The law seeks to protect the idea of 'freedom of contract', although **contractual terms** may be regulated by **statute**, particularly where the parties are of unequal bargaining strength.

- The **three essential elements** of a contract are **offer and acceptance**, **consideration** and **intention to enter into legal relations**.

- As a general rule, **a contract may be made in any form**.

- The first essential element in the formation of a binding contract is **agreement**. This is usually evidenced by **offer and acceptance**. An offer is a definite promise to be bound on specific terms, and must be distinguished from the mere **supply of information** and from an **invitation to treat**.

- An offer may only be accepted while it is still open. In the absence of an acceptance, an offer may be **terminated** in any of the following ways.

  - Rejection
  - Counter-offer
  - Lapse of time
  - Revocation by the offeror
  - Failure of a condition to which the offer was subject
  - Death of one of the parties

- **Acceptance** must be an unqualified agreement to all the terms of the offer. **Acceptance** is generally not effective until **communicated** to the offeror, except where the **'postal rule'** applies, in which case acceptance is complete and effective as soon as it is posted.

- The general rule is that acceptance **must be communicated** to the offeror and that it is not effective (and hence there is no contract) until this has been done. However, this rule does not apply in all cases.

- In certain circumstances, the courts may infer the existence of a contract without the formalities of offer and acceptance. This type of contract is a **collateral contract**.

Quick Quiz

1 How is the circulation of a price list categorised in the law of contract?

Offer	Tender
Invitation to treat	Auction

2 **Fill in the blanks** in the statements below, using the words in the box.

As a general rule, acceptance must be (1) ……………….. to the (2) ……………….. and is not effective until this has been done.

An (3) ……………….. is a definite promise to be bound on specific terms, and must be distinguished from a supply of (4) ……………….. and from an (5) ………………..

A counter-offer counts as (6) ……………….. of the original offer

• information	• offer	• invitation to treat
• rejection	• communicated	• offeror

3 Advertising an auction is an offer to sell

True ☐

False ☐

4 As a general rule, silence cannot constitute acceptance.

True ☐

False ☐

5 **Fill in the blanks** in the statement below:

A valid contract is a legally binding agreement. The three essential elements of a contract are (1) ……………….. (2) ……………….. and (3) ……………….. .

Answers to Quick Quiz

1 Invitation to treat.

2 (1) communicated (2) offeror (3) offer (4) information (5) invitation to treat (6) rejection

3 False. Advertisements for auctions are not offers to sell.

4 True. Generally, silence cannot constitute acceptance.

5 (1) offer and acceptance (agreement) (2) consideration (3) intention to create legal relations

Now try the questions below from the Practice Question Bank

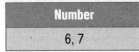

Number
6, 7

3: Formation of contract I │ Part B The law of obligations

Formation of contract II

4

Topic list	Syllabus reference
1 Consideration	B1(e)
2 Adequacy and sufficiency of consideration	B1(f)
3 Promissory estoppel	B1(e)
4 Intention to create legal relations	B1(h)
5 Privity of contract	B1(g)
6 The electronic contract	B1(a)

Introduction

In this chapter we complete our study of the essential requirements for a valid contract by looking at **consideration** and **intention**.

Consideration is what both parties bring to a contract and the key principle to remember is that it has to be **sufficient** but not necessarily **adequate**.

Agreements between family members are presumed not to have the **intention** of being legally binding, but those between strangers or businesses do have that intention.

Promissory estoppel and **privity of contract** are important concepts that could be easily used in an exam question to confuse the situation. Make sure you understand both concepts.

Finally we consider the impact of technology on contracts by examining **electronic contracts**. There is not much case law in this area, so keep an eye on the press for developments.

Study guide

		Intellectual level
B	The law of obligations	
1	Formation of contract	
(a)	Analyse the nature of a simple contract	2
(e)	Explain the need for consideration	2
(f)	Explain adequacy and sufficiency of consideration	2
(g)	Analyse the doctrine of privity	2
(h)	Distinguish the presumptions relating to intention to create legal relations	2

Exam guide

Questions may require you to identify whether a valid contract exists. They may also test your ability to spot whether acceptable consideration has passed between the parties and whether they can be legally held to have intended to be bound by the contract.

1 Consideration

FAST FORWARD

Consideration is an **essential** part of most contracts. It is what each party brings to the contract.

Key term

Consideration is what each party brings to the contract. For example one party provides goods and the other provides payment for them.

Using the language of purchase and sale, it could be said that one party must know that they have bought the other party's **promises** either by performing some act of their own or by offering a promise of their own.

Illustration

Another example of giving consideration is by suffering **detriment** as in *Carlill v Carbolic Smoke Ball Company 1883*. Mrs Carlill gave consideration by using the smoke ball as she was instructed.

1.1 Valid consideration

FAST FORWARD

Consideration may be **executed** (an act in return for a promise) or **executory** (a promise in return for a promise). It may not be **past**, unless one of three recognised exceptions applies.

There are two broad types of valid consideration – **executed** and **executory**. If consideration is **past** then it is not enforceable.

Executed consideration **is an act in return for a promise**. The consideration for the promise is a performed, or executed, act.

Illustration

A offers a reward for the return of lost property; their promise becomes binding when B performs the act of returning A's property to them. A is not bound to pay anything to anyone until the prescribed act is done. Therefore in Carlill's case, the claimant's act, in response to the Smoke Ball company's promise of reward, was executed consideration.

Key terms

> **Executed consideration** is consideration which passes when the contract is made. For example, in a shop, the goods and payment are the consideration which passes at the time the purchase is made.
>
> **Executory consideration is a promise given for a promise**. The consideration in support of each promise is the other promise, not a performed act.

Illustration

If a customer orders goods which a shopkeeper undertakes to obtain from the manufacturer, the shopkeeper promises to supply the goods and the customer promises to accept and pay for them. Neither has yet done anything but each has given a promise to obtain the promise of the other. It would be breach of contract if either withdrew without the consent of the other.

Key term

> **Executory consideration** is consideration which passes in the future. For example, goods may be delivered and payment made in a week's time.

1.1.1 Additional rules for valid consideration

As well as being either executed or executory, there are **additional** rules that must be met for consideration to be valid:

*   **Performance must be legal**. The courts will not enforce payment for illegal acts
*   **Performance must be possible**. Agreeing to perform the impossible is not a basis for a binding contract
*   **Consideration must pass from the promisee**
*   **Consideration must be sufficient but not necessarily adequate**

1.2 Past consideration

Key term

> **Past consideration** is something that has already been done when the promise is made. For example, agreeing to pay for goods which have already been delivered.

Anything which has already been done before a promise in return is given is past consideration which, as a general rule, is not sufficient to make the promise binding. The following is the key case in this area.

> *Re McArdle 1951*
>
> *The facts:* Under a will, the testator's children were entitled to a house after their mother's death. In the mother's lifetime one of the children and his wife lived in the house with the mother. The wife made improvements to the house. The children later agreed in writing to repay the wife 'in consideration of your carrying out certain alterations and improvements'. But at the mother's death they refused to do so.
>
> *Decision:* The work on the house had all been completed before the documents were signed. At the time of the promise the improvements were past consideration and so the promise was not binding.

If there is an **existing contract** and one party makes a further promise, no contract will arise. Even if the promise is directly related to the **previous bargain**, it has been made upon past consideration.

> *Roscorla v Thomas 1842*
>
> *The facts:* The claimant agreed to buy a horse from the defendant at a given price. When negotiations were over and the contract was formed, the defendant told the claimant that the horse was 'sound and free from vice'. The horse turned out to be vicious and the claimant brought an action on the warranty.
>
> *Decision:* The express promise was made after the sale was over and was unsupported by fresh consideration.

In three instances **past consideration** for a promise is sufficient to make the promise binding.

(a)   Past consideration is sufficient to create liability on a **bill of exchange** (such as a cheque). Most cheques are issued to pay existing debts.

(b)   After 6 (or, in some cases, 12) years the right to sue for recovery of a debt becomes **statute barred**. If, after that period, the debtor makes written acknowledgement of the creditor's claim, the claim is again enforceable at law.

(c)   When a request is made for a **service** this request may imply a promise to pay for it. If, after the service has been rendered, the person who made the request promises a specific reward, this is treated as fixing the amount to be paid.

Key term

> A **bill of exchange** is a negotiable instrument which entitles the holder to payment at a future date.

> *Lampleigh v Braithwaite 1615*
>
> *The facts:* The defendant had killed a man and had asked the claimant to obtain for him a royal pardon. The claimant did so at his own expense. The defendant then promised to pay him £100. He failed to pay it and was sued.
>
> *Decision:* The defendant's request was regarded as containing an implied promise to pay, and the subsequent promise merely fixed the amount.

Both parties must have **assumed** during their negotiations that the services were ultimately to be paid for.

> *Re Casey's Patents 1892*
>
> *The facts:* A and B, joint owners of patent rights, asked their employee, C, as an extra task to find licensees to work the patents. After C had done so, A and B agreed to reward him for his past services with one-third of the patent rights. A died and his executors denied that the promise was binding.
>
> *Decision:* The promise to C was binding since it merely fixed the 'reasonable remuneration' which A and B by implication promised to pay before the service was given.

2 Adequacy and sufficiency of consideration

FAST FORWARD

> The long-established rule is that consideration need **not be adequate** but it **must be sufficient**.

The court will also seek to ensure that a **particular act** or **promise** can actually be deemed to be consideration. Learn these rules:

(a)   **Consideration need not be adequate** (that is, equal in value to the consideration received in return). There is no remedy at law for someone who simply makes a poor bargain.

(b)   **Consideration must be sufficient**. It must be capable in law of being regarded as consideration by the courts.

2.1 Adequacy

It is presumed that each party is capable of serving their **own interests**, and the courts will not seek to weigh up the comparative value of the promises or acts exchanged.

> *Thomas v Thomas 1842*
>
> *The facts:* By his will, the claimant's husband expressed the wish that his widow should have the use of his house during her life. The defendants, his executors, allowed the widow to occupy the house (a) in accordance with her husband's wishes and (b) in return for her undertaking to pay a rent of £1 per annum. They later said that their promise to let her occupy the house was not supported by consideration.
>
> *Decision:* Compliance with the husband's wishes was not valuable consideration (no economic value attached to it), but the nominal rent was sufficient consideration.

2.2 Sufficiency

Consideration is sufficient if it has some **identifiable value**. The law only requires an element of bargain, not necessarily that it should be a good bargain.

> *Chappell & Co v Nestle Co 1960*
>
> *The facts:* As a sales promotion scheme, the defendant offered to supply a record to anyone who sent in a postal order for 1s.6d and three wrappers from 6d bars of chocolate made by them. The claimants owned the copyright of the tune. They sued for infringement of copyright. In the ensuing dispute over royalties the issue was whether the wrappers, which were thrown away when received, were part of the consideration for the promise to supply the record. The defendants offered to pay a royalty based on the price of 1s.6d per record, but the claimants rejected this, claiming that the wrappers also represented part of the consideration.
>
> *Decision:* The wrappers were part of the consideration as they had commercial value to the defendants.

As stated earlier, forbearance or the promise of it may be **sufficient** consideration if it has some value, or amounts to giving up something of value.

> *Horton v Horton 1961*
>
> *The facts:* Under a separation agreement, the defendant agreed to pay his wife (the claimant) £30 per month. Under the deed this amount was a net payment after deduction of income tax; for nine months the husband paid it without any deduction so that the wife had to make the deductions herself. He then signed a document agreeing to pay such amount as 'after the deduction of income tax should amount to the clear sum of £30'. He paid this for three years, then stopped, pleading that the later agreement was not supported by consideration.
>
> *Decision:* The later agreement was supported by consideration: the wife could have sued to have the original agreement rectified, but did not.

2.2.1 Performance of existing contractual duties

Performance of an **existing obligation imposed by statute** is no consideration for a promise of reward.

> *Collins v Godefroy 1831*
>
> *The facts:* The claimant had been subpoenaed to give evidence on behalf of the defendant in another case. He alleged that the defendant had promised to pay him six guineas for appearing.
>
> *Decision:* There was no consideration for this promise.

But if some **extra service** is given, that is sufficient consideration.

> **Glasbrook Bros v Glamorgan CC 1925**
>
> *The facts:* At a time of industrial unrest, colliery owners, rejecting the view of the police that a mobile force was enough, agreed to pay for a special guard on the mine. Later they repudiated liability saying that the police had done no more than perform their public duty of maintaining order, and that no consideration was given.
>
> *Decision:* The police had done more than perform their general duties. The extra services given, beyond what the police in their discretion deemed necessary, were consideration for the promise to pay.

In the *Glasbrook* case the threat to law and order was not caused by either of the parties. Where one party's actions lead to the need for heightened police presence, and the police deem this presence **necessary**, they may also be entitled to payment.

> **Harris v Sheffield United FC Ltd 1988**
>
> *The facts:* The defendants argued that they did not have to pay for a large police presence at their home matches.
>
> *Decision:* They had voluntarily decided to hold matches on Saturday afternoons when large attendances were likely, increasing the risk of disorder.

2.2.2 Promise of additional reward

If there is already a contract between A and B, and B promises **additional reward** to A if they (A) perform their existing duties, there is no consideration from A to make that promise binding.

> **Stilk v Myrick 1809**
>
> *The facts:* Two members of the crew of a ship deserted in a foreign port. The master was unable to recruit substitutes and promised the rest of the crew that they would share the wages of the deserters if they would complete the voyage home short-handed. The shipowners however repudiated the promise.
>
> *Decision:* In performing their existing contractual duties the crew gave no consideration for the promise of extra pay and the promise was not binding.

If a claimant does **more than perform an existing contractual duty**, this may amount to consideration.

> **Hartley v Ponsonby 1857**
>
> *The facts:* 17 men out of a crew of 36 deserted. The remainder were promised an extra £40 each to work the ship to Bombay. The claimant, one of the remaining crew members, sued to recover this amount.
>
> *Decision:* The large number of desertions made the voyage exceptionally hazardous, and this had the effect of discharging the original contract. The claimant's promise to complete the voyage formed consideration for the promise to pay an additional £40.

The courts now appear to be taking a slightly different line on the payment of **additional consideration**. It may be that where the party promising the additional reward has received a 'practical' benefit that will be treated as consideration even if, in law, they have received no more than they were already entitled to under the contract.

> **Williams v Roffey Bros & Nicholls (Contractors) Ltd 1990**
>
> *The facts:* The claimants agreed to do carpentry work for the defendants, who were engaged as contractors to refurbish a block of flats, at a fixed price of £20,000. The work ran late and so the defendants, concerned that the job might not be finished on time and that they would have to pay money under a penalty clause, agreed to pay the claimants an extra £10,300 to ensure the work was completed on time. They later refused to pay the extra amount.

> *Decision:* The fact that there was no apparent consideration for the promise to pay the extra was not held to be important, as in the court's view both parties derived a practical benefit from the promise. The telling point was that the defendants' promise had not been extracted by duress or fraud: it was therefore binding. The defendant had avoided the possible penalty.

Exam focus point

> *Williams v Roffey Bros* is important because it is a newer case than the bulk of contract cases, most of which were decided in the nineteenth century.

> *Re Selectmove 1994*
>
> *The facts:* A company which was the subject of a winding-up order offered to settle its outstanding debts by instalment. An Inland Revenue inspector agreed to the proposal. The company tried to enforce it.
>
> *Decision:* Despite the verdict in *Williams v Roffey Brothers* the court held that an agreement to pay in instalments is unenforceable. Even though the creditor may obtain some practical benefit this is not adequate consideration to render the agreement legally binding in respect of part-payment of debts.

2.2.3 Performance of existing contractual duty to a third party

If A promises B a reward if B will perform their **existing contract** with C, there is consideration for A's promise since they obtain a benefit to which they previously had no right, and B assumes new obligations.

> *Shadwell v Shadwell 1860*
>
> *The facts:* The claimant, a barrister, was engaged to marry E. His uncle promised the claimant that if he (the nephew) married E (as he did), the uncle would during their joint lives pay to his nephew £150 pa until such time as the nephew was earning 600 guineas pa at the bar (which never transpired). The uncle died after eighteen years owing six annual payments. The claimant claimed the arrears from his uncle's executors, who denied that there was consideration for the promise.
>
> *Decision:* Sufficient consideration was provided by the claimant.

2.2.4 Waiver of existing rights

 Illustration

If X owes Y £100 but Y agrees to accept a lesser sum, say £80, in full settlement of Y's claim, there is a promise by Y to waive their entitlement to the balance of £20. The promise, like any other, should be supported by consideration.

> *Foakes v Beer 1884*
>
> *The facts:* The defendant had obtained judgement against the claimant. Judgement debts bear interest from the date of the judgement. By a written agreement the defendant agreed to accept payment by instalments, no mention being made of the interest. Once the claimant had paid the amount of the debt in full, the defendant claimed interest, claiming that the agreement was not supported by consideration.
>
> *Decision:* She was entitled to the debt with interest. No consideration had been given by the claimant for waiver of any part of her rights against him.

There are, however, **exceptions** to the rule that the debtor (denoted by 'X' in the following paragraphs) must give consideration if the waiver is to be binding.

	Exceptions
Alternative consideration *Anon 1495* *Pinnel's Case 1602*	If X offers and Y accepts anything to which Y is not already entitled, the extra thing is sufficient consideration for the waiver • Goods instead of cash • Early payment
Bargain between the creditors *Woods v Robarts 1818*	If X arranges with creditors that they will each accept part-payment in full entitlement, that is bargain between the creditors X has given no consideration but he can hold the creditors individually to the agreed terms
Third-party part-payment *Welby v Drake 1825*	If a third-party (Z) offers part-payment and Y agrees to release X from Y's claim to the balance, Y has received consideration from Z against whom they had no previous claim
Promissory estoppel	The principle of promissory estoppel may prevent Y from retracting their promise with retrospective effect

3 Promissory estoppel

FAST FORWARD

The principle of **promissory estoppel** was developed in *Central London Property Trust v High Trees House 1947*. It means that in some cases where someone has made a promise they can be prevented from denying it.

Key term

The doctrine of **promissory estoppel** works as follows.

If a creditor (Y) makes a promise (unsupported by consideration) to the debtor (X) that Y will not insist on the full discharge of the debt, and the promise is made with the intention that X should act on it and they do so, Y is **estopped** from retracting their promise, unless X can be restored to their original position.

Central London Property Trust v High Trees House 1947

The facts: In September 1939, the claimants let a block of flats to the defendants at an annual rent of £2,500 pa. It was difficult to let the individual flats in wartime, so in January 1940 the claimants agreed in writing to accept a reduced rent of £1,250 pa. Note, no consideration passed from the defendants in return for the reduced rent. There was no time limit set on the arrangement but it was clearly related to wartime conditions. The reduced rent was paid from 1940 to 1945 and the defendants sublet flats during the period on the basis of their expected liability to pay rent under the head lease at £1,250 only. In 1945 the flats were fully let. The claimants demanded a full rent of £2,500 pa, both retrospectively and for the future.

Decision: The agreement of January 1940 ceased to operate early in 1945. The claim for full rent after the war was upheld. However, the 1940 agreement had estopped any claim for the period 1940 to 1945.

If the **defendants** in the *High Trees* case had sued on the promise, they would have **failed** as they provided no consideration to the 1940 agreement. Therefore, the principle of promissory estoppel is '**a shield not a sword**' and cannot become a cause of action in its own right. Promissory estoppel only applies to a promise of waiver which is **entirely voluntary**.

D and C Builders v Rees 1966

The facts: The defendants owed £482 to the claimants who were in acute financial difficulties. The claimants reluctantly agreed to accept £300 in full settlement. They later claimed the balance.

Decision: The debt must be paid in full. Promissory estoppel only applies to a promise voluntarily given. The defendants had been aware of and had exploited the claimants' difficulties.

4 Intention to create legal relations

FAST FORWARD

Various cases give us a set of rules to apply when determining whether the **parties** to a contract intended to be **legally bound** by it.

Where there is no express statement as to whether or not legal relations are intended, the courts apply one of two **rebuttable presumptions** to a case.

- **Social, domestic and family arrangements** are not usually intended to be binding
- **Commercial agreements** are usually intended by the parties involved to be legally binding

The word **'presumption'** means that it is assumed that something is the case, for example it is presumed that social arrangements are not deemed to be legally binding. **'Rebuttable'** means that the presumption can in some cases be refuted; the burden of proof for rebutting the presumption is on the party seeking to escape liability.

Key term

Intention to create legal relations can be defined as follows.

'An agreement will only become a legally binding contract if the parties intend this to be so. This will be strongly presumed in the case of business agreements but not presumed if the agreement is of a friendly, social or domestic nature.'

4.1 Domestic arrangements

4.1.1 Husband and wife

The fact that the parties are husband and wife does not mean that they cannot enter into a **binding contract** with one another. Contrast the following two cases.

Balfour v Balfour 1919

The facts: The defendant was employed in Ceylon. He and his wife returned to the UK on leave but it was agreed that for health reasons she would not return to Ceylon with him. He promised to pay her £30 a month as maintenance. Later the marriage ended in divorce and the wife sued for the monthly allowance which the husband no longer paid.

Decision: An informal agreement of indefinite duration made between husband and wife whose marriage had not at the time broken up was not intended to be legally binding.

Merritt v Merritt 1970

The facts: The husband had left the matrimonial home, which was owned in the joint names of husband and wife, to live with another woman. The spouses met and held a discussion, in the course of which he agreed to pay her £40 a month out of which she agreed to keep up the mortgage payments. The wife made the husband sign a note of these terms and an undertaking to transfer the house into her name when the mortgage had been paid off. The wife paid off the mortgage but the husband refused to transfer the house to her.

Decision: In the circumstances, an intention to create legal relations was to be inferred and the wife could sue for breach of contract.

Where agreements between husband and wife or other relatives relate to **property matters** the courts are very ready to impute an intention to create legal relations.

4.1.2 Relatives

Agreements between other **family members** may also be examined by the courts.

> **Jones v Padavatton 1969**
>
> *The facts:* The claimant wanted her daughter to move to England to train as a barrister, and offered to pay her a monthly allowance. The daughter did so in 1962. In 1964 the claimant bought a house in London; part of the house was occupied by the daughter and the other part let to tenants whose rent was collected by the daughter for herself. In 1967 the claimant and her daughter quarrelled and the claimant issued a summons claiming possession of the house. The daughter sued for her allowance.
>
> *Decision:* There were two agreements to consider: the daughter's agreement to read for the bar in exchange for a monthly allowance, and the agreement by which the daughter lived in her mother's house and collected the rent from tenants. Neither agreement was intended to create legal relations.

4.1.3 Other domestic arrangements

Domestic arrangements extend to those between people who are not related but who have a **close relationship** of some form. The nature of the agreement itself may lead to the conclusion that legal relations were intended.

> **Simpkins v Pays 1955**
>
> *The facts:* The defendant, her granddaughter and the claimant, a paying boarder, took part together each week in a competition organised by a Sunday newspaper. The arrangements over postage and other expenses were informal and the entries were made in the grandmother's name. One week they won £750; the paying boarder claimed a third share, but the defendant refused to pay on the grounds that there was no intention to create legal relations.
>
> *Decision:* There was a 'mutuality in the arrangements between the parties', amounting to a contract.

4.2 Commercial agreements

When business people enter into commercial agreements it is presumed that there is an intention to enter into legal relations unless this is **expressly disclaimed** or the **circumstances indicate otherwise**.

> **Rose and Frank v Crompton 1923**
>
> *The facts:* A commercial agreement by which the defendants appointed the claimant to be its distributor in the US contained a clause described as 'the Honourable Pledge Clause' which expressly stated that the arrangement was 'not subject to legal jurisdiction' in either country. The defendants terminated the agreement without giving notice as required, and refused to deliver goods ordered by the claimants although they had accepted these orders when placed.
>
> *Decision:* The general agreement was not legally binding as there was no obligation to stand by any clause in it. However the orders for goods were separate and binding contracts. The claim for damages for breach of the agreement failed, but the claim for damages for non-delivery of goods ordered succeeded.

The words relied on by a party to a commercial agreement to show that legal relations are not intended are not always clear. In such cases, the **burden of proof** is **on the party seeking to escape liability**.

> **Edwards v Skyways Ltd 1964**
>
> *The facts:* In negotiations over the terms for making the claimant redundant, the defendants gave him the choice either of withdrawing his total contributions from their contributory pension fund, or of receiving a paid-up pension. It was agreed that if he chose the first option, the defendants would make an ex gratia payment to him. He chose the first option; his contributions were refunded but the ex gratia payment was not made. He sued for breach of contract.
>
> *Decision:* Although the defendants argued that the use of the phrase ex gratia showed no intention to create legal relations, this was a commercial arrangement and the burden of rebutting the presumption of legal relations had not been discharged by the defendants.

Care needs to be taken during the negotiation stage as to whether a contract is intended. Use of the words **'subject to contract'** amounts to a strong presumption that **no** immediately binding contract is intended.

RTS Flexible Systems Ltd v Molkerei Alois Müller GmbH 2010

The facts: A letter of intent set out a draft contract which was not to become effective until signed and executed by the parties. The contract was not signed but the parties proceeded with the project of installing two production lines in the claimant's factory.

Decision: The Supreme Court held, first, that it was unrealistic to conclude that major works would have been carried out in the absence of a contract and, second, that there was evidence of an agreement and an intent to create legal relations in this case. The court made it clear that it would not always be the case, in circumstances where works commence before a contract is finalised, that the contract that exists between the parties contains the same terms as those in the negotiated contract. That would be a question of fact in all the circumstances.

4.3 Statutory provisions

Procedural agreements between **employers and trade unions** for the settlement of disputes are not intended to give rise to legal relations, in spite of their elaborate content, under the **Trade Union and Labour Relations (Consolidation) Act 1992** (HMSO, 1992).

4.4 Letters of comfort

For many years, holding companies have given **'letters of comfort'** to creditors of subsidiaries which purport to give some comfort as to the ability of the subsidiary to pay its debts. Such letters have always been presumed in the past not to be legally binding.

Kleinwort Benson Ltd v Malaysia Mining Corpn Bhd 1989

The facts: The claimants lent money to the defendant's subsidiary, having received a letter from the defendant stating 'it is our policy to ensure that the business is at all times in a position to meet its liabilities to you.' The subsidiary went into liquidation, and the bank claimed against the holding company for the outstanding indebtedness.

Decision: The letter of comfort was a statement of existing policy and not a promise that the policy would continue in the future. Because both parties were well aware that in business a 'letter of comfort' imposed moral and not legal responsibilities, it was held not to have been given with the intention of creating legal relations.

4.5 Transactions binding in honour only

If the parties state that an agreement is **'binding in honour only'**, this amounts to an express denial of intention to create legal relations.

Jones v Vernons Pools 1938

The facts: The claimant argued that he had sent to the defendant a football pools coupon on which his predictions entitled him to a dividend. The defendants denied having received the coupon. A clause on the coupon stated that the transaction should not 'give rise to any legal relationship ... but ... be binding in honour only'.

Decision: This clause was a bar to an action in court.

---

5 Privity of contract

FAST FORWARD

> As a general rule, only a person who is a party to a contract has enforceable rights or obligations under it. This is the doctrine of **privity of contract**. The Contracts (Rights of Third Parties) Act 1999 has had a fundamental effect on the doctrine.

There is a maxim in contract law which states that **consideration must move from the promisee**. As consideration is the price of a promise, the price must be paid by the person who seeks to enforce the promise. For example, A promises B that (for a consideration provided by B) A will confer a benefit on C. Therefore, C cannot as a general rule enforce A's promise since C has given no consideration for it.

Tweddle v Atkinson 1861

The facts: The claimant married the daughter of G. On the occasion of the marriage, the claimant's father and G exchanged promises that they would each pay a sum of money to the claimant. G died without making the promised payment and the claimant sued G's executor for the specified amount.

Decision: The claimant had provided no consideration for G's promise.

In *Tweddle's* case each father could have sued the other, but the claimant could not sue. The rule that consideration must move from the promisee overlaps with the rule that **only a party to a contract can enforce it**. No one may be entitled to, or bound by, the terms of a contract to which they are not an original party.

Key term

Privity of contract can be defined as follows.

As a general rule, only a person who is a party to a contract has enforceable rights or obligations under it. Third parties have no right of action save in certain exceptional instances.

The following is the **leading case** on privity of contract.

Dunlop v Selfridge 1915

The facts: The claimant supplied tyres to Dew & Co, a distributor, on terms that they would not re-sell the tyres at less than the prescribed retail price. If Dew & Co sold the tyres wholesale to trade customers, they must impose a similar condition on those buyers to observe minimum retail prices. Dew & Co resold tyres on these conditions to the defendant. Under the terms of the contract between Dew & Co and Selfridge, Selfridge was to pay to the claimant a sum of £5 per tyre if it sold tyres to customers below the minimum retail price. They sold tyres to two customers at less than the minimum price. The claimant sued to recover £5 per tyre as liquidated damages.

Decision: The claimant could not recover damages under a contract (between Dew & Co and Selfridge) to which it was not a party.

The **party** to the contract who **imposes the condition,** or obtains a promise of a benefit for a third party, can usually **enforce it**, but damages cannot be recovered on the third party's behalf, since a claimant can only recover damages for a loss they have suffered. Other remedies may be sought however.

Where the contract is one which provides something for the **enjoyment** of both the contracting party and third parties – such as a family holiday – the contracting party may be entitled to recover damages for their loss of the benefit.

5.1 Exceptions

There are a number of **exceptions** to the rule of privity of contract.

	Exceptions
The third party can sue in another capacity	*Beswick v Beswick 1968* The facts: X transferred his business to the defendant, his nephew, in consideration for a pension of £6.10s per week and, after his death, a weekly annuity to X's widow. Only one such annuity payment was made. The widow brought an action against the nephew, asking for an order of specific performance. She sued both as administratrix of her husband's estate and in her personal capacity as recipient. *Decision:* As her husband's representative, the widow was successful in enforcing the contract for a third party's (her own) benefit. In her personal capacity she had no right of action.
Collateral contracts	*Shanklin Pier Ltd v Detel Products Ltd 1951* *The facts*: Shanklin Pier contracted with painters to have the pier repainted using products from Detel. Detel had already communicated their paint's suitability to the claimants. The paint was not suitable and Shanklin took action against Detel Products even though their contract was with the painters. *Decision:* It was held that a collateral contract existed between Shanklin and Detel. Detel had confirmed the paint's suitability in return for Shanklin requiring the painters to use it.
Valid assignment	Benefit from a contract can be re-assigned from the original beneficiary to a third party if it is in writing, it transfers the same or no more benefits to the new beneficiary and has the consent of the other party.
Foreseeable loss to the third party	*Linden Gardens Trust Ltd v Lenesta Sludge Disposals Ltd 1994* The facts: Linden Gardens contracted with the defendants for work to be done on their property. The defendants knew there was the likelihood that the property would be transferred to a third party soon after. After the transfer it became apparent that the workmanship amounted to breach of contract. As the third party had no action against the defendants due to the rules on privity, Linden Gardens took action in their place. *Decision:* As the transfer was in the contemplation of both parties the original beneficiary could claim full damages on behalf of the third party.
Implied trusts	Equity may hold that an implied trust has been created. *Gregory and Parker v Williams 1817* *The facts:* P owed money to G and W. He agreed with W to transfer his property to W if W would pay his (P's) debt to G. The property was transferred, but W refused to pay G. G could not sue on the contract between P and W. *Decision:* P could be regarded as a trustee for G, and G could therefore bring an action jointly with P.
Statutory exceptions	Road Traffic Act 1972 (HMSO, 1972): A person injured in a road accident may claim against the motorist's insurers. Contracts (Rights of Third Parties) Act 1999: see below.
Agency	In normal circumstances the agent discloses to a third party with whom they contract that they are acting for a principal. The contract, when made, is between the principal and the third party. The agent has no liability under the contact and no right to enforce it.

	Exceptions
Covenants	A restrictive covenant may run with land. *Tulk v Moxhay 1848* *The facts:* The claimant owned several plots of land in Leicester Square. He sold one to X, who agreed not to build on it, but to preserve it in its existing condition. It was sold on, eventually being purchased by the defendant, who, although he was aware of the restriction, proposed to build on it. The claimant sought an injunction. *Decision:* The injunction was granted.

5.2 Contracts (Rights of Third Parties) Act 1999

The Contracts (Rights of Third Parties) Act 1999 (TSO, 1999) has a fundamental effect on the rule of **privity of contract** by setting out the circumstances in which a third party has a right to enforce a contract term or have it varied or rescinded, and a right to all the remedies that are available for breach of contract. There is a **two-limbed test** for the circumstances in which a third party may enforce a contract term.

- Whether the **contract itself expressly so provides**

- Where the **term confers a benefit on the third party**, unless it appears that the contracting parties did not intend them to have the right to enforce it

The **third party** must be **expressly identified** in the contract by name, class or description, but need not be in existence when the contract is made (for example, an unborn child or a future spouse). The Act enables a third party to take advantage of exclusion clauses as well as to enforce 'positive' rights.

The Act also **protects third parties** from the original parties varying contract terms without their consent and the **promisor is protected from double liability**. Damages awarded to the third party will be reduced by the amount of damages already awarded to the original promisee. The Act does not confer third-party rights in relation to a **company's constitution**, or **employment contracts**. So, for example, a customer of an employer cannot use this Act to enforce a term of a contract of employment against an employee.

6 The electronic contract

FAST FORWARD

The **pace of technological change** raises issues for modern contract law. Problems arise as contracts are often **electronic**, are **digitally signed**, are **accepted by email** and consideration is often provided by **credit card**.

It could be said that the case of *Byrne v Van Tienhoven*, dating from 1880, is an early example of an **electronic contract**. In that case, the sending of an acceptance by telegram was an important action in a chain of events leading to the formation of a contract. Since then, technology has permitted such actions to become **almost instantaneous**. Fax messages, emails and use of the internet may all play a part in the communication of offers and purported acceptances. This is a potentially wide-ranging topic and the law is still in its infancy. The following is a **summary** of the issues which will need to be considered.

(a) **In writing?** There are two main reasons why contracts need to be in writing.

    (i) A written contract provides evidence of the terms of the contract.

    (ii) The requirement of formality allows a weaker party to 'think twice' before entering into a transaction.

        An **electronic contract** meets the reasoning behind the requirement for writing, and can thus be said to be in writing.

(b) **Signed?** In 2000 the UK government passed legislation to give legal effect to 'digital signatures', thereby giving an electronic contract the same status as contracts in more traditional formats.

(c)   **Timing of acceptance**. A contract comes into existence when an offer is accepted; in the case of acceptance by letter, this is when the letter is posted, not when it is received. Internet email shares many of the qualities of conventional mail – it is not usually instantaneous and may be subject to delay. Therefore the postal rule, with any problems arising from it, may apply, although the point has not been tested.

(d)   **Consideration**. In the past, difficulties with credit card payments slowed the growth of electronic commerce. Although technology has improved, websites may still be insecure, and this may cause problems when it comes to payment.

Activities on the internet are largely **unregulated** at the moment, but this is likely to change, as governments recognise the business opportunities available and the EU seeks to **protect consumers**. **Basic legal principles** must, therefore, be applied.

Of course, the internet is much more than simply a means of sending and receiving messages. As the commercial applications of the **world wide web** have been exploited, a new 'shop front' has been developed. Some sites are highly automated and software handles ordering, stock checking, payment processing and despatch confirmation without human involvement.

There are risks associated with leaving commercial transactions to **automated IT programs**. Eliminating human intervention and fully automating the sales process, for example, can increase the likelihood of errors. There have been several instances of websites mis-pricing goods for sale, such as offering television sets for £2.99, rather than £299.

The following are some of the **practical legal issues** that must be faced by a **seller** when contracting online.

- Websites should be constructed as shop windows, that is, **invitations to treat** rather than offers.

- **Terms and conditions** governing electronic transactions should be made explicit and clear.

- **An indication of interest** by a purchaser visiting the website should be understood by both parties to be **an offer**, not an acceptance, which the seller is then free to accept or reject.

- Sellers can continue to use **disclaimers of liability**, clearly displayed on the website, subject to the usual **consumer protection laws** on unfair terms.

- The **law and jurisdiction** governing the transaction should be made clear, for example, 'All transactions are governed by English law'.

- The seller should make sure that any **web pages do not contravene local laws** (for example, those relating to advertising standards) in the countries targeted.

- A **time limit** should be set for all offers made on the website, which should take account of potential delays in receiving emails.

Chapter Roundup

- **Consideration** is an **essential** part of most contracts. It is what each party brings to the contract.

- Consideration may be **executed** (an act in return for a promise) or **executory** (a promise in return for a promise). It may not be **past**, unless one of three recognised exceptions applies.

- The long-established rule is that consideration need **not be adequate** but it **must be sufficient**.

- The principle of **promissory estoppel** was developed in *Central London Property Trust v High Trees House 1947*. It means that in some cases where someone has made a promise they can be prevented from denying it.

- Various cases give us a set of rules to apply when determining whether the **parties** to a contract intended to be **legally bound** by it.

- As a general rule, only a person who is a party to a contract has enforceable rights or obligations under it. This is the doctrine of **privity of contract**. The Contracts (Rights of Third Parties) Act 1999 has had a fundamental effect on the doctrine.

- The **pace of technological change** raises issues for modern contract law. Problems arise as contracts are often **electronic**, are **digitally signed**, are **accepted by email** and consideration is often provided by **credit card**.

Quick Quiz

1   Distinguish between executed and executory consideration.

2   Past consideration, as a general rule, is not sufficient to make a promise binding.

    True   ☐

    False   ☐

3   **Fill in the blanks** in the statement below.

    Consideration need not be (1) .... but it must be (2) ....

4   **Fill in the blanks** in the statement below.

    If Alice promises Ben that (for a consideration provided by Ben) Alice will confer a benefit on Charlotte, then (1)................... cannot at common law enforce Alice's promise. This is the doctrine of (2) ....

5   A promise of additional reward for the performance of existing duties is not generally binding.

    True   ☐

    False   ☐

1   Executed consideration is an **act** in return for a promise such as paying for goods when the shopkeeper hands them over. Executory consideration is a **promise** given for a promise, such as promising to pay for goods that the shopkeeper puts on order for you.

2   True. Past consideration is not valid consideration for a new contract.

3   (1) adequate, (2) sufficient

4   (1) Charlotte, (2) Privity of contract

5   True (as in *Stilk v Myrick*)

Now try the questions below from the Practice Question Bank

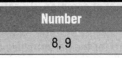

Number
8, 9

Content of contracts

5

Topic list	Syllabus reference
1 Contract terms	B2 (a)
2 Express terms and implied terms	B2 (b)
3 Conditions and warranties	B2 (b)
4 Exclusion clauses – common-law rules	B2 (c)
5 The Unfair Contract Terms Act 1977	B2 (c)
6 The Consumer Rights Act 2015	B2 (c)

Introduction

This chapter analyses the contents of a contract, specifically the different types of **contract term**.

You must be clear as to what **express terms** are and be able to distinguish them from mere **representations**. It is also important that you understand how terms can be **implied** into contracts and whether or not terms are **conditions** or **warranties**.

Once you have grasped these subjects you will be able to determine whether or not an organisation or individual has **breached** the terms of the contract and determine their liability (if any).

We complete the chapter by looking at **exclusion clauses**. You must be familiar with the legislation in this area, the effect of such clauses and how they are controlled.

Study guide

		Intellectual level
B	**The law of obligations**	
2	**Content of contracts**	
(a)	Distinguish terms from mere representations	1
(b)	Define the various contractual terms	1
(c)	Explain the control over terms in consumer contracts and the operation of exclusion clauses in non-consumer contracts	2

Exam guide

You may be asked to identify contract terms, conditions and warranties and how they are brought into a contract. Scenario questions may require you to explain if a party can rely on an exclusion clause.

1 Contract terms

FAST FORWARD

Statements made by the parties may be classified as **terms or representations**. Different **remedies** attach to breach of a term and to misrepresentation respectively.

In addition to the final contract, many statements may be made during the process of negotiation that often lead to the formation of a contract. It is important to be able to establish whether what has been written or said actually amounts to a contract term or whether it is simply a representation. **Statements may be classified as terms or as representations**.

Key term

A **representation** is something which induces the formation of a contract but which does not become a **term** of the contract. The importance of the distinction is that different remedies are available depending on whether a term is broken or a representation turns out to be untrue.

If something said in negotiations proves to be untrue, the party misled can claim for **breach of contract** if the statement became a **term** of the contract. If the pre-contract statement was merely a **representation** then the party misled can claim misrepresentation, resulting in a lesser remedy than for breach of contract. There are a number of factors that a court may consider when determining whether a statement is or is not a term.

The court will consider **when** the representation was made, to assess whether it was designed as a contract term or merely as an incidental statement. The court will also look at the **importance** the recipient of the information attached to it.

Bannerman v White 1861

The facts: In negotiations for the sale of hops the buyer emphasised that it was **essential** to him that the hops should not have been treated with sulphur adding that, if they had, he would not even bother to ask the price. The seller replied explicitly that no sulphur had been used. It was later discovered that a small proportion of the hops (five acres out of 300) had been treated with sulphur. The buyer refused to pay the price.

Decision: The representation as to the absence of sulphur was intended to be a **term** of the contract.

> **Routledge v McKay 1954**
>
> *The facts:* The defendant, in discussing the possible sale of his motorcycle to the claimant, said on 23 October that the cycle was a 1942 model; he took this information from the registration document. On 30 October the parties made a written contract which did not refer to the year of the model and the purchaser had not indicated that the age of the cycle was of critical importance to him. The actual date was 1930.
>
> *Decision:* The buyer's claim for damages failed. The reference to a 1942 model was a **representation made prior** to the contract

If the statement is made by a person with **special knowledge** it is more likely to be treated as a contract term.

> **Dick Bentley Productions v Arnold Smith Motors 1965**
>
> *The facts:* The defendants sold the claimants a car which they stated to have done only 20,000 miles since a replacement engine and gearbox had been fitted. In fact the car had covered 100,000 miles since then and was unsatisfactory.
>
> *Decision:* The defendants' statement was a term of the contract and the claimants were entitled to damages.

> **Oscar Chess v Williams 1957**
>
> *The facts:* The defendant, when selling his car to the claimant car dealers, stated (as the registration book showed) that his car was a 1948 model and the dealers valued it at £280 in the transaction. In fact it was a 1939 model, worth only £175, and the registration book had been altered by a previous owner.
>
> *Decision:* The statement was a mere representation. The seller was not an expert and the buyer had better means of discovering the truth.

2 Express terms and implied terms

FAST FORWARD As a general rule, the parties to a contract may include in the agreement whatever **terms** they choose. This is the principle of **freedom of contract**. Terms clearly included in the contract are **express terms**. The law may complement or replace terms by **implying** terms into a contract.

2.1 Express terms

Key term

An **express term** is a term expressly agreed by the parties to a contract to be a term of that contract. In examining a contract, the courts will look first at the terms expressly agreed by the parties.

An apparently binding legal agreement must be **complete in its terms** to be a valid contract.

> **Scammell v Ouston 1941**
>
> *The facts:* The defendants wished to buy a motor-van from the claimants on hire-purchase. They placed an order 'on the understanding that the balance of purchase price can be had on hire-purchase terms over a period of two years'. The hire-purchase terms were never specified.
>
> *Decision:* The court was unable to identify a contract which it could uphold because the language used was so vague.

It is always possible for the parties to leave an essential term to be **settled by other means**, for example by an independent third party.

Illustration

It may be agreed to sell at the open market price on the day of delivery, or to invite an arbitrator to determine a fair price. The price may be determined by the course of dealing between the parties.

Where an agreement appears vague or incomplete, the courts will seek to uphold it by looking at the **intention of the parties**. If the parties use standard printed conditions, some of which are inappropriate, such phrases may be disregarded.

> *Nicolene v Simmonds 1953*
>
> *The facts:* The claimant offered to buy steel bars from the defendant. A contract was made by correspondence, in which the defendant provided that 'the usual conditions of acceptance apply'. The defendant failed to deliver the goods and argued that there had been no explicit agreement.
>
> *Decision:* The words should be disregarded. The contract was complete without these words; there were no usual conditions of acceptance.

2.2 Implied terms

FAST FORWARD

Terms may be implied by the **courts**, by **statute** or by **custom**.

There are occasions where certain terms are not **expressly** adopted by the parties. Additional terms of a contract may be **implied** by law: through custom, statute or the courts to bring efficacy to the contract. Implied terms may override express terms in certain circumstances, such as where they are implied by statute.

Key term

> An **implied term** is a term deemed to form part of a contract even though it is not made expressly.

2.2.1 Terms implied by custom

The parties may enter into a contract subject to **customs** of their trade. Any express term overrides a term which might be implied by custom.

> *Hutton v Warren 1836*
>
> *The facts:* The defendant landlord gave the claimant, a tenant farmer, notice to quit the farm. He insisted that the tenant should continue to farm the land during the period of notice. The tenant asked for 'a fair allowance' for seeds and labour from which he received no benefit because he was to leave the farm.
>
> *Decision:* By custom he was bound to farm the land until the end of the tenancy; but he was also entitled to a fair allowance for seeds and labour incurred.

> *Les Affreteurs v Walford 1919*
>
> *The facts:* A charter of a ship provided expressly for a 3% commission payment to be made 'on signing the charter'. There was a trade custom that it should only be paid at a later stage. The ship was requisitioned by the French government and so no hire was earned.
>
> *Decision:* An express term prevails over a term otherwise implied by custom. The commission was payable on hire.

2.2.2 Terms implied by statute

Terms may be implied by statute. In some cases the statute may permit the parties to contract out of the **statutory terms**. In other cases the statutory terms are obligatory; for example, the protection given under consumer law to a consumer who buys goods from a trader cannot be taken away from them.

2.2.3 Terms implied by the courts

Terms may be **implied** if the court concludes that the **parties intended those terms** to apply to the contract.

> *The Moorcock 1889*
>
> *The facts:* The owners of a wharf agreed that a ship should be moored alongside to unload its cargo. It was well known that at low water the ship would ground on the mud at the bottom. At ebb tide the ship settled on a ridge concealed beneath the mud and suffered damage.
>
> *Decision:* It was an implied term, though not expressed, that the ground alongside the wharf was safe at low tide since both parties knew that the ship must rest on it.

A term of a contract which is left to be implied and is not expressed is often **something that goes without saying**; so that, if while the parties were making their bargain an officious bystander were to suggest some express provision for it, they would say 'why should we put that in? That's obvious'. The terms are required to give **efficacy** to the contract, that is, to make it work in practice.

The court may also imply terms because the court believes such a term to be a '**necessary incident**' of this type of contract.

> *Liverpool City Council v Irwin 1977*
>
> *The facts:* The defendants were tenants in a tower block owned by the claimants. There was no formal tenancy agreement. The defendants withheld rent, alleging that the claimants had breached implied terms because *inter alia* the lifts did not work and the stairs were unlit.
>
> *Decision:* Tenants could only occupy the building with access to stairs and/or lifts, so terms needed to be implied on these matters.

Where a term is implied as a 'necessary incident' it has **precedent value** and such terms will be implied into future contracts of the same type.

3 Conditions and warranties

FAST FORWARD

Statements which are classified as contract terms may be further categorised as **conditions** or **warranties**. A **condition** is a vital term going to the **root** of the **contract**, while a **warranty** is a term **subsidiary** to the main purpose of the **contract**. The remedies available for breach are different in each case.

Exam focus point

It is fundamental to be able to explain and distinguish between conditions and warranties and innominate terms.

The terms of the contract are usually classified by their relative importance as **conditions** or **warranties**.

(a)   **A condition is a vital term**, going to the root of the contract, breach of which entitles the injured party to decide to treat the contract as **discharged** and to claim damages.

(b)   **A warranty is a term subsidiary to the main purpose of the contract**, breach of which only entitles the injured party to claim damages.

Key terms

> A **condition** is a term that is deemed so important that if it is broken the contract will be destroyed.
>
> A **warranty** is a term deemed less importan than a condition.

Poussard v Spiers 1876

The facts: Mme Poussard agreed to sing in an opera throughout a series of performances. Owing to illness she was unable to appear on the opening night and the next few days. The producer engaged a substitute who insisted that she should be engaged for the whole run. When Mme Poussard recovered, the producer declined to accept her services for the remaining performances.

Decision: Failure to sing on the opening night was a breach of condition which entitled the producer to treat the contract for the remaining performances as discharged.

Bettini v Gye 1876

The facts: An opera singer was engaged for a series of performances under a contract by which he had to be in London for rehearsals six days before the opening performance. Owing to illness he did not arrive until the third day before the opening. The defendant refused to accept his services, treating the contract as discharged.

Decision: The rehearsal clause was subsidiary to the main purpose of the contract.

Classification may depend on the following issues.

(a)   **Statute** often identifies implied terms specifically as conditions or warranties. An example is the Consumer Rights Act 2015.

(b)   **Case law** may also define particular types of clauses as conditions, for example a clause as to the date of 'expected readiness' of a ship let to a charterer: *The Mihalis Angelos 1971*.

(c)   The court may construe what was the **intention of the parties** at the time the contract was made as to whether a broken term was to be a condition or a warranty: *Bunge Corporation v Tradax SA 1981*.

It is important to remember that if the injured party merely wants damages, there is **no** need to consider whether the term broken is a condition or a warranty, since either type of breach entitles the injured party to damages.

3.1 Innominate terms

FAST FORWARD   It may not be possible to determine whether a term is a condition or a warranty. Such terms are classified by the courts as **innominate terms**.

Traditionally, terms were either classified as conditions or warranties and the injured party could choose to end the contract only for breach of condition. Sometimes a warranty was broken with catastrophic results, yet the court could not permit the injured party to end the contract because the term broken was not a condition.

The courts have determined that where the breach deprives the injured party of **substantially the whole benefit** of the contract the term broken can be called '**Innominate'** and the injured party can choose to end the contract even if it could not be regarded as a condition: *Cehave v Bremer 1975*.

If the **nature and effect of the breach** is such as to deprive the injured party of most of their benefit from the contract then it will be treated as if the guilty party had breached a condition.

The doctrine was developed in the following case.

> *Hong Kong Fir Shipping Co Ltd v Kawasaki Kisa Kaisha Ltd 1961*
>
> *The facts:* The defendants chartered a ship from the claimants for a period of 24 months. A term in the contract stated that the claimants would provide a ship which was 'in every way fitted for ordinary cargo service'. Because of the engine's age and the crew's lack of competence the ship's first voyage, from Liverpool to Osaka, was delayed for five months and further repairs were required at the end of it. The defendants purported to terminate the contract, so the claimants sued for breach; the defendants claimed that the claimants were in breach of a contractual condition.
>
> *Decision:* The term was innominate and could not automatically be construed as either a condition or a warranty. The obligation of 'seaworthiness' embodied in many charterparty agreements was too complex to be fitted into one of the two categories.
>
> The ship was still available for 17 out of 24 months. The consequences of the breach were not so serious that the defendants could be justified in terminating the contract as a result.

4 Exclusion clauses – common-law rules

FAST FORWARD

> An **exclusion clause** may attempt to restrict one party's liability for breach of contract or for negligence.

Point to note

> The Unfair Contract Terms Act 1977 and Consumer Rights Act 2015 (which we shall come to shortly) are the key sources of regulation of exclusion clauses. However, the common-law must still be considered. For example, if an exclusion clause has not been validly incorporated into a contract then it will be void without having to consider the legislation.
>
> It should be noted that many of the common-law rules that we shall consider below have been incorporated in the legislation. It is important to understand the common-law rules to fully appreciate the effect and application of the legislation.

To be enforceable, **a term must be validly incorporated into a contract**. Because most disputes about whether a term has been incorporated arise in the context of exclusion clauses, much of the relevant case law surrounds exclusion clauses – and in particular:

(a)   Whether an exclusion clause (as a contract term) has been **validly incorporated** into the contract; and

(b)   If so, how the exclusion clause should be **interpreted**.

Key term

> **Exclusion clauses** are clauses that purports to exclude a party from liability or limit any damages payable. They are sometimes referred to as exemption clauses.'

There has been strong criticism of the use of exclusion clauses in contracts made between manufacturers or sellers of goods or services and private citizens as consumers. The seller puts forward standard conditions of sale which the buyer may not understand, but which they must accept if they wish to buy. With these so-called **standard form contracts**, the presence of exclusion clauses becomes an important consideration.

For many years the courts demonstrated the hostility of the common law to exclusion clauses by developing various rules of case law designed to restrain their effect. To these must also be added the considerable statutory safeguards provided by the **Unfair Contract Terms Act 1977** and the **Consumer Rights Act 2015.**

The **courts** have generally sought to protect consumers from the harsher effects of exclusion clauses in two ways.

(a)   Exclusion clauses must be **incorporated** into a contract before they have legal effect.
(b)   Exclusion clauses are **interpreted** strictly. This may prevent the application of the clause.

The wording of an exclusion clause is of great importance and it must be presented **clearly and precisely**. Any ambiguous clauses will be invalid due to the *contra proferentum* rule: *Houghton v Trafalgar Insurance 1954.*

4.1 Incorporation of exclusion clauses

FAST FORWARD

> The courts protect parties from the harsher effects of exclusion clauses by ensuring that they are properly **incorporated** into a contract and then by **interpreting** them strictly.

The law seeks to protect parties (usually the weaker party to the contract) from the full force of exclusion clauses. They do this by applying the '**letter of the law**' to see if such clauses have been incorporated correctly. Where there is uncertainty the clauses may be excluded from the contract.

Such **uncertainty** can arise in several circumstances.

- The document containing notice of the clause must be an **integral part** of the contract.
- If the document is an integral part of the contract, a term may not usually be disputed if it is included in a document which a party has **signed**.
- The term must be put forward **before** the contract is made.
- If the contact is not signed, an exclusion clause is not a binding term unless the party whose rights it restricts was made **sufficiently aware** of it at the time of agreeing to it.
- **Onerous terms** must be sufficiently highlighted (it is doubtful whether this applies to signed contracts).

4.1.1 Contractual documents

Where the exclusion clause is contained in an **unsigned document** it must be shown that this document is an integral part of the contract and is one which could be expected to contain terms.

Chapelton v Barry UDC 1940

The facts: There was a pile of deckchairs and a notice stating 'Hire of chairs 2d per session of three hours'. The claimant took two chairs, paid for them and received two tickets which were headed 'receipt' which he put in his pocket. One of the chairs collapsed and he was injured. The defendant council relied on a notice on the back of the tickets by which it disclaimed liability for injury.

Decision: The notice advertising chairs for hire gave no warning of limiting conditions and it was not reasonable to communicate them on a receipt. The disclaimer of liability was not binding on the claimant.

Thompson v LMS Railway 1930

The facts: An elderly lady who could not read asked her niece to buy her a railway excursion ticket on which was printed 'Excursion: for conditions see back'. On the back it was stated that the ticket was issued subject to conditions contained in the company's timetables. These conditions excluded liability for injury.

Decision: The conditions had been adequately communicated and therefore had been accepted.

4.1.2 Signed contracts

If a party **signs** a document containing a term, they are held to have agreed to the term even if they have not read the document. But this is not so if the party who puts forward the document for signature gives a misleading explanation of the term's legal effect.

L'Estrange v Graucob 1934

The facts: The defendant sold to the claimant, a shopkeeper, a slot machine under conditions which excluded the claimant's normal rights under the Sale of Goods Act 1893. The claimant signed the document described as a 'Sales Agreement' and including clauses in 'legible, but regrettably small print'.

Decision: The conditions were binding on the claimant since she had signed them. It was not material that the defendant had given her no information of their terms nor called her attention to them.

Curtis v Chemical Cleaning Co 1951

The facts: The claimant took her wedding dress to be cleaned. She was asked to sign a receipt on which there were conditions that restricted the cleaner's liability and in particular placed on the claimant the risk of damage to beads and sequins on the dress. The document in fact contained a clause 'that the company is not liable for any damage however caused'. The dress was badly stained in the course of cleaning.

Decision: The cleaners could not rely on their disclaimer since they had misled the claimant. She was entitled to assume that she was running the risk of damage to beads and sequins only.

4.1.3 Unsigned contracts and notices

Each party must be aware of the contract's terms before or **at the time of entering into the agreement** if they are to be binding.

Olley v Marlborough Court 1949

The facts: A husband and wife arrived at a hotel and paid for a room in advance. On reaching their bedroom they saw a notice on the wall by which the hotel disclaimed liability for loss of valuables unless handed to the management for safe keeping. The wife locked the room and handed the key in at the reception desk. A thief obtained the key and stole the wife's furs from the bedroom.

Decision: The hotel could not rely on the notice disclaiming liability since the contract had been made previously and the disclaimer was too late.

Complications can arise when it is difficult to determine at exactly **what point in time** the contract is formed so as to determine whether or not a term is validly included.

Thornton v Shoe Lane Parking Ltd 1971

The facts: The claimant wished to park his car in the defendant's automatic car park. He had seen a sign saying 'All cars parked at owner's risk' outside the car park and when he received his ticket he saw that it contained words which he did not read. In fact these made the contract subject to conditions displayed obscurely on the premises. These not only disclaimed liability for damage but also excluded liability for injury. When he returned to collect his car there was an accident in which he was badly injured.

Decision: The reference on the ticket to conditions was received too late for the conditions to be included as contractual terms. At any rate, it was unreasonable for a term disclaiming liability for personal injury to be presented so obscurely. Note that since the Unfair Contracts Terms Act 1977 the personal injury clause would be unenforceable anyway.

An exception to the rule that there should be prior notice of the terms is where the parties have had **consistent dealings** with each other in the past, and the documents used then contained similar terms.

J Spurling Ltd v Bradshaw 1956

The facts: Having dealt with a company of warehousemen for many years, the defendant gave it eight barrels of orange juice for storage. A document he received a few days later acknowledged receipt and contained a clause excluding liability for damage caused by negligence. When he collected the barrels they were empty and he refused to pay.

Decision: It was a valid clause as it had also been present in the course of previous dealings, even though he had never read it.

If the parties have had previous dealings (but not on a consistent basis), then the person to be bound by the term must be **sufficiently aware** of it at the time of making the latest contract.

> *Hollier v Rambler Motors 1972*
>
> *The facts:* On three or four occasions over a period of five years the claimant had had repairs done at a garage. On each occasion he had signed a form by which the garage disclaimed liability for damage caused by fire to customers' cars. The car was damaged by fire caused by negligence of garage employees. The garage contended that the disclaimer had, by course of dealing, become an established term of any contract made between them and the claimant.
>
> *Decision:* The garage was liable. There was no evidence to show that the claimant knew of and agreed to the condition as a continuing term of his contracts with the garage.

4.1.4 Onerous terms

Where a term is **particularly unusual** and **onerous** it should be **highlighted** (although it is doubtful whether this applies to signed contracts). Failure to do so may mean that it does not become incorporated into the contract.

> *Interfoto Picture Library Ltd v Stiletto Visual Programmes Ltd 1988*
>
> *The facts:* 47 photographic transparencies were delivered to the defendant together with a delivery note with conditions on the back. Included in small type was a clause stating that for every day late each transparency was held a 'holding fee' of £5 plus VAT would be charged. They were returned 14 days late. The claimants sued for the full amount.
>
> *Decision:* The term was onerous and had not been sufficiently brought to the attention of the defendant. The court reduced the fee to one-tenth of the contractual figure to reflect more fairly the loss caused to the claimants by the delay.

4.2 Interpretation of exclusion clauses

In deciding what an exclusion clause means, the courts interpret any ambiguity against the party who relies on the exclusion. This is known as the **contra proferentem rule**. Liability can only be excluded or restricted by clear words.

In the *Hollier* case the court decided that as a **matter of interpretation** the disclaimer of liability could be interpreted to apply:

- Only to accidental fire damage; or
- To fire damage caused in any way including negligence.

It should therefore be interpreted against the garage in the **narrower sense** of (a) so that it did not give exemption from fire damage due to negligence. If a person wishes successfully to exclude or limit liability for loss caused by **negligence** the courts require that the word 'negligence', or an accepted synonym for it, should be included in the clause.

> *Alderslade v Hendon Laundry 1945*
>
> *The facts:* The conditions of contracts made by a laundry with its customers excluded liability for loss of, or damage to, customers' clothing in the possession of the laundry. By its negligence the laundry lost the claimant's handkerchief.
>
> *Decision:* The exclusion clause would have no meaning unless it covered loss or damage due to negligence. It did, therefore, cover loss by negligence.

4.2.1 The 'main purpose' rule

When construing an exclusion clause the court will also consider the **main purpose rule**. By this, the court presumes that the clause was not intended to prevent the main purpose of the contract.

4.2.2 Fundamental breach

There is no doubt that at common law a **properly drafted** exclusion clause can cover any breach of contract.

Photo Productions v Securicor Transport 1980

The facts: The defendants agreed to guard the claimants' factory under a contract by which the defendants were excluded from liability for damage caused by any of their employees. One of the guards deliberately started a small fire which destroyed the factory and contents. It was contended that Securicor had entirely failed to perform their contract and so they could not rely on any exclusion clause in the contract.

Decision: There is no principle that total failure to perform a contract deprives the party at fault of any exclusion from liability provided by the contract. In this case the exclusion clause was drawn widely enough to cover the damage which had happened. As the fire occurred before the UCTA was in force, the Act could not apply here. But if it had done it would have been necessary to consider whether the exclusion clause was reasonable.

---

5 The Unfair Contract Terms Act 1977

FAST FORWARD

The Unfair Contract Terms Act 1977 aims to **protect parties** when they enter contracts by stating that some exclusion clauses are **void**, and considering whether others are **reasonable**.

When considering the **validity** of exclusion clauses the courts have had to strike a balance between:

- The principle that parties should have complete **freedom to contract** on whatever terms they wish; and
- The need to **protect parties** from unfair exclusion clauses.

Exclusion clauses do have a proper place in business. They can be used to **allocate contractual risk**, and thus to determine in advance who is to insure against that risk. Between businessmen with similar bargaining power, exclusion clauses are a legitimate device.

Before we consider the specific terms of the **Unfair Contract Terms Act 1977** (HMSO, 1977) (UCTA), it is necessary to describe how its **scope is restricted**.

(a) In general, the Act only applies to **business-to-business contracts** (business-to-consumer contracts are covered by the Consumer Rights Act 2015). Generally, private individuals may contract on any terms that they wish (consumer to consumer contracts).

(b) The **Act does not apply to some contracts**, for example contracts of insurance or contracts relating to the transfer of an interest in land.

(c) Specifically, the **Act applies to**:

  (i) Clauses that attempt to limit liability for **negligence**;

  (ii) Clauses that attempt to limit liability for **breach of contract**.

The Act uses two techniques for controlling exclusion clauses – some types of clauses are **void**, whereas others are subject to a **test of reasonableness**.

5.1 Clauses which are void

A clause is void in the following circumstances.

- A clause which purports to exclude or limit liability for **death or personal injury** resulting from negligence. This is the key circumstance to remember.

- In a contract for the sale or hire purchase of goods, a clause that purports to exclude the condition that the seller has a **right to sell** the goods.

5.2 Clauses which are subject to a test of reasonableness

If a clause is not automatically void, it is subject to a **statutory test of reasonableness**.

5.3 The statutory test of reasonableness

The term must be **fair and reasonable** having regard to all the circumstances which were, or which ought to have been, known to the parties when the contract was made. The burden of proving reasonableness lies on the person seeking to rely on the clause. Statutory guidelines have been included in the Act to assist the determination of reasonableness. For instance, the court will consider the following.

- The relative **strength** of the parties' bargaining positions

- Whether any **inducement** (for example, a reduced price) was offered to the customer to persuade them to accept limitation of their rights

- Whether the customer **knew or ought to have known** of the existence and extent of the clause

- If **failure to comply with a condition** (for example, failure to give notice of a defect within a short period) excludes or restricts the customer's rights, whether it was reasonable to expect when the contract was made that compliance with the condition would be practicable

- Whether the goods were made, processed or adapted to the **special order** of the customer

---

St Albans City and District Council v International Computers Ltd 1994

The facts: The defendants had been hired to assess population figures on which to base community charges (local government taxation). Their standard contract contained a clause restricting liability to £100,000. The database which they supplied to the claimants was seriously inaccurate and the latter sustained a loss of £1.3 million.

Decision: The clause was unreasonable. The defendants could not justify this limitation, which was very low in relation to the potential loss. In addition, they had aggregate insurance of £50 million. The defendants had to pay full damages.

---

6 The Consumer Rights Act 2015

FAST FORWARD

The **Consumer Rights Act 2015** provides protection for consumers in contracts with businesses.

The **Consumer Rights Act 2015** (TSO, 2015) (CTA) provides statutory control in respect of **consumer contracts** and **consumer notices** (such as signs in car parks, previously covered by the rule in the *Thornton* case). It provides that terms in contracts between a business and a consumer will only be binding on the consumer if they are **'fair'**.

6.1 Fairness

To determine whether a term is fair, the Act firstly considers whether it can be **deemed automatically unenforceable**. For example, a consumer contract or notice, **cannot limit liability for death or personal injury resulting from negligence**. Nor can it **restrict any of the consumer's legal rights** under the Act. If it does then the clause is automatically unenforceable and void, so the question of fairness is not considered any further.

If the clause is not deemed automatically unenforceable then the Act provides guidance as to whether or not it is fair. The Act states:

'A term is unfair if, contrary to the requirement of **good faith**, it causes a **significant imbalance** in the **parties' rights** and **obligations** under the contract to the **detriment of the consumer**.'

When considering whether a term is **'fair'**, a number of factors should be considered, such as whether it puts the **consumer at a disadvantage**, if there were any **relevant circumstances** when the contract was signed, as well as the **nature of the contract** itself. In addition, the Act requires that terms are set out in **plain, intelligible language** and any **relevant terms** must be **prominent**. The test is whether an **average consumer** who is reasonably well-informed, observant and circumspect would be aware of the term.

The Act also provides an **indicative list of terms which may be regarded as unfair**, and therefore void.

Some of the **terms** on the list include:

- Payment of disproportionate compensation by the consumer if they fail to perform their obligations
- Binding the consumer to terms that they had no real opportunity to read before the contract was concluded
- Allowing the business to unilaterally alter the terms of the contract with no valid reason
- Allowing the business to determine the price payable after the consumer has been bound by the contract
- Forcing the consumer to perform their obligations when the business does not perform theirs

6.1.1 Exemptions

Two types of term are **exempt from the rule on fairness**. These are **price** and **subject matter of the contract**. However, the Act states that these terms must be **sufficiently transparent** and **prominent** in the contract. If they are not, then their fairness will be considered.

6.1.2 Consumer reliance

A **consumer may rely on a term** (and therefore enforce a contract) which is deemed 'unfair'. Unfair terms do not invalidate the whole contract which will continue as far as possible.

Where a contractual term is open to **different meanings**, the meaning given to it will be the one which is most favourable to the consumer.

6.2 Businesses acting as consumers

Where a business engages in an activity which is merely **incidental to the business**, the activity will not be in the course of the business unless it is an integral part and carried on with a degree of regularity. It will therefore be acting as a consumer and the Consumer Rights Act may apply to it. However, the business must prove that it was acting as a consumer. The following case indicates how the law is likely to be applied in this area.

> *R & B Customs Brokers Ltd v United Dominions Trust Ltd 1988*
>
> *The facts:* The claimants, a company owned by Mr and Mrs Bell and operating as a shipping broker, bought a second-hand Colt Shogun. The car was to be used partly for business and partly for private use.
>
> *Decision:* This was a consumer sale, since the company was not in the business of buying cars.

Chapter Roundup

- Statements made by the parties may be classified as **terms or representations**. Different **remedies** attach to breach of a term and to misrepresentation respectively.

- As a general rule, the parties to a contract may include in the agreement whatever **terms** they choose. This is the principle of **freedom of contract**. Terms clearly included in the contract are **express terms**. The law may complement or replace terms by **implying** terms into a contract.

- Terms may be implied by the **courts**, by **statute** or by **custom**.

- Statements which are classified as contract terms may be further categorised as **conditions** or **warranties**. A **condition** is a vital term going to the **root** of the **contract**, while a **warranty** is a term **subsidiary** to the main purpose of the **contract**. The remedies available for breach are different in each case.

- It may not be possible to determine whether a term is a condition or a warranty. Such terms are classified by the courts as **innominate terms**.

- An **exclusion clause** may attempt to restrict one party's liability for breach of contract or for negligence.

- The courts protect parties from the harsher effects of exclusion clauses by ensuring that they are properly **incorporated** into a contract and then by **interpreting** them strictly.

- The Unfair Contract Terms Act 1977 aims to **protect parties** when they enter contracts by stating that some exclusion clauses are **void**, and considering whether others are **reasonable**.

- The **Consumer Rights Act 2015** provides protection for consumers in contracts with businesses.

Quick Quiz

1   **Fill in the blanks** in the statements below, using the words in the box.

A (1) ……………….. is a vital term, going to the root of the contract, breach of which entitles the injured party to treat the contract as (2) ……………….. and claim (3) ……………….. .

A (4) ……………….. is a term (5) ……………….. to the main purpose of the contract.

The consequence of a term being classified as innominate is that the court must decide what is the actual effect of its (6) ……………….. .

• breach	• condition	• subsidiary
• warranty	• damages	• discharged

2   Terms implied by custom cannot be overridden.

True ☐

False ☐

3   A business is classed as a consumer if it does not make the contract in the course of its business.

True ☐

False ☐

4   Match the laws to their jurisdictions under the law of contract

(a)   Common law   (1)   Does not apply to business-to-consumer contracts
(b)   UCTA 1977   (2)   Applies only to business-to-consumer contracts
(c)   CRA 2015   (3)   Applies to all contracts

5   What is the 'contra proferentem' rule?

Answers to Quick Quiz

1 (1) condition (2) discharged (3) damages (4) warranty (5) subsidiary (6) breach

2 False. Such terms can be overridden.

3 True. Businesses are classed as consumers if it can prove the contract was not made in the ordinary course of its business.

4 (a) (3)
   (b) (1)
   (c) (2)

5 In deciding what an exclusion clause means, the courts interpret any ambiguity against the person at fault who relies on the exclusion.

Now try the questions below from the Practice Question Bank

Number
10, 11

Breach of contract and remedies

Topic list	Syllabus reference
1 Discharge of contract	B3(a)
2 Breach of contract	B3(b)
3 Damages	B3(c)
4 Remoteness of damage	B3(c)
5 Measure of damages	B3(c)
6 Liquidated damages and penalty clauses	B3(c)
7 Other common law remedies	B3(c)
8 Equitable remedies	B3(d)

Introduction

Most contracts end with the intended result; however, many contracts end with one party breaching the **terms** of the deal. This chapter examines what breach of contract is and what the remedies are for the innocent party.

Damages are **monetary compensation** for a loss. However, there are rules concerning what damages can be claimed for and how much should be awarded. **Liquidated damages** and **penalty clauses** are contractual terms that state how damages will be calculated so both parties agree to them in advance. You should understand when these will and will not be enforced by the court.

There are also **equitable remedies** that can be claimed if damages are not suitable. You should understand all of them.

Study guide

		Intellectual level
B	**The law of obligations**	
3	**Breach of contract and remedies**	
(a)	Explain the ways in which a contract may be discharged	2
(b)	Explain the meaning and effect of breach of contract, and the remedies available in common law	2
(c)	Explain the rules relating to the award of damages	2
(d)	Analyse the equitable remedies for breach of contract	2

Exam guide

In scenario questions you may be asked to explain whether or not one party can claim damages from another. Knowledge-based questions may require you to identify the circumstances where damages and other remedies would be available.

1 Discharge of contract

FAST FORWARD

> Contracts can be discharged through **agreement, frustration, performance** and **breach**.

Contracts can be **discharged** in four ways:

- **Agreement**. Where both parties agree to end the agreement and it is supported by consideration.

- **Frustration**. Where performance of an obligation is impossible due to specific circumstances occurring after formation of the contract.

- **Performance**. The most common method of discharge. The contractual obligations are exactly or substantially met (all contract terms are performed).

- **Breach**. Where one party fails to meet its contractual obligations.

2 Breach of contract

FAST FORWARD

> A party is said to be in breach of contract where, without **lawful excuse**, they do not perform their contractual obligations precisely.

A person sometimes has a **lawful excuse** not to perform contractual obligations, if:

- Performance is **impossible**, perhaps because of some unforeseeable event.
- They have tendered performance but this has been **rejected**.
- The **other party** has made it **impossible** for them to perform.
- The contract has been discharged through **frustration**.
- The parties have by **agreement** permitted **non-performance**.

Breach of contract gives rise to a secondary **obligation to pay damages** to the other party. However, the primary obligation to perform the contract's terms remains, unless the party in default has **repudiated** the contract. This may be before performance is due, or before it has been completed, and repudiation has been accepted by the injured party.

Key term

> **Repudiation** can be defined as a breach of contract which entitles the injured party to end the contract if they so choose.

2.1 Repudiatory breach

FAST FORWARD

Breach of a **condition** in a contract or other repudiatory breach allows the injured party to **terminate** the contract unless the injured party elects to treat the contract as continuing and merely claim **damages** for their loss.

Key term

A **repudiatory breach** occurs where a party indicates, either by words or by conduct, that they do not intend to honour their contractual obligations or commits a breach of condition or commits a breach which has very serious consequences for the injured party. It usually occurs when performance is due.

It does not **automatically** discharge the contract – indeed the injured party has a choice.

- They can elect to treat the contract as repudiated by the other, **recover damages** and treat themselves as being discharged from their primary obligations under the contract.

- They can elect to **affirm** the contract.

2.1.1 Types of repudiatory breach

Repudiatory breach arises in the following circumstances.

(a) **Refusal to perform (renunciation).** One party renounces their contractual obligations by showing that they have no intention of performing them.

(b) **Failure to perform an entire obligation.** An entire obligation is said to be one where complete and precise performance of it is a precondition of the other party's performance.

(c) **Incapacitation.** Where a party prevents themselves from performing their contractual obligations they are treated as if they refused to perform them. For instance, where A sells a thing to C even though they promised to sell it to B, they are in repudiatory breach of their contract with B.

(d) **Breach of condition** (a fundamental term of the contract).

(e) **Breach of an innominate term** (a term of the contract, the effect of which cannot be determined until the contract is breached) which has the effect of depriving the injured party of substantially the whole benefit of the contract.

2.1.2 Anticipatory breach

FAST FORWARD

If there is **anticipatory breach** (one party declares in advance that they will not perform their side of the bargain when the time for performance arrives) the other party may treat the contract as discharged forthwith, or continue with their obligations until actual breach occurs. Their claim for damages will then depend upon what they have actually lost.

Repudiation may be **explicit** or **implicit**. A party may break a condition of the contract merely by declaring in advance that they will not perform it, or by some other action which makes future performance impossible. The other party may treat this as **anticipatory breach**:

- Treat the contract as **discharged** forthwith
- At their option, **allow the contract to continue** until there is an actual breach

---

Hochster v De La Tour 1853

The facts: The defendant engaged the claimant as a courier to accompany him on a European tour commencing on 1 June. On 11 May he wrote to the claimant to say that he no longer required his services. On 22 May the claimant commenced legal proceedings for anticipatory breach of contract. The defendant objected that there was no actionable breach until 1 June.

Decision: The claimant was entitled to sue as soon as the anticipatory breach occurred on 11 May.

Where the injured party allows the contract to continue, it may happen that the parties are discharged from their obligations **without** liability by some other cause which occurs later.

If the innocent party elects to treat the contract as still in force, the former may continue with their preparations for performance and **recover the agreed price** for their services. Any claim for damages will be assessed on the basis of what the claimant has really lost.

> *White & Carter (Councils) v McGregor 1961*
>
> *The facts:* The claimants supplied litter bins to local councils, and were paid not by the councils but by traders who hired advertising space on the bins. The defendant contracted with them for advertising of his business. He then wrote to cancel the contract but the claimants elected to advertise as agreed, even though they had at the time of cancellation taken no steps to perform the contract. They performed the contract and claimed the agreed payment.
>
> *Decision:* The contract continued in force and they were entitled to recover the agreed price for their services. Repudiation does not, of itself, bring the contract to an end. It gives the innocent party the choice of affirmation or rejection.

Exam focus point

Questions on breach of contract may focus on specific types of breach and the remedies available.

2.1.3 Termination for repudiatory breach

To terminate for repudiatory breach, the innocent party must **notify** the other of their decision. This may be by way of refusal to accept defects in performance, refusal to accept further performance, or refusal to perform their own obligations.

- They are not bound by their **future** or **continuing contractual obligations**, and cannot be sued on them.

- They need not **accept** nor pay for further performance.

- They can **refuse to pay** for partial or defective performance already received, unless the contract is severable.

- They can **reclaim money** paid to a defaulter if they can and do reject defective performance.

- They are **not discharged** from the contractual obligations which were due at the time of termination.

The innocent party can also claim **damages** from the defaulter. An innocent party who began to perform their contractual obligations but who was prevented from completing them by the defaulter can claim **reasonable** remuneration on a *quantum meruit* basis.

2.1.4 Affirmation after repudiatory breach

If a person is aware of the other party's repudiatory breach and of their own right to terminate the contract as a result, but still decides to treat the contract as being in existence, they are said to have **affirmed the contract**. The contract remains fully in force.

Point to note

Anticipatory breach occurs before the time that performance is due. Repudiatory breach usually occurs at the time of performance.

3 Damages

 FAST FORWARD

Damages are a common law remedy intended to restore the party who has suffered loss to the position they would have been in if the contract had been performed. The two tests applied to a claim for damages relate to **remoteness of damage** and **measure of damages**.

Key term

> **Damages** are a common law remedy intended to restore the party who has suffered loss to the same position they would have been in if the contract had been performed. The two tests applied to a claim for damages relate to **remoteness of damage** and **measure of damages**.

Damages form the **main remedy** in actions for breach of contract, but there are others: injunctions and specific performance are the most important.

In a claim for damages the first issue is **remoteness of damage**. Here, the courts consider how far down the sequence of cause and effect the consequences of breach should be traced before they should be ignored. Second, the court must decide how much money to award in respect of the breach and its relevant consequences. This is the **measure of damages**.

4 Remoteness of damage

FAST FORWARD

> **Remoteness of damage** is tested by the **two limbs** of the rule in **Hadley v Baxendale 1854**.
>
> - The first part of the rule states that the **loss must arise either naturally from the breach** or in a manner which the parties may reasonably be supposed to have contemplated when making the contract.
>
> - The second part of the rule provides that a **loss outside the usual course of events** will only be compensated if the exceptional circumstances which caused it were within the defendant's **actual or constructive knowledge** when they made the contract.

Under the rule in *Hadley v Baxendale* damages may only be awarded in respect of loss as follows.

(a)   (i)   **The loss must arise naturally** from the breach.

     (ii)   The loss must arise **in a manner which the parties may reasonably be supposed to have contemplated**, in making the contract, as the probable result of the breach of it.

(b)   A loss outside the **natural course** of events will only be compensated if the exceptional circumstances are within the defendant's knowledge when they made the contract.

> *Hadley v Baxendale 1854*
>
> *The facts:* The claimants owned a mill at Gloucester, the main crank shaft of which had broken. They made a contract with the defendant for the transport of the broken shaft to Greenwich to serve as a pattern for making a new shaft. Owing to neglect by the defendant, delivery was delayed and the mill was out of action for a longer period. The defendant did not know that the mill would be idle during this interval. He was merely aware that he had to transport a broken millshaft. The claimants claimed for loss of profits of the mill during the period of delay.
>
> *Decision:* Although the failure of the carrier to perform the contract promptly was the direct cause of the stoppage of the mill for an unnecessarily long time, the claim must fail since the defendant did not know that the mill would be idle until the new shaft was delivered. Moreover, it was not a natural consequence of delay in transport of a broken shaft that the mill would be out of action. The miller might have a spare.

The defendant is liable only if they knew of the **special circumstances** from which the abnormal consequence of breach could arise.

> **Victoria Laundry (Windsor) v Newman Industries 1949**
>
> *The facts:* The defendants contracted to sell a large boiler to the claimants 'for immediate use' in their business of launderers and dyers. Owing to an accident in dismantling the boiler at its previous site, delivery was delayed. The defendants were aware of the nature of the claimants' business and had been informed that the claimants were most anxious to put the boiler into use in the shortest possible space of time. The claimants claimed damages for normal loss of profits for the period of delay and for loss of abnormal profits from losing 'highly lucrative' dyeing contracts to be undertaken if the boiler had been delivered on time.
>
> *Decision:* Damages for loss of normal profits were recoverable since in the circumstances failure to deliver major industrial equipment ordered for immediate use would be expected to prevent operation of the plant. The claim for loss of special profits failed because the defendants had no knowledge of the dyeing contracts.

Contrast this ruling with the case below.

> **The Heron II 1969**
>
> *The facts:* K entered into a contract with C for the shipment of a cargo of sugar belonging to C to Basra. He was aware that C were sugar merchants but he did not know that C intended to sell the cargo as soon as it reached Basra. The ship arrived nine days late and in that time the price of sugar on the market in Basra had fallen. C claimed damages for the loss due to the fall in market value.
>
> *Decision:* The claim succeeded. It is common knowledge that market values of commodities fluctuate so that delay might cause loss.

If the type of loss caused is not **too remote** the defendant may be liable for serious consequences.

> **H Parsons (Livestock) v Uttley Ingham 1978**
>
> *The facts:* There was a contract for the supply and installation of a large storage hopper to hold pig foods. Owing to negligence of the defendant supplier the ventilation cowl was left closed. The pig food went mouldy. Young pigs contracted a rare intestinal disease, from which 254 died. The pig farmer claimed damages for the value of the dead pigs and loss of profits from selling the pigs when mature.
>
> *Decision:* Some degree of illness of the pigs was to be expected as a natural consequence. Since illness was to be expected, death from illness was not too remote.

5 Measure of damages

FAST FORWARD

> The **measure of damages** is that which will **compensate for the loss incurred**. It is not intended that the injured party should profit from a claim. Damages may be awarded for financial and non-financial loss.

As a general rule, the amount awarded as damages is what is needed to put the claimant in the position they would have achieved if the contract had been performed. This is sometimes referred to as protecting the **expectation interest** of the claimant.

A claimant may alternatively seek to have their **reliance interest** protected; this refers to the position they would have been in had they not relied on the contract. This compensates for wasted expenditure.

The onus is on the defendant to show that the expenditure would **not** have been recovered if the contract had been performed.

> **C & P Haulage v Middleton 1983**
>
> *The facts:* The claimants granted to the defendant a 6-month renewable licence to occupy premises as an engineering workshop. He incurred expenditure in doing up the premises, although the contract provided that he could not remove any fixtures he installed. He was ejected in breach of the licence agreement 10 weeks before the end of a 6-month term. He sued for damages.
>
> *Decision:* The defendant could only recover nominal damages. He could not recover the cost of equipping the premises (as reliance loss) as he would not have been able to do so if the contract had been lawfully terminated.

If a contract is **speculative**, it may be unclear what profit might result.

> **Anglia Television Ltd v Reed 1972**
>
> *The facts:* The claimants engaged an actor to appear in a film they were making for television. He pulled out at the last moment and the project was abandoned. The claimants claimed the preparatory expenditure, such as hiring other actors and researching suitable locations.
>
> *Decision:* Damages were awarded as claimed. It is impossible to tell whether an unmade film will be a success or a failure and, had the claimants claimed for loss of profits, they would not have succeeded.

The general principle is to compensate for **actual financial loss**.

> **Thompson Ltd v Robinson (Gunmakers) Ltd 1955**
>
> *The facts:* The defendants contracted to buy a Vanguard car from the claimants. They refused to take delivery and the claimants sued for loss of profit on the transaction. There was at the time a considerable excess of supply of such cars over demand for them and the claimants were unable to sell the car.
>
> *Decision:* The market price rule, which the defendants argued should be applied, was inappropriate in the current market as demand for such cars was so low as to effectively mean that no market for them existed. The seller had lost a sale and was entitled to the profit.

> **Charter v Sullivan 1957**
>
> *The facts:* The facts were the same as in the previous case, except that the sellers were able to sell every car obtained from the manufacturers.
>
> *Decision:* Only nominal damages were payable.

5.1 Market price rule

The measure of damages for breaches of contract for the sale of goods is usually made in relation to the **market price** of the goods. Where a seller fails to sell the goods, the buyer can go into the market and purchase **equivalent goods** instead. The seller would have to compensate the buyer for any additional cost the buyer incurred over the contract cost. The situation is reversed when the buyer fails to purchase the goods. The seller can sell the goods on the **open market** and recover any **loss of income** incurred by having to sell the goods at a lower price than what they contracted to.

5.2 Non-financial loss

In some cases, damages have been recovered for **mental distress** where that is the main result of the breach. It is uncertain how far the courts will develop this concept. Contrast the following cases.

> **Jarvis v Swans Tours 1973**
>
> *The facts:* The claimant entered into a contract for holiday accommodation at a winter sports centre. What was provided was much inferior to the description given in the defendant's brochure. Damages on the basis of financial loss only were assessed at £32.
>
> *Decision:* The damages should be increased to £125 to compensate for disappointment and distress because the principle purpose of the contract was the giving of pleasure.

> **Alexander v Rolls Royce Motor Cars Ltd 1995**
>
> *The facts:* The claimant sued for breach of contract to repair his Rolls Royce motor car and claimed damages for distress and inconvenience or loss of enjoyment of the car.
>
> *Decision:* Breach of contract to repair a car did not give rise to any liability for damages for distress, inconvenience or loss of enjoyment.

5.3 Cost of cure

Where there has been a breach and the claimant is seeking to be put in the position they would have been in if the contract had been performed, by seeking a sum of money to 'cure' the defect which constituted the breach, they may be denied the cost of cure if it is **wholly disproportionate** to the breach.

> **Ruxley Electronics and Construction Ltd v Forsyth 1995**
>
> *The facts:* A householder discovered that the swimming pool he had ordered to be built was shallower than specified. He sued the builder for damages, including the cost of demolition of the pool and construction of a new one. Despite its shortcomings, the pool as built was perfectly serviceable and safe to dive into.
>
> *Decision:* The expenditure involved in rectifying the breach was out of all proportion to the benefit of such rectification. The claimant was awarded a small sum to cover loss of amenity.

5.4 Mitigation of loss

In assessing the amount of damages it is assumed that the claimant will take any reasonable steps to reduce or **mitigate** their loss. The burden of proof is on the defendant to show that the claimant failed to take a reasonable opportunity of mitigation.

> **Payzu Ltd v Saunders 1919**
>
> *The facts:* The parties had entered into a contract for the supply of goods to be delivered and paid for by instalments. The claimants failed to pay the first instalment when due, one month after delivery. The defendants declined to make further deliveries unless the claimants paid cash in advance with their orders. The claimants refused to accept delivery on those terms. The price of the goods rose, and they sued for breach of contract.
>
> *Decision:* The seller had no right to repudiate the original contract. But the claimants should have mitigated their loss by accepting the seller's offer of delivery against cash payment. Damages were limited to the amount of their assumed loss if they had paid in advance, which was interest over the period of pre-payment.

The injured party is not required to take **discreditable** or **risky measures** to reduce their loss since these are not 'reasonable'.

> **Pilkington v Wood 1953**
>
> *The facts:* The claimant bought a house in Hampshire, having been advised by his solicitor (the defendant) that title was good. The following year, he decided to sell it. A purchaser was found but it was discovered that the house was not saleable at the agreed price, as the title was not good. The defendant was negligent in his investigation of title and was liable to pay damages of £2,000, being the difference between the market value of the house with good title and its market value with defective title. The defendant argued that the claimant should have mitigated his loss by taking action against the previous vendor for conveying a defective title.
>
> *Decision:* This would have involved complicated litigation and it was not clear that he would have succeeded. The claimant was under no duty to embark on such a hazardous venture 'to protect his solicitor from the consequences of his own carelessness'.

Exam focus point

> An article titled 'Damages' appeared in *Student Accountant* and is available on the ACCA website.

6 Liquidated damages and penalty clauses

FAST FORWARD

> To avoid later complicated calculations of loss, or disputes over damages payable, the parties may include up-front in their contract a formula (**liquidated damages**) for determining the damages payable for breach.

Key term

> **Liquidated damages** can be defined as 'a fixed or ascertainable sum agreed by the parties at the time of contracting, payable in the event of a breach, for example, an amount payable per day for failure to complete a building. If they are a genuine attempt to pre-estimate the likely loss, the court will enforce payment.'

> **Dunlop Pneumatic Tyre Co Ltd v New Garage & Motor Co Ltd 1915**
>
> *The facts:* The contract (for the sale of tyres to a garage) imposed a minimum retail price. The contract provided that £5 per tyre should be paid by the buyer if he resold at less than the prescribed retail price or in four other possible cases of breach of contract. He did sell at a lower price and argued that £5 per tyre was a 'penalty' and not a genuine pre-estimate of loss.
>
> *Decision:* As a general rule when a fixed amount is to be paid as damages for breaches of different kinds, some more serious in their consequences than others, that is not a genuine pre-estimate of loss and so it is void as a 'penalty'. In this case the formula was an honest attempt to agree on liquidated damages and would be upheld.

> **Ford Motor Co (England) Ltd v Armstrong 1915**
>
> *The facts:* The defendant had undertaken not to sell the claimant's cars below list price, not to sell Ford cars to other dealers and not to exhibit any Ford cars without permission. A £250 penalty was payable for each breach as being the agreed damage which the claimant would sustain.
>
> *Decision:* Since the same sum was payable for different kinds of loss it was not a genuine pre-estimate of loss and was in the nature of a penalty. Unlike the *Dunlop* case the figure set was held to be excessive.

The following, more recent case, indicates that courts are flexible when considering onerous liquidated damages clauses which may, in the past, have been considered penalty clauses.

> **Azimut-Benetti SpA v Darrell Marcus Healey 2010**
>
> *The facts:* The defendants entered into a shipbuilding contract with the claimants. A liquidated damages clause stated that in the event the contract is terminated by the defendants, the claimants could receive a sum equal to 20% of the contract price (€7.1 million).
>
> *Decision:* The court held that the clause represented a commercially justified balance between the parties' interests and the claimants could receive the €7.1 million when the defendants failed to pay the first instalment due.

A contractual term designed as a **penalty clause** to discourage breach is void and not enforceable. Relief from penalty clauses is an example of the influence of equity in the law of contract, and has most frequently been seen in consumer credit cases.

Key term

> A **penalty clause** is a contractual clause that provides that a specific sum of money is payable in the event of a breach of contract.

> **Bridge v Campbell Discount Co 1962**
>
> *The facts:* A clause in a hire purchase contract required the debtor to pay, on termination, both arrears of payments due before termination, and an amount which, together with payments made and due before termination, amounted to two-thirds of the HP price, and additionally to return the goods.
>
> *Decision:* This was a penalty clause and void since, in almost all circumstances, the creditor would receive on termination more than 100% of the value of the goods.

In recent times, terms have not been classified as penalty clauses unless they are considered to be penal in nature. The view is if the sum does not protect the legitimate interest of the innocent party and is excessive, then it is a penalty clause and therefore unenforceable.

The following cases have provided examples of situations where a penalty clause may be enforceable.

In *Cavendish Square Holding BV v Talal El Makdessi 2015* a test of whether a clause is a penalty or not was developed. It was held that if a clause creates an obligation to pay a party more in damages than their actual losses, it will be enforceable providing it is in proportion to the primary obligation under the contract. This will be a question of fact for the court to decide.

> **ParkingEye Limited v Beavis 2015**
>
> *The facts:* The claimant managed a car park at a retail park. There were notices around the car park stating that visitors are entitled to two hours of free parking but an £85 charge would be levied if visitors stay in excess of that time. Mr Beavis stayed in the car park for almost three hours but refused to pay the charge stating that it was a penalty.
>
> *Decision:* The Supreme Court held that a charge like this acts as a deterrent and as such should not be deemed a penalty. In this case the claimant has a legitimate secondary interest which is not satisfied by recovering damages for breach of contract. The purpose of the charge is to prevent visitors overstaying, which is important for managing the car park in the interest of all visitors (ie to stop the car park being clogged up with people staying for extended periods). There were notices displayed all around the car park and the charge was not excessive when compared to the level of parking fines generally.

7 Other common law remedies

7.1 Action for the price

FAST FORWARD

A simple **action for the price** to recover the agreed sum should be brought if breach of contract is failure to pay the price. But property must have passed from seller to buyer, and complications arise where there is anticipatory breach.

If the breach of contract arises out of one party's **failure to pay the contractually agreed price** due under the contract, the creditor should bring a personal action against the debtor to recover that sum. This is a fairly straightforward procedure but is subject to two specific limitations.

The first is that an **action for the price** under a contract for the sale of goods may only be brought if property has passed to the buyer, unless the price has been agreed to be payable on a specific date.

Second, whilst the injured party may recover an **agreed sum** due at the time of an anticipatory breach, sums which become due after the anticipatory breach may not be recovered unless they affirm the contract.

7.2 Quantum meruit

FAST FORWARD

A **quantum meruit** is a claim which is available as an alternative to damages. The injured party in a breach of a contract may claim the value of their work. The aim of such an award is to restore the claimant to the position they would have been in had the contract never been made. It is a **restitutory award**.

In particular situations, a claim may be made on a quantum meruit basis as an **alternative** to an action for damages for breach of contract.

Key term

The phrase **quantum meruit** literally means **'how much it is worth'**. It is a measure of the value of contractual work which has been performed. The aim of such an award is to restore the claimant to the position they would have been in if the contract had never been made, and is therefore known as a **restitutory award**.

Quantum meruit is likely to be sought where **one party has already performed part of their obligations** and the other party then repudiates the contract.

> *De Bernardy v Harding 1853*
>
> *The facts:* The claimant agreed to advertise and sell tickets for the defendant, who was erecting stands for spectators to view the funeral of the Duke of Wellington. The defendant cancelled the arrangement without justification.
>
> *Decision:* The claimant might recover the value of services rendered.

In most cases, a quantum meruit claim is needed because the other party has unjustifiably prevented performance. Because it is **restitutory**, a quantum meruit award is usually for a **smaller amount** than an award of damages. However, where only **nominal damages** would be awarded (say because the claimant would not have been able to perform the contract anyway) a quantum meruit claim would still be available and would yield a **higher amount**.

8 Equitable remedies

8.1 Specific performance

FAST FORWARD

An order for **specific performance** is an equitable remedy. The party in breach is ordered to perform their side of the contract. Such an order is only made where damages are inadequate compensation, such as in a sale of land, and where actual consideration has passed.

The court may at its **discretion** give an equitable remedy by ordering the defendant to perform their part of the contract instead of letting them 'buy themselves out of it' by paying damages for breach.

Specific performance is a court order for a party to perform an obligation. It is an equitable remedy awarded at the discretion of the court when damages would not be an adequate remedy. Its principal use is in contracts for the sale of land but may also be used to compel a sale of shares or debentures. It will never be used in the case of employment or other contracts involving personal services.'

An order will be made for specific performance of a contract for the **sale of land** since the claimant may need the land for a particular purpose and would not be adequately compensated by damages for the loss of their bargain.

The order will **not** be made if it would require performance over a period of time and the court could not ensure that the defendant did comply fully with the order. Therefore specific performance is not ordered for contracts of **employment** or **personal service** nor, usually, for building contracts.

8.2 Injunction

An **injunction** is a discretionary court order and an equitable remedy, requiring the defendant to observe a negative condition of a contract.

An **injunction** is a discretionary court order and an equitable remedy, requiring the defendant to observe a negative restriction of a contract.

An injunction may be made to **enforce** a contract of **personal service** for which an order of specific performance would be refused.

Warner Bros Pictures Inc v Nelson 1937

The facts: The defendant (the film star Bette Davis) agreed to work for a year for the claimants and not during the year to work for any other producer nor 'to engage in any other occupation' without the consent of the claimants. She came to England during the year to work for a British film producer. The claimants sued for an injunction to restrain her from this work and she resisted arguing that if the restriction were enforced she must either work for them or abandon her livelihood.

Decision: The court would not make an injunction if it would have the result suggested by the defendant. But the claimants merely asked for an injunction to restrain her from working for a British film producer. This was one part of the restriction accepted by her under her contract and it was fair to hold her to it to that extent.

The scope of injunctions is limited to **enforcement** of **contract terms** which are in substance negative restraints. They would **not** be made merely to **restrain** the defendant from acts inconsistent with their positive obligations.

8.2.1 Mareva or 'freezing' injunctions

The Mareva injunction is named from the case of *Mareva Compania Naviera SA v International Bulkcarriers SA 1975*, but has been given **statutory effect**. If the claimant can convince the court that they have a good case and that there is a danger of the defendant's assets being exported or dissipated, they may be awarded an injunction which restricts the defendant's dealing with the assets.

8.3 Rescission

Strictly speaking the equitable right to **rescind** an agreement is not a remedy for breach of contract – it is a right which exists in certain circumstances, such as where a contract is **voidable**.

Rescinding a contract means that it is cancelled or rejected and the parties are restored to **their pre-contract condition**. Four conditions must be met.

- It **must be possible** for each party to be returned to the pre-contract condition *(restitutio in integrum)*.

- An **innocent third party** who has acquired rights in the subject matter of the contract will prevent the original transaction being rescinded.

- The right to rescission must be exercised within a **reasonable time** of it arising.

- Where a person **affirms** a contract expressly or by conduct it **may not then be rescinded**.

Exam focus point

> Questions may ask whether a particular remedy, say specific performance, is appropriate in any given situation.

Chapter Roundup

- Contracts can be discharged through **agreement**, **frustration**, **performance** and **breach**.

- A party is said to be in breach of contract where, without **lawful excuse**, they do not perform their contractual obligations precisely.

- **Breach** of a **condition** in a contract or other repudiatory breach allows the injured party to **terminate** the contract unless the injured party elects to treat the contract as continuing and merely claim **damages** for their loss.

- If there is **anticipatory breach** (one party declares in advance that they will not perform their side of the bargain when the time for performance arrives) the other party may treat the contract as discharged forthwith, or continue with their obligations until actual breach occurs. Their claim for damages will then depend upon what they have actually lost.

- **Damages** are a common law remedy intended to restore the party who has suffered loss to the position they would have been in if the contract had been performed. The two tests applied to a claim for damages relate to **remoteness of damage** and **measure of damages**.

- **Remoteness of damage** is tested by the **two limbs** of the rule in **Hadley v Baxendale 1854**.

    - The first part of the rule states that the **loss must arise either naturally from the breach** or in a manner which the parties may reasonably be supposed to have contemplated when making the contract.

    - The second part of the rule provides that a **loss outside the usual course of events** will only be compensated if the exceptional circumstances which caused it were within the defendant's **actual or constructive knowledge** when they made the contract.

- The **measure of damages** is that which will **compensate for the loss incurred**. It is not intended that the injured party should profit from a claim. Damages may be awarded for financial and non-financial loss.

- To avoid later complicated calculations of loss, or disputes over damages payable, the parties may include up-front in their contract a formula (**liquidated damages**) for determining the damages payable for breach.

- A simple **action for the price** to recover the agreed sum should be brought if breach of contract is failure to pay the price. But property must have passed from seller to buyer, and complications arise where there is anticipatory breach.

- A **quantum meruit** is a claim which is available as an alternative to damages. The injured party in a breach of a contract may claim the value of their work. The aim of such an award is to restore the claimant to the position they would have been in had the contract never been made. It is a **restitutory award**.

- An order for **specific performance** is an equitable remedy. The party in breach is ordered to perform their side of the contract. Such an order is only made where damages are inadequate compensation, such as in a sale of land, and where actual consideration has passed.

- An **injunction** is a discretionary court order and an equitable remedy, requiring the defendant to observe a negative condition of a contract.

1   **Fill in the blanks** in the statements below, using the words in the box.

(1) ……………….. are a (2) ……………….. remedy designed to restore the injured party to the position they would have been in had the contract been (3) ………………..

A loss outside the natural course of events will only be compensated if the (4) ……………….. circumstances are within the (5) ………………..'s knowledge at the time of making the contract.

In assessing the amount of damage it is assumed that the (6) ……………….. will (7) ……………….. their loss.

A contractual term designed as a (8) ……………….. is (9) ……………….. .

• mitigate	• performed	• claimant
• penalty clause	• exceptional	• damages
• common law	• void	• defendant

2   **Fill in the blanks** in the statements below.

When anticipatory breach occurs, the injured party has two options. These are

(1) ………………..

(2) ………………..

3   The amount awarded as damages is what is needed to put the claimant in the position they would have achieved if the contract had been performed. What interest is being protected here?

expectation
reliance

4   A court will never enforce a liquidated damages clause, as any attempt to discourage breach is void.

True   ☐

False   ☐

5   Are each of the following remedies based on (i) equity or (ii) common law?

(a)   Quantum meruit
(b)   Injunction
(c)   Action for the price
(d)   Rescission
(e)   Specific performance

1   (1)   damages   (2)   common law   (3)   performed
    (4)   exceptional   (5)   defendant   (6)   claimant
    (7)   mitigate   (8)   penalty clause   (9)   void

2   (1)   Treat the contract as discharged forthwith
    (2)   Allow the contract to continue until there is an actual breach

3   Expectation

4   False. Courts will enforce liquidated damages clauses if they are genuine.

5   (a)   Common law
    (b)   Equity
    (c)   Common law
    (d)   Equity
    (e)   Equity

Now try the questions below from the Practice Question Bank

Number
12, 13, 14

The law of torts and professional negligence

Topic list	Syllabus reference
1 Tort and other wrongs	B4(a), B4(b)
2 The tort of negligence	B4(c)
3 Duty of care	B4(c)
4 Breach of duty of care	B4(c)
5 Causality and remoteness of damage	B4(d)
6 Defences to negligence	B4(e)
7 Professional advice	B4(f)
8 The Caparo decision	B4(f)

Introduction

In this chapter we introduce the law of torts.

Torts are **wrongful acts** against an **individual**, a **company** or their **property** that give rise to a **civil liability** against the person who committed them.

There are a number of torts, however **negligence** is the one that will concern you most in your studies.

Your syllabus requires you to understand the **nature** of torts and to explain the **factors** that must be present for claims to succeed. By focusing on the rules and their related **cases** you will be able to apply them to any case given to you in an exam question.

Study guide

		Intellectual level
B	**The law of obligations**	
4	**The law of torts and professional negligence**	
(a)	Explain the meaning of tort	2
(b)	Explain the tort of 'passing off'	2
(c)	Explain the tort of negligence including the duty of care and its breach, and the concept of vicarious liability	2
(d)	Explain the meaning of causality and remoteness of damage	2
(e)	Discuss defences to actions in negligence	2
(f)	Explain and analyse the duty of care of accountants and auditors	2

Exam guide

There are a number of ways tort could be examined. Scenario questions may require you to identify whether a tort has been committed, whether a duty of care exists or if there is sufficient link between the actions and resulting damage for liability to be established. Other questions may require you to identify the different types of tort and the circumstances that create a liability for damages.

1 Tort and other wrongs

FAST FORWARD

> The law gives various rights to persons. When such a right is infringed the wrongdoer is liable in **tort**.

1.1 Tort

Tort is **distinguished** from other legal wrongs.

(a) It is **not** a **breach of contract**, where the obligation which is alleged to have been breached arose under an agreement between two parties.

(b) It is **not** a **crime**, where the object of proceedings is to punish the offender rather than compensate the victim.

Key term

> A **tort** is a civil wrong and the person wronged sues in a **civil court** for compensation or an injunction. The claimant's claim generally is that they have suffered a loss such as personal injury at the hands of the defendant and the defendant should pay damages.
>
> **In tort no previous transaction or contractual relationship need exist**: the parties may be complete strangers; such as when a motorist knocks down a pedestrian in the street. The claim in tort is based on the general law of duties and rights.

1.2 Types of tort

The two main types of tort that you need to understand for your exam are 'passing-off' and negligence.

1.2.1 'Passing-off'

Passing-off is the use of a name, mark or description by one business that **misleads a consumer** to believe that their business is that of another. This tort often occurs when expensive 'designer' products such as watches or clothing are copied and sold as 'originals' to unsuspecting customers.

The development of the **Internet** has seen the routine selling of domain names to those who wish to buy them. This has created the opportunity for individuals to set up a website that has the intention of mimicking an established brand and stealing their customers.

The issue of what is **misleading** under the tort of passing-off has been the subject of numerous cases, but it appears that the businesses do have to be very similar indeed. In *Stringfellow v McCain Foods GB 1984* the owner of a famous nightclub failed to prevent a manufacturer of long, thin oven chips from calling their product by the same name. When Midland Bank in the UK rebranded as HSBC they were subject to a passing-off claim from the long established HFC Bank. The case failed on the grounds of there being insufficient chance of public confusion: *HFC Bank v Midland Bank 2000*. We shall consider passing-off further when we look at company names in a later chapter.

We shall come back to the tort of 'passing-off' in more detail later on when we consider the rules on company names.

1.2.2 Negligence

In simple terms, negligence is the **carelessness** of an individual or company which causes damage (physical or financial) to the claimant. Negligent acts tend to be **inadvertent** or **reckless**, but not normally intentional.

2 The tort of negligence

FAST FORWARD

Negligence is the most important modern tort. To succeed in an action for negligence the claimant must prove that:

- The defendant had **a duty of care** to avoid causing injury, damage or loss
- There was **a breach of that duty** by the defendant
- **In consequence** the claimant suffered **injury, damage or loss**

2.1 Definition

There is a **distinct tort of negligence** which is causing loss by a failure to take reasonable care when there is a duty to do so. This is the most important and far reaching modern tort.

FAST FORWARD

The term negligence is used to describe **carelessly** carrying out an **act** and breaking a **legal duty of care** owed to another causing them **loss or damage**.

Exam focus point

Two articles on the tort of negligence have appeared in *Student Accountant* and are available on the ACCA website. They are titled 'Key aspects of the law of contract and the tort of negligence' and 'The tort of negligence'.

2.2 Liability

Any **legal person** can commit and therefore be **liable for a tort** providing the three stage test is passed. This includes, for example, a car driver who injures a pedestrian, or a company that causes death or injury to a customer. Also, an employer can be **vicariously liable** for the acts of an employee. This means an employer may be liable for loss or damage caused by an employee, providing the acts were committed whilst the employee was performing the duties they were employed to do.

3 Duty of care

FAST FORWARD

In the landmark case of *Donoghue v Stevenson 1932* the House of Lords ruled that a person might **owe a duty of care to another with whom they had no contractual relationship** at all. The doctrine has been refined in subsequent rulings, but the principle is unchanged.

3.1 The basic rule

The question of whether or not a duty of care exists in any situation is generally decided by the courts on a **case by case basis**, with each new case setting a precedent based on its own particular facts.

In the case described below, the House of Lords was attempting to establish a **general duty** that could be applied to all subsequent cases and situations.

Donoghue v Stevenson 1932

The facts: A purchased a bottle of ginger beer for consumption by B. B drank part of the contents, which contained the remains of a decomposed snail, and became ill. The manufacturer argued that as there was no contract between himself and B he owed her no duty of care and so was not liable.

Decision: The House of Lords laid down the general principle that every person owes a duty of care to his 'neighbour', to 'persons so closely and directly affected by my act that I ought reasonably to have them in contemplation as being so affected'.

3.2 Development of the doctrine

This narrow doctrine has been much refined over the years since the snail made its celebrated appearance. For any duty of care to exist, it was stated in *Anns v Merton London Borough Council 1977* that two stages must be tested:

- Is there sufficient **proximity** between the parties, such that the harm suffered was **reasonably foreseeable**?

- Should the duty be **restricted** or **limited** for reasons of economic, social or public policy?

The latest stage in the doctrine's development came in *Caparo Industries plc v Dickman 1990* that established a three stage test for establishing a duty of care that still stands:

- Was the harm **reasonably foreseeable**?
- Was there a relationship of **proximity** between the parties?
- Considering the circumstances, is it **fair, just and reasonable** to impose a duty of care?

4 Breach of duty of care

FAST FORWARD

The second element that must be proven by a claimant in an action for negligence is that there was a **breach of the duty** of care by the defendant.

4.1 The basic rule

Breach of duty of care is the second issue to be considered in a negligence claim. The standard of reasonable care requires that the person concerned should do what a **reasonable man** would do, and should not do what a reasonable man would not do: *Blyth v Birmingham Water Works 1856*. This will also mean the reasonable **employer**, or the reasonable **adviser**.

The following factors should be considered when deciding if a duty of care has been breached:

(a) **Probability of injury**

It is presumed that a reasonable man takes **greater precautions** when the risk of injury is high: *Bolton v Stone 1951*. Therefore when the risk is higher the defendant must do more to meet their duty. In *Glasgow Corporation v Taylor 1922* a local authority was held to be negligent when children ate poisonous berries in a park. A warning notice was not considered to be sufficient to protect children.

(b) **Seriousness** of the risk

The young, old or disabled may be prone to more serious injury than a fit able-bodied person. The **'egg-shell skull'** rule means that you must take your victim as they are. Where the risk to the vulnerable is high, the level of care required is raised: *Smith v Leech Brain & Co 1962.*

> *Paris v Stepney Borough Council 1951*
>
> *The facts:* P was employed by K on vehicle maintenance. P had already lost the sight of one eye. It was not the normal practice to issue protective goggles since the risk of eye injury was small. A chip of metal flew into P's good eye and blinded him.
>
> *Decision:* There was a higher standard of care owed to P because an injury to his remaining good eye would blind him.

(c) Issues of **practicality and cost**

It is not always reasonable to ensure all possible precautions are taken. Where the **cost** or **disruption** caused to eliminate the danger far **exceeds the risk** of it occurring it is likely that defendants will be found not to have breached their duty if they do not implement them.

> *Latimer v AEC Ltd 1952*
>
> *The facts:* The defendants owned a factory that became flooded after a period of heavy rain. The water mixed with oil on the factory floor causing it to become very slippery. Sawdust was applied to the majority of the areas affected, but the claimant slipped on one of the few areas that was not treated.
>
> *Decision:* The defendant did all that was necessary to reduce the risk to its employees and was not held liable. The only other option was to close the factory, however no evidence could be provided that would indicate a reasonable employer would have taken that course of action. Closing the factory would have outweighed the risk to the employees.

(d) **Common practice**

Where an individual can prove their actions were in line with **common practice** or **custom** it is likely that they would have met their duty of care. This is unless the common practice itself is found to be negligent.

(e) **Social benefit**

Where an action is of **some benefit** to society, defendants may be **protected** from liability even if their actions create risk. For example, a fire engine that speeds to a major disaster provides a social benefit that may outweigh the greater risk to the public.

(f) **Professions and skill**

Persons who hold themselves out to possess a particular skill should be judged on what a **reasonable person possessing the same skill** would do in the situation rather than that of a reasonable man. Professions are able to set their own **standards of care** for their members to meet and therefore members should be judged against these standards rather than those laid down by the courts.

4.2 Res ipsa loquitur

In some circumstances the claimant may argue that the **facts speak for themselves** (*res ipsa loquitur*) – want of care being the only possible explanation for what happened, negligence on the part of the defendant must be presumed.

Res ipsa loquitur can be defined as: 'The thing speaks for itself'. If an accident occurs which appears to be most likely caused by negligence, the court may apply this maxim and infer negligence from mere proof of the facts. The burden of proof is reversed and the defendant must prove that they were not negligent.

The **claimant must demonstrate** the following to rely on this principle:

(a) The thing which caused the injury was under the **management and control** of the defendant.

(b) The accident was such that it would not occur if those in control used **proper care**. Therefore in *Richley v Faull 1965* the fact that a car skidded to the wrong side of the road was enough to indicate careless driving.

4.3 Example

In *Mahon v Osborne 1939* a surgeon was required to prove that leaving a swab inside a patient after an operation was not negligent.

5 Causality and remoteness of damage

Finally the claimant must demonstrate that they suffered injury or loss as a **result** of the breach.

5.1 Damage or loss

This is the third element of a negligence claim. A claim for compensation for negligence will not succeed if **damage** or **loss** is not proved. A person will only be compensated if they have suffered actual loss, injury, damage or harm **as a consequence** of another's actions. Examples of such loss may include:

- Personal injury
- Damage to property
- Financial loss which is directly connected to personal injury, for example, loss of earnings
- Pure financial loss is rarely recoverable

5.1.1 Pure financial loss

Pure financial loss, also known as **economic loss,** is loss which is **unconnected with physical damage**. It is not usually recoverable. For example in *Spartan Steel and Alloys Ltd v Martin & Co Ltd 1973* it was held that general loss of profits due to interruption caused by a prolonged loss of power to a manufacturing plant as a whole was not recoverable. However, the claimants were able to recover losses from physical damage to a particular furnace, and loss of profit on the damaged products in the furnace, which occurred as a direct result of power being unexpectedly cut.

5.2 The 'But for' test

To satisfy the requirement that harm must be caused by another's actions, the **'But for' test** is applied. The claimant must prove that if it was not 'but for' the other's actions they would not have suffered damage. Therefore claimants are **unable** to claim for any harm that would have happened to them **anyway** irrespective of the defendant's actions.

Barnett v Chelsea and Kensington HMC 1969

The facts: A casualty doctor sent a patient home without treatment, referring him to his own doctor. The patient died of arsenic poisoning.

Decision: Whilst the doctor was held negligent, the negligence did not cause the patient's death because he would have died anyway.

5.2.1 Multiple causes

The courts often have difficulty in determining **causation** where there are a number of possible causes of injury including the negligent act. The courts must decide on the **facts** if the negligent act was the one that most likely caused the injury.

> *Wilsher v Essex AHA 1988*
>
> *The facts:* A premature baby suffered blindness after birth. It was claimed that a doctor failed to notice that the baby received high doses of oxygen and this caused the blindness.
>
> *Decision:* Evidence was provided that there were six possible causes of the blindness including the one claimed. However, the court could not ascertain which of the six actually occurred and therefore could not create a direct causal link.

The case below indicates the court's flexibility when applying legal principles in **exceptional** cases.

> *Fairchild v Glenhaven Funeral Services Ltd & Others 2002*
>
> *The facts:* The claimants all contracted a disease caused by contact with asbestos over extended periods of time with several different employers. The defence claimed that the disease could be contracted by exposure to one asbestos fibre and as the claimants were employed by a number of employers it could not be established at which employer they contracted the disease.
>
> *Decision:* The House of Lords held that all the employers (who had failed to take reasonable care), contributed to the cause and were all liable.

5.3 Novus actus interveniens

Courts will only impart liability where there is a cause of events that are a **probable** result of the defendant's actions. Defendants will not be liable for damage when the chain of events is broken. There are **three types** of intervening act that will break the chain of causation.

5.3.1 Act of the claimant

The actions of the claimant themselves may **break** the chain of causation. The rule is that where the act is **reasonable** and in the **ordinary course of things** an act by the claimant will not break the chain.

> *McKew v Holland, Hannen and Cubbitts (Scotland) Ltd 1969*
>
> *The facts:* The claimant had a leg injury which was prone to causing his leg to give way from time to time. Whilst at work he failed to ask for assistance when negotiating a flight of stairs. He fell and was injured as a result.
>
> *Decision:* The fact that the claimant failed to seek assistance was unreasonable and was sufficient to break the chain of causality.

5.3.2 Act of a third party

Where a **third party** intervenes in the course of events the defendant will normally only be liable for damage **until** the intervention. For example, in *Knightley v Johns 1982* the defendant caused a road traffic accident. A police inspector negligently handled traffic control following the accident. This negligence led to the claimant, a police officer, being killed. The defendant who caused the accident successfully argued that the negligent handling by the police inspector broke the chain of causation between his negligence and the death of the officer.

> **Lamb v Camden LBC 1981**
>
> *The facts:* The defendant negligently caused a house to be damaged, and as a result it had to be vacated until it could be repaired. During the vacant period, squatters took up residence and the property suffered further damage.
>
> *Decision:* Intrusion by squatters was a possibility that the defendant should have considered, but it was not held to be a likely event. Therefore the defendant should not be liable for the additional damage caused by the intervening actions of the squatters.

5.3.3 Natural events

The chain of causality is **not automatically** broken due to an intervening natural event. In situations where the breach puts the claimant at risk of **additional** damage caused by a natural event the chain will not be broken. However, where the natural event is **unforeseeable**, the chain will be broken.

> **Carslogie Steamship Co Ltd v Royal Norwegian Government 1952**
>
> *The facts:* A ship owned by the claimants was damaged as a result of the defendant's negligence and required repair. During the trip to the repair site the ship was caught in severe weather conditions that resulted in additional damage being caused and therefore a longer repair time was required. The claimants claimed loss of charter revenue for the period the ship was out of action for repairs caused by the original incident.
>
> *Decision:* The House of Lords held that the defendants were liable for loss of profit suffered as result of the defendants' wrongful act only. Whilst undergoing repairs, the ship ceased to be a profit-earning machine as the weather damage had rendered her unseaworthy. The weather conditions created an intervening act and the claimants had sustained no loss of profit due to the ship being out of action as it would have been unavailable for hire anyway due to the weather damage.

5.4 Remoteness of damage

Even where causation is proved, a negligence claim can still fail if the damage caused is *'too remote'*. The test of **reasonable foresight** developed out of *The Wagon Mound (1961)*. Liability is limited to damage that a **reasonable man** could have foreseen. This does not mean the exact event must be foreseeable in detail, just that the eventual outcome is foreseeable.

> **The Wagon Mound 1961**
>
> *The facts:* A ship was taking on oil in Sydney harbour. Oil was spilled onto the water and it drifted to a wharf 200 yards away where welding equipment was in use. The owner of the wharf carried on working because he was advised that the sparks were unlikely to set fire to furnace oil. Safety precautions were taken. A spark fell onto a piece of cotton waste floating in the oil, thereby starting a fire which damaged the wharf. The owner of the wharf sued the charterers of the Wagon Mound.
>
> *Decision:* The claim must fail. Pollution was the foreseeable risk: fire was not.

The House of Lords decided in the case of *Jolley v London Borough of Sutton 2000* that the remoteness test can be passed if **some** harm is foreseeable even if the exact nature of the injuries could not be.

> **Jolley v London Borough of Sutton 2000**
>
> *The facts:* The defendants should have removed a boat which had been dumped two years previously. A teenage boy was injured while attempting to repair it.
>
> *Decision:* Even though the precise incident was not foreseeable, the authority should have foreseen that some harm could be caused since they knew children regularly played on the abandoned boat.

6 Defences to negligence

FAST FORWARD

The amount of damages awarded to the claimant can be reduced if it is shown that they **contributed** to their injury. The defendant can be **exonerated** from paying damages if it can be proved that the claimant **expressly** or **impliedly** consented to the risk. In employment situations, an employer may be held **vicariously liable** for the actions of their employee.

6.1 Contributory negligence

A court may **reduce** the amount of damages paid to the claimant if the defendant establishes that they **contributed** to their own **injury** or **loss**, this is known as **contributory negligence**.

Sayers v Harlow UDC 1958

The facts: The claimant was injured whilst trying to climb out of a public toilet cubicle that had a defective lock.

Decision: The court held that the claimant had contributed to her injuries by the method by which she had tried to climb out.

If the defendant proves that the claimant was at least **partially** at fault, courts will reduce the damages awarded to them by a **percentage** that is **just** and **reasonable**. This percentage is calculated according to what is established as the **claimant's share of the blame**. This is typically in the range of 10% to 75%, however it is possible to reduce the claim by up to 100%.

In *Fitzgerald v Lane & Patel 1989* the claimant crossed the road whilst the lights were at red for pedestrians. The first defendant driver collided with him and the claimant was thrown from the bonnet of that car into the road, where he was run over by a car driven by the second defendant. The claimant suffered severe spinal injuries that led to partial paralysis, but it could not be proven which impact caused the paralysis. In awarding damages the House of Lords attributed blame in the proportion of 50% against the claimant and 25% each against the two speeding drivers. Damages were thus awarded in those relative proportions.

6.2 Volenti non fit injuria

Where a defendant's actions carry the risk of a tort being committed they will have a defence if it can be proved that the claimant consented to the risk. *Volenti non fit injuria* literally means the **voluntary acceptance** of the **risk of injury**.

This defence is available to the defendant where both parties have **expressly** consented to the risk (such as waiver forms signed by those taking part in dangerous sports), or it may be **implied** by the **conduct** of the claimant.

ICI v Shatwell 1965

The facts: The claimant and his brother disregarded safety precautions whilst using detonators, resulting in injury to the claimant.

Decision: The court upheld the defence of *volenti non fit injuria*. The claimant disregarded his employer's statutory safety rules and consented to the reckless act willingly.

An **awareness** of the risk **is not sufficient to establish consent**. For this defence to be successful the defendant must **prove** that the claimant was **fully informed** of the **risks** and that they consented to them.

This point was made in *Dann v Hamilton 1939* where a girl passenger in a car driven by a drunk driver was injured. The defendant established that she was aware of the risk but could offer no evidence that she consented to it. As a result of this case the defence of *volenti* is unlikely to succeed in cases where consent is **implied**.

6.3 Vicarious liability

In employment situations, an employee can avoid liability for negligence if they were acting on their **employer's business** at the time of the incident. For the employer to be **vicariously liable**, the employee must have been following their **employer's instructions**, even if the manner of how they were carrying them out was not how the employer told them to.

In *Limpus v London General Omnibus Co 1862* a bus company was found vicariously liable for a bus driven negligently by a bus driver against their instructions. However, in *Beard v London General Omnibus Co 1900*, the bus company was not found vicariously liable where a bus conductor (who was not authorised to drive a bus) drove a bus negligently. In that case, the employee was held liable.

The law relating to whether an employee was acting in the course of their employment has been revised considerably by the following case:

Lister and ors v Hesley Hall Ltd 2001

The facts: The warden of a boarding school was found guilty of abusing children resident there.

Decision: The school was vicariously liable. The nature of the warden's work created a sufficient connection between the acts of abuse which he had committed and the work which he was employed to do.

Obviously, in this case, the school did not employ the warden for the purposes of abusing the children. In that sense, he was not acting in the course of his employment when he carried out the crime. However, it was decided that the acts that he carried out were so **closely connected** with the nature of his work, that it was fair and just to hold the employer liable. In other words, he was employed to look after the children, and the torts committed were in his work time, in the place where he was employed and while he was carrying out his employed duty to care for the children.

Whether this 'close connection' between the employee's tort and his employment exists must be decided by the **court on the facts of each case**. The following is another case in which the test has been applied since the *Lister* case.

Dubai Aluminium Co Ltd v Salaam and ors 2002

The facts: A, a solicitor, drafted bogus agreements.

Decision: The drafting of agreements of this nature (but for a proper purpose) would be within the ordinary course of business for a solicitor. Therefore the dishonest acts were sufficiently closely connected to the course of his business for his employers to be vicariously liable for those acts.

---

7 Professional advice

FAST FORWARD

Professional individuals and organisations have a special relationship with their clients and those who rely on their work. This is because they act in an **expert capacity**.

7.1 Development

We shall now turn our attention to how the law relating to negligent professional advice, and in particular **auditors**, has been developed through the operation of precedent, being refined and explained with each successive case that comes to court. It illustrates the often step-by-step development of English law, which has gradually refined the principles laid down in *Donoghue v Stevenson* and *Anns v Merton London Borough Council* to cover **negligent misstatements** which cause **pure financial loss**.

7.2 The special relationship

Before 1963, it was held that any liability for careless statements was limited in scope and depended upon the existence of a **contractual** or **fiduciary relationship** between the parties. Lord Denning's tests of a further (later termed 'special') relationship were laid down in the Court of Appeal in his dissenting judgement on *Candler v Crane, Christmas & Co 1951*.

FAST FORWARD

> According to Lord Denning, to establish a **special relationship** the person who made the statement must have done so in some professional or expert capacity which made it likely that others would rely on what they said. This is the position of an adviser such as an accountant, banker, solicitor or surveyor.

It follows that a duty could not be owed to complete strangers, but Lord Denning also stated at the time: 'Accountants owe a duty of care not only to their own clients, but also to **all those whom they know will rely on their accounts** in the transactions for which those accounts are prepared.' This was to prove a significant consideration in later cases.

However, Lord Denning's view was a dissenting voice in 1951 in the *Candler* case, where the Court of Appeal held that the defendants were **not** liable (for a bad investment based upon a set of negligently prepared accounts) because there was no direct contractual or fiduciary relationship with the claimant investor.

It was 12 years later that the **special relationship** was accepted as a valid test. Our starting point is a **leading case** (*Hedley*) on negligent misstatement which was the start of a **new judicial approach** to cases involving negligent misstatement. You must make sure that you are familiar with it.

> *Hedley Byrne & Co Ltd v Heller and Partners Ltd 1963*
>
> *The facts:* HB were advertising agents acting for a new client, Easipower Ltd. HB requested information from Easipower's bank (HP) on its financial position. HP returned non-committal replies, which expressly disclaimed legal responsibility, and which were held to be a negligent misstatement of Easipower's financial resources.
>
> *Decision:* While HP were able to avoid liability by virtue of their disclaimer, the House of Lords went on to consider whether there ever could be a duty of care to avoid causing financial loss by negligent misstatement where there was no contractual or fiduciary relationship. It decided (as *obiter dicta*) that HP were guilty of negligence having breached the duty of care, because a special relationship did exist. Had it not been for the disclaimer, a claim for negligence would have succeeded.

Point to note

> As you already know, *obiter dicta* such as those made in 1963 do not form part of the *ratio decidendi*, and are not binding on future cases. They will, however, be **persuasive**.

Note that at the time liability did not extend to those who the advisor might merely **foresee as a possible user** of the statement.

However in a subsequent case, the courts extended potential liability, and started to take account of third parties not known to the adviser.

The following case echoed the principles laid down in *Anns* and addressed the question of **reasonable foresight** being present to create a duty of care.

> *JEB Fasteners Ltd v Marks, Bloom & Co 1981*
>
> *The facts:* The defendants, a firm of accountants, prepared an audited set of accounts showing overvalued stock and hence inflated profit. The auditors knew there were liquidity problems and that the company was seeking outside finance. The claimants were shown the accounts; they took over the company for a nominal amount, since by that means they could obtain the services of the company's two directors. At no time did MB tell JEB that the stock value was inflated. With the investment's failure, JEB sued MB, with the following claims.
>
> (a) The accounts had been prepared negligently.
> (b) They had relied on those accounts.
> (c) They would not have invested had they been aware of the company's true position.
> (d) MB owed a duty of care to all persons whom they could reasonably foresee would rely on the accounts.
>
> *Decision:* Even though JEB had relied on the accounts (b), they would not have acted differently if the true position had been known (c), since they had really wanted the directors and not the company. Hence the accountants were not the cause of the consequential harm and were not liable. Significantly (although this did not affect the decision as to liability) it was the judge's view that MB did indeed owe a duty of care through foresight (d) and had been negligent in preparing the accounts (a).

Decisions since *JEB Fasteners* have, however, shied away from the foresight test and gone back to looking at whether the adviser has **knowledge of the user** and the **use to which the statement will be put**.

8 The Caparo decision

FAST FORWARD

> The **Caparo case** is fundamental to understanding professional negligence. It was decided that **auditors do not owe a general duty of care to the public at large** or to **shareholders increasing their stakes in the company in question**.

This important and controversial case made considerable changes to the tort of negligence as a whole, and the negligence of **professionals** in particular. It set a precedent which forms the basis for courts when considering the liability of professional advisers.

> *Caparo Industries plc v Dickman and Others 1990*
>
> *The facts:* Caparo, which already held shares in Fidelity plc, bought more shares and later made a takeover bid, after seeing accounts prepared by the defendants that showed a profit of £1.3m. Caparo claimed against the directors and the auditors for the fact that the accounts should have shown a loss of £400,000. The claimants argued that the auditors owed a duty of care to investors and potential investors in respect of the audit. They should have been aware that a press release stating that profits would fall significantly had made Fidelity vulnerable to a takeover bid and that bidders might well rely upon the accounts.
>
> *Decision:* The auditor's duty did not extend to potential investors nor to existing shareholders increasing their stakes. It was a duty owed to the body of shareholders as whole.

In the *Caparo* case the House of Lords decided that there were **two** very different situations facing a person giving professional advice.

(a) Preparing information in the knowledge that a **particular person** was contemplating a transaction and would rely on the information in deciding whether or not to proceed with the transaction (the 'special relationship').

(b) Preparing a statement for **general circulation**, which could forseeably be relied upon by persons unknown to the professional for a variety of different purposes.

It was held therefore that a public company's auditors owe **no general duty of care to the public at large** who rely on an audit report when deciding to invest – and, in purchasing additional shares, an existing shareholder is in no different position to the public at large.

In *MacNaughton (James) Papers Group Ltd v Hicks Anderson & Co 1991*, it was stated that it was necessary to examine each case in the light of the following.

- Foreseeability
- Proximity
- Fairness

This is because there could be **no single overriding principle** that could be applied to all individual cases. Lord Justice Neill set out the matters to be taken into account in considering this.

- The purpose for which the statement was **made**
- The purpose for which the statement was **communicated**
- The **relationship** between the maker of the statement, the recipient and any third party
- The **size** of any class to which the recipient belonged
- The **state of knowledge** of the maker
- Any **reliance** by the recipient

8.1 Non-audit role

The duty of care of accountants is held to be higher when advising on takeovers than when auditing. The directors and financial advisors of the target company in a contested takeover bid owe a duty of care to a **known** takeover bidder in respect of express representations made about financial statements prepared for the purpose of contesting the bid on which they knew the bidder would rely: *Morgan Crucible Co plc v Hill Samuel Bank Ltd and others 1991*.

8.2 The law since *Caparo*

A more recent case highlighted the need for a cautious approach and careful evaluation of the circumstances when giving **financial advice**, possibly with the need to issue a disclaimer.

ADT Ltd v BDO Binder Hamlyn 1995

The facts: Binder Hamlyn was the joint auditor of BSG. In October 1989, BSG's audited accounts for the year to 30 June 1989 were published. Binder Hamlyn signed off the audit as showing a true and fair view of BSG's position. ADT was thinking of buying BSG and, as a potential buyer, sought Binder Hamlyn's confirmation of the audited results. In January 1990, the Binder Hamlyn audit partner attended a meeting with a director of ADT. This meeting was described by the judge as the 'final hurdle' before ADT finalised its bid for BSG. At the meeting, the audit partner specifically confirmed that he 'stood by' the audit of October 1989. ADT proceeded to purchase BSG for £105m. It was subsequently alleged that BSG's true value was only £40m. ADT therefore sued Binder Hamlyn for the difference, £65m plus interest.

Decision: Binder Hamlyn assumed a responsibility for the statement that the audited accounts showed a true and fair view of BSG which ADT relied on to its detriment. Since the underlying audit work had been carried out negligently, Binder Hamlyn was held liable for £65m. The courts expect a higher standard of care from accountants when giving advice on company acquisitions since the losses can be so much greater.

This situation was different from *Caparo* since the court was specifically concerned with the **purpose of the statement made at the meeting**. Did Binder Hamlyn **assume any responsibility** as a result of the partner's comments? The court decided that it did. The court did not need to consider the question of duty to individual shareholders, because *Caparo* had already decided that there was none.

Following the *ADT* case, another case tested the court's interpretation.

> **NRG v Bacon and Woodrow and Ernst & Young 1995**
>
> *The facts:* NRG alleged that the defendants had failed to suggest the possibility that certain companies it was targeting might suffer huge reinsurance losses. They had also failed to assess properly whether these losses could be protected against, because defective actuarial methods had been used. As a result, it overpaid for these companies by £255m.
>
> *Decision:* The judge observed that accountants owe a higher standard of care when advising on company purchases, because the potential losses are so much greater, following *ADT*. However, applying this higher standard of care to the facts, it was decided that NRG had received the advice that any competent professional would have given, because the complex nature of the losses that the companies were exposed to were not fully understood at the time. In addition, the use of defective actuarial methods had not led directly to the losses, because NRG would have bought the companies anyway.

There have been some other **important clarifications** of the law affecting accountants' liability in the area of responsibility towards non-clients. The following two cases both concern auditors' liability to group companies.

> **Barings plc v Coopers & Lybrand 1997**
>
> *The facts:* Barings collapsed in 1995 after loss-making trading by the general manager of its Singapore subsidiary, BFS. BFS was audited by the defendant's Singapore firm, which provided Barings directors with consolidation schedules and a copy of the BFS audit report. The defendant tried to argue that there was no duty of care owed to Barings, only to BFS.
>
> *Decision:* A duty of care was owed to Barings, as the defendants must have known that their audit report and consolidation schedules would be relied upon at group level.

> **BCCI (Overseas) Ltd v Ernst & Whinney 1997**
>
> *The facts:* In this case, the defendants audited the group holding company's accounts, but not those of the claimant subsidiary. The claimant tried to claim that the defendants had a duty of care to them.
>
> *Decision:* No duty of care was owed to the subsidiary because no specific information is normally channelled down by a holding company's auditor to its subsidiaries.

8.3 Extension of liability to third parties

Although the *Caparo* case states that **no general duty** is owed by auditors to third parties, a number of cases have found that an **auditor can owe a duty** in **limited circumstances**.

In *Law Society v KPMG Peat Marwick 2000* it was held that an accountant who reported on a solicitor's client accounts owed a duty to the solicitor's regulator as well as to the solicitor. This is because a solicitor is legally and professionally required to obtain an accountant's report on their client accounts by their regulator (then the Law Society, now the Solicitors Regulation Authority), and the regulator may be liable to pay compensation to clients of a solicitor who has mismanaged their accounts.

In *Royal Bank of Scotland v Bannerman Johnstone Maclay 2005* it was held that a third party can be owed a duty of care where auditors know their identity, the use to which the information would be put and that the third party intends to rely on it.

In this case, the banker and major financier to a company was entitled to the monthly management accounts and audited financial statements as part of its lending agreement. Over a number of years, the bank acquired a majority shareholding in the business but the accounts on which they relied were misstated and the business collapsed with debts of £13 million owed to the bank. The duty of care was owed as a consequence of the auditors being aware that the accounts would be sent to the bank as part of the lending agreement and would therefore be relied upon. The auditors could have disclaimed responsibility to the bank if they wanted to avoid liability.

The Bannerman case was upheld in the decision of *Barclays Bank plc v Grant Thornton UK LLP 2015*. In this case, the auditors disclaimed liability on the face of its audit reports which were relied upon by the lender of a hotel chain that went into administration. The court struck out the case brought by the bankers who claimed that the disclaimer was not valid in law. The court held that it is not unreasonable for auditors to include a disclaimer stating that they do not accept responsibility to anyone other than the addressees of the audit report.

To counter the risk of liability to clients and third parties, UK accountancy firms have been investigating ways of **limiting liability** in the face of increasing litigation. KPMG, for example, incorporated its audit practice in 1995.

In 2000, the **Limited Liability Partnerships Act 2000** (TSO, 2000) was passed, and limited liability partnerships have been permitted under law since 2001.

This **protects the partners** of accountancy firms from the financial consequences of **negligent actions** as their liability to third parties (previously unlimited) can now be limited.

Chapter Roundup

- The law gives various rights to persons. When such a right is infringed the wrongdoer is liable in **tort**.

- **Negligence** is the most important modern tort. To succeed in an action for negligence the claimant must prove that:

    - The defendant had **a duty of care** to avoid causing injury, damage or loss
    - There was **a breach of that duty** by the defendant
    - **In consequence** the claimant suffered **injury, damage or loss**

- The term negligence is used to describe **carelessly** carrying out an **act** and breaking a **legal duty of care** owed to another causing them **loss or damage**.

- In the landmark case of *Donoghue v Stevenson 1932* the House of Lords ruled that a person might **owe a duty of care to another with whom they had no contractual relationship** at all. The doctrine has been refined in subsequent rulings, but the principle is unchanged.

- The second element that must be proven by a claimant in an action for negligence is that there was a **breach of the duty** of care by the defendant.

- Finally the claimant must demonstrate that they suffered injury or loss as a **result** of the breach.

- The amount of damages awarded to the claimant can be reduced if it is shown that they **contributed** to their injury. The defendant can be **exonerated** from paying damages if it can be proved that the claimant **expressly** or **impliedly** consented to the risk. In employment situations, an employer may be held **vicariously liable** for the actions of their employee.

- Professional individuals and organisations have a special relationship with their clients and those who rely on their work. This is because they act in an **expert capacity**.

- According to Lord Denning, to establish a **special relationship** the person who made the statement must have done so in some professional or expert capacity which made it likely that others would rely on what they said. This is the position of an adviser such as an accountant, banker, solicitor or surveyor.

- The **Caparo case** is fundamental to understanding professional negligence. It was decided that **auditors do not owe a general duty of care to the public at large** or to **shareholders increasing their stakes in the company in question**.

BPP
LEARNING MEDIA

Quick Quiz

1   In tort no previous transaction or contractual relationship need exist.

True ☐

False ☐

2   The 'neighbour' principle was established by the landmark case

A   *Caparo v Dickman 1990*
B   *Anns v Merton London Borough Council 1977*
C   *Donoghue v Stevenson 1932*
D   *The Wagon Mound 1961*

3   When the court applies the maxim *res ipsa loquitur*, it is held that the facts speak for themselves and the defendant does not have to prove anything, since the burden of proof is on the claimant.

True ☐

False ☐

4   Under which circumstance will a court reduce the award of damages to a claimant?

A   The claimant intervened in the chain of causality
B   A natural event occurred which caused additional damage
C   The claimant contributed to the loss they suffered
D   The defendant acknowledged they were to blame

5   'A public company's auditors owe no general duty of care to the public at large who rely on the audit report in deciding to invest.'

This is the decision from *Caparo*.

True ☐

False ☐

Answers to Quick Quiz

1   True. No transaction or relationship is needed.

2   C. *Donoghue v Stevenson 1932*

3   False. The burden of proof under *res ipsa loquitur* is reversed, the defendant must prove that they were not negligent.

4   C. This option is contributory negligence.

5   True. Auditors do not owe a general duty of care to the public at large.

Now try the questions below from the Practice Question Bank

Number
15, 16

P
A
R
T

C

Employment law

8

Contract of employment

Topic list	Syllabus reference
1 What is an employee?	C1(a)
2 Why does it matter?	C1(a)
3 Employment contract: basic issues	C1(b)
4 Common law duties	C1(b)
5 Statutory duties	C1(b)
6 Varying the terms of an employment contract	C1(b)
7 Continuous employment	C1(b)

Introduction

We begin our study of employment law by looking at the **distinction** between the **employed** and the **self-employed**. This distinction is very important because it has implications regarding employee **rights** and **liabilities**.

The chapter continues by examining the **contents** of an employment contract. Like any other contract it may include **express** and **implied terms** and you should be able to explain how these terms are included.

Employers and employees owe certain **duties** to one another; breach of these duties may result in legal action against the party who breached their duty. Learn these duties and the supporting case law as they are an important part of your syllabus.

This chapter is based on the Employment Rights Act 1996 (TSO, 1996) *and Small Business, Enterprise and Employment Act 2015* (TSO, 2015) *unless otherwise noted.*

Study guide

		Intellectual level
C	**Employment law**	
1	**Contract of employment**	
(a)	Distinguish between employees and the self-employed	2
(b)	Explain the nature of the contract of employment and common law and statutory duties placed on the employer and employee	2

Exam guide

Questions may be set that require you to identify the differences between the employed and the self-employed and the implications to an individual of being classed as one or the other.

You may also be tested on the various duties that employees and employers have to each other.

1 What is an employee?

FAST FORWARD

It is important to distinguish between a **contract of service** (employment) and a **contract for services** (independent contractor). Each type of contract has different rules for taxation, health and safety provisions, protection of contract and vicarious liability in tort and contract.

A contract of service is **distinguished** from a contract for services usually because the parties **express** the agreement to be one of service. This does not always mean that an employee will not be treated as an independent contractor by the court, however; much depends on the three tests.

- Control test
- Integration test
- Economic reality test

A general rule is that an employee is someone who is employed under a **contract of service**, as distinguished from an independent contractor, who is someone who works under a **contract for services**.

However, it is important to note that some **statutory provisions** apply to '**workers**' and this term is wider than '**employees**' and includes those personally performing work or services unless they are truly self-employed. Examples of workers include agency workers, short-term casual workers and some freelancers. Workers benefit from some **basic employment rights** and **protections** although these rights are generally not as wide-ranging as someone who is employed.

Key terms

> An **employee** is an individual who has entered into, or works under, a contract of employment.
>
> A **contract of employment** is a contract of service or apprenticeship, whether express or implied, and (if it is express) whether it is oral or in writing.
>
> A **worker** is any individual who works for an employer, whether under a contract of employment, or any other contract where an individual undertakes to do or perform personally any work or service.

In practice this distinction depends on **many factors** and it can be very important to know whether an individual is an employee or an independent contractor. The courts will apply a series of **tests**.

Primarily, the court will look at the **reality of the situation**. This may be in spite of the form of the arrangement.

Exam focus point

> The various tests applied by the courts in determining whether someone is employed or self-employed could easily be tested in any type of question.

> *Ferguson v John Dawson & Partners 1976*
>
> *The facts*: A builder's labourer was paid his wages, without deduction of income tax or National Insurance contributions, and worked as a self-employed contractor providing services. His 'employer' could dismiss him, decide on which site he would work and direct him as to the work he should do. It also provided the tools which he used. He was injured in an accident and sued his employers on the basis that they owed him legal duties as his employer.
>
> *Decision*: On the facts taken as a whole, he was an employee working under a contract of employment.

Where there is some **doubt** as to the nature of the relationship the courts will then look at any **agreement between the parties**.

> *Massey v Crown Life Assurance 1978*
>
> *The facts*: The claimant was originally employed by an insurance company as a departmental manager; he also earned commission on business which he introduced. At his own request he changed to a self-employed basis. Tax and other payments were no longer deducted by the employers but he continued to perform the same duties. The employers terminated these arrangements and the claimant claimed compensation for unfair dismissal.
>
> *Decision*: As he had opted to become self-employed and his status in the organisation was consistent with that situation, his claim to be a dismissed employee failed.

It can still be unclear whether a person is an employee or an independent contractor. Historically, the tests of **control, integration** into the employer's organisation, and **economic reality** (or the multiple test) have been applied in such cases.

The fundamental prerequisite of a contract of employment is that there must be **mutual obligations** on the employer to provide, and the employee to perform, work.

1.1 The control test

The court will consider whether the employer has **control** over the way in which the employee performs their duties.

> *Mersey Docks & Harbour Board v Coggins & Griffiths (Liverpool) 1947*
>
> *The facts:* Stevedores (dockworkers) hired a crane with its driver from the harbour board under a contract which provided that the driver (appointed and paid by the harbour board) should be the employee of the stevedores. Owing to the driver's negligence a checker was injured. The case was concerned with whether the stevedores or the harbour board were vicariously liable as employers.
>
> *Decision:* It was decided that the issue must be settled on the facts and not on the terms of the contract. The stevedores could only be treated as employers of the driver if they could control in detail how he did his work. But although they could instruct him what to do, they could not control him in how he operated the crane. The harbour board (as 'general employer') was therefore still the driver's employer.

Another example of this test is in *Walker v Crystal Palace FC 1910* where it was held that a **professional footballer** was employed because he was subject to the control of his club in the form of training, discipline and method of pay.

There must be a **contractual right of control** over the employee; it is not simply about who controls their day-to-day work (*Troutbeck SA v White and Todd 2013*).

1.2 The integration test

The courts consider whether the employee is so skilled that they cannot be controlled in the performance of their duties. Lack of control indicates that an employee is **not integrated** into the employer's organisation, and therefore not employed.

BPP
LEARNING MEDIA

> **Cassidy v Ministry of Health 1951**
>
> *The facts:* The full-time assistant medical officer at a hospital carried out a surgical operation in a negligent fashion. The patient sued the Ministry of Health as employer. The Ministry resisted the claim arguing that it had no control over the doctor in his medical work.
>
> *Decision:* In such circumstances the proper test was whether the employer appointed the employee, selected him for his task and so integrated him into the organisation. If the patient had chosen the doctor the Ministry would not have been liable as employer. But here the Ministry (the hospital management) made the choice and so it was liable.

The control and integration tests are important, but **no longer decisive** in determining whether a person is an employee.

1.3 The multiple (economic reality) test

Courts also consider whether the employee was **working on their own account** and require numerous factors to be taken into account.

> **Ready Mixed Concrete (South East) v Ministry of Pensions & National Insurance 1968**
>
> *The facts:* The driver of a special vehicle worked for one company only in the delivery of liquid concrete to building sites. He provided his own vehicle (obtained on hire purchase from the company) and was responsible for its maintenance and repair. He was free to provide a substitute driver. The vehicle was painted in the company's colours and the driver wore its uniform. He was paid gross amounts (no tax, etc deducted) on the basis of mileage and quantity delivered as a self-employed contractor. The Ministry of Pensions claimed that he was, in fact, an employee for whom the company should make the employer's insurance contributions.
>
> *Decision:* In such cases the most important test is whether the worker is working on his own account. On these facts the driver was a self-employed transport contractor and not an employee.

In the above case, the judge held that a contract of service existed where:

- There is **agreement** from the worker that they will provide work for their master in exchange for remuneration.

- The worker agrees either expressly or impliedly that their master can exercise **control** over their performance.

- There are other **factors** included in the contract that make it **consistent** with a contract of service.

The fact that the drivers could appoint a **replacement** for themselves was a major factor in the decision that found them as contractors rather than employees.

1.4 Agency workers

The status of agency workers has been the subject of numerous cases in recent years, as the numbers employed under such contracts have increased. Two key cases have considered **length of service** of agency workers and **control** that the client of the agency has over the worker.

(a) **Length of service**

In *Franks v Reuters Ltd 2003*, the agency worker had been providing services to the client for some **six years** engaged in a variety of jobs, and was effectively so thoroughly integrated with the employer's organisation as to be **indistinguishable** from the employer's staff.

The case was remitted to the tribunal for further consideration, but the length of an assignment of an agency worker clearly has implications for the development of other indications of an employment relationship, with those utilising the services of the worker forgetting the true nature of the relationship and behaving towards the worker as if they were an employee. It may be that at this point the relevant approach also starts to involve the 'integration' test'.

(b) **Control over the worker**

Where the client of the agency has **sufficient control** over the employee provided by the agency, it could be held that they are in fact the true employer.

Motorola v Davidson and Melville Craig 2001

The facts: Davidson was contracted with the Melville Craig agency and was assigned to work for Motorola. Both the agency and Motorola had agreed that Davidson could be sent back to the agency if his work was unacceptable. Following a disciplinary hearing Davidson was found unacceptable and returned to the agency. Davidson took Motorola to an employment tribunal for unfair dismissal.

Decision: Motorola had sufficient control over Davidson to make them the employer. It was held that the court should look beyond the pure legal situation and look at the practical control aspects in such cases as well.

1.5 Relevant factors

Significant factors that you should consider when deciding whether or not a person is employed or self-employed are as follows.

- Does the employee use their **own tools and equipment** or does the employer provide them?

- Does the alleged employer have the power to **select or appoint** its employees, and may it dismiss them?

- **Payment of salary** is a fair indication of there being a contract of employment.

- **Working for a number of different people** is not necessarily a sign of self-employment. A number of assignments may be construed as 'a series of employments.'

In difficult cases, courts will consider whether the employee can **delegate** all their obligations, whether there is restriction as to place of work, whether there is a **mutual obligation** and whether holidays and hours of work are agreed.

O'Kelly v Trusthouse Forte plc 1983

The facts: The employee was a 'regular casual' working when required as a waiter. There was an understanding that he would accept work when offered and that the employer would give him preference over other casual employees. The employment tribunal held that there was no contract of employment because the employer had no obligation to provide work and the employee had no obligation to accept work when offered.

Decision: The Court of Appeal agreed with this finding. Whether there is a contract of employment is a question of law but it depends entirely on the facts of each case; here there was no 'mutuality of obligations' and hence no contract.

The decision whether to classify an individual as an employee or not is also influenced by **policy considerations**. For example, an employment tribunal might regard a person as an employee for the purpose of unfair dismissal despite the fact that the tax authorities treated them as self-employed.

Airfix Footwear Ltd v Cope 1978

The facts: The case concerned a classic outworking arrangement under which the applicant (having been given training and thereafter supplied with the necessary tools and materials) generally worked five days a week making heels for shoes manufactured by the respondent company. She was paid on a piecework basis without deduction of income tax or NIC.

Decision: Working for some seven years, generally for five days a week, resulted in the arrangement being properly classified as employment under a contract of employment.

The case below marks an important shift away from courts accepting as fact the **contents of an employment contract** towards looking at the **actual working arrangement** when deciding on an employee's employment status. It also means that the **relative bargaining power** between the parties should be considered.

Autoclenz v Belcher 2011

The facts: A group of individuals worked as car valeters. Their contracts stated that they were self-employed contractors, that there was no obligation to provide them with work, that they had to provide their own materials and that they could substitute others to work in their place.

Decision: The reality of the situation did not agree with the contracts. The workers would arrive each day and be provided with work, there was never any substitution of labour, the workers had to provide advance notice if they would not be available to work and they were provided with cleaning materials for a small charge. In the court's opinion, the contract did not genuinely reflect the reality of the situation and should be set aside. There was a difference in the relative bargaining power between the parties which indicated an employer/employee relationship.

The question of whether someone who is described as **'self-employed'** is actually self-employed was asked in *Tiffin v Lester Aldridge LLP 2012*. This case considered whether partners in a partnership can be employees. It was held that **partners with equity stakes** in a partnership **cannot be employees**. However, each case should be determined on its facts and it is likely that a salaried partner (without an equity stake) will be deemed an employee for employment law purposes.

2 Why does it matter?

> The distinction between **employed** and **self-employed** is important as to whether certain **rights** are available to an individual and how they are treated for **tax purposes**.

The first thing that it is important to note is that much of the legislation which gives protection to employees **extends further than employees**. Much of it is drafted to cover 'workers', a term which has a wide definition to cover most people providing services to others outside of the course of (their own) business. This has reduced the importance of the **distinction** between employee and independent contractor in this area. However, there are several other **practical reasons** why the distinction between a contract of service and a contract for services is important.

Significance of the distinction		
	Employed	**Self-employed**
Social security	Employers must pay secondary Class 1 National Insurance contributions on behalf of employees Employees make primary Class 1 National Insurance contributions There are also differences in statutory sick pay and levies for industrial training purposes	Independent contractors pay Class 2 and 4 contributions
Taxation	Deductions must be made for income tax by an employer under PAYE from salary paid to employee	The self-employed are taxed under self-assessment for income tax and are directly responsible to HM Revenue & Customs for tax due
Employment protection	There is legislation which confers protection and benefits upon employees under a contract of service, including • Minimum periods of notice • Remedies for unfair dismissal	Employment protection is not available for contractors

Significance of the distinction		
	Employed	**Self-employed**
Tortious acts	Employers are generally vicariously liable for tortious acts of employees, committed in the course of employment	Liability of the person hiring an independent contractor for the contractor's acts is severely limited unless there is strict liability
Implied terms	There are rights and duties implied by statute for employers and employees This will affect things such as copyrights and patents	These implied rights and duties do not apply to such an extent to a contract for services.
VAT	Employees do not have to register for, or charge, VAT	An independent contractor may have to register for, and charge, VAT
Bankruptcy	In an employer's liquidation, an employee has preferential rights as a creditor for payment of outstanding salary and redundancy payments, up to a statutory limit	Contractors are treated as non-preferential creditors if their employer is liquidated
Health and safety	There is significant common law and legislation governing employers' duties to employees with regard to health and safety	The common law provisions and much of the legislation relating to employees also relates to independent contractors

3 Employment contract: basic issues

FAST FORWARD

There are no particular legal rules relating to the commencement of employment – it is really **just like any other contract** in requiring offer and acceptance, consideration and intention to create legal relations.

An employment contract is a contract of service which may be **express** or **implied**. If express, it can be either **oral** or **written**. This means that employment contracts can be simple, straightforward agreements. The contract must, of course, comply with the usual rules relating to the formation of a valid contract. At the one extreme, an employment contract may be a **document** drawn up by solicitors and signed by both parties; at the other extreme it may consist of a **handshake** and a 'See you on Monday'. In such cases the court has to clarify the agreement by determining what the parties must be taken to have agreed.

The case of *Preston (formerly Moore) v President of the Methodist Conference 2013* demonstrates the importance of **intention to create legal relations** in an employment contract. In this case, a Methodist **church minister was held not to be an employee** because the arrangements, such as the lifelong commitment to the church by the minister, and the payment of maintenance and support, rather than a salary, was inconsistent with an intention to be legally bound.

Senior personnel may sign a contract specially drafted to include terms on **confidentiality** and **restraint of trade**. Other employees may sign a standard form contract, exchange letters with the new employer or simply agree terms orally at interview.

Each of these situations will form a valid contract of employment, subject to the requirements regarding written particulars, as long as there is **agreement** on **essential terms** such as hours and wages. Nor should it be forgotten that even prior to employment commencing the potential employer has legal obligations: for example, not to discriminate in recruitment.

3.1 Implied terms

Implied terms usually arise out of **custom** and **practice** within a profession or industry. In *Henry v London General Transport Services Ltd 2001* it was held that four requirements should be met before such terms can be read into a contract.

- The terms must be **reasonable**, **certain** and **notorious**
- They must represent the **wishes** of both parties
- **Proof** of the custom or practice must be provided by the party seeking to rely on the term
- A **distinction** must be made between implying terms that make **minor,** and terms that make **fundamental** changes to the contract

3.2 Requirement for written particulars

Within two months of the beginning of the employment, the employer must give to an employee a written **statement of prescribed particulars** of their employment.

The statement should identify the following.

- The names of **employer** and **employee**
- The **date** on which employment began
- Whether any service with a previous employer forms part of the employee's **continuous period** of employment
- **Pay** – scale or rate and intervals at which paid
- **Hours** of work (including any specified 'normal working hours')
- Any **holiday** and **holiday pay** entitlement (for a person working five days per week, the holiday entitlement is 5.6 weeks or 28 days, which may include bank and public holidays depending on the contract of employment)
- **Sick leave** and **sick pay** entitlement
- **Pensions** and pension **schemes**
- Length of **notice** of termination to be given on either side
- The **title** of the job which the employee is employed to do (or a brief job description)

A **'principal statement'**, which must include the **first six items** above and the **title** of the job, must be provided, but other particulars may be given by way of separate documents.

If the employee has a **written contract of employment** covering these points and has been given a copy it is not necessary to provide them with separate written particulars.

According to the **Employment Act 2002** (TSO, 2002), the written particulars must also contain details of **disciplinary procedures** and **grievance procedures** or reference to where they can be found.

If the employer fails to comply with these requirements the employee may apply to an **employment tribunal** for a declaration of what the terms should be. The Employment Act 2002 allows a tribunal to award compensation to an employee claiming unfair dismissal if the particulars are incomplete.

4 Common law duties

FAST FORWARD

The **employer** has an implied **duty at common law** to take **reasonable care** of their employees; they must select proper staff, materials and provide a safe system of working.

The **employee** has a duty of **faithful service** and to exercise **care and skill** in performance of their duties.

4.1 Employee's duties

The employee has a **fundamental duty of faithful service** to their employer. All other duties are features of this general duty.

Hivac Ltd v Park Royal Scientific Instruments Ltd 1946

The facts: In their spare time certain of the claimant's employees worked for the defendant company, which directly competed with the claimant.

Decision: Even though the employees had not passed on any confidential information, they were still in breach of their duty of fidelity to the claimants.

This duty also extends after the employment where **trade secrets** are concerned. Employees will be in breach of their duty if they disclose such secrets to their new employer.

The **facts of the case** and the **nature of employment** should be considered when making a decision, for example customer lists of a chicken-selling business was not considered a trade secret when a sales manager set up their own competing organisation *(Faccenda Chicken Ltd v Fowler 1986)*.

The **implied** duties of the employee include the following.

(a) **Reasonable competence** to do their job.

(b) **Obedience** to the employer's instructions unless they require them to do an unlawful act or to expose themselves to personal danger (not inherent in their work) or are instructions outside the employee's contract.

Pepper v Webb 1969

The facts: The defendant, a gardener, refused to obey instructions from his employer regarding planting in the garden. He also swore at him.

Decision: The gardener was in breach of his implied duty to obey as the instructions were lawful and reasonable.

(c) **Duty to account for all money and property** received during the course of their employment except what is customary to be received or is trivial.

Boston Deep Sea Fishing and Ice Co v Ansell 1888

The facts: The defendant, who was managing director of the claimant company, accepted personal commissions from suppliers on orders which he placed with them for goods supplied to the company. He was dismissed and the company sued to recover from him the commissions.

Decision: The company was justified in dismissing the claimant and he must account to it for the commissions.

(d) **Reasonable care and skill** in the performance of their work. What is reasonable depends on the degree of skill and experience which the employee professes to have.

(e) **Personal service** – the contract of employment is a personal one and so the employee may not delegate their duties without the employer's express or implied consent.

4.2 Employer's duties

There is an overriding **duty of mutual trust and confidence** between the employer and the employee. Examples of where this duty has been breached include:

- A director calling their secretary 'an intolerable bitch on a Monday morning' – *Isle of Wight Tourist Board v Coombes 1976*

- Failure to investigate a sexual harassment claim – *Bracebridge Engineering v Darby 1990*

The employer usually also has the following duties at common law:

(a) To **pay remuneration** to employees. If there is no rate fixed by the parties, this duty is to pay **reasonable** remuneration.

(b) To **indemnify the employee** against expenses and losses incurred in the course of employment.

(c) To take care of the employees' **health and safety** at work. This is also provided for in statute.

(d) To **provide work**, where:

   –   The employee is an apprentice.

   –   The employee is paid with reference to work done.

   –   The opportunity to work is the essence of the contract (for example, for actors).

   –   There is work available to be done (subject to contractual terms to the contrary) **and** the relevant employee is a skilled worker who needs work to preserve their skills.

There is no breach of duty if there is **no work** available and the employer continues to pay its employees. However, if an employee was appointed to a **particular role** and no work was provided there may be a breach of duty to provide work if it denies the employee the opportunity to maintain their skills

There is no duty to provide a **reference** when employees leave service. Employers may be liable under negligence for not taking reasonable care over accuracy and fairness if they do provide one.

The **importance** of these common law implied duties on both parties is that:

• **Breach of a legal duty**, if it is important enough, may entitle the injured party to treat the contract as **discharged** and to claim damages for breach of contract at common law; and

• In an employee's claim for compensation for unfair dismissal, the employee may argue that it was a case of **constructive dismissal** by the employer, or the employer may seek to justify their express dismissal of the employee by reference to their conduct.

5 Statutory duties

FAST FORWARD

Statute implies terms into employment contracts, which may not usually be overridden, regarding pay and equality, maternity leave and work/life balance generally, time off, health and safety and working time.

Various matters are implied into contracts of employment by statute. Some of them build upon the **basic matters** covered by the common law. Most of the employment statutes in this area implement European Directives on employment law issues. An **employer** has **statutory duties** in the following areas:

• Pay and equality
• Time off work
• Maternity rights and the 'work/life balance'
• Health and safety
• Working time

5.1 Pay and equality

There are two key pieces of legislation in relation to pay. These are the **National Minimum Wage Act 1998** and the **Equality Act 2010**.

5.1.1 National Minimum Wage Act 1998

A **national minimum hourly wage** was introduced in the UK in 1999 by the **National Minimum Wage Act 1998** (TSO, 1998) and the rate is reviewed annually. It is a criminal offence, and a company will be penalised financially, if it does not pay all or some of its employees the statutory minimum. The penalty is calculated on a per worker basis.

5.1.2 Equality Act 2010

The **Equality Act 2010** (TSO, 2010) seeks to ensure **equal treatment** in **employment** and **access to employment** for employees, applicants for employment and contract workers, and therefore to **outlaw direct discrimination** (including associative and perceived discrimination), **harassment** (including harassment by a third party), **victimisation** and **disability-related discrimination at work**.

Under this Act, contractual **employment terms should be at least as favourable as those given to an employee of the opposite sex**. The Act covers terms such as pay, sick pay, holiday pay and working hours and it applies to all forms of full-time and part-time work.

The Act is applied on the basis of **'protected characteristics'**, namely:

- Age
- Disability
- Sex (including sexual orientation or gender re-assignment)
- Race (that is colour, nationality and ethnic or national origins)
- Religion or belief
- Marriage or civil partnership
- Pregnancy or maternity

In the future, **discrimination judgements** shall be viewed in light of a single **'objective justification' test**. This means employers need to prove their actions were a **'proportionate means of meeting a legitimate aim'**. What this means in practice will be decided by the courts and employment tribunals, though it is expected that where previous legislation allowed or prevented certain types of discrimination, this will continue under the new Act.

The **'objective justification' test** is based on **the Employment Statutory Code of Practice** which identifies that the meaning of the terms **'proportionate'** and **'legitimate aims' derive from EU law**.

Proportionate means:

- The discriminatory effect should be significantly outweighed by the benefits of achieving the aim.

- There is no reasonable alternative. If the aim can be achieved with less discrimination, that option should be followed.

The **Employment Statutory Code of Practice** states that EU law views treatment as proportionate if it is an 'appropriate and necessary' means of achieving a legitimate aim. But 'necessary' does not mean that the provision, criterion or practice is the only possible way of achieving the legitimate aim; it is sufficient that the same aim could not be achieved by less discriminatory means.

Legitimate aims include:

- Business needs and efficiency
- Health and safety reasons
- Particular training requirements of the job

The **Employment Statutory Code of Practice** states that the aim of the provision, criterion or practice should be legal, should not be discriminatory in itself, and must represent a real, objective consideration. The health, welfare and safety of individuals may qualify as legitimate aims provided that risks are clearly specified and supported by evidence. Although reasonable business needs and economic efficiency may be legitimate aims, an employer solely aiming to reduce costs cannot expect to satisfy the test. For example, the employer cannot simply argue that to discriminate is cheaper than avoiding discrimination.

5.1.3 Pay statements

Under the Employment Rights Act 1996 (TSO, 1996), employers are obliged to provide an itemised pay statement.

5.2 Time off work

In addition to the rights relating to maternity and parental leave, statute lists several occasions when an employee has a right to time off work.

(a) **Trade union officials** are entitled to time off on full pay at the employer's expense to enable them to carry out **trade union duties**.

(b) An employee who has been given notice of dismissal for **redundancy** may have time off to look for work or to arrange training for other work.

(c) A member of a recognised independent **trade union** may have time off work (without statutory right to pay) for **trade union activities**, for example, attending a branch meeting.

(d) Employers also have a duty to allow an employee to have reasonable time off to carry out certain **public duties**, for example performing their duties as a magistrate. There is **no statutory provision** entitling an employee to time off for jury service, but prevention of a person from attending as a juror is contempt of court.

5.3 Maternity rights and the 'work/life balance'

A **woman** who is pregnant is given **substantial rights** under statute, including:

- The right to **time off work** for ante-natal care
- The right to **ordinary maternity leave**
- The right to **additional maternity leave**
- The right to **maternity pay**
- The right to **return to work** after maternity leave
- If dismissed, a claim for **unfair dismissal**

Much recent employment legislation has been concerned with the introduction of **family-friendly** employment policies and the 'work/life balance'. The law has developed as a result in the areas of maternity leave and pay, paternity leave, rights of adoptive parents and a right to request flexible working.

5.3.1 Ante-natal care

An employee has a right not to be **unreasonably refused time** off for ante-natal care during working hours.

5.3.2 Maternity leave and pay

Every woman who is an employee is entitled to **statutory maternity leave** of up to **52 weeks** if she gives 15 weeks' notice of her due date to her employer. **Statutory maternity pay** is paid for **39 weeks** during statutory maternity leave but is only paid if the woman has at least 26 weeks' service at the time of giving her notice and earns more than a statutory minimum. The amount of maternity pay received is based on the woman's salary and is subject to a **statutory maximum**. A woman must take a minimum of two weeks' leave after the birth of her baby (four weeks for factory workers) but has the option to share the balance of her maternity leave and pay allowance with her partner if she wishes. This is known as **shared parental leave** and **statutory shared parental pay**.

5.3.3 Paternity leave and pay

To qualify for paternity leave a man must qualify as an employee and generally have been with the employer for at least 26 weeks before the 15th week before the baby is due. On giving the required notice, eligible employees are entitled to take either **one week** or **two consecutive weeks** paid paternity leave. The leave must be completed within 56 days of the actual birth of the child and, like maternity pay, paternity pay is based on salary and subject to a statutory maximum.

5.3.4 Adoption leave and pay

Parents who adopted their child have a right to **statutory adoption leave** (SAL) and **statutory adoption pay** (SAP). The rules for qualifying for this, and the amounts of leave and pay, are the same as for statutory maternity leave and pay.

5.3.5 Flexible working

Employees have the **right** to apply for a change in terms and conditions of employment in respect of hours, time and place of work and not to be unreasonably refused.

The employer may **reasonably refuse** a request on the grounds of:

- The burden of additional cost
- A detrimental effect on ability to meet customer demand
- An inability to re-organise the work amongst existing staff or to recruit additional staff
- A detrimental impact on quality or performance
- Insufficiency of work during the periods the employee proposes to work, or
- Planned structural changes

5.3.6 Parental leave

Any employee with a year's continuous service who has parental responsibility is entitled to **unpaid parental leave** of 18 weeks to care for each child up to the child's eighteenth birthday. This is different to, and should not be confused with, shared parental leave that we saw earlier.

5.4 Health and safety

The key legislation under which an employer has a duty to their employees with regard to **health and safety** is the Health and Safety at Work Act 1974 (HMSO, 1974), which has been augmented by subsequent regulations, notably the Management of Health and Safety at Work Regulations 1999 (TSO, 1999).

This **duty** includes the following issues:

- Provide and maintain plant and systems of work which are safe and without risk
- Make arrangements to ensure safe use, handling, storage and transport of articles/substances
- Provide adequate information, instruction, training and supervision
- Maintain safe places of work and ensure that there is adequate access in and out
- Provide a safe and healthy working environment

Under the **Enterprise and Regulatory Reform Act 2013** (TSO, 2013), employers are only liable to pay compensation to employees injured at work if they are found to have acted negligently. Employees are not entitled to compensation if their employer has taken all reasonable steps to prevent injury.

5.4.1 Employment rights

The contract of employment contains an **implied right not to be subjected to detriment** by the employer on grounds of health and safety. Specifically, the employee has a right not to be subjected to detriment on the ground that they intended to, or did:

- Carry out activities designated to them in connection with preventing/reducing health and safety risks at work

- Perform duties as a representative of workers on issues of health and safety

- Take part in consultation with the employer under health and safety regulations

- Leave their place of work or refused to work in circumstances which they reasonably believed to be serious or imminent and they could not reasonably be expected to avert

- Take appropriate steps to protect themselves or others from circumstances of danger which they believed to be serious and imminent

5.5 Working time

The Working Time Regulations 1998 (TSO, 1998) provide broadly that a worker's **average working time in a 17-week period** (including overtime) shall **not exceed 48 hours for each 7-day period**, unless the worker has agreed in writing that this limit shall not apply.

6 Varying the terms of an employment contract

A contract of employment can only be **varied** if the contract **expressly** gives that right, or if all parties consent to the variation.

It should be clear, from your earlier studies of general contract law, that a change in contract terms **can only be made with the consent of both parties** to the contract.

6.1 Varying terms without changing the contract

There may be circumstances in which an employer can vary the terms of an employment contract without actually needing to vary the contract itself. For example, there may be an **express term** in the contract which itself gives rights of variation, for example to allow a change in area of work.

Alternatively, an **implied term** may act to vary the contract.

(a)   A sales representative may be required to take responsibility for such area as their employer considers necessary in order to meet changing market conditions.

(b)   Terms may also be implied by custom; for example, where a steel erector is required at the request of their employer to change sites: *Stevenson v Teeside Bridge & Engineering Co Ltd 1971*.

6.2 Changing the existing contract

The existing contract can be changed by **consent**. Consent might be demonstrated by **oral agreement** to new terms, by the **signing** of a new statement of terms and conditions or by the employee showing acceptance by **working** under the new terms. If an employee's contract is varied without consent, the employee may have a claim for **constructive dismissal**.

6.3 Signing a new contract

The third option open to the employer is to give contractual notice to the employee and then offer a new contract on the new terms. This opens the employer to a **potential claim** for unfair dismissal. It is generally best for the employer to obtain consent to vary the terms of an existing contract.

7 Continuous employment

Many rights given to employees under the **Employment Rights Act 1996** are only available if an employee has a specified period of **continuous employment**.

You may have noticed a couple of references to '**continuous employment**' in the previous sections. Most of the employment protection which is available is only given to employees who have one year's continuous service.

Exam focus point

> You need to learn that one year's continuous service is required to qualify for employment protection and then learn the **exceptions** to this rule which are pointed out for you where they are discussed.

There are provisions in statute for how the year's continuous service should be calculated, and what counts as service and what does not. **The basic rule is that a year is 12 calendar months.**

Certain weeks might not be taken into account in calculating continuous service, but they do not break the period of continuous service. This might be the case if the employee takes part in a strike, or is absent due to service in the armed forces.

Illustration

If Ben was employed for eight months and then was given leave to do some service in the army for five months, on his return to the employer he would have been employed for 13 calendar months.

However, until he completes another four months of service he will not be eligible for the employment protection given to those employees with a year's continuous service. Once he has completed those four months, the eight months prior, and the four months subsequent, to the armed service will count as continuous service, despite being split by a period away from the employer.

7.1 Transfer of undertakings

Another factor that impacts on continuous service is when a business or undertaking is transferred by one person to another. Where the business is transferred, so that an employee works for a new employer, this change represents **no break in the continuous service of the employee**.

Chapter Roundup

- It is important to distinguish between a **contract of service** (employment) and a **contract for services** (independent contractor). Each type of contract has different rules for taxation, health and safety provisions, protection of contract and vicarious liability in tort and contract.

- A contract of service is **distinguished** from a contract for services usually because the parties **express** the agreement to be one of service. This does not always mean that an employee will not be treated as an independent contractor by the court, however; much depends on the three tests.

  - Control test
  - Integration test
  - Economic reality test

- The distinction between **employed** and **self-employed** is important as to whether certain **rights** are available to an individual and how they are treated for **tax purposes**.

- There are no particular legal rules relating to the commencement of employment – it is really **just like any other contract** in requiring offer and acceptance, consideration and intention to create legal relations.

- The **employer** has an implied **duty at common law** to take **reasonable care** of their employees; they must select proper staff, materials and provide a safe system of working.

- The **employee** has a duty of **faithful service** and to exercise **care and skill** in performance of their duties.

- **Statute** implies terms into employment contracts, which may not usually be overridden, regarding pay and equality, maternity leave and work/life balance generally, time off, health and safety and working time.

- A contract of employment can only be **varied** if the contract **expressly** gives that right, or if all parties consent to the variation.

- Many rights given to employees under the **Employment Rights Act 1996** are only available if an employee has a specified period of **continuous employment**.

Quick Quiz

1   **Fill in the blanks** in the statements below.

What tests are applied by the courts to answer these questions?
Has the employer control over the way in which the employee performs their duties? (1) ....
Is the skilled employee part of the employer's organisation? (2) ....
Is the employee working on their own account? (3)....................

2   Working for a number of different people is an automatic sign of self employment?

True ☐
False ☐

3   A 'principal statement' must include the following (tick all that apply)

(a)   Names of parties ☐
(b)   Job title ☐
(c)   Date employment began ☐
(d)   Notice details ☐
(e)   Details of continuous employment ☐
(f)   Pay details ☐
(g)   Pensions and pension scheme details ☐
(h)   Holiday entitlement ☐

4   What is an employee's fundamental duty?

5   How can an employee show acceptance when the terms of their employment contract have changed?

(i)   Signing a wholly new contract
(ii)   Working under the new terms
(iii)   Agreeing verbally

A   (iii) only
B   (i) and (ii) only
C   (ii) and (iii) only
D   (i), (ii) and (iii)

1   (1)   control test
    (2)   integration test
    (3)   multiple (economic reality) test

2   False. Other facts will be considered.

3   (a) (c) (e) (f) (h). The other options must be included in the written statement of prescribed particulars but are not included in a 'principal statement'.

4   Faithful service to their employer

5   D. All the options are acceptable methods of showing agreement to the new terms.

Now try the questions below from the Practice Question Bank

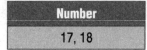

Number
17, 18

BPP LEARNING MEDIA

9

Dismissal and redundancy

Topic list	Syllabus reference
1 Termination by notice	C2(a)
2 Termination of employment by breach of contract	C2(b)
3 Wrongful dismissal	C2(c)
4 Remedies for wrongful dismissal	C2(c)
5 Unfair dismissal	C2(d)
6 Unfair dismissal – justification of dismissal	C2(d)
7 Remedies for unfair dismissal	C2(e)
8 Redundancy	C2(f)

Introduction

The Employment Rights Act 1996 (TSO, 1996) and the Small Business, Enterprise and Employment Act 2015 (TSO, 2015) apply to this chapter unless otherwise noted.

Ending an employment contract can be a traumatic time for all involved and it can result in legal action. Both employees and employers must know their rights and obligations to minimise the risk of such action.

Study guide

		Intellectual level
C	**Employment law**	
2	**Dismissal and redundancy**	
(a)	Explain termination of employment by notice	2
(b)	Distinguish between summary and constructive dismissal	2
(c)	Explain wrongful dismissal	2
(d)	Explain unfair dismissal, including the procedure, and fair and unfair reasons for dismissal	2
(e)	Discuss the remedies available to those who have been subject to unfair dismissal	2
(f)	Explain what is meant by redundancy and the operation of the rules relating to it.	2

Exam guide

Multiple choice questions are likely to focus on distinguishing wrongful, unfair and constructive dismissal.

1 Termination by notice

FAST FORWARD

When an employment contract is terminated by notice there is **no** breach of contract unless the **contents** of the notice (such as notice period) are themselves in breach.

A contract of employment may be terminated by **notice**. The following rules apply.

(a) The period of notice given must **not be less than the statutory minimum**, whatever the contract may specify.

(b) It **may be given without specific reason** for so doing, unless the contract requires otherwise.

(c) If the contract states that notice may **only be given in specific circumstances** then generally it may **not** be given for any other reason.

Although there is no breach of contract, **termination by notice** or **non-renewal** qualifies as 'dismissal' under the statutory code. This means that the employee may be entitled to compensation for unfair dismissal.

Statute imposes a **minimum period of notice** of termination to be given on either side.

1.1 Minimum period of notice

FAST FORWARD

Where employment is **terminated by notice** the period given must **not be less** than the **statutory minimum**.

If an **employer terminates the contract** of employment by giving notice, the **minimum period of notice** to be given is determined by the employee's length of continuous service for the employer as follows.

(a) An employee who has been continuously employed for **one month or more** but less than two years is entitled to not less than **one week's** notice.

(b) An employee who has been continuously employed for **two years or more** but less than twelve years is entitled to **one week's notice for each year of continuous employment.**

(c)   Any employee who has been employed for **12 years** or more is entitled to not less than **12 weeks'** notice.

If the **employee** gives notice, the minimum period required is **one week** if they have been employed for at least one month.

The notice must specify the **date of its expiry**. Either party may waive their entitlement to notice or accept a sum in lieu of notice.

The statutory rules on length of notice merely prescribe a **minimum**. If the contract provides for a longer period, notice must be given in accordance with the contract.

During the period of notice an employee is entitled to pay at a rate not less than the **average** of their **earnings** over the **previous 12 weeks**.

If the employee is **dismissed** in any way they may request their employer gives them a **written statement of the reasons** for their dismissal and **the employer must provide it** within 14 days. The statement must contain at the least a simple summary of the reasons for dismissal and can be used as **admissible evidence** before an employment tribunal.

Dismissal is the word used to describe **termination of an employment contract by the employer**. Here are a few definitions relating to dismissal.

Key terms

> **Summary dismissal** is where the employer dismisses the employee without notice. They may do this if the employee has committed a serious breach of contract.
>
> **Constructive dismissal** is where the employer commits a breach of contract, thereby causing the employee to resign. By implication, this is also dismissal without notice.
>
> **Wrongful dismissal** is a common law concept arising in specific circumstances. It gives the employee an action for breach of contract.
>
> **Unfair dismissal** is a statutory concept introduced by employment protection legislation. As a general rule, employees have the right not to be unfairly dismissed.
>
> Correspondingly, **fair dismissal** is a statutory concept where a person has been dismissed as a result of a fair reason under legislation.

Exam focus point

> Note that the distinction between wrongful and unfair dismissal depends not so much upon the nature of the dismissal, as on the **remedies available**.

2 Termination of employment by breach of contract

FAST FORWARD

> Breach of the employment contract occurs where there is **summary dismissal**, **constructive dismissal**, **inability** on the employer's side to **continue employment**, or **repudiation** of the contract by the employee.

An employment contract is **terminated by breach in the following circumstances**.

- Summary dismissal
- Constructive dismissal
- Inability on the employer's behalf to continue
- Repudiation of the contract by the employee

The concepts of **summary dismissal** and **constructive dismissal** are both examples of **dismissal without proper notice**. A dismissal with proper notice is generally held to be lawful, unless it is shown to be wrongful or unfair. However, the **reason for dismissal** has to be determined in relation to both when the notice is given and when the employment is terminated.

2.1 Summary dismissal

Summary dismissal occurs where the employer dismisses the employee without notice. They may do this if the employee has committed a serious breach of contract and, if so, the employer incurs no liability.

If, however, they have **no sufficient justification** the employer is liable for **breach of contract** and the employee may claim a remedy for wrongful dismissal. Whether the employee's conduct justifies summary dismissal will vary according to the circumstances of the case.

Wilson v Racher 1974

The facts: A gardener swore at his employer using extreme obscenities.

Decision: His action for wrongful dismissal succeeded, as the employer's own conduct had provoked the outburst. This was a solitary outburst following a history of diligence and competence.

Contrast this with *Pepper v Webb 1969*. The decision in this case favoured the employer as the incident also included the employee's **refusal to obey a reasonable** and **lawful instruction**.

2.2 Constructive dismissal

Constructive dismissal occurs where the employer, although willing to continue the employment, repudiates some **essential term** of the contract, for example by the imposition of a complete change in the employee's duties, and the employee resigns. The employer is liable for breach of contract.

2.2.1 Mobility clauses

Employers may include **mobility clauses** in the employment contracts of employees. These clauses state that the employer may require the employee to work in various locations or areas, including different countries. Very often an employee will generally be based in a single location, but a dispute arises when the employer's circumstances change and they invoke the clause in order to move the employee to a different site. This may happen, for instance, where an employer decides to close down a particular office and, to avoid making an employee redundant, decides to move their place of work.

Generally, these clauses are **valid** and will be upheld by the courts if they are **reasonable**. If they are not held to be valid, the employee will have been **constructively dismissed**.

2.2.2 Establishing constructive dismissal

To establish constructive dismissal, an **employee** must show that:

- His employer has committed a serious breach of contract (a repudiatory breach).
- He left because of the breach.
- He has not 'waived' the breach, thereby affirming the contract.

The breach must be serious. Examples of breaches of contract which have lead to claims of **constructive dismissal** include the following.

- A reduction in pay
- A complete change in the nature of the job
- A failure to follow the prescribed disciplinary procedure
- A failure to provide a suitable working environment
- A failure to implement a proper procedure

Where there is more than one cause for the employee's resignation, the claimant must prove that the employer's repudiation was '**an** effective cause' rather than '**the** effective cause' of the resignation.

In *Wright v North Ayrshire Council 2013*, it was held that the claimant's resignation was due, in part, to the need to care for their partner, but because the employer had not dealt with their grievances properly, this was sufficient to be considered as a cause of the resignation and therefore the claim of constructive dismissal was upheld.

2.3 Employer's inability to continue employment

If a personal employer dies, an employing firm of partners is dissolved, an employing company is **compulsorily wound up**, a receiver is appointed or the employee's place of employment is permanently closed, the employer may become unable to continue to employ the employee.

2.4 Repudiation of the contract by the employee

Resignation, striking or failing to perform the contract and to observe its conditions, is **breach of contract** by the employee. The employer may dismiss them or treat the contract as discharged by the employee's breach.

2.5 Employment tribunals

Employment tribunals have jurisdiction to deal with all manner of employment-related disputes, such as wrongful and unfair dismissal and redundancy, which formerly had to be heard in the civil courts. The Employment Tribunals (Constitution and Rules of Procedure) Regulations 2013 (TSO, 2013) apply to them.

The objective of an employment tribunal is to resolve **employment disputes**. A hearing is normally convened with an Employment Judge and two other individuals. Each side makes its case and a decision is made. In some cases, the parties will be encouraged to settle their dispute informally through **mediation**.

The first stage of a tribunal is where the claimant submits a **claim form** that sets out their case. The other party submits a **response form** that sets out their case. The second, **'sift' stage** involves an Employment Judge reviewing all the documentation and deciding whether the case should go to a hearing. A case may be rejected if there is no case for the respondent to answer or if the matter is outside the scope of a tribunal. A **preliminary hearing** is set where any case management or other issues are heard and this may be converted into a **final hearing** if no party is materially prejudiced. Otherwise, a final hearing date is set, when the case is heard before the tribunal panel and a decision is reached.

There are processes in place under the **Small Business, Enterprise and Employment Act 2015** (TSO, 2015) that aim to **manage the tribunal process efficiently** by minimising the postponement of hearings. Also, where a tribunal settlement is not paid on time or in full, the company will face a financial penalty.

2.6 Settlement agreements and early conciliation

The **Enterprise and Regulatory Reform Act 2013** (TSO, 2013) aims to reduce the number of employment disputes that go to tribunal, to save the cost and time involved in them. The Act allows employers and employees to use settlement agreements to part company on agreed terms.

The Act also requires employees to contact **Acas** (the government-sponsored organisation that aims to prevent and resolve employment disputes) before filing a claim at an employment tribunal. This allows the parties to resolve the situation before incurring the expense of going to tribunal.

3 Wrongful dismissal

FAST FORWARD

Where the employer has **summarily dismissed** an employee without notice (as where the employer becomes insolvent), there may be a claim for **damages** at common law for **wrongful dismissal**.

An action for wrongful dismissal derives from the employee's **common law** rights in contract. Therefore, claimants must show that they were **dismissed in breach of contract**, for example with less than the statutory minimum period of notice and that they have **as a result suffered loss**.

As the action is taken for a breach of contract, the hearing will usually only **award damages** for the **loss of notice period**. A dismissal will not be wrongful if it is **justified**.

3.1 Justification of dismissal

The following have been taken as **justifiable circumstances**.

(a)   **Wilful disobedience of a lawful order** if it amounts to wilful and serious defiance of authority.

(b)   **Misconduct**, in connection with the business or outside it, if it is sufficiently grave. For example, acceptance of a secret commission, disclosure of confidential information, assault on a fellow employee or fraud by an employee in a position of trust.

(c)   **Dishonesty**, where the employee is in a position of particular trust.

(d)   **Incompetence or neglect**, insofar as the employee lacks or fails to use skills which they profess to have.

(e)   **Gross negligence**, depending on the nature of the job.

(f)   **Immorality**, only if it is likely to affect performance of duties or the reputation of the business.

(g)   **Drunkenness**, only if it occurs in aggravated circumstances such as when driving a vehicle or a train, or is repeated.

4 Remedies for wrongful dismissal

FAST FORWARD

> Generally, the **only effective remedy** available to a **wrongfully dismissed** employee is a claim for **damages** based on the **loss of earnings**. The measure of damages is usually the sum that would have been earned if **proper notice** had been given.

As with any other case of compensation, the wronged party is expected to **mitigate** their loss by, say, seeking other employment.

Where a breach of contract leaves the **employer as the injured party**, they may dismiss the employee and withhold wages. The employer may recover confidential papers, or apply for an injunction to enforce a valid restrictive covenant.

5 Unfair dismissal

FAST FORWARD

> Certain employees have a right not to be **unfairly dismissed**. Breach of that right allows an employee to claim compensation from a tribunal. To claim for unfair dismissal, the employee must satisfy certain criteria.

Unfair dismissal is an extremely important element of employment protection legislation. The remedies available following a successful action for **wrongful dismissal** are **limited to damages** compensating for the sum which would have been earned **if proper notice had been given**.

Legislation seeks to **widen the scope of protection** and **increase the range of remedies** available to an employee who has been unfairly dismissed. Under the terms of the **Employment Rights Act 1996** (TSO, 1996) a statutory maximum **compensatory award** is set every year which a tribunal may award to an employee who is unfairly dismissed.

5.1 Scope

Every **employee who qualifies** under the criteria (a) and (b) below has a statutory right not to be unfairly dismissed. Certain categories of employee are **excluded** from the statutory unfair dismissal code.

*   Persons employed to work **outside the UK**
*   Employees dismissed while taking **unofficial strike** or other industrial action
*   Other categories, including members of the police

In order to **obtain a statement of reasons for dismissal, compensation** or **other remedies** for **unfair dismissal** the employee must satisfy several criteria. The employee must:

(a) Have been **continuously employed for two years** full-time or part-time (under the Unfair Dismissal and Statement of Reasons for Dismissal (Variation of Qualifying Period) Order 2012) (TSO, 2012).

(b) Have been **dismissed**. This may have to be determined by the tribunal, for example if the employee resigned claiming constructive dismissal.

(c) Have been **unfairly** dismissed. Dismissal may be unfair, even though it is not a breach of contract by the employer.

There are some **exceptions** to the continuous service qualification. These are:

- Where the matter concerns a **safety representative** being penalised for carrying out legitimate health and safety activities

- Where an employee is being **denied a statutory** right (for example an unlawful deduction from wages)

- Where the employee is **pregnant**

The **effective date** of **dismissal** is reckoned as follows.

- Where there is termination by notice, the date on which the notice expires
- Where there is termination without notice, the date on which the termination takes effect
- Where an employee's fixed-term contract is not renewed, the date on which that term expires

5.2 Making a claim

There are four steps to making a claim for **compensation** for unfair dismissal.

Step 1   The **employee** must **apply to a tribunal** within **three months** of dismissal.

Step 2   The **employee** must **show** that they are a **qualifying employee** and that they have in fact been **dismissed**.

Step 3   Then the **employer** must **demonstrate**:

      (a) What was the alleged **only or principal reason** for dismissal

      (b) That it was one of the statutory fair reasons for dismissal or was otherwise a '**substantial reason** of a kind such as to be capable of justifying the dismissal of an employee' in this position.

Step 4   Then the tribunal must decide if the **principal reason** did in fact **justify the dismissal** and whether the employer acted reasonably in treating the reason as sufficient.

If the employer cannot show that the principal reason allegedly justifying the dismissal was one of the **fair reasons** given in statute the dismissal is unfair. Dismissal may be **identified** in three circumstances.

(a) **Actual dismissal** can usually be clearly recognised from the words used by an employer.

(b) **Constructive dismissal**, as described earlier, involves a fundamental breach of the employment contract by the employer.

(c) **Expiry of a fixed-term contract** without renewal amounts to a dismissal.

The employee must show that they have in fact been dismissed. The courts often have to debate whether or not the use of **abusive language** by employers constitutes mere abuse or indicates dismissal.

5.3 The reason for dismissal

As noted above, if the principal reason for dismissal was not one of the statutory fair reasons, then dismissal will be unfair. However, even if the employer shows that they dismissed the employee for a reason which is recognised as capable of being sufficient, **a tribunal may still decide that the dismissal was unfair**. It may do this if it considers that on the basis of **equity and the merits** of the case, **the employer acted unreasonably** in dismissing the employee.

5.3.1 Reasonableness of employer

The **employment tribunal** is required to review the circumstances and to decide whether it was reasonable to dismiss the employee for the reasons given.

Determining whether the **employer has acted reasonably** requires the tribunal to ask:

- Has the correct **procedure** been applied?
- Did the employer take all **circumstances** into consideration?
- What would any **reasonable employer** have done?

The employer does not act reasonably unless they **take account of the relevant circumstances**. If an inexperienced employee is struggling to do their work, the employer is expected to help by advice or supervision in the hope that they may improve. **One or more warnings** should be given before dismissing the employee, so that they may heed the warning and amend their conduct or their performance.

5.3.2 Disciplinary procedure

Employers are required to follow Acas's statutory Code of Practice on Disciplinary and Grievance Procedures. This provides basic practical guidance to employers, employees and their representatives, and sets out principles for handling disciplinary and grievance situations in the workplace.

A **failure to follow the Code** does not, in itself, make a person or organisation liable to proceedings. However, employment tribunals take the Code into account when considering relevant cases, and they are also able to adjust any awards made in relevant cases by up to 25% for unreasonable failure to comply with any provision of the Code. Therefore, if the tribunal feels that an employer has unreasonably failed to follow the Code, it can increase any award it has made by up to 25%. Conversely, it can reduce an award by up to 25% if it feels an employee has unreasonably failed to follow the Code.

The **Code** aims to ensure fairness in any **disciplinary procedure**, and this includes the following elements:

Stage 1   The **employer investigates the matter** to establish the facts of the case

Stage 2   The **employee is informed** of the problem

Stage 3   A **meeting is held** between the parties to discuss the problem (the **employee** has the right to be **accompanied**)

Stage 4   A **decision is made** and appropriate **action taken**

Stage 5   The **employee** has an **opportunity to appeal** the decision

A similar process applies to a **grievance process** instituted by the employee. During either process **both parties should act promptly** without causing undue delay and **be consistent** in their actions.

5.3.3 Warnings

Except in severe cases, it is **not reasonable for an employer to dismiss an employee without first warning them** that if they continue or repeat their behaviour they are likely to be dismissed.

5.3.4 Concluding on reasonableness

In reaching its conclusion on the issue of reasonableness, **the tribunal should not substitute what it would have done if placed in the employer's situation**. It is necessary to set the rights and interests of the employee against the interests of the employer's business and then decide whether **any reasonable employer could have come to a different conclusion**.

Unreasonableness and **breach of contract by the employer must be distinguished.** Some unreasonable conduct by the employer may be serious enough to repudiate the contract, and if the employee leaves they can claim for constructive dismissal by the employer. If the employer acts **unreasonably** but in a manner which does not amount to repudiation of the contract, any resigning employee cannot claim constructive dismissal.

6 Unfair dismissal – justification of dismissal

Dismissal must be **justified** if it is related to the employee's capability or qualifications, the employee's conduct, redundancy, legal prohibition or restriction on the employee's continued employment or some other substantial reason.

Dismissal is **automatically unfair** if it is on the grounds of trade union membership or activities, refusal to join a trade union, pregnancy, redundancy when others are retained, a criminal conviction which is 'spent' under the Rehabilitation of Offenders Act 1974, or race or sex.

6.1 Potentially fair reasons for dismissal

Under the **Employment Rights Act 1996** (TSO, 1996), to justify dismissal as fair dismissal, employers must show their **principal reason** relates to either:

(a)   The **capability or qualifications** of the employee for performing work of the kind which they were employed to do

(b)   The **conduct** of the employee

(c)   **Redundancy**

(d)   **Legal prohibition** or restriction that prevents the employee from lawfully working in the position which they held. For example, if a doctor is struck off the relevant professional register, or an employee loses their driving licence which they need to be able to do their job

(e)   **Some other substantial reason** which justifies dismissal

6.1.1 Capability/qualifications

If the employer dismisses for want of **capability** on the part of the employee, the employer has to establish that fault.

- What does the contract require?
- What is the general standard of performance of their employees in this trade?
- What is the previous standard of performance of the dismissed employee themselves?

If the employee is **incompetent** it must be of such a nature and quality as to justify dismissal. For example, a shop manageress who left her shop dirty and untidy and who failed to maintain cash registers: *Lewis Shops Group Ltd v Wiggins 1973*.

'Capability' is to be assessed by reference to skills, aptitude, health or any other physical or mental quality. **'Qualification'** means any academic or technical qualifications relevant to the position that the employee holds. **'Reasonableness'** on the part of the employer is required, for example:

- **Consultation** with the employee to determine areas of difficulty
- Allowing a **reasonable time** for improvement
- Providing **training** if necessary
- Considering **all alternatives** to dismissal

If the employer relies on **ill health** as the grounds of incapability there must be **proper medical evidence**. The employer is entitled to consider their own business needs. A reasonable procedure involves cautions, confrontation with records and the granting of a period for improvement.

LEARNING MEDIA

Part C Employment law | **9: Dismissal and redundancy**   **151**

> *International Sports Ltd v Thomson 1980*
>
> *The facts*: The employee had been away from work for around 25% of the time, suffering from a number of complaints, all of which were certified by medical certificates. She received a number of warnings. Prior to dismissal the company consulted their medical adviser. As the illnesses were unrelated and unverifiable, he did not consider an examination worthwhile. She was dismissed.
>
> *Decision*: The dismissal was fair.

6.1.2 Misconduct

It is usual to apply the common law distinction between **gross misconduct**, which justifies summary dismissal on the first occasion and **ordinary misconduct**, which is not usually sufficient grounds for dismissal unless it is persistent.

 Illustration

Assault on a fellow employee, conduct exposing others to danger (for example, smoking in an area where it was prohibited for safety reasons), unpleasant behaviour towards customers and persistent absences from work have been treated as sufficient misconduct to justify dismissal.

6.1.3 Redundancy

If an employee is dismissed mainly or only on the ground of **redundancy**, they may claim remedies for unfair dismissal if they can show one of the following.

(a)   There were other employees in similar positions who might have been made redundant and that **selection for redundancy was in breach of a customary arrangement or agreed procedure**.

(b)   He was selected for a reason connected with **trade union membership**.

A redundancy selection procedure should be in conformity with **good industrial relations practice** which requires consultation and objective criteria of selection. The criteria set out by the Employment Appeals Tribunal in *Williams v Compair Maxam Ltd 1982* have been accepted as standards of behaviour.

(a)   The employer should give as much **warning** as possible of impending redundancies.

(b)   The employer should **consult with the trade union** as to the best means of achieving the desired management result.

(c)   It should be possible to check **criteria** for selection against such things as attendance records, efficiency at the job and length of service.

(d)   The employer should ensure that the selection is made **fairly**.

(e)   The employer should consider whether an **offer of alternative employment** can be made.

6.1.4 Other substantial reason

The category of **other substantial reason** permits the employer to rely on some factor which is unusual and likely to affect them adversely. An employer has justified dismissal on specific grounds.

(a)   The employee was married to one of their competitors.

(b)   The employee refused to accept a reorganisation. For example, a change of shift working made in the interests of the business and with the agreement of a large majority of other employees.

6.1.5 Automatically fair reasons for dismissal

Other reasons are designated as being **automatically fair** by legislation.

• Taking part in **unofficial industrial action**
• Being a **threat to national security** (to be certified by the Government)

An employee who strikes or refuses to work normally may be fairly dismissed unless the industrial action has been **lawfully organised** under the protection conferred by the Employment Relations Act 1999 (TSO, 1999). Where dismissal results from a lock-out or a strike, the tribunal cannot deal with it as a case of alleged unfair dismissal unless victimisation is established.

6.1.6 Automatically unfair reasons for dismissal

Some reasons are automatically unfair (known as **'inadmissible reasons'**). Examples include:

- Pregnancy or other maternity-related grounds
- A spent conviction under the Rehabilitation of Offenders Act 1974
- Trade union membership or activities
- Dismissal on transfer of an undertaking (unless there are 'economic, technical or organisational reasons' justifying the dismissal)
- Taking steps to avert danger to health and safety at work
- Seeking to enforce rights relating to the national minimum wage
- Exercising rights under the Working Time Regulations 1998
- Refusing or opting out of Sunday working (in the retail sector)
- Making a protected disclosure order under the Public Interest Disclosure Act 1998

Dismissal on grounds of pregnancy or pregnancy-related illness is automatically unfair, **regardless of length of service** as it amounts to **gender discrimination**.

6.2 Proving what was the reason for dismissal

The employer may be required to give to the employee a **written statement** of the **reason for dismissal**. If an employee is dismissed for trying to **enforce their employment rights**, for example by requesting a written statement of particulars or an itemised pay statement, they may claim unfair dismissal **regardless of the length of service** and hours worked.

Exam focus point

> Exam questions may test fair and unfair reasons for dismissal and the meaning and effect of constructive dismissal.

7 Remedies for unfair dismissal

FAST FORWARD

> Remedies for **unfair dismissal** include:
> - **Reinstatement**
> - **Re-engagement**
> - **Compensation**

Under the **Employment Rights Act 1996** (TSO, 1996) an employee who alleges unfair dismissal must present their complaint to an **employment tribunal** within three months of the effective date of termination. The dispute is referred to a Conciliation Officer and only comes before the tribunal if their efforts to promote a settlement fail.

7.1 Reinstatement

If unfair dismissal is established, the tribunal first considers the possibility of ordering reinstatement.

Key term

> **Reinstatement** is return to the same job without any break of continuity.

7.2 Re-engagement

The tribunal may alternatively order **re-engagement**. The new employment must be of the same status and comparable with the old role or otherwise suitable.

> **Re-engagement** means that the employee is given new employment with the employer (or their successor or associate) on terms specified in the order.

In deciding whether to exercise these powers, the tribunal must take into account whether the complainant wishes to be reinstated and, whether it is practicable and just for the employer to comply. **Such orders are in fact very infrequent**.

The **Employment Appeal Tribunal** has ruled that an order for re-engagement should not be made if there has been a breakdown in confidence between the parties.

7.3 Compensation

If the tribunal does not order reinstatement or re-engagement the tribunal may award **compensation**, which may be made in three stages, as follows.

(a) A **basic award** calculated as follows. Those aged 41 and over receive one-and-a-half weeks' pay (up to a statutory maximum per week) for each year of service up to a maximum of 20 years. In other age groups the same provisions apply, except that the 22–40 age group receive one week's pay per year and the 21-and-under age group receive half a week's pay.

(b) A **compensatory award** for any additional loss of earnings, expenses and benefits, on common law principles of damages for breach of contract. This is to compensate the employee for financial loss suffered as a result of unfair dismissal insofar as that loss is attributable to action taken by the employer. This is limited to a statutory maximum and may be awarded in cases where reinstatement or re-engagement are deemed inappropriate by the tribunal.

(c) If the employer does not comply with an order for reinstatement or re-engagement, and does not show that it was impracticable to do so, a punitive **additional award** is made of between 26 and 52 weeks' pay (again subject to a statutory weekly maximum).

The tribunal may **reduce the amount** of the award in any of the following circumstances.

- If the employee **contributed** in some way to their own dismissal
- If they have **unreasonably refused** an offer of reinstatement
- If it is **just and equitable** to reduce the basic award by reason of some matter which occurred before dismissal.

8 Redundancy

> Dismissal is caused by **redundancy** when the employer has ceased to carry on the business in which the employee has been employed or the business no longer needs employees to carry on that work. In these circumstances, dismissal is **presumed** by the courts to be by redundancy unless otherwise demonstrated.

An employee may claim a **redundancy payment** where they are:
- Dismissed by their employer by reason of redundancy
- Laid off or kept on short time

8.1 What is redundancy?

> A dismissal is treated as caused by **redundancy** if the only or main reason is that:
>
> - The employer has ceased, or intends to cease, to carry on the business (or the local establishment of the business) in which the employee has been employed
>
> - The requirements of that business for employees to carry on the work done by the employee have ceased or diminished (or are expected to)

If the employee's contract has a **mobility clause** (a clause that allows the employer to change the place of work) there is no redundancy if the employee is relocated. However, in some cases it might be classed as constructive dismissal.

A key test for determining whether or not an employee is redundant is to see whether there has been a reduction of the employers' requirements for employees to work **at the place where the person concerned is employed**.

High Table Ltd v Horst and Others 1997

The facts: High Table Ltd, contract caterers, employed waitresses who had worked for several years at one company. The client company told High Table that the waitresses were no longer required, so they were dismissed by High Table on the grounds of redundancy. The waitresses, who had mobility clauses in their contracts, alleged unfair dismissal since High Table had not tried to re-employ them somewhere else.

Decision: The Court of Appeal ruled against them, saying that the place of work was at the client company premises and the dismissals were for genuine redundancy.

In considering whether the requirements of the business for staff have diminished, it is the **overall** position which must be considered. If, for example, A's job is abolished and A is moved into B's job and B is dismissed, that is a case of redundancy although B's job continues.

In *British Broadcasting Corporation v Farnworth 1998* a radio producer's fixed-term contract was not renewed and the employer advertised for a radio producer with more experience. It was held by the Employment Appeal Tribunal (EAT) that the less-experienced radio producer was indeed redundant as the **requirement for her level of services had diminished**.

If the employer **reorganises their business** or alters their methods so that the same work has to be done by different means which are beyond the capacity of the employee, that is not redundancy.

North Riding Garages v Butterwick 1967

The facts: A garage reorganised its working arrangements so that the workshop manager's duties included more administrative work . He was dismissed when it was found he could not perform these duties.

Decision: His claim for redundancy pay must fail since it was not a case of redundancy.

Vaux and Associated Breweries v Ward 1969

The facts: The owners of a public house renovated their premises and as part of the new image they dismissed the middle-aged barmaid and replaced her with a younger employee.

Decision: The claim for redundancy pay must fail since the same job still existed.

8.2 Calculation of redundancy pay

Redundancy pay is calculated on the same basis as the **basic compensation for unfair dismissal**.

8.3 Exceptions to the right to redundancy payment

A person is **excluded** from having a right to redundancy payment where:

- They do not fit the **definition** of 'employee' given in statute
- They have not been **continuously employed** for **two** years
- They have been or could be dismissed for **misconduct**
- An offer to **renew the contract** is unreasonably **refused**
- Claim is made **out of time** (after six months)
- The **employee leaves** before being made redundant, having been notified of the possibility of redundancies

8.3.1 Misconduct of the employee

An employee who is dismissed for **misconduct** is **not entitled to redundancy pay** even though they may become redundant.

> *Sanders v Neale 1974*
>
> *The facts*: In the course of a dispute employees refused to work normally. The employer dismissed them and closed down his business. The employees claimed redundancy pay.
>
> *Decision*: The claim must be dismissed since the employees had repudiated the contract before the employer's decision to close down made them redundant.

An employee can be dismissed for misconduct but still claim redundancy pay in the event of a **strike** if the strike occurs after the notice of termination of the contract from the employer, or after the employee has given notice claiming redundancy pay on account of lay-off or short time.

8.3.2 Offer of further employment

The employer may offer a redundant employee alternative employment for the future. If the employee then unreasonably refuses the offer, they lose their entitlement to redundancy pay.

The offer must be of alternative employment **in the same capacity**, at the same place and on the same terms and conditions as the previous employment. It should not be perceived as being lower in status.

When there is a difference between the terms and conditions of a new contract and the previous contract, the employee is entitled to a **four-week trial** period in the new employment. If either party terminates the new contract during the trial period, it is treated as a case of dismissal for redundancy at the expiry date of the previous employment. The employee can also still bring claims for unfair dismissal.

8.4 Lay-off and short time

An employee's exact remuneration may depend on the employer providing work. They are 'laid off' in any week in which they earn nothing by reason of lack of work or they are '**kept on short time**', which is any week in which they earn less than half a normal week's pay.

When an employee is **laid off** or **kept on short time** for 4 or more consecutive weeks, or 6 weeks in a period of 13 weeks, they **may claim redundancy** pay by giving notice to the employer of their intention to claim. In addition to their **notice of claim** the employee must also give notice to the employer to terminate the contract of employment.

8.5 Strike action

Employees involved in **strike action** after redundancy notice is served **will** be entitled to redundancy payments. However, if they are **on strike** when the notice is served they will **not** be eligible for the payment.

Chapter Roundup

- When an employment contract is terminated by notice there is **no** breach of contract unless the **contents** of the notice (such as notice period) are themselves in breach.

- Where employment is **terminated by notice** the period given must **not be less** than the **statutory minimum**.

- **Breach of the employment contract** occurs where there is **summary dismissal**, **constructive dismissal**, **inability** on the employer's side to **continue employment**, or **repudiation** of the contract by the employee.

- Where the employer has **summarily dismissed** an employee without notice (as where the employer becomes insolvent), there may be a claim for **damages** at common law for **wrongful dismissal**.

- Generally, the only **effective remedy** available to a **wrongfully dismissed** employee is a claim for **damages** based on the **loss of earnings**. The measure of damages is usually the sum that would have been earned if **proper notice** had been given.

- Certain employees have a right not to be **unfairly dismissed**. Breach of that right allows an employee to claim compensation from a tribunal. To claim for unfair dismissal, the employee must satisfy certain criteria.

- Dismissal must be **justified** if it is related to the employee's capability or qualifications, the employee's conduct, redundancy, legal prohibition or restriction on the employee's continued employment or some other substantial reason.

- Dismissal is **automatically unfair** if it is on the grounds of trade union membership or activities, refusal to join a trade union, pregnancy, redundancy when others are retained, a criminal conviction which is 'spent' under the Rehabilitation of Offenders Act 1974 or race or sex.

- Remedies for **unfair dismissal** include:

    - **Reinstatement**
    - **Re-engagement**
    - **Compensation**

- Dismissal is caused by **redundancy** when the employer has ceased to carry on the business in which the employee has been employed or the business no longer needs employees to carry on that work. In these circumstances, dismissal is **presumed** by the courts to be by redundancy unless otherwise demonstrated.

Quick Quiz

1   **Fill in the blanks** below, using the words in the box.

To claim (1) ……………….. for unfair dismissal, three issues have to be considered.

The employee must show that they are a (2) ……………….. employee and that they have been (3) ………………..

The (4) ……………….. must show what the (5) ……………….. was for dismissal

Application has to be made to the (6) ……………….. within (7) ……………….. months of the dismissal

• qualifying	• dismissed	• employer
• reason	• three	• compensation
• employment tribunal		

2   Expiry of a fixed-term contract without renewal amounts to a dismissal.

True ☐

False ☐

3   Which one of the following is **not** a question that a tribunal, when considering an employer's reasonableness in an unfair dismissal claim, will want to answer?

    A   What would a reasonable employer have done?
    B   Has the correct procedure been applied?
    C   Has any employee been dismissed in this way before?
    D   Did the employer take all circumstances into consideration?

4   Which is the most common remedy awarded for unfair dismissal?

compensation
re-engagement
re-instalment

5   An employee is not entitled to redundancy pay if they resign voluntarily before being made redundant even if they were aware of the possibility of redundancy.

True ☐

False ☐

Answers to Quick Quiz

1   (1) compensation (2) qualifying (3) dismissed (4) employer (5) reason (6) employment tribunal (7) three

2   True. Non-renewal constitutes dismissal.

3   C. The question is irrelevant to the employee's situation.

4   Compensation, as in most cases the working relationship would have been irrevocably damaged.

5   True, as they are not being made redundant.

Now try the questions below from the Practice Question Bank

Number
19, 20, 21

The formation and constitution of business organisations

Agency law

Topic list	Syllabus reference
1 Role of agency and agency relationships	D1(a)
2 Formation of agency	D1(b)
3 Authority of the agent	D1(c)
4 Relations between agents and third parties	D1(d)

Introduction

In this chapter we examine how an **agency relationship** arises and how the **agent's authority** is acquired and defined. Agency is the foundation of most business relationships where more than one person engages in commerce together. Examples include **partnerships** and **companies**, which we shall introduce in the next chapter.

'Agents' are employed by **'principals'** to perform tasks which the principals cannot or do not wish to perform themselves. This is often because the principal does not have the time or expertise to carry out the task.

If businesspeople did not employ the services of agents, they would be weighed down by the contractual details, and would probably get little else done!

When parties enter into an **agency arrangement**, the principal gives a measure of authority to the agent to carry out tasks on their behalf. The agent **contracts and deals with third parties** on behalf of the principal.

Study guide

		Intellectual level
D	**The formation and constitution of business organisations**	
1	**Agency law**	
(a)	Define the role of the agent and give examples of such relationships paying particular regard to partners and company directors	2
(b)	Explain the formation of the agency relationship	2
(c)	Define the authority of the agent	2
(d)	Explain the potential liability of both principal and agent	2

Exam guide

Agency may form a multiple choice question requiring you to identify types of agent, how agency relationships are established and an agent's authority and liability to others.

1 Role of agency and agency relationships

> **FAST FORWARD**
>
> **Agency** is a relationship which exists between two legal persons (the **principal** and the **agent**) in which the function of the agent is to form a **contract between their principal and a third party**. Partners, company directors, factors, brokers and commercial agents are all acting as agents.

Agency is a very important feature of **modern commercial life**. It can be represented diagrammatically as follows:

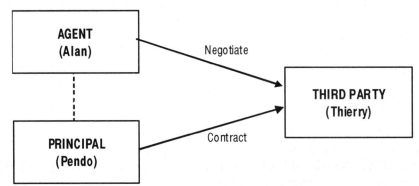

For instance Pendo may ask Alan to take Pendo's shoes to be repaired. Pendo and Alan expressly agree that Alan is to do this on Pendo's behalf. In other words, Alan becomes the agent in negotiating a contract between Pendo and Thierry, the shoe repairer, for Pendo's shoes to be mended.

1.1 Types of agent

In practice, there are many **examples of agency relationships** of which you are probably aware in everyday life, although you might not know that they illustrate the law of agency. The most important agency relationships in this syllabus are those of partners and company directors.

Types of agent	
Partners	This is a particularly important example of agency in your syllabus, as accountants who own and run an accountancy practice together are partners, and are therefore agents of each other.
Company directors	This is another important example of agency in your syllabus. Company directors act as agents of their company.

Types of agent	
Promoters	A promoter is someone (except professionals acting in their professional capacity) who undertakes to form a company.
Factors	A factor, sometimes called a mercantile agent, is a person whose job is to sell or buy goods on behalf of another person. For example, motor dealers are often factors.
Brokers	A broker may operate in many trades. They are essentially an intermediary who arranges contracts in return for commission. For example, an insurance broker.
Auctioneers	Auctioneers are agents authorised to sell property at auction on behalf of the seller. When an auctioneer accepts a bid from a buyer, they become the agent of the buyer for the purpose of making a record of the sale.
Commercial agents	A commercial agent is an independent agent who has continuing authority in connection with the sale or purchase of goods.

2 Formation of agency

FAST FORWARD

The relationship of principal and agent is created by **mutual consent** in the vast majority of cases. This **agreement does not have to be formal or written**.

The mutual consent comes about usually by **express agreement**, even if it is informal. However, it may also be **implied agreement**, due to the **relationship** or **conduct** of the parties.

2.1 Express agreement

This is where the agent is **expressly appointed** by the principal. This may be orally, or in writing. In most commercial situations, the appointment would be made in writing to ensure that everything was clear. An agent expressly appointed by the principal has **actual authority** of the principal to act on their behalf.

2.2 Implied agreement

An agency relationship between two people may be implied by their **relationship** or by their **conduct**.

For example, if an employee's duties include making contracts for their employer, say by ordering goods on their account, then they are, by implied agreement, the agent of the employer for this purpose. An agent authorised in this way is said to have implied authority.

2.3 Ratification of an agent's act: retrospective agreement

FAST FORWARD

A principal may subsequently **ratify** an act of an agent retrospectively.

An agency relationship may be created **retrospectively**, by the 'principal' **ratifying** the act of the 'agent'. Therefore it is created after the 'agent' has formed a contract on behalf of the 'principal'. If the principal agrees to the acts of the agent after the event, they may approve the acts of the agent and make it as if they had been principal and agent at the time of the contract.

The **conditions for ratification** are:

- The principal must have **existed** at the time of the contract made by the agent
- The principal must have had **legal capacity** at the time the contract was made
- The ratification must take place **within reasonable time**
- They ratify the contract in its **entirety**
- They **communicate** their ratification to the third party sufficiently clearly

Once a contract has been ratified by the principal, the effect is that it is as if the agency relationship had been **expressly formed before** the contract made by the agent took place.

2.4 Formation of agency agreement without consent

FAST FORWARD

An agency may be created, or an agent's authority may be extended, without express consent. This happens **by estoppel**, when the principal **'holds out'** a person to be their agent, and when there is an **agent of necessity**.

2.4.1 Implied agreement

In some cases, an agency created by implied agreement might result in the agent having **more implied authority** than the principal might have consented to.

2.4.2 Agent by estoppel

An agency relationship may be formed by implication when the **principal holds out to third parties** that a person is their agent, even if the principal and the 'agent' do not agree to form such a relationship. In such a case, the principal is estopped from denying the agent's apparent/ostensible authority, hence the name **'agent by estoppel'**. An agency relationship is not so formed if it is the 'agent' who creates the impression that they are in an agency relationship with a 'principal'.

2.4.3 Agent by necessity

In some rare situations, it may be necessary for a person to take action in respect of someone else's goods in an **emergency situation**. That person can become an **agent of necessity** of the owner of the goods, as they take steps in respect of the goods.

Illustration

A seller is shipping frozen goods to a buyer in another country. While the ship is docked, the freezers in the ship break down and the relevant part required to fix them cannot be obtained. If the ship's captain (acting as the agent of necessity) cannot make contact with the owner of the goods, they might, of necessity, sell the goods while they are still frozen, rather than allow them to spoil by defrosting.

This is particularly rare, because it would only occur when the 'agent' could not make contact with the 'principal', which in the modern world is **extremely unlikely**.

This principle is a historic part of English shipping and merchant law and you should be aware that it might be possible, but do not worry about the other details of the doctrine.

3 Authority of the agent

FAST FORWARD

If an agent acts within the limits of their authority, any contract they make on the principal's behalf is **binding** on both principal and third party. The extent of the agent's authority may be **express, implied** or **ostensible**. Express and implied authority are both forms of **actual authority**.

A principal does not give the agent unlimited authority to act on their behalf. A **contract** made by the agent is **binding** on the principal and the other party **only if** the **agent was acting within the limits of their authority** from their principal.

In analysing the **limits of an agent's authority**, three distinct sources of authority can be identified:

- Express authority
- Implied authority
- Ostensible authority

3.1 Express authority

Express authority is a matter between principal and agent. This is authority explicitly given by the principal to the agent to perform particular tasks, along with the powers necessary to perform those tasks.

The extent of the agent's express authority will depend on the **construction of the words used on their appointment**. If the appointment is in **writing**, then the document will need to be examined. If it is oral, then the scope of the agent's authority will be a matter of evidence. If the agent contracts outside the scope of their express (actual) authority, they may be **liable** to the principal and the third party for **breach of warrant of authority**.

Illustration

A board of directors may give an individual direct express authority to enter the company into a specific contract. The company would be bound to this contract, but not to one made by the individual director outside the express authority.

3.2 Implied authority

Where there is no express authority, authority may be **implied** from the **nature** of the agent's activities or from what is **usual** or **customary** in the **circumstances**. Between principal and agent, the latter's express authority is paramount. The agent cannot contravene the principal's express instructions by claiming that they had implied authority for acting in the way they did. As far as **third parties** are concerned, they are entitled to assume that the agent has implied usual authority unless they know to the contrary.

Watteau v Fenwick 1893

The facts: The owner of a hotel (F) employed the previous owner (H) to manage it. F forbade H to buy cigars on credit but H did buy cigars from W. W sued F for payment but F argued that he was not bound by the contract, since H had no actual authority to make it, and that W believed that H still owned the hotel.

Decision: It was within the usual authority of a manager of a hotel to buy cigars on credit and F was bound by the contract (although W did not even know that H was the agent of F) since his restriction of usual authority had not been communicated.

Hely-Hutchinson v Brayhead Ltd 1968

The facts: The chairman and chief executive of a company acted as its de facto managing director, but he had never been formally appointed to that position. Nevertheless, he purported to bind the company to a particular transaction. When the other party to the agreement sought to enforce it, the company claimed that the chairman had no authority to bind it.

Decision: Although the director derived no authority from his position as chairman of the board, he did acquire authority from his position as chief executive. Therefore the company was bound by the contract as it was within the implied authority of a person holding such a position.

Illustration

A principal employs a stockbroker to sell shares. It is an implied term of the arrangement between them that the broker shall have **actual authority** to do what is usual in practice for a broker selling shares for a client. Any person dealing with the broker is entitled to assume (unless informed to the contrary) that the broker has the usual authority of a broker acting for a client.

3.3 Actual authority

Express and implied authority are sometimes referred to together as **actual authority**. This distinguishes them from **ostensible** or **apparent authority**.

> **Actual authority** is a legal relationship between principal and agent created by a consensual agreement between them.

3.4 Apparent/ostensible authority

> An agent's **apparent** or **ostensible authority** may be greater than their express or implied authority. This occurs where a **principal** holds it out to be so to a third party, who relied on the representation and altered their position as a result. It may be **more extensive** than what is usual or incidental.

The **ostensible** (or **apparent**) authority of an agent is what a principal **represents** to other persons that they have given to the agent (authority by **'holding out'**). As a result, an agent with **express** or **implied** authority which is limited can be held, in practice, to have a more extensive authority.

Apparent/ostensible authority usually **arises** either

(a)   Where the **principal** has **represented** the agent as having authority even though they have not actually been appointed; or

(b)   Where the **principal** has **revoked** the agent's **authority** but the **third party** has **not had notice** of this.

3.4.1 The extent of ostensible authority

Ostensible authority is not restricted to what is usual and incidental. The principal may expressly or by inference from their conduct **confer on the agent any amount of ostensible authority**.

3.4.2 Example: partnership

A **partner** has considerable but **limited implied authority** by virtue of being a partner. If, however, the other partners allow them to exercise greater authority than is implied, they have represented that they have wider authority. They will be bound by the contracts which they make within the limits of this **ostensible authority**.

3.4.3 Example: companies

> *Freeman & Lockyer v Buckhurst Park Properties (Mangal) Ltd 1964*
>
> *The facts:* K and H carried on business as property developers through a company which they owned in equal shares. Each appointed another director, making four in all. H lived abroad and the business of the company was left entirely under the control of K. As a director K had no actual or apparent authority to enter into contracts as agent of the company, but he did make contracts as if he were a managing director without authority to do so. The other directors were aware of these activities but had not authorised them. The claimants sued the company for work done on K's instructions.
>
> *Decision:* There had been a representation by the company through its board of directors that K was the authorised agent of the company. The board had authority to make such contracts and also had power to delegate authority to K by appointing him to be Managing Director. Although there had been no actual delegation to K, the company had by its acquiescence led the claimants to believe that K was an authorised agent and the claimants had relied on it. The company was bound by the contract made by K under the principle of 'holding out' (or estoppel). The company was estopped from denying (that is, not permitted to deny) that K was its agent, although K had no actual authority from the company.

It can be seen that it is the **conduct** of the '**principal**' which **creates ostensible authority**. It does not matter whether there is a pre-existing agency relationship or not.

This is important – ostensible authority arises in two distinct ways. It may arise where a **person makes a representation to third parties** that a particular person has the authority to act as their agent, without actually appointing them as their agent. Alternatively, it may arise where a **principal has previously represented to a third party** that an agent has authority to act on their behalf.

3.4.4 Representations creating ostensible authority

The **representation must be made by the principal or an agent acting on their behalf.** It cannot be made by the agent who is claiming ostensible authority.

It must be a **representation of fact, not law**, and must be **made to the third party**. This distinguishes ostensible authority from actual authority, where the third party need know nothing of the agent's authority.

3.4.5 Reliance on representations

It must be shown that the **third party relied on the representation**. If there is no causal link between the third party's loss and the representation, the third party will not be able to hold the principal as liable.

Illustration

If the third party did not believe that the agent had authority, or if they positively knew they did not, then ostensible authority cannot be claimed. This is true even if the agent appeared to have authority.

3.4.6 Alteration of position following a representation

It is enough that the third party **alters their position as a result of reliance on the representation**. They do not have to suffer any detriment as a result, but damages would in such an event be minimal.

3.5 Revocation of authority

Where a principal has represented to a third party that an agent has authority to act, and has subsequently **revoked the agent's authority**, this may be **insufficient to escape liability**. The principal should inform third parties who have previously dealt with the agent of the change in circumstances. This is particularly relevant to partnerships and the position when a partner leaves a partnership.

3.6 Termination of agency

FAST FORWARD 〉〉 Agency is terminated by **agreement** or by **operation of law** (death, insanity, insolvency).

Agency is terminated when the **parties agree** that the relationship should end.

It may also be terminated by **operation of law** in the following situations:

- Principal or agent dies

- Principal or agent becomes insane

- Principal becomes bankrupt, or the agent becomes bankrupt and this interferes with their position as agent

Termination brings the **actual authority** of the agent to an end. However, third parties are allowed to enforce contracts made later by the 'agent' until they are actively or constructively informed of the termination of the agency relationship.

4 Relations between agents and third parties

An agent usually has **no liability** for a contract entered into as an agent, nor any **right to enforce it**. Exceptions to this would include when an agent is **intended** to have liability; where it is **usual business practice** to have liability; when the agent is actually acting on their own behalf; where agent and principal have joint liability.

A third party to a contract entered into with an agent acting outside their ostensible authority can sue for breach of **warranty of authority**.

4.1 Liability of the agent for contracts formed

An agent contracting for their principal within their actual and/or apparent authority generally **has no liability** on the contract and **is not entitled to enforce it**. However, there are **circumstances** when the **agent will be personally liable** and can enforce it.

(a)   When they **intended to undertake personal liability** – for example, where they sign a contract as party to it without signifying that they are an agent.

(b)   Where it is **usual business practice or trade custom** for an agent to be liable and entitled.

(c)   Where the agent **is acting on their own behalf** even though they purport to act for a principal.

Where an agent enters into a **collateral contract** with the third party with whom they have contracted on the principal's behalf, there is separate liability and entitlement to enforcement on that collateral contract.

It can happen that there is **joint liability** of agent and principal. This is usually the case where an agent did not disclose that they acted for a principal.

4.2 Breach of warranty of authority

An agent who **exceeds their authority** will generally have **no liability to their principal**, since the latter will not be bound by the unauthorised contract made for him. But the agent **will be liable** in such a case **to the third party** for breach of warranty of authority.

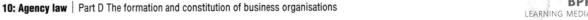

BPP
LEARNING MEDIA

Chapter Roundup

- **Agency** is a relationship which exists between two legal persons (the **principal** and the **agent**) in which the function of the agent is to form a **contract between their principal and a third party**. Partners, company directors, factors, brokers and commercial agents are all acting as agents.

- The relationship of principal and agent is created by **mutual consent** in the vast majority of cases. This **agreement does not have to be formal or written**.

- The mutual consent comes about usually by **express agreement**, even if it is informal. However, it may also be **implied agreement**, due to the **relationship** or **conduct** of the parties.

- A principal many later **ratify** an act of an agent retrospectively.

- An agency may be created, or an agent's authority may be extended, without express consent. This happens **by estoppel**, when the principal **'holds out'** a person to be their agent, and when there is an **agent of necessity**.

- If an agent acts within the limits of their authority, any contract they make on the principal's behalf is **binding** on both principal and third party. The extent of the agent's authority may be **express, implied** or **ostensible**. Express and implied authority are both forms of **actual authority**.

- An agent's **apparent** or **ostensible authority** may be greater than their express or implied authority. This occurs where a **principal** holds it out to be so to a third party, who relied on the representation and altered their position as a result. It may be **more extensive** than what is usual or incidental.

- Agency is terminated by **agreement** or by **operation of law** (death, insanity, insolvency).

- An agent usually has **no liability** for a contract entered into as an agent, nor any **right to enforce it**. Exceptions to this would include when an agent is **intended** to have liability; where it is **usual business practice** to have liability; when the agent is actually acting on their own behalf; where agent and principal have joint liability.

- A third party to a contract entered into with an agent acting outside their ostensible authority can sue for breach of **warranty of authority**.

Quick Quiz

1   **Fill in the blanks** in the statements, using the words in the boxes below.

Agency is the (1)......................... which exists between two (2)....................... persons. They are the (3)............... and the agent, in which the function of the agent is to form a (4)................ between their (5)................ and a (6)...............

• relationship	• contract	• legal
• third party	• principal	• principal

2   A principal may, in certain circumstances, ratify the acts of the agent which has retrospective effect.

True   ☐

False   ☐

3   What is the best definition of ostensible authority?

(a)   The authority which the principal represents to other persons that they have given to the agent.
(b)   The authority implied to other persons by the agent's actions.

4   What point of law is explained in the case of *Freeman & Lockyer v Buckhurst Park Properties (Mangal) Ltd 1964?*

5   Which of the following are circumstances where an agent may enforce a contract?

(a)   Where the agent is intended to take personal liability
(b)   Where it is usual business practice to allow enforcement
(c)   Where the agent acts on their own behalf even if they purport to act for a principal

(i)   (a), (b)
(ii)   (b), (c)
(iii)   (a), (c)
(iv)   (a), (b) and (c)

Answers to Quick Quiz

1   (1)   relationship   (2)   legal   (3)   principal
    (4)   contract   (5)   principal   (6)   third party

2   True. Principals may ratify retrospectively.

3   (a). The key word is 'represents'.

4   A director may have ostensible authority to contract if, although they do not have their express permission, the other directors are aware that contracts are being made and do nothing to prevent it.

5   (iv). They are all valid circumstances.

Now try the questions below from the Practice Question Bank

Number
22, 23

11

Partnerships

Topic list	Syllabus reference
1 Partnerships	D2(a)
2 Forming an unlimited liability partnership	D2(b)
3 Terminating an unlimited liability partnership	D2(e)
4 Authority of partners in an unlimited liability partnership	D2(c)
5 Liability of partners in an unlimited liability partnership	D2(d)
6 Limited liability partnerships	D2(a–e)

Introduction

Partnerships are a common form of business organisation and are commonly used for **small businesses** and some **professional businesses**, for example accountants.

A partnership is a group of individuals who have an **agency** relationship with each other. We shall look at how partnerships are **formed** and later **terminated**, then at how **relationships** with other partners and with third parties work.

Study guide

		Intellectual level
D	**The formation and constitution of business organisations**	
2	**Partnerships**	
(a)	Demonstrate a knowledge of the legislation governing the partnership, both unlimited and limited	1
(b)	Discuss the formation of a partnership	2
(c)	Explain the authority of partners in relation to partnership activity	2
(d)	Analyse the liability of various partners for partnership debts	2
(e)	Explain the termination of a partnership and partners' subsequent rights and liabilities	2

Exam guide

Partnership is highly suited to scenario questions where you may be required to identify who is liable for partnership debts.

1 Partnerships

FAST FORWARD

Partnership is defined as 'the relation which subsists between persons carrying on a business in common with a view of profit'. A partnership is **not** a separate legal person distinct from its members, it is merely a 'relation' between persons. Each partner (there must be at least two) is **personally liable** for all the debts of the firm.

Partnership is a common form of business association. It is **flexible**, because it can either be a **formal** or **informal** arrangement, so can be used for large organisations or a small husband-and-wife operation.

Partnership is normal practice in the **professions**, as most professions prohibit their members from carrying on practice through limited companies (though some professions permit their members to trade as limited liability partnerships which have many of the characteristics of companies). Business people are not so restricted and generally prefer to trade through a limited company for the advantages this can bring.

Applying the law on partnerships and companies to meet the needs of your clients is a way of meeting the requirement of PO1 for those working in public practice. You need to keep your knowledge of partnership and company law up-to-date in order to provide the best possible advice to clients.

Exam focus point

Your syllabus requires you to demonstrate knowledge of the legislation governing both limited and unlimited liability partnerships. You should, therefore, make careful note of the rules regarding the Partnership Act 1890, the Limited Partnership Act 1907 and the Limited Liability Partnership Act 2000.

1.1 Definition of partnership

Key term

Partnership is the relation which subsists between persons carrying on a business in common with a view of profit.

The **Partnership Act 1890** (HMSO, 1890) covers unlimited partnerships. We shall look at how the Act applies the above definition.

1.1.1 The relation which subsists between persons

'Person' includes a corporation such as a **registered company** as well as an **individual** living person.

There must be at least **two** partners. If, therefore, two people are in partnership, one dies and the survivor carries on the business, that person is a sole trader. There is no longer a partnership.

1.1.2 Carrying on a business

Business can include **every trade**, **occupation** or **profession**. But three points should be noted.

(a)   A business is a **form of activity**. If two or more persons are merely the passive joint owners of revenue-producing property, such as rented houses, that fact does not make them partners.

(b)   A business can consist of a **single transaction**. These situations are often described as 'joint ventures'.

(c)   Carrying on a business must have a **beginning and an end**. A partnership begins when the partners agree to conduct their **business activity** together.

1.1.3 In common

Broadly this phrase means that the partners must be associated in the business as **joint proprietors**. The evidence that this is so is found in their taking a share of the profits, especially **net profit**.

1.1.4 A view of profit

If persons enter into a partnership with a **view of making profits** but they actually suffer losses, it is still a partnership. The test to be applied is one of **intention**. If the intention of trading together is just to gain experience, for example, there is no partnership.

1.2 Consequences of the definition

In most cases there is no doubt about the existence of a partnership. The partners declare their intention by such steps as signing a **written partnership agreement** and adopting a **firm name**. These outward and visible signs of the existence of a partnership are not essential however – a partnership can exist without them.

1.2.1 Terminology

The word 'firm' is correctly used to denote a partnership. It is **not** correct to apply it to a registered company (though the newspapers often do so).

The word 'company' may form part of the name of a partnership, for example, 'Smith and Company'. But 'limited company' or 'registered company' is **only** applied to a properly registered company.

1.3 Liability of the partners

Every partner is liable **without limit** for the debts of the partnership. This means that a creditor can require a partner to settle an invoice if the partnership fails to pay, and partners must make good the partnership's debts if the partnership is terminated and does not have sufficient assets to pay what it owes.

It is possible to register a limited partnership in which one or more individual partners has limited liability, but the limited partners may not take part in the management of the business.

The **limited partnership** is useful where one partner wishes to invest in the activities of the partnership without being involved in its day-to-day operation. Such partners are entitled to inspect the accounts of the partnership.

Under the **Limited Liability Partnership Act 2000** it is possible to register a partnership with limited liability (an LLP).

2 Forming an unlimited liability partnership

FAST FORWARD

Partnerships can be **formed** very informally, but there may be complex formalities to ensure clarity.

Under the Partnership Act 1890 (HMSO, 1890) a partnership can be a very **informal arrangement**. This is reflected in the procedure to form a partnership.

A partnership is **formed when two or more people agree to run a business together**. Partnerships can be formed in any trade or occupation or profession.

In order to be a partnership, the business must be **'carried on in common'**, meaning that all parties must have **responsibility** for the business. In other words, there is **more than one proprietor**. A husband and wife who run a shop together are partners, but a shop owner and their employee are not. In law then, the formation of a partnership is essentially straightforward. People **make an agreement** together to run a business, and **carry that agreement out**.

2.1 Common formation formalities

In practice, the formalities of setting up a partnership may be more **complex** than simple agreement. Many professional people use partnerships. These business associations can be vast organisations with substantial revenue and expenditure, such as the larger accountancy firms and many law firms.

Such organisations have so many partners that the relationships between them has to be **regulated**. Thus forming some partnerships can involve creating **detailed partnership agreements** which lay out terms and conditions of partnership.

2.2 The partnership agreement

A **written partnership agreement** is **not legally required**. In practice there are advantages in setting down, in writing, the terms of the partners' association.

(a)   It **fills** in the **details** which the law would not imply – the nature of the firm's business, its name, and the bank at which the firm will maintain its account, for instance.

(b)   A written agreement serves to **override terms**, otherwise implied by the Partnership Act 1890, which may be inappropriate to the partnership. The Act, for example, implies that partners share profits equally.

(c)   Additional clauses can be developed. **Expulsion clauses** are an example and they provide a mechanism to expel a partner, where there would be no ability to do so otherwise.

3 Terminating an unlimited liability partnership

FAST FORWARD

Partnerships may be **terminated** by passing of time, termination of the underlying venture, death or bankruptcy of a partner, illegality, notice, agreement or by order of the court.

Termination is, quite simply, when the partnership comes to an end.

Illustration

Alison, Ben, Caroline and David are in partnership as accountants. Caroline decides to change career and become an interior designer. In her place, Alison, Ben and David invite Emily to join the partnership.

As far as third parties are concerned, a partnership offering accountancy services still exists. In fact, however, the old partnership (ABCD) has been dissolved, and a new partnership (ABDE) has replaced it.

3.1 Events causing termination

The **Partnership Act 1890** (HMSO, 1890) states that partnership is terminated in the following instances.

- **Passing of time**, if the partnership was entered into for a fixed term
- **Termination of the venture**, if entered into for a single venture
- The **death or bankruptcy** of a partner (partnership agreement may vary this)
- **Subsequent illegality**
- **Notice** given by a partner, if it is a partnership of indefinite duration
- **Order of the court** granted to a partner
- **Agreement** between the partners

In the event of the **termination** of a partnership, the partnership's **assets are realised** and the proceeds applied in this order.

- Paying off **external debts**
- Repaying to the **partners** any **loans** or **advances**
- Repaying the partners' **capital contribution**
- Anything left over is then **repaid** to the **partners** in the **profit-sharing ratio**

The partnership agreement can exclude some of these provisions and can **avoid dissolution** in the following circumstances.

- **Death** of a partner
- **Bankruptcy** of a partner

It is wise to make such provisions to give **stability** to the partnership.

4 Authority of partners in an unlimited liability partnership

FAST FORWARD

> The **authority** of partners to bind each other in contract is based on the principles of agency.

In simple terms, a partner is the **agent of the partnership and their co-partners**. This means that some of their acts bind the other partners, either because they have, or because they appear to have, authority. The **Partnership Act 1890** (HMSO, 1890) **defines** the **authority** of a partner to make contracts as follows.

Authority of a partner

Every partner is an **agent** of the firm and their other partners for the purpose of the business of the partnership, and the acts of every partner who does any act for carrying on the **usual way** of business if the kind carried on by the firm of which they are a member **bind the firm** and their partners, **unless** the partner so acting has **in fact no authority** to act for the firm in the particular matter, **and the person with whom they are dealing** either **knows that they have no authority**, or **does not know or believe them to be a partner**.

Where a partner pledges the credit of the firm for a **purpose apparently not connected** with the firm's ordinary course of business, the **firm is not bound, unless** they are in fact **specially authorised** by the other partners: but this section does not affect any personal liability incurred by an individual.

If it has been **agreed between the partners** that any **restriction** shall be placed on the power of any one or more of them to bind the firm, **no act** done in contravention of the agreement is **binding** on the firm with respect to **persons having notice of the agreement**.

The key point to note about authority of partners is that, other than when the partner has actual authority, the authority often **depends on the perception of the third party**. If the third party genuinely believes that the partner has authority, the partner is likely to bind the firm.

Partners are also **jointly liable** for **crimes** and **torts** committed by one of their number in the course of business.

5 Liability of partners in an unlimited liability partnership

Partners are **jointly liable** for all partnership debts that result from contracts that the partners have made which bind the firm.

Under the **Partnership Act 1890** (HMSO, 1890), partners are **jointly liable** for all partnership debts that result from contracts made by other partners which bind the firm. The **Civil Liability (Contribution) Act 1978** (HMSO, 1978) provides that judgement against one partner does not prevent subsequent actions against other partners. The link between authority and liability can be seen in the following diagram.

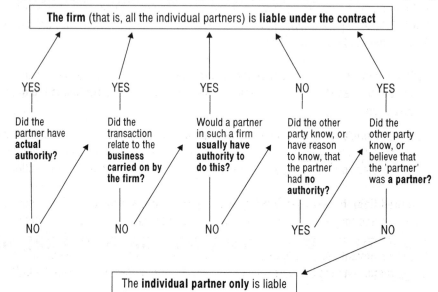

There are particular rules on liability for new and retiring partners.

Partner	Partner liability
New partners	A new partner admitted to an existing firm is liable for **debts incurred** only **after** they become a partner. They are not liable for debts incurred before they were a partner unless they agree to become liable.
Retiring partners	A partner who retires is still **liable** for any **outstanding debts** incurred while they were a partner, unless the creditor has agreed to release them from liability. They are also **liable** for debts of the firm **incurred after their retirement** if the creditor knew them to be a partner (before retirement) and has not had **notice** of their retirement. Therefore, it is **vital** on retirement that a partner **gives notice** to all the creditors of the firm. The retiring partner may have an indemnity from the remaining partners with respect to this issue.

5.1 Supervision and regulation

There is **no formal statutory supervision** or **regulation** of partnerships. Their accounts need not be in prescribed form nor is an audit necessary. The public has no means or legal right of inspection of the firm's accounts or other information such as companies must provide. If, however, the partners carry on business under a firm name which is not the surnames of them all, say, 'Smith, Jones & Co', they are required to disclose the **names** of the **partners** on their letterheads and at their places of business. They are required to make a **return** of their **profits** for income tax and **usually** to **register** for VAT.

5.2 Property

Partnerships **can** grant a **mortgage** or **fixed charge** over property, but **cannot** grant **floating changes**.

6 Limited liability partnerships

FAST FORWARD

A limited liability partnership combines the features of a traditional partnership with the limited liability and creation of legal personality more usually associated with limited companies.

6.1 Definition of limited liability partnership

Another form of partnership commonly used in England, particularly for professional partnerships, is the **limited liability partnership (LLP)**. This type of business association was created by the Limited Liability Partnership Act 2000 (TSO, 2000).

LLPs are similar to limited companies in that they have separate legal identity and unlimited liability for debts, but the liability of the individual partners (or members) is **limited to the amount of their capital contribution**.

LLPs have similar requirements for **governance** and **accountability** as limited companies. They are generally set up by firms of professionals such as accountants and lawyers, who are required by the rules of their professions to operate as partnerships but who seek to have the protection of limited liability.

Key term

> A **limited liability partnership (LLP)** is a corporate body which has separate legal personality from its members and therefore some of the advantages and disadvantages of a company.

The **main advantage of an LLP** over a traditional partnership is that the LLP will be liable for its own debts, rather than the partners. All contracts with third parties will be with the LLP.

6.2 Formation

A limited liability partnership may be formed by persons associating to carry on lawful business with a view to profit, but it **must be incorporated** to be recognised. LLPs can have an unlimited number of partners. To be incorporated, the subscribers must send an **incorporation document** and a **statement of compliance** to the Registrar of Companies.

The **document must be signed** and **state** the following:

- The **name** of the LLP
- The **location** of its **registered office** (England and Wales/Wales/Scotland)
- The **address** of the registered office
- The name and address of all the **members** of the LLP
- Which of the members are to be **designated members**

A **registration fee** is also payable to Companies House.

6.3 Internal regulation

LLPs are more **flexible** than companies as they provide **similar protection** for the owners, but **with less statutory rules** on areas such as meetings and management. No board of directors is needed. As can be seen in the incorporation procedures, LLPs come under the supervision of the **Registrar of Companies** (the Registrar). The members of the LLP are those who **subscribe** to the original incorporation document, and those admitted afterwards in accordance with the terms of the partnership agreement.

The **rights and duties** of the **partners** will usually be set out in a **partnership agreement**. In the absence of a partnership agreement, the rights and duties are set out in regulations under the Act. LLPs must have **two designated members**, who take responsibility for the publicity requirements of the LLP.

Examples of **duties** of an LLP's **designated members** include:

- **Filing** certain notices with the Registrar, such as when a member leaves and the Register of People With Significant Interest

- Signing and filing **accounts**

- Appointing **auditors** if appropriate

The Registrar will maintain a file containing the **publicised documents** of the LLP at Companies House.

6.4 External relationships

Every member is an **agent** of the LLP. As such, where the member has authority, the LLP will be bound by the acts of the member.

The **LLP will not be bound by the acts of the member where:**

- They have no authority and the third party is aware of that fact
- They have ceased to be a member, and the third party is aware of that fact

6.5 Dissolution

An LLP **does not dissolve when a member leaves** in the same way that a traditional partnership does. Where a member has died or (for a corporate member) been wound up, that member ceases to be a member, but the LLP continues in existence.

An **LLP must therefore be wound up** when the time has come for it to be dissolved. This is achieved under provisions **similar to company winding-up** provisions.

6.6 Limited partnership

The other form of partnership that is seen, rarely, in the UK is the **limited partnership**. Under the Limited Partnership Act 1907 (HMSO, 1907), a partnership may be formed in which at least one partner (the general partner) must have **full, unlimited liability**. The other partners have **limited liability** for the debts of the partnership beyond the extent of the capital they have contributed. The rules are as follows:

- Limited partners may not withdraw their capital

- Limited partners may not take part in the management of the partnership

- Limited partners cannot bind the partnership in a contract with a third party without losing the benefit of limited liability

- The partnership must be registered with Companies House

Exam focus point

Partnership questions in scenarios often revolve around a partner's authority to enter into contracts and the liability of all the partners when debts are incurred.

Chapter Roundup

- **Partnership** is defined as 'the relation which subsists between persons carrying on a business in common with a view of profit'. A partnership is **not** a separate legal person distinct from its members, it is merely a 'relation' between persons. Each partner (there must be at least two) is **personally liable** for all the debts of the firm.

- **'Person'** includes a corporation such as a **registered company** as well as an **individual** living person.

- Partnerships can be **formed** very informally, but there may be complex formalities to ensure clarity.

- Partnerships may be **terminated** by passing of time, termination of the underlying venture, death or bankruptcy of a partner, illegality, notice, agreement or by order of the court.

- The **authority** of partners to bind each other in contract is based on the principles of agency.

- Partners are **jointly liable** for all partnership debts that result from contracts that the partners have made which bind the firm.

- **A limited liability partnership** combines the features of a traditional partnership with the limited liability and creation of a legal personality more usually associated with limited companies.

Quick Quiz

1   Which one of the following statements about traditional (unlimited) partnerships is **incorrect**?

   A   In England a partnership has no existence distinct from the partners.
   B   A partnership must have a written partnership agreement.
   C   A partnership is subject to the Partnership Act.
   D   Each partner is an agent of the firm.

2   An LLP dissolves when a member leaves.

   True   ☐

   False   ☐

3   Which one of the following statements about the liability of a new partner in a partnership is **correct**?

   A   New partners automatically assume liability for existing partnership debts when they join the firm and for new debts incurred after they join
   B   New partners are only liable for partnership debts that they personally authorise
   C   New partners are not liable for existing partnership debts when they join but are liable for new partnership debts incurred after they join
   D   New partners become liable for new partnership debts when they meet the creditors personally

4   It is the LLP itself, rather than the partners personally, that enjoys the benefit of limited liability.

   True   ☐

   False   ☐

5   There is no legal requirement for an LLP to be audited.

   True   ☐

   False   ☐

Answers to Quick Quiz

1   B. A written agreement is not needed.

2   False. LLPs are only dissolved when they cease to trade.

3   C. New partners are only liable for partnership debts incurred after they join a firm.

4   False. It is the partners of an LLP that enjoy limited liability.

5   False. An LLP may be required to appoint auditors if it fulfils certain criteria.

Now try the questions below from the Practice Question Bank

Number
24, 25

12

Corporations and legal personality

Topic list	Syllabus reference
1 Sole traders' and companies' legal identities	D3(a)
2 Limited liability of members	D3(b)
3 Types of company	D3(c)
4 Additional classifications	D3(c)
5 Effect of legal personality	D3(d)
6 Ignoring separate personality	D3(e)
7 Comparison of companies and partnerships	D3(a)

Introduction

Companies, as business vehicles, are distinct from sole traders and partnerships. The key difference between them is the concept of **separate legal personality**. This chapter outlines this doctrine, and also discusses its implications (primarily **limited liability** for members) and the exceptions to it (lifting the **veil of incorporation**).

The Companies Act 2006 (TSO, 2006) and the Small Business, Enterprise and Employment Act 2015 (TSO, 2015) apply to this and all chapters from this point onwards unless otherwise stated.

Study guide

		Intellectual level
D	**The formation and constitution of business organisations**	
3	**Corporations and legal personality**	
(a)	Distinguish between sole traders, partnerships and companies	1
(b)	Explain the meaning and effect of limited liability	2
(c)	Analyse different types of companies, especially private and public companies	2
(d)	Illustrate the effect of separate personality and the veil of incorporation	2
(e)	Recognise instances where separate personality will be ignored (lifting the veil of incorporation)	2

Exam guide

You must be able to compare and contrast companies and partnerships, and to identify which business vehicle would be the best form of business organisation in a particular situation.

Two articles on the Companies Act 2006 appeared in *Student Accountant* and are available on the ACCA website.

1 Sole traders' and companies' legal identities

FAST FORWARD

In a **sole tradership**, there is no legal distinction between the individual and the business.

1.1 Sole traders

A **sole trader owns** and **runs a business**. They contribute capital to start the enterprise, run it with or without employees, and earn the profits or stand the losses of the venture.

Sole traders are found mainly in the **retail trades** (local newsagents), **small-scale service industries** (plumbers), and **small manufacturing** and **craft industries**. An accountant may operate as a sole trader.

1.2 Legal status of the sole trader

While the business is a separate accounting entity the business is **not legally distinct** from the person who owns it. In law, the person and the business are viewed as the same entity.

The **advantages** of being a sole trader are as follows.

(a) **No formal procedures** are required to set up in business. However, for certain classes of business a licence may be required (eg retailing wines and spirits), and VAT registration is often necessary.

(b) **Independence** and **self-accountability**. A sole trader does not need to consult anybody about business decisions and is not required to reveal the state of the business to anyone (other than the tax authorities each year).

(c) **Personal supervision** of the business by the sole trader should ensure its effective operation. Personal contact with customers may enhance commercial flexibility.

(d) **All** the **profits** of the business **accrue** to the sole trader. This can be a powerful motivator, and satisfying to the individual whose ability/energy results in reward.

The **disadvantages** of being a sole trader include the following.

(a) If the business gets into debt, a sole trader's **personal wealth** (for example, private house) might be lost if the debts are called in, as they are the same legal entity.

(b) Expansion of the business is usually only possible by **ploughing back** the **profits** of the business as further capital, although loans or overdraft finance may be available.

(c) The business has a **high dependence** on the **individual** which can mean long working hours and difficulties during sickness or holidays.

(d) The **death** of the proprietor may make it **necessary** to **sell** the **business** in order to pay the resulting tax liabilities, or family members may not wish to continue the business anyway.

(e) The **individual** may **only have one skill**. A sole trader may be, say, a good technical engineer or craftsman but may lack the skills to market effectively or to maintain accounting records to control the business effectively.

(f) Other **disadvantages** include lack of diversification, absence of economies of scale and problems of raising finance.

1.3 Companies

FAST FORWARD

A company has a **legal personality** separate from its owners (known as members). It is a formal arrangement, surrounded by formality and publicity, but its chief advantage is that members' **liability** for the company's debts is typically **limited**.

A company is the most popular form of **business association** and, by its nature, it is more **formal** than a partnership or a sole trader. There is often substantially **more legislation** on the formation and procedures of companies than any other business association.

The key reason why the company is a popular form of business association is that the **liability of its members to contribute to the debts of the entity is significantly limited**. For many people, this benefit outweighs the disadvantage of the formality surrounding companies, and encourages them not to trade as sole traders or (unlimited) partnerships.

Exam focus point

A two-part article titled 'The Companies Act 2006' was included in *Student Accountant* and is available on the ACCA website.

1.4 Definition of a company

Key terms

For the purposes of this Study Text, a **company** is an entity registered as such under the Companies Act 2006.

The key feature of a company is that it has a **legal personality** (existence) distinct from its members and directors.

1.5 Legal personality

A person possesses **legal rights** and is subject to **legal obligations**. In law, the term 'person' is used to denote two categories of legal person.

- An individual human being is a **natural person**. A sole trader is a natural person, and there is legally no distinction between the individual and the business entity in sole tradership.

- The law also recognises **artificial persons** in the form of companies and limited partnerships. Unlimited partnerships are not artificial persons.

> **Corporate personality** is a common law principle that grants a company a legal identity, separate from the members who comprise it. It follows that the property of a company belongs to that company; debts of the company must be satisfied from the assets of that company; and the company has perpetual succession until wound up.

A corporation is a **legal entity** separate from the natural persons connected with it, for example as members or directors.

2 Limited liability of members

> The fact that a company's members – not the company itself – have **limited liability** for its debts **protects the members** from the company's creditors and ultimately from the full risk of business failure.

A key consequence of the fact that the company is distinct from its members is that its members have **limited liability**.

> **Limited liability** is a protection offered to members of certain types of company. In the event of business failure, the members will only be asked to contribute identifiable amounts to the assets of the business.

2.1 Protection for members against creditors

The **company** itself is **liable without limit for its own debts**. If the company buys plastic from another company, for example, it owes the other company money.

Limited liability is a benefit to members. They own the business, so might be the people whom the creditors logically ask to pay the debts of the company if the company is unable to pay them itself.

Limited liability prevents this by stipulating the **creditors** of a limited company **cannot demand payment of the company's debts** from members of the company.

2.2 Protection from business failure

As the company is liable for all its own debts, limited liability only becomes an issue in the event of a business failure when the **company is unable to pay its own debts**.

This will result in the **winding up** of the company and enables the creditors to be paid from the proceeds of any assets remaining in the company. It is at winding up that limited liability becomes most relevant.

2.3 Members asked to contribute identifiable amounts

Although the creditors of the company cannot ask the members of the company to pay the debts of the company, there are some amounts that **members are required to pay in the event of a winding up**.

Type of company	Amount owed by member at winding up
Company limited by shares	Any **outstanding amount** from when they originally purchased their shares from the company
	If the member's shares are fully paid, they **do not have to contribute anything in the event of a winding up**
Company limited by guarantee	The **amount they guaranteed** to pay in the event of a winding up

2.4 Liability of the company for tort and crime

As a company has a **separate legal identity**, it may also have liabilities in **tort** and **crime**. Criminal liability of companies in particular is a topical area, but is outside the scope of your syllabus.

3 Types of company

Most companies are those **incorporated** under the **Companies Act 2006** (TSO, 2006). However, there are other types of company such as **corporations sole**, **chartered corporations**, **statutory corporations** and **community interest companies**.

Corporations are **classified** in one of the following categories.

Categories	Description
Corporations sole	A corporation sole is an **official position** which is filled by one person who is replaced from time to time. The Public Trustee and the Treasury Solicitor are corporations sole.
Chartered corporations	These are usually **charities** or bodies such as the Association of Chartered Certified Accountants, formed by Royal Charter.
Statutory corporations	Statutory corporations are formed by special Acts of Parliament. This method is little used now, as it is slow and expensive. It was used in the nineteenth century to form railway and canal companies.
Registered companies	Registration under the Companies Act is the normal method of incorporating a commercial concern. Any body of this type is properly called a company.
Community Interest Companies (CICs)	A special form of company for use by 'social' enterprises pursuing purposes that are beneficial to the community, rather than the maximisation of profit for the benefit of owners, created by the Companies (Audit, Investigation and Community Enterprise) Act 2004 (TSO, 2004).

3.1 Limited companies

The meaning of limited liability has already been explained. It is the **member**, not the company, whose liability for the company's debts may be limited.

3.1.1 Liability limited by shares

Liability is usually **limited by shares**. This is the position when a company which has share capital states in its constitution that 'the liability of members is limited'.

3.1.2 Liability limited by guarantee

Alternatively a company may be **limited by guarantee.** Its constitution states the amount which each member **undertakes** to **contribute** in a winding up (also known as a liquidation). A creditor has no direct claim against a member under their guarantee, nor can the company require a member to pay up under their guarantee until the company goes into liquidation.

Companies limited by guarantee are appropriate to **non-commercial activities**, such as a charity or a trade association which is non-profit making but wishes to have a form of reserve capital if it becomes insolvent. They do not have **share capital**.

3.2 Unlimited liability companies

Key term

An **unlimited liability company** is a company in which members do not have limited liability. In the event of business failure, the liquidator can require members to contribute as much as may be required to pay the company's debts in full.

An unlimited company **can only be a private company**; by definition, a **public company is always limited**. An unlimited company need not **file** a copy of its **annual accounts** and reports with the Registrar, unless during the relevant accounting reference period:

(a)   It is (to its knowledge) a **subsidiary** of a limited company.

(b)   **Two** or more **limited companies** have **exercised rights** over the **company**, which (had they been exercised by only one of them) would have **made** the **company** a **subsidiary** of that one company.

(c)   It is the **parent company** of a limited liability company.

The unlimited company certainly has its uses. It provides a **corporate body** (a separate legal entity) which can conveniently hold assets to which liabilities do not attach.

3.3 Public and private companies

FAST FORWARD

A company may be **private** or **public**. Only the latter may offer its share to the public.

Key terms

> A **public company** is a company whose constitution states that it is public and that it has complied with the registration procedures for such a company.
>
> A **private company** is a company which has not been registered as a public company under the Companies Act. The major practical distinction between a private and public company is that the former may not offer its securities to the public.

A **public** company is a company registered as such under the Companies Act with the Registrar. **Any company not registered as public is a private company**. A public company may be one which was **originally incorporated** as a public company or one which re-registered as a public company having been previously a private company.

3.4 Conditions for being a public company

FAST FORWARD

To trade, a public company must hold a **Registrar's trading certificate** having met the requirements, including **minimum capital** of **£50,000**.

3.4.1 Registrar's trading certificate

Before it can trade a company originally incorporated as a public company must have a **trading certificate** issued by the Registrar. The conditions for this are:

*   The **name** of the company identifies it as a public company by ending with the words 'public limited company' or 'plc'; or their Welsh equivalent, 'ccc', for a Welsh company.

*   The **constitution** of the company states 'the company is a public company' or words to that effect.

*   The **allotted share capital** of the company is at least the authorised minimum, which is £50,000.

*   It is a **company** limited by shares.

With regard to the **minimum share capital** of £50,000.

*   A company originally incorporated as a public company will not be permitted to trade until its **allotted** share capital is at least £50,000.

*   A private company which re-registers as a public company will not be permitted to trade until it has **allotted** share capital of at least £50,000; this needs only be paid up to one-quarter of its nominal value (plus the whole of any premium).

*   A private company which has share capital of £50,000 or more may, of course, continue as a private company; it is always **optional** to become a public company.

A **company limited by guarantee** which has no share capital, and an **unlimited company**, **cannot** be **public companies**.

3.4.2 Minimum membership and directors

A **public company** must have a minimum of **one member**. This is the same as a private company. However, unlike a private company it must have at least **two directors**. A private company must have at least one. Directors do not usually have liability for the company's debts.

3.5 Private companies

A **private company** is the **residual category** and so does not need to satisfy any special conditions. They are generally small enterprises in which some if not all shareholders are also directors and **vice versa**. Ownership and management are combined in the same individuals.

Therefore, it is unnecessary to impose on the directors complicated restrictions to safeguard the interests of members and so the number of rules that apply to public companies are reduced for private companies.

3.6 Differences between private and public companies

FAST FORWARD

The main differences between public and private companies relate to: **capital**; **dealings** in **shares**; **accounts**; **commencement of business**; **general meetings**; **names**; **identification**; and **disclosure requirements**.

The more **important differences** between public and private companies relate to the following factors.

3.6.1 Capital

The **main differences** are:

(a)   There is a minimum amount of **£50,000** for a **public company**, but **no minimum** for a **private** company.

(b)   A public company may **raise capital** by **offering** its **shares** or debentures to the public; a **private** company is **prohibited** from doing so.

(c)   Both **public** and **private companies** must generally **offer** to **existing members first** any ordinary shares to be allotted for cash. However, a **private** company **may permanently disapply** this rule.

3.6.2 Dealings in shares

Only a **public company** can obtain a listing for its shares on the **stock exchange** or other investment exchange. To obtain the advantages of listing, the company must agree to elaborate conditions contained in particulars in a **listing agreement** with the stock exchange. However, not all public companies are listed.

3.6.3 Accounts

(a)   A **public company** has **six months** from the end of its accounting reference period in which to produce its statutory audited accounts. The period for a **private company** is **nine months**.

(b)   A **private** company, if qualified by its size, may have **partial exemption** from various **accounting provisions**. These exemptions are not available to a public company or to its subsidiaries (even if they are private companies).

(c)   A **listed public company** must publish its full accounts and reports on its **website**.

(d)   **Public companies** must **lay their accounts** and reports before a **general meeting annually**. Private companies have no such requirement.

3.6.4 Commencement of business

A **private** company can commence business **as soon** as it is **incorporated**. A **public** company, if incorporated as such, must first **obtain a trading certificate from the Registrar**.

3.6.5 General meetings

Private companies are not required to hold annual general meetings (AGMs). **Public companies** must hold one within six months of their financial year end.

3.6.6 Names and identification

The **rules on identification** as public or private are as follows.

* The word **'limited'** or **'Ltd'** in the name denotes a private company; **'public limited company'** or **'plc'** must appear at the end of the name of a public company.

* The **constitution** of a **public** company must state that it is a public company. A **private company** should be identified as private.

3.6.7 Disclosure requirements

There are **special disclosure and publicity requirements** for public companies.

The **main advantage** of carrying on business through a public, rather than a private, company is that a public company, by the issue of listing particulars, may obtain a **listing** on the stock exchange and so mobilise capital from the investing public generally.

Attention!

There is an important distinction between public companies and **listed public companies**. Listed (or quoted) companies are those which trade their shares (and other securities) on stock exchanges. Not all public companies sell their shares on stock exchanges (although, in law, they are entitled to sell their shares to the public). **Private** companies are not entitled to sell shares to the public in this way.

In practice, only public companies meeting certain criteria would be allowed to obtain such a listing by the stock exchange.

Private companies may be broadly **classified** into two groups: **independent** (also called **free-standing)** private companies and **subsidiaries** of other companies.

4 Additional classifications

FAST FORWARD

There are a number of other ways in which companies can be **classified**.

4.1 Parent (holding) and subsidiary companies

There is a distinction between an 'accounting' definition of a parent company, and a 'legal' definition under the Companies Act 2006 (TSO, 2006). A company will be the **parent** (or **holding) company** of another company, its **subsidiary company**, if any of the rules apply.

Key term

Parent company

(a)   It holds a **majority of the voting rights** in the subsidiary.

(b)   **It is a member of the subsidiary and has the right to appoint or remove a majority of its board of directors**.

(c)   **It has the right to exercise a dominant influence over the subsidiary**:

    (i)   By virtue of provisions contained in the subsidiary's articles
    (ii)   By virtue of a control contract

(d)   **It is a member of the subsidiary and controls alone**, under an agreement with other members, **a majority of the voting rights in the company.**

(e)   **A company is also a parent if:**

   (i)   It has the power to exercise, or actually exercises, a dominant influence or control over the subsidiary.

   (ii)   It and the subsidiary are managed on a unified basis.

(f)   **A company is also treated as the parent of the subsidiaries of its subsidiaries.**

A company (A Ltd) is a **wholly owned subsidiary** of another company (B Ltd) if it has no other members except B Ltd and its wholly owned subsidiaries, or persons acting on B Ltd's or its subsidiaries' behalf.

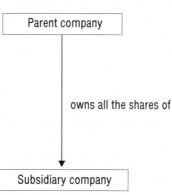

The diagram illustrates a **simple group**. In practice, such groups might be much larger and much more complex.

The **importance** of the **parent** and **subsidiary company relationship** is recognised in company law in a number of rules.

(a)   A parent company must generally prepare **group accounts** in which the financial situation of parent and subsidiary companies is consolidated as if they were one person.

(b)   A subsidiary may **not ordinarily be a member** of its parent company.

(c)   Since directors of a parent company can **control** its **subsidiary**, some rules designed to regulate the dealings of companies with directors also apply to its subsidiaries, particularly loans to directors.

PO7 requires you to prepare financial statements in accordance with legal and regulatory requirements. This section will help you to identify whether a group (or combined entity) exists. This should assit you in preparing financial statements which are appropriate to the type of entity concerned.

4.2 Quoted companies

As we have seen, public companies may seek a listing on a **public exchange**. This option is not open to private companies, who are not allowed to offer their shares for sale to the public. Listed companies are sometimes referred to as **quoted companies** (because their shares are quoted publicly).

4.3 Small companies regime

Small companies benefit from the **small companies regime's** reduced legal requirements in terms of filing accounts with the Registrar and obtaining an audit. The definitions of a small company for the purposes of accounting and auditing are almost identical.

In **accounting terms**, a company is small if it meets two of the following applicable criteria:

(a)   Balance sheet total of not more than £5.1 million
(b)   Turnover of not more than £10.2 million
(c)   50 employees or fewer on average

For **audit purposes**, a company is classed as small if it qualifies on the above criteria, but must **meet both** of conditions (a) and (b).

4.4 Micro-entities regime

A **micro-entity** has to option to take advantage of certain **accounting exemptions**. These include using **simple profit and loss accounts** and **balance sheets** and only providing a **minimum of accounting information** (referred to in the regulations as minimum accounting terms).

An **entity** is classed as **'micro'** if it meets at least **two** of the following **conditions**:

(a)   Annual turnover must be not more than £632,000
(b)   The balance sheet total must be not more than £316,000
(c)   The average number of employees must be not more than 10

4.5 Multinational companies

The vast majority of companies will simply operate in one country. However, some of the larger companies in the world will operate in more than one country. Such companies are **multinational**.

Key term

> A **multinational company** is a company that produces and markets its products in more than one country.

4.5.1 Examples: multinational companies

Some examples of well-known multinational companies are Walmart Stores, Royal Dutch Shell, Exxon Mobil and Toyota.

5 Effect of legal personality

FAST FORWARD

> The case of *Salomon v Salomon & Co Ltd 1897* clearly demonstrates the **separate legal personality** of companies.

Salomon v Salomon & Co Ltd 1897

The facts: The claimant, S, had carried on business for 30 years. He decided to form a limited company to purchase the business, so he and six members of his family each subscribed for one share.

The company then purchased the business from S for £38,782, the purchase price being payable to the claimant by way of the issue of 20,000 £1 shares, the issue of £10,000 of debentures and £8,782 in cash.

The company did not prosper and was wound up a year later, at which point its liabilities exceeded its assets. The liquidator, representing unsecured trade creditors of the company, claimed that the company's business was, in effect, still the claimant's (he owned 20,001 of 20,007 shares). Therefore he should bear liability for its debts and that payment of the debenture debt to him should be postponed until the company's trade creditors were paid.

Decision: The House of Lords held that the business was owned by, and its debts were liabilities of, the company. The claimant was under no liability to the company or its creditors, his debentures were validly issued and the security created by them over the company's assets was effective. This was because the company was a legal entity separate and distinct from S.

The **principle of separate legal personality** was confirmed in the following case.

Lee v Lee's Air Farming Ltd 1960

The facts: Mr Lee, who owned the majority of the shares of an aerial crop-spraying business, and was the sole working director of the company, was killed while piloting the aircraft.

Decision: Although he was the majority shareholder and sole working director of the company, he and the company were separate legal persons. Therefore he could also be an employee with rights against it when killed in an accident in the course of his employment.

The following is a more **recent case** on separate legal personality, which confirms the previous case law is still valid.

MacDonald v Costello 2011

The facts: Mr and Mrs Costello entered into an agreement with MacDonald (a firm of builders) to develop land which they owned. For tax purposes, the Costellos used a special purpose vehicle (Oakwood Residential Limited) to finance the work and the contract was between Oakwood and MacDonald. Oakwood had been used in previous dealings between the parties. Oakwood failed to pay some invoices when there was disagreement about the work which had been done. MacDonald was awarded a payment order against Oakwood and an award in restitution against the Costellos personally for unjust enrichment. The Costellos appealed the award for unjust enrichment.

Decision: Although the Costellos had been enriched by the work done by MacDonald, it was decided that the award against them should not be upheld. They were not party to the contract and, as shareholders of Oakwood, they were protected by the veil of incorporation.

5.1 Veil of incorporation

FAST FORWARD

> Incorporation 'veils' members from outsiders' view, but this veil may be lifted in **some circumstances** so creditors and others can seek redress directly from members. The veil may be lifted: by statute to enforce the law; to prevent the evasion of obligations; and in certain situations where companies trade as a group.

Because a company has **separate legal personality** from the people who own or run it (the members/shareholders/directors), people can look at a company and not know who or what owns or runs it.

The fact that members are 'hidden' in this way is sometimes referred to as the '**veil of incorporation**'. Literally, the members are 'veiled' from view.

6 Ignoring separate personality

FAST FORWARD

> It is sometimes necessary by law to look at who the owners of a company are. This is referred to as '**lifting the veil**'.

Separate personality can be **ignored** to:

- **Identify** the **company** with its **members** and/or directors
- Treat a **group of companies** as a **single commercial entity** (if a company is owned by another company)

The more important of these two reasons is the first one, although the second reason can sometimes be more complex. The main instances for lifting the veil are to **enforce the law**, **prevent evasion of obligations** and in some **group situations**. However, with the establishment of the concept of **corporate manslaughter** it is likely that directors will increasingly face prosecution and custodial sentences where they are found personally accountable for a death where the death can be connected with how they ran their business. The veil of incorporation will no longer protect them: *R v OLL Ltd 1994*.

6.1 Lifting the veil by statute to enforce the law

Lifting of the veil is **permitted under a number of statutes** to enforce the law.

6.1.1 Liability for trading without trading certificate

A public company must obtain a trading certificate from the Registrar before it may commence to trade. Failure to do so leads to **personal liability** of the directors for any loss or damage suffered by a third party resulting from a transaction made in contravention of the trading certificate requirement. They are also liable for a fine.

6.1.2 Fraudulent and wrongful trading

When a company is wound up, it may appear that its business has been carried on with **intent** to **defraud creditors** or others. In this case the court may decide under the Insolvency Act 1986 (HMSO, 1986) that the persons (usually the directors) who were knowingly parties to the **fraudulent trading** shall be **personally responsible** under civil law for debts and other liabilities of the company.

Fraudulent trading is also a criminal offence. Under the Companies Act 2006 (TSO, 2006) any person guilty of the offence, even if the company has not been, or is not being, wound up, is liable for a fine or imprisonment for up to ten years.

If a company in insolvency proceedings is found to have traded when there is no reasonable prospect of avoiding insolvent liquidation, its directors may be liable under civil law for **wrongful trading**. Under the Insolvency Act 1986 a court may order such directors to make a contribution to the company's assets.

6.1.3 Disqualified directors

Directors who participate in the management of a company in contravention of an order under the Company Directors Disqualification Act 1986 (HMSO, 1986) will be **jointly** or **severally liable** along with the company for the company's debts.

6.1.4 Abuse of company names

In the past there were a number of instances where directors of companies which went into **insolvent liquidation** formed another company with an identical or similar name. This new company bought the original company's business and assets from its liquidator.

The Insolvency Act 1986 makes it a criminal offence, and the directors personally liable, where they are a director of a company that goes into insolvent liquidation **and** they become involved with the directing, managing or promoting of a business which has an **identical name** to the original company, or a **name similar** enough to suggest a connection.

Exam focus point

Questions in this area may require the identification of circumstances where the veil of incorporation will be lifted.

6.2 Lifting the veil to prevent evasion of obligations

A company may be identified with those who control it, for instance to determine its residence for tax purposes. The courts may also ignore the distinction between a company and its members and managers if the latter use that distinction to **evade** their **existing legal obligations**.

> *Gilford Motor Co Ltd v Home 1933*
>
> *The facts:* The defendant had been employed by the claimant company under a contract which forbade him to solicit its customers after leaving its service. After the termination of his employment he formed a company of which his wife and an employee were the sole directors and shareholders. However he managed the company and through it evaded the covenant that prevented him from soliciting customers of his former employer.
>
> *Decision:* An injunction requiring observance of the covenant would be made both against the defendant and the company which he had formed as a 'a mere cloak or sham'.

6.2.1 Public interest

In time of war a company is not permitted to trade with '**enemy aliens**'. The courts may draw aside the veil if, despite a company being registered in the UK, it is suspected that it is controlled by aliens: *Daimler Co Ltd v Continental Tyre and Rubber Co (GB) Ltd 1916*. The question of nationality may also arise in peacetime, where it is convenient for a foreign entity to have a British **facade** on its operations.

> *Re F G Films Ltd 1953*
>
> *The facts:* An English company was formed by an American company to 'make' a film which would obtain certain marketing and other advantages from being called a British film. Staff and finance were American and there were neither premises nor employees in England. The film was produced in India.
>
> *Decision:* The British company was the American company's agent and so the film did not qualify as British. Effectively, the corporate entity of the British company was swept away and it was exposed as a 'sham' company.

6.2.2 Evasion of liabilities

The veil may also be lifted where directors **ignore** the separate legal personality of two companies and transfer assets from one to the other in disregard of their duties, in order to avoid an existing liability.

> *Re H and Others 1996*
>
> *The facts:* The court was asked to rule that various companies within a group, together with the minority shareholders, should be treated as one entity in order to restrain assets prior to trial.
>
> *Decision:* The order was granted. The court thought there was evidence that the companies had been used for the fraudulent evasion of excise duty.

6.2.3 Evasion of taxation

Courts may lift the veil of incorporation where it is being used to **conceal** the nationality of the company.

> *Unit Construction Co Ltd v Bullock 1960*
>
> *The facts:* Three companies, wholly owned by a UK company, were registered in Kenya. Although the companies' constitutions required board meetings to be held in Kenya, all three were, in fact, managed entirely by the holding company.
>
> *Decision:* The companies were resident in the UK and liable to UK tax. The Kenyan connection was a sham, the question being not where they ought to have been managed, but where they were actually managed.

6.2.4 Quasi-partnership

An application to wind up a company on the 'just and equitable' ground under the Insolvency Act 1986 may involve the court lifting the veil to reveal the company as a **quasi-partnership.** This may happen where the company only has a few members, all of whom are actively involved in its affairs. Typically the individuals have operated contentedly as a company for years but then fall out, and one or more of them seeks to remove the others.

The courts are willing in such cases to treat the **central relationship** between the directors as being that of partners, and rule that it would be unfair therefore to allow the company to continue with only some of its original members. This is illustrated by the case of *Ebrahimi v Westbourne Galleries Ltd 1973.*

6.3 Lifting the veil in group situations

The principle of the veil of incorporation extends to the holding (parent) company/subsidiary relationship. Although holding companies and subsidiaries are part of a group under company law, they retain their **separate legal personalities**. There is also some precedent for treating separate companies as a group (*DHN Food Distributors v Tower Hamlets LBC 1976)* although doubt has since been cast on this by subsequent cases.

In *Adams v Cape Industries plc 1990*, three reasons were put forward for identifying the companies as one, and lifting the veil of incorporation. They are:

- The subsidiary is acting as **agent** for the holding company.
- The group is to be treated as a **single economic entity** because of statutory provision.
- The **corporate structure** is being used as a **facade** (or sham) to conceal the truth.

Adams v Cape Industries plc 1990

The facts: Cape, an English company, headed a group which included many wholly owned subsidiaries. Some of these mined asbestos in South Africa, and others marketed the asbestos in various countries including the US.

Several hundred claimants had been awarded damages by a Texas court for personal injuries suffered as a result of exposure to asbestos dust. The defendants in Texas included one of Cape's subsidiaries, NAAC. The courts also considered the position of AMC, another subsidiary, and CPC, a company linked to Cape Industries.

Decision: The judgement would not be enforced against the English holding company, either on the basis that Cape had been 'present' in the US through its local subsidiaries or because it had carried on business in the US through the agency of NAAC. Slade LJ commented, in giving the judgement, that English law 'for better or worse recognises the creation of subsidiary companies ... which would fail to be treated as separate legal entities, with all the rights and liabilities which would normally be attached to separate legal entities'.

Whether desirable or not, English law allowed a group structure to be used so that legal liability fell on an individual member of a group rather than the group as a whole.

Exam focus point

Lifting the veil in group situations is easily forgotten. Ensure you know the *Cape Industries* case and the three reasons for lifting the veil in groups which it sets out.

6.4 Summary of situations in which the veil can be lifted

The instances in which the veil will be lifted are as follows.

Lifting the veil by statute to enforce the law	• Liability for trading without a trading certificate • Fraudulent and wrongful trading • Disqualified directors • Abuse of company names
Evasion of obligations	• Evasion of legal obligations • Public interest • Evasion of liabilities • Evasion of taxation • Quasi-partnership
Group situations	• Subsidiary acting as agent for the holding company • The group is to be treated as a single economic entity • The corporate structure is being used as a sham

6.5 Lifting the veil and limited liability

The above examples of lifting the veil include examples of where, if they have broken the law, **directors** can be made **personally liable** for a company's debts. This is very rare. If those directors are also members, then limited liability **does not apply**. This is the only time that limited liability is overridden and that the **member** becomes **personally liable** for the company's debts **due to their actions as a director**.

7 Comparison of companies and partnerships

FAST FORWARD

Because it is a separate legal entity, a company has a number of features which are different from a partnership. The most important difference between a company and a traditional partnership is that a company has a **separate legal personality** from its members, while a traditional partnership does not.

7.1 The differences

The **separate legal personality** of a company gives rise to a number of characteristics which mark it out from a traditional partnership. **Revise** this table when you have studied the rest of the book and know more of the details concerning the distinctive factors of companies.

Factor	Company	Traditional partnership
Entity	Is a legal entity separate from its members	Has no existence outside of its members
Liability	Members' liability can be limited	Partners' liability is usually unlimited
Size	May have any number of members (at least one)	Some partnerships are limited to 20 members (professional partnerships excluded)
Succession	Perpetual succession – change in ownership does not affect existence	Partnerships are dissolved when any partner leaves
Owners' interests	Members own transferable shares	Partners cannot assign their interests in a partnership
Assets	Company owns the assets	Partners own assets jointly
Management	Company must have at least one director (two for a public company)	All partners can participate in management
Constitution	Company must have a written constitution	A partnership may have a written partnership agreement, but also may not

Factor	Company	Traditional partnership
Accounts	A company must usually deliver accounts to the Registrar	Partners do not have to send their accounts to the Registrar
Security	A company may offer a floating charge over its assets	A partnership may not usually give a floating charge on assets
Withdrawal of capital	Strict rules concerning repayment of subscribed capital	More straightforward for a partner to withdraw capital
Taxation	Company pays tax on its profit Directors are taxed through PAYE system Shareholders receive dividends which are taxed ten months after the tax year	Partners extract 'drawings' weekly or monthly No tax is deducted as income tax is payable on final profit for the year
Management	Members elect directors to manage the company	All partners have a right to be involved in management

Chapter Roundup

- In a **sole tradership**, there is no legal distinction between the individual and the business.

- A company has a **legal personality** separate from its owners (known as members). It is a formal arrangement, surrounded by formality and publicity, but its chief advantage is that members' **liability** for the company's debts is typically **limited**.

- The fact that a company's members – not the company itself – have **limited liability** for its debts **protects** the **members** from the company's creditors and ultimately from the full risk of business failure.

- Most companies are those **incorporated** under the **Companies Act 2006** (TSO, 2006). However, there are other types of company such as **corporations sole, chartered corporations, statutory corporations** and **community interest companies**.

- A company may be **private** or **public**. Only the latter may offer its shares to the public.

- To trade, a public company must hold a **Registrar's trading certificate** having met the requirements, including **minimum capital** of **£50,000**.

- The main differences between public and private companies relate to: **capital**; **dealings** in **shares**; **accounts**; **commencement of business**; **general meetings**; **names**; **identification**; and **disclosure requirements**.

- There are a number of other ways in which companies can be **classified**.

- The case of *Salomon v Salomon & Co Ltd 1897* clearly demonstrates the **separate legal personality** of companies.

- Incorporation '**veils**' members from outsiders' view, but this veil may be lifted in **some circumstances** so creditors and others can seek redress directly from members. The veil may be lifted: by statute to enforce the law; to prevent the evasion of obligations; and in certain situations where companies trade as a group.

- It is sometimes necessary by law to look at who the owners of a company are. This is referred to as '**lifting the veil**'.

- Because it is a separate legal entity, a company has a number of features which are different from a partnership. The most important difference between a company and a traditional partnership is that a company has a **separate legal personality** from its members, while a traditional partnership does not.

1   Which two of the following statements are true? A private company…

   A   Is defined as any company that is not a public company

   B   Sells its shares on the junior stock market known as the Alternative Investment Market and on the Stock Exchange

   C   Must have at least one director with unlimited liability

   D   Is a significant form of business organisation in areas of the economy that do not require large amounts of capital

2   Under which circumstance would a member of a limited company have to contribute funds on winding up?

   A   Where there is not enough cash to pay the creditors
   B   Where they have an outstanding amount from when they originally purchased their shares
   C   To allow the company to repurchase debentures it issued
   D   Where the company is a community interest company and the funds are required to complete a community project

3   The minimum share capital of a public limited company is:

   A   £12,500
   B   £50,000
   C   £100,000
   D   £500,000

4   Which two of the following are correct? A public company or plc …

   A   Is defined as any company which is not a private company
   B   Has a legal personality that is separate from its members or owners
   C   Must have at least one director with unlimited liability
   D   Can own property and make contracts in its own name

5   Businesses in the form of sole traders are legally distinct from their owners.

   True   ☐

   False   ☐

1   A and D are correct. A private company cannot sell its shares to the public on any stock market, so B is incorrect. Directors need not have unlimited liability, so C is incorrect.

2   B   Members only have a liability for any outstanding amounts of share capital partly paid for.

3   B   £50,000 is the minimum.

4   B and D are correct. A public company has to be defined as such in its constitution so A is incorrect. No directors **need** have unlimited liability, so C is incorrect.

5   False. Sole trader businesses are not legally distinct from their owners.

Now try the questions below from the Practice Question Bank

Number
26, 27

13

Company formation

Topic list	Syllabus reference
1 Promoters and pre-incorporation contracts	D4(a)
2 Pre-incorporation expenses and contracts	D4(b)
3 Registration procedures	D4(c)
4 Statutory books and records	D4(d)
5 Confirmation statements	D4(d)

Introduction

This chapter concentrates on the **procedural aspects** of **company formation**. Important topics in these sections include the **formalities** that a company must observe in order to be formed, and the liability of **promoters for pre-incorporation contracts**.

This chapter also considers the concept of the **public accountability** of **limited companies** in terms of the records they must keep and returns they must make.

Study guide

		Intellectual level
D	**The formation and constitution of business organisations**	
4	**The formation and constitution of a company**	
(a)	Explain the role and duties of company promoters, and the breach of those duties and remedies available to the company	2
(b)	Explain the meaning of, and the rules relating to, pre-incorporation contracts	2
(c)	Describe the procedure for registering companies, both public and private, including the system of streamlined company registration	1
(d)	Describe the statutory books, records and returns, including the confirmation statement and the register of people with significant control, that companies must keep or make	1

Exam guide

Questions could be set on the procedures that need to be followed in order to set up a private or public limited company. You may also be tested on the potential liability of a promoter.

1 Promoters and pre-incorporation contracts

FAST FORWARD

> A promoter **forms** a company. They must act with **reasonable skill** and **care**, and if shares are to be allotted they are the agent of the prospective shareholders, with an agent's fiduciary duties.

A company cannot form itself. The person who forms it is called a '**promoter**'. A promoter is an example of an **agent**.

Key term

> A **promoter** is one who undertakes to form a company with reference to a given project and to set it going and who takes the necessary steps to accomplish that purpose.

In addition to the person who takes the procedural steps to get a company incorporated, the term 'promoter' includes anyone who makes **business preparations** for the company. **However**, a person who acts **merely** in a **professional capacity** in company formation, such as a solicitor or an accountant, **is not** on that account a **promoter**.

1.1 Duties of promoters

Promoters have a general duty to exercise **reasonable skill and care**.

If the **promoter** is to be the **owner** of the company there is **no conflict of interest** and it does not matter if the promoter obtains some advantage from this position, for example, by selling their existing business to the company for 100% of its shares.

If, however, **some or all the shares** of the company when formed **are to be allotted to other people**, the promoter acts as their **agent**. This means the promoter has the customary **duties** of an agent and the following fiduciary duties.

(a) A promoter must account for any **benefits obtained** through acting as a promoter.

(b) Promoters must not put themselves in a position where their own **interests conflict** with those of the company.

(c)   A promoter must provide **full information** on their transactions and account for all monies arising from them. The promoter must therefore make **proper disclosure** of any personal advantage to **existing** and **prospective** company **members** or to an **independent board of directors**.

A promoter may make a **profit** as a result of their position.

(a)   A **legitimate** profit is made by a promoter who acquires interest in property **before promoting** a company and then makes a profit when they sell the property to the promoted company, provided they disclose it.

(b)   A **wrongful** profit is made by a promoter who enters into and makes a profit personally in a contract as a promoter. They are in breach of fiduciary duty.

A promoter of a public company makes their **disclosure of legitimate profit** through listing particulars or a prospectus. If they make proper disclosure of a legitimate profit, they may retain it.

1.1.1 Remedy for breach of promoter's fiduciary duty

If the promoter does not make a proper disclosure of legitimate profits, or if they make wrongful profits, the primary remedy of the company is to **rescind** the **contract** and **recover its money**: *Erlanger v New Sombrero Phosphate Co 1878*.

However, sometimes it is too late to rescind because the property can no longer be returned or the company prefers to keep it. In such a case the company can **only recover** from the promoter their **wrongful profit**, unless some special circumstances dictate otherwise.

Where shares are sold under a **prospectus offer**, promoters have a statutory liability to compensate any person (who acquires securities to which the prospectus relates) who suffered loss as a result of any untrue or misleading statement or omission. **Statutory** and **listing regulations**, together with **rigorous investigation** by merchant banks, have greatly lessened the problem of the dishonest promoter.

2 Pre-incorporation expenses and contracts

FAST FORWARD

A promoter has **no automatic right** to be reimbursed **pre-incorporation expenses** by the company, though this can be expressly agreed.

2.1 Pre-incorporation expenses

A promoter usually incurs **expenses** in preparations, such as drafting legal documents, made before the company is formed. They have **no automatic right to recover these** 'pre-incorporation expenses' from the company. However they can generally arrange that the first directors, of whom they may be one, **agree** that the company shall pay the bills or refund to them their expenditure. They could also include a special article in the company's constitution containing an indemnity for the promoter.

2.2 Pre-incorporation contracts

FAST FORWARD

Pre-incorporation contracts **cannot** be ratified by the company. A new contract on the same terms must be expressly created.

Key term

> A **pre-incorporation contract** is a contract purported to be made by a company or its agent at a time before the company has been formed.

In agency law a principal may ratify a contract made by an agent retrospectively. However, a company can **never ratify** a contract made on its behalf **before it was incorporated**. This is because it did not exist when the pre-incorporation contract was made, so one of the conditions for ratification fails.

A company may enter into a **new contract** on **the same or similar terms** after it has been incorporated (**novation**). However, there must be **sufficient evidence** that the company has made a new contract. Mere recognition of the pre-incorporation contract by performing it, or accepting benefits under it, is not the same as making a new contract.

2.3 Liability of promoters for pre-incorporation contracts

A company's **promoter** is **liable** on all contracts to which they are deemed to be a party. This means they may also be entitled to enforce such contracts against the other party and so they could transfer the right to **enforce** the contract to the company.

2.4 Other ways of avoiding liability as a promoter for pre-incorporation contracts

There are various other ways for **promoters** to **avoid liability** for a **pre-incorporation contract**.

(a) The contract remains as a **draft** (so not binding) until the company is formed. The promoters are the directors, and the company has the power to enter the contract. Once the company is formed, the directors take office and the company enters into the contract.

(b) If the contract has to be finalised before incorporation, it should contain a clause that the personal liability of promoters is to cease if the company, when formed, enters a **new contract** on identical terms. This is known as **novation**.

(c) A common way to avoid the problem concerning pre-incorporation contracts is to buy a company **'off the shelf'**. Even if a person contracts on behalf of the new company before it is bought, the company should be able to ratify the contract since it existed 'on the shelf' at the time the contract was made.

<table>
<tr><td>**Exam focus point**</td><td>You should consider the status of pre-incorporation contracts as a highly examinable topic.</td></tr>
</table>

3 Registration procedures

<table>
<tr><td>**FAST FORWARD**</td><td>A **company** is **formed and registered** under the Companies Act 2006 when it is issued with a **certificate of incorporation** by the Registrar, after submission to the Registrar of a number of documents and a fee.</td></tr>
</table>

Most companies are **registered** under the Companies Act 2006 (TSO, 2006).

A company is formed under the Companies Act 2006 by one or more persons **subscribing to a memorandum of association** who comply with the requirements regarding registration. A company may not be formed for an unlawful purpose.

3.1 Documents to be delivered to the Registrar

To obtain r**egistration** of a company limited by shares, an **application for registration**, **various documents** and a **fee** must be sent to the Registrar (usually electronically).

3.1.1 Application for registration

The Companies Act requires an **application for registration** to be made and submitted to the Registrar.

The **application** must contain:

- The company's **proposed name**
- The **location** of its **registered office** (England and Wales, Wales, Scotland or Northern Ireland)
- A statement that the **liability of members** is to be **limited** by **shares** or **guarantee**
- Whether the company is to be **private** or **public**
- A statement of the **intended address** of the **registered office**

Documents to be delivered	Description
Memorandum of association	This is a **prescribed form** signed by the subscribers. The memorandum states that the subscribers wish to form a company and they agree to become members of it. If the company has share capital each subscriber agrees to subscribe for at least one share.
Articles of association (only required if the company does not adopt model articles)	Articles are signed by the same subscriber(s), dated and witnessed. **Model articles** are provided by statute and can be adopted by a new company if: • No other articles are registered, or • If the articles supplied do not exclude or modify the model articles
Statement of proposed officers	The statement gives the particulars of the proposed **director(s)** and **company secretary** if applicable. The persons named as directors must consent to act in this capacity. When the company is incorporated they are deemed to be appointed.
Statement of compliance	The statement that the **requirements** of the **Companies Act** in respect of registration have been **complied** with.
Statement of capital and initial shareholdings (only required for companies limited by shares)	A statement of capital and initial shareholdings must be delivered by all companies with **share capital**. Alternatively, a statement of guarantee is required by companies limited by guarantee.
Registration fee	A **registration fee** is also payable on registration.

3.2 Certificate of incorporation

The Registrar considers whether the documents are formally in order. If satisfied, the company is given a **registered number**. A **certificate of incorporation is** issued and notice of it is publicised.

A company is registered by the inclusion of the company in the register, and the issue of a **certificate of incorporation** by the Registrar. The certificate:

- Identifies the company by its **name** and **registered number**
- States that it is **limited** (if appropriate) and whether it is a **private** or **public** company
- States whether the **registered office** is in England and Wales, Wales, Scotland or Northern Ireland
- States the **date of incorporation**
- Is **signed** by the **Registrar**, or authenticated by the Registrar's official seal

Key term

A **certificate of incorporation** is a certificate issued by the Registrar which denotes the date of incorporation, 'the subscribers, together with any persons who from time to time become members, become a body corporate capable of exercising all the functions of an incorporated company'.

The **certificate of incorporation** is **conclusive evidence** that:

- All the **requirements** of the **Companies Act** have been **followed**
- The company is a **company authorised** to be **registered** and has been **duly registered**
- If the certificate states that the company is a **public company** it is conclusive

If irregularities in formation procedure, or an error in the certificate itself, are later discovered, the certificate is nonetheless **valid** and **conclusive**: *Jubilee Cotton Mills Ltd v Lewes 1924.*

Upon incorporation persons named as **directors** and **secretary** in the statement of proposed officers automatically become such officers.

3.3 Companies 'off the shelf'

Buying a company 'off the shelf' avoids the administrative burden of registering a company.

Despite the **Small Business, Enterprise and Employment Act 2015** (TSO, 2015) introducing changes to streamline company administration, the registration of a new company can be a lengthy business and it is often easiest for people wishing to operate as a company to purchase an **'off-the-shelf' company**.

This is possible by contacting enterprises specialising in registering a **stock of companies**, ready for sale when a person comes along who needs the advantages of incorporation.

Normally the persons associated with the company formation enterprise are registered as the company's subscribers, and its first secretary and director. When the company is purchased, the **shares** are **transferred** to the **buyer**, and the Registrar is notified of the director's and the secretary's resignation.

The principal **advantages** for the purchaser of purchasing an off-the-shelf company are as follows.

(a)   The **following documents** will **not need** to be **filed** with the Registrar by the purchaser:

   (i)   Memorandum and articles (unless the articles are not model articles)
   (ii)   Application for registration
   (iii)   Statement of proposed officers
   (iv)   Statement of compliance
   (v)   Statement of capital and initial shareholdings
   (vi)   Fee

   This is because the specialist has already registered the company. It will therefore be a quicker, and very possibly cheaper, way of incorporating a business.

(b)   There will be **no risk** of **potential liability** arising from pre-incorporation contracts. The company can trade without needing to worry about waiting for the Registrar's certificate of incorporation.

The **disadvantages** relate to the changes that will be required to the off-the-shelf company to make it compatible with the members' needs.

(a)   The off-the-shelf company is likely to have **model articles**. The directors may wish to amend these.

(b)   The directors may want to **change** the **name** of the company.

(c)   The **subscriber shares** will need to be **transferred**, and the transfer recorded in the register of members. Stamp duty will be payable.

3.4 Re-registration procedures

A **private company** with share capital may be able to re-register as a **public company** if the share capital requirement is met. A public company may re-register as a private one.

Note. For a private company to re-register as a public company it must fulfil the share capital requirement of a public company: its allotted share capital must be at least £50,000, of which a quarter must be paid up, plus the whole of any premium.

	Re-registering as a public company	Re-registering as a private company
Resolution	The **shareholders must agree** to the company going public <ul><li>Convene a general meeting</li><li>Pass a **special resolution** (75% majority) – alters the constitution</li></ul>	The **shareholders must agree** to the company going private <ul><li>Convene a general meeting</li><li>Pass a **special resolution** (75% majority of those present and voting) – alters the constitution</li></ul>

	Re-registering as a public company	Re-registering as a private company

Application	The **company must** then **apply** to the Registrar to go public
	
	• Send application to the Registrar
	• Send additional information to the Registrar, comprising
	  – Copy of the special resolution
	  – Copy of proposed new public company articles
	  – Statement of the company's proposed name on re-registration
	  – Statement of proposed company secretary
	  – Balance sheet and related auditors' statement which states that at the balance sheet date the company's net assets are not less than its called-up share capital and undistributable reserves.
	  – Statement of compliance
	  – Valuation report regarding allotment of shares for non-cash consideration since the balance sheet date
		The **company must** then **apply** to the Registrar to go private
		
		• Send the application to the Registrar
		• Send additional information to the Registrar, comprising
		  – Copy of the special resolution
		  – Copy of altered new private company articles
		  – Statement of compliance
		  – Statement of the company's proposed name on re-registration

Approval	The Registrar must accept the statement of compliance as sufficient evidence that the company is entitled to be re-registered as public. A certificate of incorporation on re-registration is issued.	The Registrar issues a certificate of incorporation on re-registration.
Compulsory re-registration	If the **share capital** of a public company **falls below £50,000**, it must re-register as a private company.	There is **no such compulsion** for a private company.

3.4.1 Limited company to unlimited company re-registration

Although less common, it is also possible for a **private limited company to re-register as an unlimited**. This requires the **approval of all the members** of the company and is only permitted if the company has not previously re-registered as a limited company. On application to the Registrar, the company must submit its proposed name, the resolution, proposed new articles and a statement of compliance that the requirements for re-registration have been complied with.

3.4.2 Unlimited company to limited company re-registration

An **unlimited company may re-register as limited** if it passes a **special resolution** to that effect and is only permitted if the company has not previously re-registered as unlimited. The company should then apply to the Registrar, submitting a copy of the resolution (which must state whether the company is to be limited by shares or guarantee), its proposed name, a statement of guarantee (if the company is to be limited by guarantee), a statement of capital (if the company has share capital) and a statement of compliance that confirms the requirements for re-registration have been complied with.

3.5 Commencement of business rules

To **trade** or **borrow**, a public company needs a **trading certificate**. Private companies may commence business on **registration**.

3.5.1 Public companies

A **public company** incorporated as such may not do business or exercise any borrowing powers unless it has obtained a **trading certificate** from the Registrar. This is obtained by sending an application to the Registrar. A private company which is re-registered as a public company is not subject to this rule.

The **application**:

- States the nominal value of the allotted share capital is not less than £50,000, or prescribed euro equivalent
- States the particulars of preliminary expenses and payments or benefits to promoters
- Must be accompanied by a statement of compliance

If a public company does business or borrows before obtaining a certificate the other party is protected since the **transaction is valid**. However, the company and any officer in default have committed an offence **punishable** by a **fine**. They may also have to indemnify the third party.

Under the Insolvency Act 1986 (TSO, 1986) a court may **wind up** a public company which does not obtain a trading certificate within **one year** of incorporation.

3.5.2 Private company

A **private company** may do business and exercise its borrowing powers from the date of its incorporation. After registration the following procedures are important.

(a) A **first meeting** of the directors should be held at which the chairman, secretary and sometimes the auditors are appointed, shares are allotted to raise capital, authority is given to open a bank account and other commercial arrangements are made.

(b) A **return of allotments** should be made to the Registrar.

(c) The company may give notice to the Registrar of the **accounting reference date** on which its annual accounts will be made up. If no such notice is given within the prescribed period, companies are deemed to have an accounting reference date of the **last day of the month** in which the **anniversary of incorporation** falls.

4 Statutory books and records

4.1 The requirement for public accountability

The price of limited liability is greater **public accountability** via the Companies Registry, registers, the *London Gazette* and company letterheads.

Under company law the **privileges of trading** through a separate corporate body are matched by the duty to provide information which is available to the public about the company.

Basic sources of information on UK companies
The Registrar keeps a file at **Companies House** which holds all documents delivered by the company for filing. Any member of the public, for example someone who intends to do business with the company, may inspect the file (usually electronically).
The **registers and other documents** which the company is required to hold at its registered office (or another registered address).
The *London Gazette*, a specialist publication, in which the company itself or the Registrar is required to publish certain notices or publicise the receipt of certain documents.
The **company's letterheads** and other forms which must give particulars of the company's place of registration, its identifying number and the address of its office.

4.2 The Registrar of Companies

The **Registrar of Companies** (the Registrar) and the Registrar's department within the Government is usually called Companies House (in full it is 'the Companies Registration Office').

For **English** and **Welsh** companies the Registrar is located at Companies House in **Cardiff**; for **Scottish** companies the Registrar is in **Edinburgh**.

The company is identified by its **name** and **serial number** which must be stated on every document sent to Companies House for filing.

On incorporation, the company's file includes a copy of its **certificate of incorporation** and the **original documents** presented to secure its incorporation.

Once a company has been in existence for some time the **file is likely to include** the following.

- Certificate of incorporation
- Public company trading certificate
- Each year's annual accounts and return
- Copies of special and some ordinary resolutions
- A copy of the altered articles of association if relevant
- Notices of various events, such as a change of directors or secretary
- If a company issues a prospectus, a signed copy with all annexed documents

4.3 Statutory books

FAST FORWARD

A company must keep **registers** of certain aspects of its constitution, including the registers of members, and directors.

Under the Companies Act 2006 (TSO, 2006) various people are entitled to have access to **registers** and copies of records that the company must keep. To enable the documents to be found easily the company must keep them at its **registered office** or a **single alternative inspection location** (SAIL) which is registered with Companies House. All documents may be kept at either location or a combination of the two. Companies are not permitted to have more than one single alternative inspection location.

Private companies are permitted to file their registers of members, directors and secretaries, people with significant control (PSC) and directors' residential addresses at **Companies House** instead of a registered office or SAIL.

Register/copies of records
Register of **members**
Register of **people with significant control (PSC)**
Register of directors (and secretaries)
Register of **directors' residential addresses**

Register/copies of records
Records of **directors' service contracts and indemnities**
Records of **resolutions and meetings** of the company
Register of **debentureholders**
Register of disclosed **interests** in shares (public company **only**)

4.4 Register of members

Every company must keep a **register of members**. It must contain:

(a)   The **name** and **address** of **each member**

(b)   **The shareholder class** (if more than one) to which they belong, unless this is indicated in the particulars of their shareholding

(c)   If the company has a share capital, the **number of shares** held by each member. In addition:

   (i)   If the shares have **distinguishing numbers**, the member's shares must be identified in the register by those numbers

   (ii)   If the company has more than one class of share, the member's shares must be **distinguished** by their **class**, such as preference, ordinary, or non-voting shares

(d)   The date on which each member **became,** and eventually the date on which they **ceased** to be, a member

Any member of the company can inspect the **register of members** of a company without charge. A member of the public must pay but has the right of inspection. The right of inspection is subject to a number of criteria, including whether the person requesting the information has a **'proper purpose'** for that information. In *Fox-Davis v Burberry (2017),* it was held that a tracing agent (a person who traces lost members of public quoted companies) did not have a proper purpose for the information because they used it to charge the lost members a fee for reuniting them with the company they own shares in.

A company with more than **50 members** must keep a separate index of those members, unless the register itself functions as an index.

4.5 Register of people with significant control (PSC)

All private and public companies are required to keep a **register of people with significant control**. This register contains information on individuals who own or control over 25% of a company's shares or voting rights, or who exercise control over the company and its management in other ways (for example through the ability to appoint or remove directors).

The information which is required to be collected includes the individual's **name**, **date of birth**, **nationality** and **service address** and **details of their interest in the company**. Any changes to the PSC have to be notified to the Registrar within 14 days of the change. It an **offence** not to comply with the requirement to file this register.

4.6 Register of directors

The **register of directors** must contain the following details for all directors.

•   **Present** and **former** forenames and surnames

•   A **service address** (may be the company's registered address rather than their home address)

•   **Residency** and **nationality**

•   **Business occupation** (if any)

•   **Date of birth**

The register does not include shadow directors and it must be **open to inspection** by a member (free of charge), or by any other person (for a fee).

Note the company must keep a separate **register** of **directors' residential addresses** but this is not available to members or the general public.

4.7 Records of directors' service contracts

The company should keep **copies** or written memoranda of all **service contracts** for its directors, including contracts for services which are not performed in the capacity of director. Members are entitled to view these copies for free, or request a copy on payment of a set fee.

Key term

A director's **service contract** means a contract under which:

(a) A director of the company undertakes personally to perform services (as director or otherwise) for a company, or for a subsidiary of the company, or

(b) Services (as director or otherwise) that a director of the company undertakes personally to perform, that are made available by a third party to the company, or to a subsidiary of the company.

4.8 Register of debentureholders

Companies with debentures issued nearly always keep a **register of debentureholders** but there is no statutory compulsion to do so.

4.9 Accounting records

FAST FORWARD

Companies must keep **sufficient accounting records** to explain the company's transactions and its financial position, in other words so that a profit and loss account and balance sheet can be prepared.

A company is required to keep **accounting records** sufficient to **show and explain** the company's transactions. At any time, it should be possible:

- To **disclose** with reasonable accuracy the **company's financial position** at intervals of not more than six months

- For the directors to ensure that any accounts required to be prepared **comply** with the **Act** and **International Accounting Standards**

Certain **specific records** are required by the Act.

(a) Daily entries of **sums paid** and **received**, with details of the source and nature of the transactions

(b) A **record** of **assets** and **liabilities**

(c) **Statements of stock** held by the company at the end of each financial year

(d) **Statements of stocktaking** to back up the records in (c)

(e) **Statements of goods bought and sold** (except retail sales), together with details of buyers and sellers sufficient to identify them

The requirements (c) to (e) above apply only to businesses involved in **dealing in goods**.

Accounting records must be kept for **three** years in the case of a **private** company, and **six** years in that of a **public** one.

Accounting records should be kept at the company's **registered office** or at some other place thought fit by the directors. Accounting records should be open to **inspection** by the **company's officers**. Shareholders have **no statutory rights** to inspect the records, although they may be granted the right by the articles.

Failure in respect of these duties is an **offence** by the officers in default.

4.10 Annual accounts

A registered company must prepare **annual accounts** showing a true and fair view, lay them and various reports before members, and file them with the Registrar following directors' approval.

For each **accounting reference period** (usually 12 months) of the company the directors must prepare accounts. Where they are prepared in Companies Act format they must include a **balance sheet** and **profit and loss account** which give a **true and fair view** of the individual companies and the group.

- Assets
- Liabilities
- Financial position
- Profit or loss

The accounts can either be in **Companies Act format** or prepared in accordance with **International Accounting Standards (IAS)**. Where international accounting standards are followed, a note to this effect must be included in the notes to the accounts. Most private companies are permitted to file **abbreviated accounts**.

The company's board of directors must **approve** the **annual accounts** and they must be signed by a director on behalf of the board. If directors approve annual accounts that do not comply with the Act or IAS they are **guilty** of an **offence**.

A public company is required to **lay its accounts**, and the **directors' report**, before **members in general meeting**. A quoted company must also lay the directors' remuneration report before the general meeting.

A company must file its annual accounts and its report with the **Registrar** within a maximum period reckoned from the date to which the accounts are made up. The standard permitted interval between the end of the accounting period and the filing of accounts is **six months** for a **public** and **nine months** for a **private company**.

The accounts must be **audited**. The **auditors' report** must be attached to the copies issued to members, filed with the Registrar or published. Exemptions apply to **small and dormant companies**, though members may require an audit. The accounts must also be accompanied by a **directors' report** giving information on a number of prescribed matters. These include (where an audit was necessary) a statement that there is no relevant information of which the auditors are unaware, and another statement from the directors that they exercised due skill and care in the period. Quoted companies must submit the **directors' remuneration report**.

Under the Companies Act 2006 (Strategic Report and Directors' Report) Regulations 2013 (TSO, 2013), large companies must prepare a **strategic report** as part of their financial statements.

The purpose of the strategic report is to inform members of the company and help them **assess how the directors have performed** their duty to promote the success of the company.

The strategic report must contain a **fair review of the company's business**, and a description of the principal risks and uncertainties facing the company.

The review required is a **balanced and comprehensive analysis** of the development and performance of the company's business during the financial year, and the position of the company's business at the end of that year, consistent with the size and complexity of the business.

Each **member** and **debentureholder** is entitled to be sent a copy of the **annual accounts**, together with the directors' and auditor's reports. In the case of public companies, they should be sent at least 21 days before the meeting at which they shall be laid. In the case of private companies they should be sent at the same time as the documents are filed, if not earlier.

Anyone else entitled to **receive** notice of a general meeting, including the company's auditor, should **also receive** a copy. At any other time any member or debentureholder is entitled to a copy free of charge within **seven days** of requesting it.

All companies may prepare summary financial statements to be circulated to members instead of the full accounts, subject to various requirements as to form and content being met. However, members have the right to receive full accounts should they wish to.

Quoted companies must make their annual accounts and reports available on a website which identifies the company and is maintained on the company's behalf. The documents must be made available as soon as reasonably practicable and access should not be conditional on the payment of a fee nor subject to other restrictions.

Where the company or its directors **fail to comply** with the Act, they may be subject to a **fine**.

PO7 requires you to prepare financial statements in accordance with relevant accounting standards, policies and legislation. This section will help you understand some legal requirements relating to when the financial reports should be published and their contents.

5 Confirmation statements

FAST FORWARD

Every twelve months a company must send a **confirmation statement** to the Registrar.

Under the Companies Act 2006 (TSO, 2006) every company must send a **confirmation statement** to the Registrar. The statement can be sent at any time, but no more than twelve months may elapse between statement submissions.

The purpose of the **confirmation statement** is to keep the Registrar informed about certain changes to the company. Much of this information would have been submitted when the company is formed.

They are used to **confirm** that there have been **no changes** to items listed on the confirmation statement during the previous twelve months, if none have been made. If changes have been made, it records just the changes that have occurred.

Examples of information requiring confirmation are:

- The address of the **registered office** of the company

- The address (if different) at which the **register of members** or **debentureholders** is kept

- The type of company and its principal **business activities**

- The total number of **issued shares,** their **aggregate nominal value** and the amounts paid and unpaid on each share

- For each **class of share**, the **rights** of those shares, the **total number** of shares in that class and their **total nominal value**

- Particulars of **members** of the company

- Particulars of those who have **ceased** to be members since the last return

- The number of shares of each **class** held by members at the return date, and transferred by members since incorporation or the last return date

- The particulars of **directors,** and **secretary (if applicable)**

Chapter Roundup

- A promoter **forms** a company. They must act with **reasonable skill** and **care**, and if shares are to be allotted they are the agent of the prospective shareholders, with an agent's fiduciary duties.

- A promoter has **no automatic right** to be reimbursed **pre-incorporation expenses** by the company, though this can be expressly agreed.

- Pre-incorporation contracts **cannot** be ratified by the company. A new contract on the same terms must be expressly created.

- A **company** is **formed and registered** under the Companies Act 2006 when it is issued with a **certificate of incorporation** by the Registrar, after submission to the Registrar of a number of documents and a fee.

- Buying a company **'off the shelf'** avoids the administrative burden of registering a company.

- A **private company** with share capital may be able to re-register as a **public company** if the share capital requirement is met. A public company may re-register as a private one.

- To **trade** or **borrow**, a public company needs a **trading certificate**. Private companies may commence business on **registration**.

- The price of limited liability is greater **public accountability** via the Companies Registry, registers, the *London Gazette* and company letterheads.

- A company must keep **registers** of certain aspects of its constitution, including the registers of members, and directors.

- Companies must keep **sufficient accounting records** to explain the company's transactions and its financial position, in other words so that a profit and loss account and balance sheet can be prepared.

- A registered company must prepare **annual accounts** showing a true and fair view, lay them and various reports before members, and file them with the Registrar following directors' approval.

- Every twelve months a company must send a **confirmation statement** to the Registrar.

1   A company can confirm a pre-incorporation contract by performing it or obtaining benefits from it.

     True   ☐

     False   ☐

2   If a public company does business or borrows before obtaining a trading certificate from the Registrar, the transaction is:

     A   Invalid, and the third party cannot recover any loss
     B   Invalid, but the third party may recover any loss from the directors
     C   Valid, and the directors are punishable by a fine
     D   Valid, but the third party can sue the directors for further damages

3   A company must keep a register of directors. What details must be revealed?

     Select all that apply.

     A   Full name
     B   Service address
     C   Nationality
     D   Date of birth
     E   Business occupation

4   An accountant or solicitor acting in their professional capacity during the registration of a company may be deemed a promoter.

     True   ☐

     False   ☐

5   If a certificate of incorporation is dated 6 March, but is not signed and issued until 8 March, when is the company deemed to have come into existence?

Answers to Quick Quiz

1   False. The company must make a new contract on similar terms.

2   C. The directors are punished for allowing the company to trade before it is allowed to.

3   All of them.

4   False. A person acting in a professional capacity will not be deemed a promoter.

5   6 March. The date on the certificate is conclusive.

Now try the questions below from the Practice Question Bank

Number
28, 29

Constitution of a company

Topic list	Syllabus reference
1 Memorandum of association	D4(e)
2 A company's constitution	D4(e), D4(f), D4(g)
3 Company objects and capacity	D4(e)
4 The constitution as a contract	D4(e)
5 Company name and registered office	D4(h)

Introduction

The **articles of association** is one of the documents that may be required to be submitted to the Registrar when applying for registration. The articles, together with any resolutions and agreements which may affect them, form the company's **constitution**.

The constitution sets out what the company does; if there are no restrictions specified then the company may do anything provided it is legal. Clearly this includes the capacity to contract, an important aspect of legal personality. Also significant is the concept of *ultra vires*, a term used to describe transactions that are outside the scope of the company's capacity.

Study guide

		Intellectual level
D	**The formation and constitution of business organisations**	
4	**The formation and constitution of a company**	
(e)	Analyse the effect of a company's constitutional documents	2
(f)	Describe the contents of model articles of association	1
(g)	Explain how articles of association can be changed	2
(h)	Explain the controls over the names that companies may or may not use	2

Exam guide

A company's constitution could easily be examined in either a knowledge or an application question. You may be asked to explain any of the constitutional documents and how they may be altered.

1 Memorandum of association

FAST FORWARD

> The memorandum is a **simple document** which states that the subscribers wish to form a company and become members of it.

Before the Companies Act 2006, the **memorandum of association** was an extremely important document containing information concerning the relationship between the company and the outside world – for example its aims and purpose (its objects).

The position changed with the 2006 Act and much of the information contained in the old memorandum is now to be found in the Articles of Association, which we will come to shortly. The **essence** of the memorandum has been retained, although it is now a very simple historical document which states that the **subscribers** (the initial shareholders):

(a)   Wish to **form a company** under the Act, and

(b)   Agree to **become members** of the company and to take at least one share each if the company is to have share capital.

The memorandum must be in the **prescribed form** and must be **signed** by each subscriber.

It has been deemed by the Companies Act 2006 (TSO, 2006) that companies which were incorporated under a **previous** Act and whose memorandum contains provisions now found in the articles, shall have these provisions interpreted as if they are part of the articles.

2 A company's constitution

FAST FORWARD

> A **company's constitution** comprises the **Articles of Association** and any **resolutions and agreements** it makes which affect the constitution.

According to the Companies Act 2006 (TSO, 2006), the constitution of a company consists of:

- The **Articles of Association**
- **Resolutions and agreements** that it makes that affect the constitution

We shall consider resolutions and agreements first. This will help explain how the Articles of Association are amended.

2.1 Resolutions and agreements

In addition to the main **constitutional document** (the Articles of Association), **resolutions** and **agreements** also form part of a company's constitution.

Resolutions are decisions passed by members which directly affect the company's constitution as they are used to **introduce**, **amend** or **remove** provisions in the articles. **Agreements** made, for example between the company and members, are also deemed as amending the constitution.

Copies of resolutions, or agreements that amend the constitution, must be sent to the Registrar within **15 days** of being passed or agreed. If a company fails to do this then every officer who is in default commits an offence punishable by fine. Where a **resolution** or **agreement** which affects a company's constitution is **not in writing**, the company is required to send the registrar a **written memorandum** that sets out the terms of the resolution or agreement in question.

2.2 Articles of association

Key term

> The **articles of association** consist of the internal rules that relate to the management and administration of the company.

The articles contain detailed **rules** and **regulations** setting out how the company is to be **managed** and **administered**. The Act states that the registered articles should be contained in a **single document** which is divided into **consecutively numbered paragraphs**. Articles should contain rules on a number of areas, the most important being summarised in the table below.

Contents of articles	
Appointment and dismissal of directors	Communication with members
Powers, responsibilities and liabilities of directors	Class meetings
Directors' meetings	Issue of shares
General meetings: calling, conduct and voting	Transfer of shares
Members' rights	Documents and records
Dividends	Company secretary

2.2.1 Model articles

Rather than each company having to draft their own articles, and to allow companies to be set up **quickly** and **easily**, the Act allows the Secretary of State to provide **model** (or standard) **articles** that companies can adopt. Different models are available for different types of company; most companies would adopt model **private** or **public company** articles.

Companies are free to use **any** of the model articles that they wish to by registering them on incorporation. If **no articles** are registered then the company will be **automatically incorporated** with the **default model articles** which are relevant to the type of company being formed. Model articles can be **amended** by the members and therefore tailored to the specific needs of the company.

Model articles are effectively a **'safety net'** which allow directors and members to take decisions if the company has failed to include suitable provisions in its registered articles or registered no articles at all.

2.2.2 Alteration of the articles

FAST FORWARD

> The articles may be altered by a **special resolution**. The basic test is whether the alteration is for the **benefit of the company as a whole**.

Any company has a statutory power to alter its articles by **special resolution**. A private company may pass a **written resolution** with a **75% majority**. The alteration will be valid and binding on **all** members of

the company. **Copies** of the amended articles must be sent to the **Registrar** within 15 days of the amendment taking effect.

2.2.3 Making the company's constitution unalterable

There are devices by which some provisions of the company's constitution can be made **unalterable** unless the member who wishes to prevent any alteration consents.

(a)   The articles may give a member **additional votes** so that they can block a resolution to alter articles on particular points (including the removal of their weighted voting rights from the articles). However, to be effective, the articles must also limit the powers of members to alter the articles that give extra votes.

(b)   The articles may provide that when a meeting is held to vote on a proposed alteration of the articles the **quorum present must include** the **member concerned**. They can then deny the meeting a quorum by absenting themselves.

(c)   The Act permits companies to **'entrench' provisions** in their articles. This means specific provisions may only be **amended** or **removed** if certain **conditions** are met which are more restrictive than a special resolution such as agreement of all the members. However, such 'entrenched provisions' **cannot** be drafted so that the articles can never be amended or removed.

2.2.4 Restrictions on alteration

Even when it is possible to hold a meeting and pass a special resolution, alteration of the articles is **restricted** by the following principles.

(a)   The alteration is **void** if it **conflicts with the Companies Act** or with general law.

(b)   In various circumstances, such as to protect a minority, the **court may order** that an alteration be made or, alternatively, that an existing article shall not be altered.

(c)   An existing **member may not be compelled** by alteration of the articles to **subscribe for additional shares** or to accept increased liability for the shares which they hold unless they have given their consent.

(d)   An alteration of the articles which varies the rights attached to a class of shares may only be made if the **correct rights variation procedure** has been followed to obtain the consent of the class. A 15 per cent minority may apply to the court to cancel the variation.

(e)   A person whose **contract** is contained in the articles cannot obtain an injunction to prevent the articles being altered, **but** they may be entitled to **damages** for breach of contract. Alteration cannot take away rights already acquired by performing the contract.

(f)   An alteration may be **void** if the **majority** who approve it are **not acting *bona fide* in what they deem to be the interests of the company as a whole**.

The case law on the **bona fide test** is an effort to hold the balance between two principles:

(a)   The **majority** are **entitled** to **alter articles** even though a minority considers that the alteration is prejudicial to its interests.

(b)   A minority is entitled to protection against an alteration which is intended to **benefit** the **majority** rather than the company and which is **unjustified discrimination** against the minority.

Principle (b) tends to be **restricted** to cases where the majority seeks to expel the minority from the company.

The most elaborate analysis of this subject was made by the Court of Appeal in the case of *Greenhalgh v Arderne Cinemas Ltd 1950*. Two main propositions were laid down by the judge.

(a)   '**Bona fide for the benefit of the company as a whole**' is a **single test** and also a **subjective test** (what did the majority believe?). The court will not substitute its own view.

(b)   'The company as a whole' means, in this context, **the general body of shareholders**. The test is whether every 'individual hypothetical member' would, in the honest opinion of the majority, benefit from the alteration.

If the purpose is to benefit the company as a whole the alteration is valid, even though it can be shown that the **minority does in fact suffer special detriment** and that other members escape loss.

2.2.5 Expulsion of minorities

Expulsion cases are concerned with:

*   Alteration of the articles for the purpose of **removing** a **director from office**

*   Alteration of the articles to permit a majority of members to **enforce** a **transfer** to themselves of the shareholding of a minority

The action of the majority in altering the articles to achieve 'expulsion' will generally be treated as **valid** even though it is discriminatory, if the majority were concerned to **benefit the company** or to remove some detriment to its interests.

If, on the other hand, the majority was **blatantly seeking** to secure an **advantage** to themselves by their discrimination, the alteration made to the articles by their voting control of the company will be invalid. The cases below illustrate how the distinctions are applied in practice.

Sidebottom v Kershaw, Leese & Co Ltd 1920

The facts: The articles were altered to enable the directors to purchase at a fair price the shareholding of any member who competed with the company in its business. The minority against whom the new article was aimed did carry on a competing business. They challenged the validity of the alteration on the ground that it was an abuse of majority power to 'expel' a member.

Decision: There was no objection to a power of 'expulsion' by this means. It was a justifiable alteration if made *bona fide* in the interests of the company as a whole. On the facts this was justifiable.

Brown v British Abrasive Wheel Co 1919

The facts: The company needed further capital. The majority who held 98% of the existing shares were willing to provide more capital but only if they could buy up the 2% minority. As the minority refused to sell, the majority proposed to alter the articles to provide for compulsory acquisition on a fair value basis. The minority objected to the alteration.

Decision: The alteration was invalid since it was merely for the benefit of the majority. It was not an alteration 'directly concerned with the provision of further capital' and therefore not for the benefit of the company.

Dafen Tinplate Co Ltd v Llanelly Steel Co (1907) Ltd 1920

The facts: The claimant was a minority shareholder which had transferred its custom from the defendant company to another supplier. The majority shareholders of the defendant company sought to protect their interests by altering the articles to provide for compulsory acquisition of the claimant's shares.

The new article was not restricted (as it was in *Sidebottom's* case above) to acquisition of shares on specific grounds where benefit to the company would result. It was simply expressed as a power to acquire the shares of a member. The claimant objected that the alteration was invalid since it was not for the benefit of the company.

Decision: The alteration was invalid because it 'enables the majority of the shareholders to compel any shareholder to transfer his shares'. This wide power could not 'properly be said to be for the benefit of the company'. The mere unexpressed intention to use the power in a particular way was not enough.

Therefore if the majority intend that the **power to acquire the shares of a minority** is to be **restricted** to specific circumstances for the benefit of the company, they should ensure that this restriction is included in the new article.

Exam focus point

Scenario questions on this area of law may concern a majority wishing to amend the company's articles to allow the expulsion of a minority. If this is the case, pay close attention to the resolution as it may be invalid under one of the cases above.

2.2.6 Filing of alteration

Whenever any alteration is made to the articles a copy of the altered articles must be delivered to the Registrar within **15 days**, together with a signed copy of the special resolution making the alteration.

2.2.7 Interaction of statute and articles

There are **two aspects** to consider.

(a) If a company's articles restrict an activity that the Companies Act allows, then the company must **alter** the articles to remove the restriction before it may exercise the statutory power.

(b) The Companies Act will **override** the articles:

   (i) If the Companies Act **prohibits something**

   (ii) If something is permitted by the Companies Act **only** by a **special procedure** (such as passing a special resolution in general meeting)

3 Company objects and capacity

> **FAST FORWARD**
>
> A **company's objects** are its aims and purposes. If a company enters into a contract which is outside its objects, that contract is said to be *ultra vires*. However, the rights of third parties to the contract are protected.

3.1 The objects

The objects are the **'aims'** and **'purposes'** of a company. Under previous companies legislation they were held in a specific clause within the memorandum of association. This clause set out everything the company could do, including being a 'general commercial company' which meant it could pretty much do anything.

The Companies Act 2006 (TSO, 2006) changed matters. The objects could now be found in the **articles** but most articles will **not** mention any objects. This is because under the Act a company's objects are **completely unrestricted** (ie it can carry out any lawful activity). Only where the company wishes to restrict its activities is there an inclusion of those **restrictions** in the articles.

3.1.1 Alteration of the objects

As a company's objects are located in its articles, it may alter its objects by **special resolution** for any reason. The procedure is the same as for any other type of alteration.

3.2 Contractual capacity and *ultra vires*

> **FAST FORWARD**
>
> Companies may only act in accordance with their **objects**. If the directors permit an act which is restricted by the company's objects then the act is *ultra vires*.

> *Ultra vires* is where a company exceeds its objects and acts outside its capacity.
>
> Companies which have **unrestricted objects** are highly unlikely to act *ultra vires* since their constitution permits them to do anything. Where a company has restrictions placed on its objects, and it breaches these restrictions, then it would be acting *ultra vires*.

The approach taken by the Companies Act 2006 is to give **security** to commercial transactions for **third parties**, whilst preserving the rights of shareholders to restrain directors from entering an *ultra vires* action.

There are two important sections of the Companies Act 2006 concerning *ultra vires* contracts:

Section 39 provides as follows:

'the validity of an act done by a company shall not be called into question on the ground of lack of capacity by reason of anything in the company's constitution.'

Section 40 provides as follows:

'in favour of a person dealing with a company in good faith, the power of the directors to bind the company, or authorise others to do so, shall be deemed to be free of any limitation under the company's constitution.'

There are a number of **points to note** about s 40.

(a) The section applies in favour of the **person dealing with the company**; it does not apply to the members.

(b) In contrast with s 39, **good faith** is required on the part of the third party. The company has, however, to prove lack of good faith in the third party and this may turn out to be quite difficult.

(c) The **third party** is not required to **enquire** whether or not there are any **restrictions** placed on the power of directors. They are free to assume the directors have any power they profess to have.

(d) The section covers not only acts beyond the capacity of the company, but acts beyond **'any limitation under the company's constitution'**.

Whilst sections 39 and 40 deal with the company's transactions with **third parties**, the **members** may take action against the directors for permitting *ultra vires* acts. Their action will be based on the fact that the **objects specifically restricted** the particular act and **directors** have a statutory duty to **abide** by the **company's constitution**.

The main problem for **members** is that they are most likely to be **aware** of the *ultra vires* act only **after** it has occurred. Therefore they are not normally in a position to prevent it, although in theory they could seek an **injunction** if they found out about the potential *ultra vires* act before it took place.

> Make sure you understand how s 39 and s 40 protect third parties.

3.3 Transactions with directors

The Companies Act 2006 also applies when the company enters into a contract with one of its **directors**, or its holding company, or any **person connected** with such a director. Contracts made between the company and these parties are **voidable** by the company if the director acts outside their capacity.

Whether or not the contract is avoided, the party and any **authorising director are liable to repay any profit** they made or make good any losses that result from such a contract.

4 The constitution as a contract

The articles **constitute a contract** between:

- Company and members
- Members and the company
- Members and members

The articles **do not constitute** a contract between the **company** and **third parties**, or members in a **capacity** other than as **members** (the *Eley* case).

4.1 Effect

A **company's constitution binds**:

- Members to company
- Company to members
- Members to members

The company's constitution does **not** bind the company to third parties.

This principle applies only to rights and obligations which affect members **in their capacity as members**.

Hickman v Kent or Romney Marsh Sheepbreeders Association 1915

The facts: The claimant (H) was in dispute with the company which had threatened to expel him from membership. The articles provided that disputes between the company and its members should be submitted to arbitration. H, in breach of that article, began an action in court against the company.

Decision: The proceedings would be stayed since the dispute (which related to matters affecting H as a member) must, in conformity with the articles, be submitted to arbitration.

The principle that only rights and obligations of members are covered applies when an outsider, who is also a member, seeks to rely on the articles in support of a claim made as an **outsider**.

Eley v Positive Government Security Life Assurance Co 1876

The facts: E, a solicitor, drafted the original articles and included a provision that the company must always employ him as its solicitor. E became a member of the company some months after its incorporation. He later sued the company for breach of contract in not employing him as its solicitor.

Decision: E could not rely on the article since it was a contract between the company and its members and he was not asserting any claim as a member.

The members are able to compel the company to obey the articles: *Pender v Lushington 1877*.

4.2 Constitution as a contract between members

The Companies Act gives to the **constitution** contractual effect between (a) the **company** and (b) its **members individually**. It can also impose a contract on the members in their dealings with each other.

Rayfield v Hands 1958

The facts: The articles required that (a) every director should be a shareholder and (b) the directors must purchase the shares of any member who gave them notice of his wish to dispose of them. The directors, however, denied that a member could enforce the obligation on them to acquire his shares.

Decision: There was 'a contract ... between a member and member-directors in relation to their holdings of the company's shares in its articles' and the directors were bound by it.

Articles and resolutions are usually **drafted** so that each stage is a dealing between the company and the members, so that:

(a) A member who intends to transfer their shares must, if the articles so require, give notice of their intention to the company.

(b) The company must then give notice to other members that they have an option to take up their shares.

4.3 Constitution as a supplement to contracts

FAST FORWARD

The constitution can be used to **establish the terms** of a contract existing elsewhere.

If an **outsider** makes a **separate contract** with the company and that contract contains no specific term on a particular point but the constitution does, then the contract is deemed to incorporate the constitution to that extent.

If a contract incorporates terms of the articles it is subject to the company's **right** to **alter** its articles. However, a company's articles cannot be altered to deprive another person of a right already earned, say for services rendered **prior** to the alteration.

Point to note

Remember the articles only create contractual rights/obligations in relation to rights **as a member**.

4.4 Shareholder agreements

FAST FORWARD

Shareholders' agreements sometimes supplement a company's constitution.

Shareholder agreements are concerned with the **running of the company**; in particular they often contain terms by which the shareholders agree how they will vote on various issues.

They offer more protection to the interests of shareholders than do the articles of association. Individuals have a **power of veto** over any proposal which is contrary to the terms of the agreement. This enables a minority shareholder to protect their interests against unfavourable decisions of the majority.

5 Company name and registered office

FAST FORWARD

Except in **certain circumstances** a company's name must end with the words limited (Ltd), public limited company (plc) or the Welsh equivalents.

A company's name is its **identity**. There are a number of rules which restrict the choice of name that a company may adopt.

5.1 Statutory rules on the choice of company name

FAST FORWARD

No company may use a name which is:

– The **same** as an existing company on the Registrar's index of company names
– A **criminal offence, offensive,** or **'sensitive'**
– Suggestive of a **connection** with the **Government or local authority** (unless approved)

Under the Companies Act 2006 (TSO, 2006) the **choice of name** of a limited company must conform to the following rules.

(a) The name must **end** with the word(s):

(i) **Public limited company** (abbreviated **plc**) if it is a public company

      (ii)   **Limited** (or Ltd) if it is a private limited company, unless permitted to omit 'limited' from its name

      (iii)   The **Welsh equivalents** of either (i) or (ii) may be used by a Welsh company

(b)   No company may have a name which is the **same** as any other company appearing in the statutory index at Companies House. For this purpose two names are treated as 'the same' in spite of minor or non-essential differences. For instance the word 'the' as the first word in the name is ignored. 'John Smith Limited' is treated the same as 'John Smith' (an unlimited company) or 'John Smith & Company Ltd'. Where a company has a name which is the same or too similar to another, the Secretary of State may direct the company to **change its name**.

(c)   No company may have a name the use of which would be a **criminal** offence or which is considered **offensive** or **'sensitive'** (as defined by the Secretary of State).

(d)   Official approval is required for a name which in the Registrar's opinion suggests a **connection** with the **government** or a **local authority** or which is subject to **control**.

      A name which suggests some professional expertise such as 'optician' will only be permitted if the appropriate representative association has been consulted and raises no objection.

The general purpose of the rule is to **prevent** a company **misleading** the public as to its real circumstances or activities. Certain names may be approved by the Secretary of State on written application.

5.2 Omission of the word 'limited'

A **private company** which is a **charity** or a **company limited by shares** or **guarantee** and **licensed** to do so **before 25 February 1982** may omit the word 'limited' from its name if the following conditions are satisfied.

(a)   The objects of the company must be the **promotion** of either commerce, art, science, education, religion, charity or any profession (or anything incidental or conducive to such objects).

(b)   The memorandum or articles must require that the **profits** or other income of the company are to be **applied to promoting** its objects and no dividends or return of capital may be paid to its members. Also, on liquidation the **assets** (otherwise distributable to members) are to be **transferred** to another body with similar objects. The articles must not then be altered so that the company's status to omit 'Limited' is lost.

5.3 Change of name

A company may decide to **change its name** by:

(a)   Passing a **special resolution**

(b)   **Any other means** provided for in the **articles** (in other words the company can specify its own procedure for changing its name)

Where a **special resolution** has been passed, the **Registrar** should be notified and a copy of the resolution sent. If the change was made by **any other procedure** covered by (b), the Registrar should be notified and a statement provided which states that the change has been made in accordance with the articles.

The change is effective from when a new **incorporation certificate is issued**, although the company is still treated as the same legal entity as before. The same limitations as above apply to adoption of a name by change of name as by incorporation of a new company.

5.4 Passing-off action

A person who considers that their rights have been infringed can apply for an injunction to restrain a company from using a name (**even if** the name has been duly registered). It can do this if the name suggests that the latter company is carrying on the business of the complainant or is otherwise connected with it.

A company can be **prevented** by an **injunction** issued by the court in a **passing-off action** from **using** its **registered name**, if in doing so it causes its goods to be confused with those of the claimant.

Ewing v Buttercup Margarine Co Ltd 1917

The facts: The claimant had since 1904 run a chain of 150 shops in Scotland and the north of England through which he sold margarine and tea. He traded as 'The Buttercup Dairy Co'. The defendant was a registered company formed in 1916 with the name above. It sold margarine as a wholesaler in the London area. The defendant contended that there was unlikely to be confusion between the goods sold by the two concerns.

Decision: An injunction would be granted to restrain the defendants from the use of its name since the claimant had the established connection under the Buttercup name. He planned to open shops in the south of England and if the defendants sold margarine retail, there could be confusion between the two businesses.

If, however, the two companies' **businesses are different**, confusion is unlikely to occur, and hence the courts will refuse to grant an injunction. The complaint will also not succeed if the **claimant lays claim to the exclusive use of a word** which has a **general use**.

5.5 Appeal to the Company Names Adjudicators

A company which feels that another company's name is **too similar** to its own may object to the Company Names Adjudicator under the Companies Act. The Adjudicator will review the case and, within **90 days**, make their decision and provide their reasons for it in public. In most cases the Adjudicator will require the offending company to **change its name** to one which does not breach the rules. In some cases the **Adjudicator may determine** the new name.

An appeal against the decision may be made in Court. The Court may **reverse** the Adjudicator's decision, **affirm** it and may even **determine** a new name.

5.6 Publication of the company's name

The **company's name** must **appear legibly** and **conspicuously**:

- **Outside** the **registered office** and all **places of business**

- On all **business letters, order forms**, **notices** and **official publications**

- On all **receipts** and **invoices** issued on the company's behalf

- On all **bills of exchange**, **letters of credit**, **promissory notes**, **cheques** and **orders** for money or goods purporting to be signed by, or on behalf, of the company

- On its **website**

5.7 Business names other than the corporate name

A **business name** is a name used by a company which is different from the company's corporate name or by a firm which is different from the name(s) of the proprietor or the partners.

Most companies trade under their own **registered names**. However, a company may prefer to use some other name.

The rules require any person (company, partnership or sole trader) who carries on business under a **different name** from their own:

(a) To **state** its **name**, registered **number** and registered **address** on all **business letters (including emails)**, invoices, receipts, written orders for goods or services and written demands for payment of debts

(b)   To **display** its **name** and **address** in a **prominent position** in any **business premises** to which its customers and suppliers have access

(c)   On **request** from any **person** with whom it does business to give **notice** of its name and address

5.8 Registered office

The Companies Act 2006 provides that a company must at all times have a **registered office** to which all communications and notices can be sent. Its location in England and Wales, or just in Wales or Scotland, determines its domicile. A company may **change its registered office** (but not its domicile), but for a period of 14 days after notice is served any person may validly present documents to the previous address.

Chapter Roundup

- The memorandum is a **simple document** which states that the subscribers wish to form a company and become members of it.

- A **company's constitution** comprises the **Articles of Association** and any **resolutions and agreements** it makes which affect the constitution.

- The articles may be altered by a **special resolution**. The basic test is whether the alteration is for the **benefit of the company as a whole**.

- A **company's objects** are its aims and purposes. If a company enters into a contract which is outside its objects, that contract is said to be **_ultra vires_**. However, the rights of third parties to the contract are protected.

- Companies may only act in accordance with their **objects**. If the directors permit an act which is restricted by the company's objects then the act is _ultra vires_.

- The articles **constitute** a **contract** between:

  - Company and members
  - Members and the company
  - Members and members

- The articles **do not constitute** a contract between the **company** and **third parties**, or members in a **capacity** other than as **members** (the _Eley_ case).

- The constitution can be used to **establish the terms** of a contract existing elsewhere.

- **Shareholders' agreements** sometimes supplement a company's constitution.

- Except in **certain circumstances** a company's name must end with the words limited (Ltd), public limited company (plc) or the Welsh equivalents.

- No company may use a name which is:

  - The **same** as an existing company on the Registrar's index of company names
  - A **criminal offence, offensive,** or **'sensitive'**
  - Suggestive of a **connection** with the **Government** or **local authority** (unless approved)

1   Percy Limited has recently formed a contract with a third party which is restricted by the objects in the company's constitution.

Which of the following statements is/are correct?

A   The validity of the act cannot be questioned on the grounds of lack of capacity by reason of anything in the company's constitution.

B   The act may be restrained by the members of Percy Ltd.

C   The act may be enforced by the third party.

D   The directors have a duty to observe any limitation on their powers flowing from the company's constitution.

2   If a company wishes to restrict its objects, what kind of resolution is required?

A   Special resolution
B   Special resolution with special notice
C   Ordinary resolution with special notice
D   Ordinary resolution

3   A company has been formed within the last six months. Another long-established company considers that because of similarity between their names there may be confusion between it and the new company. The only action the long-established company can take is to bring a passing-off action if it is to prevent the new company using its name.

True   ☐

False   ☐

4   Which of the following persons are **not** bound to one another by the constitution?

A   Members to company
B   Company to members
C   Members to members
D   Company to third parties

5   How long does a company have to file amended articles with the Registrar if they have been altered?

A   14 days
B   15 days
C   21 days
D   28 days

Answers to Quick Quiz

1   A, C and D are correct. Members can only act before the contract is signed, so B is incorrect.

2   A. A special resolution is required to restrict the objects as with any alteration to the articles in general.

3   False. The long-established company can also complain to the Company Names Adjudicator.

4   A, B and C are correct. D is incorrect, illustrated by *Eley v Positive Government Security Life Assurance Co Ltd 1876.*

5   B. A company has 15 days to file amended articles with the Registrar.

Now try the questions below from the Practice Question Bank

Number
30, 31, 32

14: Constitution of a company | Part D The formation and constitution of business organisations

BPP
LEARNING MEDIA

Capital and the financing of companies

15

Share capital

Topic list	Syllabus reference
1 Members	E1(a)
2 The nature of shares and capital	E1(a)
3 Types of share	E1(b)
4 Allotment of shares	E1(c)
5 Issuing shares at a premium or at a discount	E1(d)

Introduction

In this chapter the nature of share capital is explained. You should note (and **not** confuse) the different types of capital that are important for company law purposes.

The rest of the chapter discusses procedural matters relating to the **issue** and **transfer** of shares. You will see that there are built-in safeguards to protect members' rights, **pre-emption rights** and the necessity for directors to be authorised to **allot** shares. There are also safeguards that ensure that a company receives **sufficient consideration** for its shares.

Study guide

		Intellectual level
E	**Capital and the financing of companies**	
1	**Share capital**	
(a)	Examine the different types of capital	2
(b)	Illustrate the difference between various classes of shares, including treasury shares, and the procedure for altering class rights	2
(c)	Explain allotment of shares and distinguish between rights issue and bonus issue of shares	2
(d)	Examine the effect of issuing shares at either a discount, or at a premium	2

Exam guide

Share capital is an important syllabus area that lends itself well to different types of question. You may be tested on the different types of share, what class rights are and how they can be altered.

1 Members

FAST FORWARD

Under the Companies Act 2006 (TSO, 2006) a member of a company is a person who has **agreed to become a member**, and whose name has been **entered** in the **register of members**. This may occur by: subscription to the memorandum; applying for shares; the presentation to the company of a transfer of shares to the prospective member; applying as personal representative of a deceased member or a trustee of a bankrupt.

1.1 Becoming a member

Key term

A **member** of a company is a person who has agreed to be a member and whose name has been entered in the register of members.

Entry in the register is **essential**. Mere delivery to the company of a transfer of shares does not make the transferor a member – until the transfer is entered in the register.

1.2 Subscriber shares

Subscribers to the memorandum are deemed to have agreed to become members of the company. As soon as the company is formed their names should be entered in the register of members.

Other persons may **acquire shares** and become members:

- By **applying** and being allotted shares
- By presenting to the company for registration a **transfer** of shares to them
- By applying as **personal representative** or **trustee** of a:
  - Deceased member
  - Bankrupt member

1.3 Ceasing to be a member

FAST FORWARD

There are **eight** ways in which a member ceases to be so.

A **member ceases** to be a member in any of the following circumstances.

- They **transfer** all their shares to another person and the transfer is registered
- The member **dies**
- The **shares** of a bankrupt member are **registered** in the name of their trustee
- A **member who is a minor repudiates their shares**
- The **trustee** of a **bankrupt member disclaims** their shares
- The **company forfeits** or **accepts** the **surrender of shares**
- The **company** sells them in exercise of a lien
- The **company is dissolved** and **ceases to exist**

1.4 The number of members

Public and **private companies** must have a minimum of **one** member. There is **no maximum** number.

Public and private companies must have a minimum **of one member**. There is **no maximum** number. Where a company has a sole member, the following rules will apply.

(a) The **register of members** must contain a statement that there is **only one member** and give their address.

(b) **Quorum**. The Act **automatically permits** a **quorum of one** for general meetings.

2 The nature of shares and capital

Under the Companies Act 2006 (TSO, 2006) a **share** is a transferable form of property, carrying rights and obligations, by which the interest of a member of a company limited by shares is measured.

2.1 Shares

Key term

A **share** is the interest of a shareholder in the company measured by a sum of money, for the purpose of a liability in the first place, and of interest in the second, but also consisting of a series of mutual covenants entered into by all the shareholders *inter se*.

The **key points** in this definition are:

- The share must be **paid for** ('liability'). The nominal value of the share fixes this liability: it is the base price of the share eg a £1 ordinary share.

- It gives a **proportionate entitlement** to dividends, votes and any return of capital ('interest').

- It is a form of **bargain** ('mutual covenants') between shareholders which underlies such principles as majority control and minority protection.

Key term

A share's **nominal value** is its face value. So a £1 ordinary share for instance, has a nominal value of £1. No share can be issued at a value below its nominal value.

A **share** is a form of **personal property**, carrying **rights** and **obligations**. It is, by its nature, **transferable**.

A member who holds one or more shares is a **shareholder**. However, some companies (such as most companies limited by guarantee) do not have a share capital. So they have members who are not also shareholders.

Information about any **special rights** attached to shares is obtainable from one of the following documents which are on the file at Companies House:

- The **articles**, which are the normal context in which share rights are defined.

- A **resolution** or agreement incidental to the creation of a new class of shares (copies must be delivered to the Registrar).

- A **statement of capital** given to the Registrar within one month of **allotment**, together with the return of allotment.

2.2 Types of capital

FAST FORWARD

> The term **'capital'** is used in several senses in company legislation, to mean issued, allotted or called up share capital or loan capital.

2.2.1 Authorised share capital

Under previous company legislation, companies had to specify a **maximum authorised share capital** that it could issue. Under the 2006 Act, the concept of authorised share capital was removed.

2.2.2 Issued and allotted share capital

Key terms

> **Issued** and **allotted share capital** is the type, class, number and amount of the shares issued and allotted to specific shareholders, including shares taken on formation by the subscribers to the memorandum.

A company need not issue all its share capital at once. If it retains a part, this is **unissued share capital**.

Issued share capital can be **increased** through the allotment of shares.

Rights issues and the issue of **bonus shares** will also increase the amount of a company's capital.

2.2.3 Called up and paid up share capital

Key terms

> **Called up share capital** is the amount which the company has required shareholders to pay now or in the future on the shares issued.
>
> **Paid up share capital** is the amount which shareholders have actually paid on the shares issued and called up.

For example, a company has issued and allotted 70 £1 (nominal value) shares, has received 25p per share on application and has called on members for a second 25p. Therefore its issued and allotted share capital is £70 and its **called up** share capital is £35 (50p per share). When the members pay the call, the **'paid up'** share capital is then £35 also. Capital not yet called is **'uncalled capital'**. Called capital which is not yet paid is termed **'partly paid'**; the company therefore has an outstanding claim against its shareholders and this debt is transferred to the new shareholder if the share is transferred.

As we saw earlier, on **allotment public companies** must receive at least **one-quarter of the nominal value** of the shares paid up, plus the whole of any premium.

2.2.4 Loan capital

Key term

> **Loan capital** comprises debentures and other long-term loans to a business.

Loan capital, in contrast with the above, is the term used to describe **borrowed money** obtained usually by the issue of debentures. **It is nothing to do with shares**.

2.3 Market value

Shares of a public company are **freely transferable** (providing the appropriate procedures are followed) and therefore may be subsequently sold by some or all of the shareholders. The sale price will not necessarily be the nominal value, rather it will reflect the prospects of the company and therefore may be greater or less than the nominal value.

3 Types of share

FAST FORWARD

If the constitution of a company states no differences between shares, it is assumed that they are all **ordinary** shares with parallel rights and obligations. There may, however, be other types, notably **preference shares**.

3.1 Ordinary shares (equity)

Under the Companies Act 2006 (TSO, 2006) if no differences between shares are expressed then all shares are equity shares with the **same rights**, known as ordinary shares.

Key terms

Equity is the residual interest in the assets of the company after deducting all its liabilities. It comprises issued share capital excluding any part that does not carry any right to participate beyond a specified amount in a distribution.

Equity share capital is a company's issued share capital less capital which carries preferential rights.

Ordinary shares are shares which entitle the holders to the remaining divisible profits (and, in a liquidation, the assets) after prior interests, eg creditors and prior charge capital, have been satisfied.

3.2 Class rights

Key term

Class rights are rights which are attached to particular types of shares by the company's constitution.

A company may at its option attach **special rights** to different shares regarding:

* Dividends
* Return of capital
* Voting
* The right to appoint or remove a director

Shares which have different rights from others are grouped together with other shares carrying identical rights to form a **class**. The most common types of share capital with different rights are **preference shares** and **ordinary shares**. There may also be ordinary shares with voting rights and ordinary shares without voting rights.

3.3 Preference shares

FAST FORWARD

The most common right of preference shareholders is a **prior right** to receive a fixed dividend. This right is not a right to **compel payment** of a dividend, but it is **cumulative** unless otherwise stated. Usually, preference shareholders **cannot participate** in a dividend over and above their fixed dividend and **cease to be entitled to arrears of undeclared dividends** if the company goes into liquidation.

Key term

Preference shares are shares carrying one or more rights such as a fixed rate of dividend or preferential claim to any company profits available for distribution.

A preference share may, and generally will, carry a **prior right** to receive an annual dividend of fixed amount, say 6% of the share's nominal value. **Ordinary** and **preference shares** are **deemed** to have **identical rights**. However, a company's articles or resolutions may create differences between them.

As regards the **priority dividend entitlement**, four points should be noted.

(a) **The right is merely to receive a dividend at the specified rate before any other dividend may be paid or declared**. It is **not** a right to compel the company to pay the dividend. The company can decline to pay the dividend if it decides to transfer available profits to reserves instead of using the profits to pay the preference dividend.

(b) **The right to receive a preference dividend is deemed to be cumulative unless the contrary is stated.** If, therefore, a 6% dividend is not paid in Year 1, the priority entitlement is normally carried forward to Year 2, increasing the priority right for that year to 12% – and so on.

When arrears of cumulative dividend are paid, the holders of the shares at **the time when the dividend is declared** are entitled to the whole of it even though they did not hold the shares in the year to which the arrears relate. An intention that preference shares should not carry forward an entitlement to arrears is usually expressed by the word **'non-cumulative'**.

(c) **If a company which has arrears of unpaid cumulative preference dividends goes into liquidation, the preference shareholders cease to be entitled to the arrears unless**:

(i) A **dividend** has been **declared** though **not yet paid** when liquidation commences.

(ii) The **articles** (or other terms of issue) **expressly provide** that in a liquidation arrears are to be paid in priority to return of capital to members.

(d) **Holders of preference shares have no entitlement to participate in any additional dividend over and above their specified rate.** If, for example, a 6% dividend is paid on 6% preference shares, the entire balance of available profit may then be distributed to the holders of ordinary shares.

This rule also may be expressly overridden by the terms of issue. For example, the articles may provide that the preference shares are to receive a priority 6% dividend and are also to participate equally in any dividends payable after the ordinary shares have received a 6% dividend. Preference shares with these rights are called **participating preference shares**.

In all other respects preference shares carry the **same** rights as ordinary shares **unless otherwise stated**. If they do rank equally they carry the same rights, no more and no less, to return of capital, distribution of surplus assets and voting. In practice, it is **unusual** to issue preference shares on this basis. More usually, it is expressly provided that:

(a) The preference shares are to carry a **priority right** to **return of capital**.

(b) They are **not to carry a right to vote, or voting is permitted in specified circumstances**. For example failure to pay the preference dividend, variation of their rights or a resolution to wind up.

When preference shares carry a **priority right** to **return** of **capital**, the result is that:

(a) The amount paid up on the preference shares, say £1 on each £1 share, is to be repaid in liquidation before anything is repaid to ordinary shareholders.

(b) Unless otherwise stated, the holders of the preference shares are **not** entitled to share in surplus assets when the ordinary share capital has been repaid.

3.3.1 Advantages and disadvantages of preference shares

The advantages of preference shares are **greater security of income** and (if they carry priority in repayment of capital) **greater security of capital**. However, in a period of persistent inflation, the benefit of entitlement to fixed income and to capital fixed in money terms is an illusion.

A number of other **drawbacks** and **pitfalls**, such as loss of arrears, winding up and enforced payment, have been indicated above. Preference shares may be said to fall between the two stools of risk and reward (as seen in ordinary shares) and security (debentures).

3.4 Redeemable shares

Redeemable shares are shares issued on terms that they may be bought back by a company either at a future specific date or at the shareholder's or company's option.

3.5 Treasury shares

Treasury shares are created when a **private** or **public limited company** legitimately **purchases its own shares** out of **cash** or **distributable profit**. The purchased shares are then held by the company 'in treasury' which means the company can re-issue them without the usual formalities. They can only be sold for cash and the company cannot exercise the **voting rights** which attach to them.

3.5.1 Variation of class rights

FAST FORWARD

The holders of **issued** shares have **vested rights** which can only be varied by following a strict procedure. The standard procedure is by **special resolution** passed by at least **three-quarters** of the votes cast at a **separate class meeting** or by written consent.

Key term

A **variation of class rights** is an alteration in the position of shareholders with regard to those rights or duties which they have by virtue of their shares.

Examples of rights that attach to shares (**class rights**) include **voting rights**, a right to **dividends** and a right to a **return of capital** when a company is wound up. Rights attach to a particular class of shares if the holders of shares in that class enjoy rights that are not enjoyed by the holders of shares in another class.

These class rights can only be varied by the company with the consent of all the shareholders in the class, or with such consent of a majority as is specified (usually) in the articles. The standard procedure for variation of class rights requires that a **special resolution** shall be passed by a **three-quarters majority** cast either at a **separate meeting** of the class, or by **written consent**. If any other requirements are imposed by the company's articles then these must also be followed.

3.5.2 When variation rules apply

FAST FORWARD

It is **not** a variation of class rights to issue shares to new members, to subdivide shares of another class, to return capital to preference shareholders, or to create a new class of preference shareholders.

It is only necessary to follow the variation of class rights procedure **if what is proposed amounts to a variation of class rights**. The following examples do not constitute a variation of class rights.

3.5.3 Examples: Not a variation of class rights

(a) **To issue shares of the same class to allottees who are not already members of the class** (unless the defined class rights prohibit this).

> *White v Bristol Aeroplane Co Ltd 1953*
>
> *The facts:* The company made a bonus issue of new ordinary and preference shares to the existing ordinary shareholders who alone were entitled under the articles to participate in bonus issues. The existing preference shareholders objected. They stated that reducing their proportion of the class of preference shares (by issuing the bonus of preference shares) was a variation of class rights to which they had not consented.
>
> *Decision:* This was not a variation of class rights since the existing preference shareholders had the same number of shares (and votes at a class meeting) as before.

(b) **To subdivide shares of another class with the incidental effect of increasing the voting strength of that other class**

> *Greenhalgh v Arderne Cinemas Ltd 1946*
>
> *The facts:* The company had two classes of ordinary shares, 50p shares and 10p shares. Every share carried one vote. A resolution was passed to subdivide each 50p share into five 10p shares, thus multiplying the votes of that class by five.
>
> *Decision:* The rights of the original 10p shares had not been varied since they still had one vote per share as before.

(c) **To return capital to the holders of preference shares**

(d) **To create and issue a new class of preference shares with priority over an existing class of ordinary shares**

The cases cited in the preceding paragraph illustrate the principle that without a '**literal variation**' of class rights there is no alteration of rights to which the safeguards of proper procedure and appeal to the court apply. The fact that the **value** of existing rights may be affected will not concern the court if the rights are unchanged.

<table>
<tr><td>**Exam focus point**</td><td>Knowledge of what does **not** constitute a variation of class rights is vital in this area.</td></tr>
</table>

3.5.4 Special situations

To deal with unusual **situations** which in the past caused some difficulty, the following rules apply.

(a) If the class rights are set **by the articles** and they **provide** a **variation procedure**, that procedure must be followed for any variation even if it is different to the statutory procedure.

(b) If class **rights** are **defined otherwise than by the articles** and there is **no variation procedure**, consent of a **three-quarters majority** of the class is both necessary and sufficient.

The rules on **notice, voting, polls, circulation of resolutions** and **quorum** relating to general meetings relate also to class meetings when voting on alteration of class rights.

3.5.5 Minority appeals to the court for unfair prejudice

FAST FORWARD

A **dissenting minority** holding 15% or more of the issued shares may apply to the court within 21 days of class consent to have the variation cancelled as 'unfairly prejudicial'.

Whenever class rights are varied under a procedure contained in the constitution, a **minority of holders of shares of the class** may apply to the court to have the variation cancelled.

The **objectors together** must:

- Hold **not less** than **15%** of the **issued shares** of the class in question
- **Not** themselves have **consented** to or voted in favour of the variation
- **Apply** to the court within **21 days** of the consent being given by the class

The **court** can either **approve the variation** as made or cancel it as '**unfairly prejudicial**'. It cannot, however, modify the terms of the variation. To establish that a variation is 'unfairly prejudicial' to the class, the minority must show that the majority was seeking **some advantage** to themselves as **members** of a **different class**, instead of considering the interests of the class in which they were then voting.

3.6 Statement of capital and initial shareholdings

A return known as a **statement of capital and initial shareholdings** is required to be made to the **Registrar** when a company is registered, and therefore applies only to the **shares of the subscribers**. This statement must give the following details in respect of the company's **share capital** and be **up to date** as of the statement date.

(a)   The **total number of shares** of the company

(b)   The **aggregate nominal value of the shares**

(c)   For **each class** of share:

 (i)   The **prescribed particulars** of any rights attached
 (ii)   The **total number of shares** in the class
 (iii)   The **aggregate nominal value** of shares in the class

(d)   The **aggregate amount unpaid** on the **total number of shares**

(e)   **Information that identifies the subscribers to the memorandum of association**

(f)   In respect of **each subscriber**, the **number**, **nominal value** and **class of shares** taken by them on formation and the **amount** to be **paid up**

4 Allotment of shares

FAST FORWARD

Directors exercise the **delegated power** to allot shares, either by virtue of the articles or a resolution in general meeting.

4.1 Definition

Key term

> **Allotment of shares** is the issue and allocation to a person of a certain number of shares under a contract of allotment. Once the shares are allotted and the holder is entered in the register of members, the holder becomes a member of the company. The member is issued with a share certificate.

Allotment of shares is governed by the Companies Act 2006 (TSO, 2006). The allotment of shares is a **form of contract**. The intending shareholder applies to the company for shares, and the company accepts the offer. The terms '**allotment**' and '**issue**' have different meanings.

(a)   A share is **allotted** when the person to whom it is allotted acquires an unconditional right to be entered in the register of members as the holder of that share. That stage is reached when the board of directors (to whom the power to allot shares is usually given) considers the application and formally resolves to allot the shares.

However if the directors imposed a **condition**, for instance that the shares should be allotted only on receipt of the subscription money, the allotment would only take effect when payment was made.

(b)   The **issue** of shares is not a defined term but is usually taken to be a later stage at which the allottee **receives** a **letter of allotment** or share certificate issued by the company.

The allotment of shares of a **private company** is a **simple** and **immediate matter**. The name of the allottee is entered in the register of members soon after the allotment of shares and they become a member.

4.2 Public company allotment of shares

There are various **methods of selling shares** to the public.

Key terms

> **Public offer:** where members of the public subscribe for shares directly to the company.
> **Offer for sale:** an offer to members of the public to apply for shares based on information in a prospectus.
> **Placing:** a method of raising share capital where shares are offered in a small number of large 'blocks', to persons or institutions who have previously agreed to purchase the shares at a predetermined price.

4.3 Private company allotment of shares

The **allotment of shares** in a **private company** is more **straightforward**. The rule to remember is that private companies cannot sell shares to the public. An application must be made to the directors directly. After that, shares are allotted and issued, and a return of allotment made to the Registrar, as for a public company.

4.3.1 Directors' powers to allot shares

Directors of **private companies** with **one class of share** have the **authority** to allot shares **unless restricted** by the articles.

Directors of **public companies,** or **private companies with more than one class of share, may not allot shares** (except to subscribers to the memorandum and to employees' share schemes) **without authority from the members.** Any director who allots shares **without authority** commits an **offence** under the Companies Act 2006 and may be fined. However, the allotment remains **valid**.

4.4 Pre-emption rights

FAST FORWARD

If the directors propose to allot 'equity securities' wholly for cash, there is a general requirement to offer these shares to **holders** of **similar shares** in proportion to their holdings.

Key term

Pre-emption rights are the rights of existing ordinary shareholders to be offered new shares issued by the company *pro rata* to their existing holding of that class of shares.

If a company proposes to allot ordinary shares wholly for cash, it has a **statutory obligation** to offer those shares first to holders of similar shares in **proportion to their holdings** and on the same or more favourable terms as the main allotment. This is known as a **rights issue**.

4.5 Rights issues

Key term

A **rights issue** is a right given to a shareholder to subscribe for further shares in the company, usually *pro rata* to their existing holding in the company's shares.

A rights issue must be made **in writing** (hard copy or electronic) in the same manner as a notice of a general meeting is sent to members. It must specify a period of **not less than 21 days** during which the offer may be accepted but may not be withdrawn. If not accepted or renounced in favour of another person within that period the offer is deemed to be declined.

Equity securities which have been offered to members in this way but are **not accepted** may then be allotted on the same (or less favourable) terms to non-members. If equity securities are allotted in breach of these rules the members to whom the offer should have been made may, within the ensuing two years, recover **compensation** for their loss from those in default. The allotment will generally be valid.

4.5.1 Exclusion of pre-emption rights

A **private** company may by its articles permanently exclude these rules so that there is no statutory right of first refusal.

4.5.2 Disapplication of pre-emption rights

Any company may, by special resolution, resolve that the statutory right of first refusal shall not apply. Such a resolution to 'disapply' the right may either:

(a)   Be combined with the grant to directors of authority to allot shares; or

(b)   Simply permit an offer of shares to be made for cash to a non-member (without first offering the shares to members) on a particular occasion.

4.6 Bonus issues

> A **bonus issue** is the capitalisation of the reserves of a company by the issue of additional shares to existing shareholders, in proportion to their holdings. Such shares are normally fully paid-up with no cash called for from the shareholders.

A bonus issue is more correctly, but less often, called a '**capitalisation issue**' (also called a 'scrip' issue). The articles of a company usually give it power to apply its reserves to paying up unissued shares wholly or in part, and then to allot these shares as a bonus issue to members.

5 Issuing shares at a premium or at a discount

> In issuing shares, a company must fix a **price** which is **equal** to, or **more than**, the **nominal value of the shares**. It may not allot shares at a discount to the nominal value.

The Companies Act 2006 (TSO, 2006) states that every share has a **nominal value** and **may not be allotted at a discount** to that.

In allotting shares, every company is required to obtain in money or money's worth, consideration of a value at least equal to the nominal value of the shares plus the whole of any premium. To issue shares '**at par**' is to obtain equal value, say, £1 for a £1 share.

> *Ooregum Gold Mining Co of India v Roper 1892*
>
> *The facts:* Shares in the company, although nominally £1, were trading at a market price of 12.5p. In an honest attempt to refinance the company, new £1 preference shares were issued and credited with 75p already paid, so the purchasers of the shares were actually paying twice the market value of the ordinary shares. When, however, the company subsequently went into insolvent liquidation the holders of the new shares were required to pay a further 75p.

If shares are allotted at a discount to their nominal value, the allottee, if they agree to the issue, must nonetheless pay the **full nominal value** with **interest** at the appropriate rate. Any subsequent holder of such a share who knew of the underpayment must make good the shortfall.

Consideration for shares	
Partly paid shares	The no-discount rule only requires that, in allotting its shares, a company shall not fix a price which is less than the nominal value of the shares. It may leave part of that price to be paid at some later time. Thus £1 shares may be issued partly paid – 75p on allotment and 25p when called for or by instalment. The unpaid capital passes with the shares. If transferred, they are a debt payable by the holder at the time when payment is demanded.
Underwriting fees	A company may pay underwriting or other commission in respect of an issue of shares if so permitted by its Articles. This means that, if shares are issued at par, the net amount received will be below par value.
Bonus issue	The allotment of shares as a 'bonus issue' is for full consideration since reserves, which are shareholders' funds, are converted into fixed capital and are used to pay for the shares.
Money's worth	The price for the shares may be paid in **money** or '**money's worth**', including goodwill and know-how. It need not be paid in cash and the company may agree to accept a '**non-cash' consideration** of sufficient value. For instance, a company may issue shares in payment of the price agreed in the purchase of a property.

5.1 Private companies

FAST FORWARD

Private companies may issue shares for **inadequate consideration** provided the directors are behaving reasonably and honestly.

A private company may allot shares for **inadequate consideration** by acceptance of goods or services at an overvalue. This loophole has been allowed to exist because in some cases it is very much a matter of opinion whether an asset is or is not of a stated value.

The **courts** therefore have **refused** to overrule directors in their valuation of an asset acquired for shares if it appears **reasonable** and **honest**. However, a blatant and unjustified overvaluation will be declared **invalid**.

5.2 Public companies

FAST FORWARD

There are **stringent rules** on consideration for shares in public companies.

More **stringent rules** apply to **public companies**.

(a) The company must, at the time of allotment, receive **at least one-quarter of the nominal value** of the shares and the **whole** of any premium.

(b) Any **non-cash consideration** accepted must be **independently valued**.

(c) **Non-cash consideration** may **not** be accepted as payment for shares if an undertaking contained in such consideration is to be, or may be, **performed more than five years after the allotment.** This relates to, say, a property or business in return for shares. To enforce the five-year rule, the law requires that:

  (i) At the time of the allotment the **allottee** must **undertake** to **perform** their side of the agreement within a specified period, which must not exceed five years. If no such undertaking is given the **allottee** becomes **immediately liable** to pay cash for their shares as soon as they are allotted.

  (ii) If the **allottee later fails** to **perform** their undertaking to transfer property at the due time, they become liable to pay **cash** for their shares when they default.

(d) An **undertaking to do work or perform services is not to be accepted as consideration**. A public company may, however, allot shares to discharge a debt in respect of services already rendered.

  If a public company, against the above rule, accepts future services as consideration, the shareholder must pay the company, in cash, their **nominal value** plus any **premium** treated as paid-up, and **interest** at 5% on any such amount.

(e) Within **two years of receiving its trading certificate**, a public company **may not receive a transfer of non-cash assets from a subscriber** to the memorandum. This is unless its value is less than 10% of the issued nominal share capital and it has been independently valued and agreed by an ordinary resolution.

5.2.1 Valuation of non-cash assets

When a public company allots shares for a non-cash consideration the company must usually obtain a **report on its value** from an independent valuer.

The **valuation report** must be made to the company within the six months before the allotment. On receiving the report the company must send a copy to the proposed allottee and later to the Registrar.

The independent valuation rule does not apply to an allotment of shares made in the course of a **takeover bid**.

5.3 Allotment of shares at a premium

If shares are issued at a premium, the **excess** must be credited to a **share premium** account.

Key term

Share premium is the excess received, either in cash or other consideration, over the nominal value of the shares issued.

An established company may be able to obtain consideration for new shares in excess of their nominal value. The excess, called 'share premium', must be credited to a **share premium account**.

Exam focus point

Exam questions may test your knowledge of the meaning and effect of issuing shares at a premium and at a discount.

If a company obtains non-cash consideration for its shares which exceeds the nominal value of the shares, the excess should also be credited to the **share premium account**.

5.3.1 Example: Using a share premium account

If a company allots its £1 (nominal) shares for £1.50 in cash, £1 per share is credited to the share capital account, and 50p to the share premium account.

 Illustration

We will use the above example to illustrate the effects of the transaction on the balance sheet. The company has issued 100 shares.

	Before share issue £	After share issue £
Cash	100	250
Share capital	100	200
Share premium	–	50
	100	250

The general rule is that reduction of the share premium account is subject to the **same** restrictions as reduction of share capital. You should learn the fact that **a company cannot distribute any part of its share premium account as dividend**.

5.4 Uses of the share premium account

Use of the share premium account is limited. It is most often used for **bonus issues**.

Under the Companies Act, the **permitted uses of share premium** are to pay:

- **Fully paid shares under a bonus issue** since this operation merely converts one form of fixed capital (share premium) into another (share capital)

- **Issue expenses** and **commission** in respect of a **new share issue**

Additionally, the share premium account may be used to finance any premium due when **redeemable shares** are redeemed.

Chapter Roundup

- Under the Companies Act 2006 (TSO, 2006) a member of a company is a person who has **agreed to become a member**, and whose name has been **entered** in the **register of members**. This may occur by: subscription to the memorandum; applying for shares; the presentation to the company of a transfer of shares to the prospective member; applying as personal representative of a deceased member or a trustee of a bankrupt.

- There are **eight** ways in which a member ceases to be so.

- **Public** and **private companies** must have a minimum of **one** member. There is **no maximum** number.

- Under the Companies Act 2006 (TSO, 2006) a **share** is a transferable form of property, carrying rights and obligations, by which the interest of a member of a company limited by shares is measured.

- The term **'capital'** is used in several senses in company legislation, to mean issued, allotted or called up share capital or loan capital.

- If the constitution of a company states no differences between shares, it is assumed that they are all **ordinary** shares with parallel rights and obligations. There may, however, be other types, notably **preference shares**.

- The most common right of preference shareholders is a **prior right** to receive a fixed dividend. This right is not a right to **compel payment** of a dividend, but it is **cumulative** unless otherwise stated. Usually, preference shareholders **cannot participate** in a dividend over and above their fixed dividend and **cease to be entitled to arrears of undeclared dividends** if the company goes into liquidation.

- The holders of **issued** shares have **vested rights** which can only be varied by following a strict procedure. The standard procedure is by **special resolution** passed by at least **three-quarters** of the votes cast at a **separate class meeting** or by written consent.

- It is **not** a variation of class rights to issue shares to new members, to subdivide shares of another class, to return capital to preference shareholders, or to create a new class of preference shareholders.

- A **dissenting minority** holding 15% or more of the issued shares may apply to the court within 21 days of class consent to have the variation cancelled as 'unfairly prejudicial'.

- Directors exercise the **delegated power** to allot shares, either by virtue of the articles or a resolution in general meeting.

- If the directors propose to allot 'equity securities' wholly for cash, there is a general requirement to offer these shares to **holders** of **similar shares** in proportion to their holdings.

- In issuing shares, a company must fix a **price** which is **equal** to, or **more than**, the **nominal value of the shares**. It may not allot shares at a discount to the nominal value.

- Private companies may issue shares for **inadequate consideration** provided the directors are behaving reasonably and honestly.

- There are **stringent rules** on consideration for shares in public companies.

- If shares are issued at a premium, the **excess** must be credited to a **share premium** account.

- Use of the share premium account is limited. It is most often used for **bonus issues**.

1   If a company fails to pay preference shareholders their dividend, they can bring a court action to compel the company to pay it.

True ☐

False ☐

2   Which two of the following are implied rights of preference shareholders?

A   The right to receive a dividend is cumulative.

B   If the company goes into liquidation, preference shareholders are entitled to claim all arrears of dividend from the liquidator.

C   As well as rights to their preference dividends, preference shareholders can share equally in dividends payable to ordinary shareholders.

D   Preference shareholders have equal voting rights to ordinary shareholders.

3   If a company issues new ordinary shares for cash, the general rule is that:

A   The shares must first be offered to existing members in the case of a public but not a private company.

B   The shares must first be offered to existing members whether the company is public or private.

C   The shares must first be offered to existing members in the case of a private but not a public company.

D   The shares need not be issued to existing members.

4   What is the minimum number of members that a plc must have?

A   One
B   Two
C   Three
D   Four

5   A share premium account can be used for bonus issues of shares or issue costs for new share issues.

True ☐

False ☐

1   False. The company may decide not to pay any dividend, or may be unable to because it does not have any distributable profits. What the preference shareholders have is a right to receive their dividends before other dividends are paid or declared.

2   A and D are implied rights; the others have to be stated explicitly.

3   B. The shares must be first offered to existing members whether the company is public or private.

4   A. All companies must have a minimum of one member.

5   True. Both are acceptable uses for the share premium account.

Now try the questions below from the Practice Question Bank

Number
33, 34

16

Loan capital

Topic list	Syllabus reference
1 Borrowing	E2(a)
2 Debentures and loan capital	E2(b), E2(c)
3 Charges	E2(d)
4 Registration of charges	E2(e)
5 Debentureholders' remedies	E2(b), E2(c)

Introduction

In this chapter on **borrowing** and **loan capital**, you should note that the interests and position of a lender are very different from those of a shareholder.

We shall be looking at how loan capital holders protect themselves, specifically through taking out **fixed or floating charges** over company assets. 'Charges' give the lender the right to sell assets which are subject to the charge in order to recover money owed to them if the borrower does not repay the debt.

You need to understand the differences between fixed and floating charges, and also how they can protect loan creditors, for example by giving chargeholders the ability to appoint a **receiver**.

Study guide

		Intellectual level
E	**Capital and the financing of companies**	
2	**Loan capital**	
(a)	Define companies' borrowing powers	1
(b)	Explain the meaning of loan capital and debenture	2
(c)	Distinguish loan capital from share capital and explain the different rights held by shareholders and debenture holders	2
(d)	Explain the concept of a company charge and distinguish between fixed and floating charges	2
(e)	Describe the need and the procedure for registering company charges	2

Exam guide

Loan capital may crop up in questions involving insolvency and corporate finance in general. However, it is a topic that could also be examined in a scenario question. You may be required to identify instances where a company has exceeded its borrowing powers or the differences between types of charges.

1 Borrowing

FAST FORWARD

Companies have an **implied power** to borrow for purposes incidental to their trade or business.

All companies registered under the Companies Act 2006 (TSO, 2006) have an **implied power to borrow** for purposes **incidental to their trade or business**. A company formed under earlier Acts will have an implied power to borrow if its object is to carry on a trade or business. In delegating the company's power to borrow to the directors, it is usual, and essential in the case of a company whose shares are quoted on the stock exchange, to impose a **maximum limit** on the **borrowing** arranged by directors.

A **contract** to **repay borrowed money** may in principle be **unenforceable** if either:

- It is money borrowed for an **ultra vires** (or restricted) purpose, and this is known to the lender.
- The directors **exceed their borrowing powers** or have no powers to borrow.

However:

- In both cases the lender will probably be **able** to **enforce** the contract.
- If the contract is within the capacity of the company but beyond the delegated powers of the directors the company may **ratify** the **loan contract**.

Case law has determined that if a company has power to borrow, it also has power to **create charges** over the company's assets as **security** for the loan.

1.1 Personal guarantees

Some lenders may require directors and/or members to agree to repay a loan out of their **personal wealth** should the company default on the debt. This is known as **requesting a personal guarantee**, which is a **promise by a person** (the directors or shareholders) to **assume a debt obligation** in the event of non-payment by the borrower (the company). Personal guarantees are a **means of protecting the lender** by preventing the shareholders/members from hiding behind the protection of limited liability. It is commonly used where the lender is very powerful (such as a bank) and where the borrower (such as a new or small company) has no other source of funds available to it.

2 Debentures and loan capital

2.1 Loan capital

FAST FORWARD

Loan capital comprises all the longer-term borrowing of a company. It is distinguished from share capital by the fact that, at some point, borrowing must be repaid. Share capital, on the other hand, is only returned to shareholders if the company is wound up.

A company's **loan capital** comprises all amounts which it borrows for the long term, such as **permanent overdrafts** at the bank, **unsecured loans** from a bank or other party and **loans secured** on assets, from a bank or other party. Companies often issue long-term loans as capital in the form of **debentures**.

2.2 Debentures

FAST FORWARD

A **debenture** is a document stating the terms on which a company has borrowed money. There are three main types.

- A **single debenture**

- **Debentures issued as a series** and usually registered

- **Debenture stock** subscribed to by a large number of lenders. Only this form requires a **debenture trust deed**, although the others may often incorporate one

Key term

A **debenture** is the written acknowledgement of a debt by a company, normally containing provisions as to payment of interest and the terms of repayment of principal. A debenture may be secured on some or all of the assets of the company or its subsidiaries.

A debenture may create a **charge** over the company's assets as security for the loan. However, a document relating to an unsecured loan is also a debenture in company law.

2.3 Types of debenture

A debenture is usually a **formal legal document**. Broadly, there are **three main types**.

(a) **A single debenture**

If, for example, a company obtains a secured loan or overdraft facility from its bank, the latter is likely to insist that the company seals the **bank's standard form of debenture** creating the charge and giving the bank various safeguards and powers.

(b) **Debentures issued as a series and usually registered**

Different lenders may provide **different amounts** on **different dates**. Although each transaction is a separate loan, the intention is that the lenders should rank equally *(pari passu)* in their right to repayment and in any security given to them. Each lender therefore receives a debenture in identical form in respect of their loan. The debentures are **transferable securities**.

(c) **The issue of debenture stock subscribed to by a large number of lenders**
Only a public company may use this method to **offer its debentures to the public** and any such offer is a prospectus; if it seeks a listing on the stock exchange, then the rules on listing particulars must be followed. Each lender has a right to be **repaid** their **capital** at the **due time** (unless they are perpetual) and to receive **interest** on it until **repayment**. This form of borrowing is treated as a single loan 'stock' in which each debenture stockholder has a specified fraction (in money terms) which they or some previous holder contributed when the stock was issued. Debenture stock is transferable in multiples of, say, £1 or £10.

One **advantage of debenture stock** over debentures issued as single and indivisible loan transactions is that the holder of debenture stock can sell part of their holding, say £1,000 (nominal), out of a larger amount.

Debenture stock must be created using a **debenture trust deed**, though single and series debentures may also use a debenture trust deed.

2.4 Debenture trust deed

Major elements of a debenture trust deed for debenture stock
The appointment usually of a trustee for prospective debenture stockholders. The trustee is usually a bank, insurance company or other institution but may be an individual.
The nominal amount of the debenture stock is defined, which is the maximum amount which may be raised then or later. The date or period of repayment is specified, as is the rate of interest and half-yearly interest payment dates.
If the debenture stock is secured **the deed creates a charge or charges** over the assets of the company.
The trustee is authorised to **enforce the security** in case of default and, in particular, to appoint a receiver with suitable powers of management.
The company enters into **various covenants**, for instance to keep its assets fully insured or to limit its total borrowings; breach is a default by the company.
There may be elaborate provisions for **transfer of stock** and **meetings** of debenture stockholders.

Advantages of a debenture trust deed for debenture stock
The **trustee** with appropriate powers can **intervene promptly** in case of default.
Security for the debenture stock in the form of charges over property can be **given to a single trustee**.
The **company** can **contact a representative of the debentureholders** with whom it can negotiate.
By calling a **meeting of debentureholders**, the trustee can consult them and obtain a decision binding on them all.
The **debentureholders** will be able to **enjoy the benefit of a legal mortgage** over the company's land.

2.5 Register of debentureholders

Company law does not specifically require a **register of debentureholders** be maintained. When there is a register of debentureholders, the following **regulations** apply.

(a)   The company is required by law to keep the **register** at its registered office, or at an **address** notified to the registrar.

(b)   The register must be open to **inspection** by **any person** unless the constitution or trust deed provide otherwise. Any person may obtain a copy of the register or part of it for a fee. A holder of debentures issued under a trust deed may require the company (on payment) to supply them with a copy of the deed.

Under the Companies Act 2006 (TSO, 2006) a company has **five days** to respond to an inspection request or seek exemption to do so from the court.

(c)   The register should be **properly kept** in accordance with the requirements of the Companies Act.

2.6 Rights of debentureholders

The **position of debentureholders** is best described by **comparison** with that of **shareholders**. At first sight the two appear to have a great deal in common.

- Both **own transferable company securities** which are usually long-term investments in the company.

- The **issue procedure** is much the same. An offer of either shares or debentures to the public is a prospectus as defined by the Act.

- The **procedure** for **transfer** of registered shares and debentures is the same.

But there are **significant differences**.

Differences	Shareholder	Debentureholder
Role	Is a proprietor or owner of the company	Is a creditor of the company
Voting rights	May vote at general meetings	May not vote
Cost of investment	Shares may not be issued at a discount to nominal value	Debentures may be offered at a discount to nominal value
Return	Dividends are only paid • Out of distributable profits • When directors declare them	Interest must be paid when it is due
Redemption	Statutory restrictions on redeeming shares	No restriction on redeeming debentures
Liquidation	Shareholders are the last people to be paid in a winding up	Debentures must be paid back before shareholders are paid

From the investor's standpoint debenture stock is often **preferable to preference shares**. Although both yield a fixed income, debenture stock offers greater security.

2.6.1 Advantages and disadvantages of debentures (for the company)

Advantages	Disadvantages
Easily traded	May have to pay high interest rates to make them attractive
Terms clear and specific	Interest payments mandatory
Assets subject to a floating charge may be traded	Interest payments may upset shareholders if dividends fall
Popular due to guaranteed income	Debentureholder's remedies of liquidators or receivers may be disastrous for the company
Interest tax-deductible	Crystallisation of a floating charge can cause trading difficulties for a company
No restrictions on issue or purchase by a company	

3 Charges

FAST FORWARD

A charge over the assets of a company gives a creditor a **prior claim** over other creditors to payment of their debt out of these assets.

Charges may be either **fixed**, which attach to the relevant asset on creation, or **floating**, which attach on 'crystallisation'. For this reason it is not possible to identify the assets to which a **floating** charge relates (until **crystallisation**).

3.1 Definition

Key term

> A **charge** is an encumbrance upon real or personal property granting the holder certain rights over that property. They are often used as security for a debt owed to the chargeholder. The most common form of charge is by way of legal mortgage, used to secure the indebtedness of borrowers in house purchase transactions. In the case of companies, charges over assets are most frequently granted to persons who provide loan capital to the business.

A charge **secured** over a company's assets gives to the creditor (called the 'chargee') a prior claim (over other creditors) to payment of their debt out of those assets. Charges are of two kinds, fixed and floating.

3.2 Fixed charges

Key term

> A **fixed charge** is a form of protection given to secured creditors relating to specific assets of a company. The charge grants the holder the right of enforcement against the identified asset (in the event of default in repayment or some other matter) so that the creditor may realise the asset to meet the debt owed. Fixed charges rank first in order of priority in liquidation.

Fixed (or specific) charges attach to the relevant asset as soon as the charge is created. By its nature a fixed charge is best suited to assets which the company is likely to retain for a long period. A mortgage is an example of a fixed charge.

If the company disposes of the charged asset it will either **repay the secured debt** out of the proceeds of sale so that the charge is discharged at the time of sale, or **pass the asset over to** the purchaser still subject to the charge.

3.3 Floating charges

Key term

> A **floating charge** has been defined in case law as:
>
> (a) A charge on a class of assets of a company, present and future ...
>
> (b) Which class is, in the ordinary course of the company's business, changing from time to time and ...
>
> (c) Until the holders enforce the charge the company may carry on business and deal with the assets charged.

Floating charges do not attach to the relevant assets until the charge crystallises.

A floating charge is **not restricted** to assets such as **receivables** or **inventory**. A floating charge over 'the undertaking and assets' of a company (the most common type) applies to future as well as to current assets.

3.4 Identification of charges as fixed or floating

It is not always **immediately apparent** whether a charge is fixed or floating. Chargees often do not wish to identify a charge as being floating as it may get paid later than preferential debts in insolvency proceedings.

A charge contract may declare the charge as fixed, or fixed and floating, whether it is or not. **The label attached** by parties in this way is **not a conclusive statement of the charge's legal nature**.

The general rule is that a **charge over assets will not be registered as fixed if it envisages that the company will still be able to deal with the charged assets without reference to the chargee**.

R in Right of British Columbia v Federal Business Development Bank 1988

The facts: In this Canadian case the Bank had a charge over the company's entire property expressed as 'a fixed and specific mortgage and charge'. Another term allowed the company to continue making sales from stock in the ordinary course of business until notified in writing by the bank to stop doing so.

Decision: The charge was created as a floating, not a fixed, charge.

However, the courts have found **exceptions** to the general rule concerning permission to deal.

(a)   In *Re GE Tunbridge Ltd 1995* it was held that the charge over certain fixed assets was a floating charge, even though the company was required to obtain the chargee's permission before dealing with the assets.

(b)   In *Re Cimex Tissues Ltd 1994* the court decided that the charge in dispute was a fixed charge. The assets did not in the ordinary course of business change from time to time. This was despite the company being able to deal with the assets without the chargee's permission.

3.4.1 Charges over receivables

Charges expressed to be fixed which cover **present and future receivables** (book debts) are particularly tricky.

Again the general rule applies. If the company is allowed to deal with money collected from customers without notifying the chargee, the courts have decided that the charge is floating. If the money collected must be paid to the chargee, say in reduction of an overdraft, the courts have determined that the charge is fixed: *Siebe Gorman & Co Ltd v Barclays Bank Ltd 1979*.

In 2005 the House of Lords held in *Re Spectrum Plus* that there can be no fixed charge over a company's book debts.

3.5 Creating a floating charge

A **floating charge** is **often created by express words**. However, no special form of words is essential. If a **company** gives to a chargee rights over its assets while **retaining freedom to deal with them in the ordinary course of business** until the charge crystallises, that will be a charge which 'floats'. The particular assets subject to a floating charge cannot be identified until the charge attaches by crystallisation.

3.6 Crystallisation of a floating charge

FAST FORWARD

Floating charges **crystallise** or harden (convert into a fixed charge) on the happening of certain relevant events.

Key term

Crystallisation of a floating charge occurs when it is converted into a fixed charge: that is, a fixed charge on the assets owned by the company at the time of crystallisation.

Events causing crystallisation
The **liquidation** of the company
Cessation of the company's **business**
Active intervention by the chargee, generally by way of appointing a receiver
If the **charge contract so provides**, when notice is given by the chargee that the charge is converted into a fixed charge (on whatever assets of the relevant class are owned by the company at the time of the giving of notice)
The **crystallisation** of **another floating charge** if it causes the company to cease business.

Floating charge contracts sometimes make provision for '**automatic crystallisation**'. This is where the charge is to crystallise when a **specified event** – such as a breach of some term by the company – occurs, regardless of whether:

- The chargee learns of the event
- The chargee wants to enforce the charge as a result of the event

Such clauses have been accepted by the courts if they state that, on the event happening, the floating charge is **converted** to a fixed one. Clauses which provide only that a company is to cease to deal with charged assets on the occurrence of a particular event have been rejected.

3.7 Comparison of fixed and floating charges

FAST FORWARD

Floating charges rank **behind** a number of other creditors on liquidation, in particular preferential creditors such as employees.

A **fixed charge** is normally the more satisfactory form of security since it **confers immediate rights** over identified assets. A **floating charge** has some advantage in being applicable to **current assets which may be easier to realise** than long-term assets subject to a fixed charge. If, for example, a company becomes insolvent it may be easier to sell its inventory than its empty factory.

The principal disadvantages of floating charges
The **holder** of a floating charge **cannot be certain** until the charge crystallises which assets will form their security.
Even when a floating charge has crystallised over an identified pool of assets, the **chargeholder** may find themself **postponed** to the claim of **other creditors** as follows. (a) A **judgement creditor or landlord** who has seized goods and sold them may retain the proceeds if received before the appointment of the debentureholder's receiver. (b) **Preferential debts** such as wages may be paid out of assets subject to a floating charge unless there are other uncharged assets available for this purpose. (c) The **holder** of a **fixed charge** over the same assets will usually have priority over a floating charge on those assets even if that charge was created before the fixed charge. (d) A creditor may have sold goods and delivered them to the company on condition that they are to retain legal ownership until they have been paid (a **Romalpa** clause).
A **floating charge** may become **invalid automatically** if the company creates the charge to secure an existing debt and goes into liquidation within a year thereafter. The period is only six months with a fixed charge.

3.8 Priority of charges

FAST FORWARD

If more than one charge exists over the **same class of property** then legal rules must be applied to see which takes priority in the event the company goes into liquidation.

Different charges over the **same** property may be given to different creditors. It will be necessary in such cases to determine which party's claim has **priority**.

Illustration

If charges are created over the same property to secure a debt of £5,000 to X and £7,000 to Y and the property is sold yielding only £10,000, either X or Y is paid in full and the other receives only the balance remaining out of £10,000 realised from the security.

Priority of charges
Fixed charges rank according to the **order of their creation**. If two successive fixed charges over the same factory are created on 1 January and 1 February the earlier takes priority over the later one.
A floating charge created before a fixed charge will only take priority if, when the latter was created, the **fixed chargee** had **notice** of a clause in the floating charge that prevents a later prior charge.
A **fixed charge created before** a **floating one** has **priority**.
Two floating charges take priority according to the **time of creation**.

If a floating charge is existing and a fixed charge over the same property is created later the fixed charge has priority. This is unless the fixed chargeholder knew of the floating charge. The **fixed** charge ranks **first** since it attached to the property at the time of **creation** but the **floating** charge attaches at the time of **crystallisation**. Once a floating charge has crystallised it becomes a fixed charge and a fixed charge created subsequently ranks after it.

3.8.1 Negative pledge clauses

A floating chargeholder may seek to protect themselves against losing their priority by including in the terms of their floating charge a prohibition against the company creating a fixed charge over the same property (sometimes called a **'negative pledge clause'**).

If the company **breaks that prohibition** the creditor to whom the fixed charge is given nonetheless obtains priority, unless at the time when their charge is created they have **actual** knowledge of the prohibition.

3.8.2 Sale of charged assets

If a company sells a charged asset to a **third party** the following rules apply.

- A chargee with a fixed charge still has recourse to the property in the hands of the third party – the **charge** is **automatically** transferred with the property.

- Property only remains charged by a floating charge if the **third party** had **notice** of it when they acquired the property.

Exam focus point

You should be prepared to work out the priority of charges in a scenario.

4 Registration of charges

> To be valid and enforceable, charges must be **registered** within **21 days** of creation with the Registrar.

Certain types of **charge** created by a company **should be registered** within **21 days** with the Registrar by either the company or a person interested in it (eg the debenture trustee). Charges securing a **debenture issue** and **floating charges** are **specifically registrable**.

Other charges that are **registrable** include charges on:

- Uncalled share capital or calls made but not paid
- Land or any interest in land, other than a charge for rent
- Receivables (book debts)
- Goodwill or any intellectual property
- Ships or aircraft or any share in a ship

4.1 The registration process

The **company is responsible for registering the charge** but the charge **may** also **be registered** as a result of an application **by another person** interested in the charge.

The Registrar should be sent **the instrument** by which the charge is created or evidenced. The Registrar also has to be sent **prescribed particulars of the charge**.

- The date when the charge was created
- The amount of the debt which it secures
- Short particulars of the property to which the charge applies
- The person entitled to it

The Registrar files the particulars in the company's 'charges' register and notes the date of delivery. They also issue a **certificate** which is **conclusive evidence** that the **charge had been duly registered**.

The 21-day period for registration runs from the **creation** of the **charge**, or the acquisition of property charged, and not from the making of the loan for which the charge is security. Creation of a charge is usually effected by **execution of a document**.

4.2 Rectification of register of changes

A **mistake** or **omission** in registered particulars can only be rectified by the court ordering an extension of the period for registration, and with the subsequent rectification of the register. The court will only make the order if the error or omission was accidental or if it is just and equitable to do so.

4.3 Failure to deliver particulars

The duty to deliver particulars falls upon the **company** creating the charge; if no one delivers particulars within 21 days, the **company and its officers are liable to a fine**.

Non-delivery in the time period results in the **charge** being **void** against an administrator, liquidator or any creditor of a company.

Non-delivery of a charge means that the sum secured by it is **payable forthwith on demand**.

4.3.1 Late delivery of particulars

The rules governing late delivery are the **same** as governing registration of **further particulars**, that is, a **court order** is required for registration.

A **charge** can only be **registered late** if it **does not prejudice the creditors** or **shareholders of the company**. Therefore a correctly registered fixed charge has priority over a fixed charge created earlier but registered after it, if that charge is registered late.

BPP
LEARNING MEDIA

4.4 Register of charges

As you already know, every company is under an obligation to keep a copy of documents creating charges, and a register of charges, at its **registered office** or **single alternative inspection location**.

5 Debentureholders' remedies

5.1 Rights of unsecured debentureholders

FAST FORWARD

A debentureholder **without security** has the same rights as any other creditor.

Any **debentureholder** is a **creditor** of the company with the normal remedies of an unsecured creditor. They could:

- **Sue** the company for debt and seize its property if their judgement for debt is unsatisfied

- Present a petition to the court for the **compulsory liquidation** of the company

- Apply to the court for an **administration order**, that is, a temporary reprieve to try and rescue a company

5.2 Rights of secured debentureholders

FAST FORWARD

A **secured** debentureholder may enforce the security if the company defaults on payment of interest or repayment of capital. They may take possession of the asset subject to the charge and sell it or apply to the court for its transfer to their ownership by a foreclosure order. They may also appoint a receiver or administrator of it. A floating chargeholder may place the company into administration.

A **secured** debentureholder (or the trustee of a debenture trust deed) may enforce the security. They may:

- Take **possession of the asset** subject to the charge if they have a fixed charge (if they have a floating charge they may only take possession if the contract allows)

- **Sell it** (provided the debenture is executed as a deed)

- Apply to the court for its **transfer** to their ownership by foreclosure order (rarely used and only available to a legal chargee)

- Appoint a **receiver** of it, provided an **administration order** is not in effect, or (in the case of floating chargeholders) appoint an administrator without needing to apply to the court

Chapter Roundup

- Companies have an **implied power** to borrow for purposes incidental to their trade or business.

- **Loan capital** comprises all the longer-term borrowing of a company. It is distinguished from share capital by the fact that, at some point, borrowing must be repaid. Share capital, on the other hand, is only returned to shareholders if the company is wound up.

- A **debenture** is a document stating the terms on which a company has borrowed money. There are three main types.

    - A **single debenture**

    - **Debentures issued as a series** and usually registered

    - **Debenture stock** subscribed to by a large number of lenders. Only this form requires a **debenture trust deed**, although the others may often incorporate one

- A charge over the assets of a company gives a creditor a **prior claim** over other creditors to payment of their debt out of these assets.

- Charges may be either **fixed**, which attach to the relevant asset on creation, or **floating**, which attach on 'crystallisation'. For this reason it is not possible to identify the assets to which a **floating** charge relates (until **crystallisation**).

- Floating charges **crystallise** or harden (convert into a fixed charge) on the happening of certain relevant events.

- Floating charges rank **behind** a number of other creditors on liquidation, in particular preferential creditors such as employees.

- If more than one charge exists over the **same class of property** then legal rules must be applied to see which takes priority in the event the company goes into liquidation.

- To be valid and enforceable, charges must be **registered** within **21 days** of creation with the Registrar.

- A debentureholder **without security** has the same rights as any other creditor.

- A **secured** debentureholder may enforce the security if the company defaults on payment of interest or repayment of capital. They may take possession of the asset subject to the charge and sell it or apply to the court for its transfer to their ownership by a foreclosure order. They may also appoint a receiver or administrator of it. A floating chargeholder may place the company into administration.

1   Which of the following are correct statements about the relationship between a company's ordinary shares and its debentures?

Select all that apply.

A   Debentures do not confer voting rights, whilst ordinary shares do.
B   The company's duty is to pay interest on debentures, and to pay dividends on ordinary shares.
C   Interest paid on debentures is deducted from pre-tax profits, dividends are paid from net profits.
D   A debentureholder takes priority over a member in liquidation.

2   A fixed charge:

A   Cannot be an informal mortgage
B   Can be a legal mortgage
C   Can only attach to land, shares or book debts
D   Cannot attach to land

3   Company law requires a company to maintain a register of charges, but not a register of debentureholders.

True   ☐

False   ☐

4   In which of the following situations will crystallisation of a floating charge occur?

Select all that apply.

A   Liquidation of the company
B   Disposal by the company of the charged asset
C   Cessation of the company's business
D   After the giving of notice by the chargee if the contract so provides

5   Certain types of charges need to be registered within 28 days of creation.

True   ☐

False   ☐

Answers to Quick Quiz

1   A, C and D are correct. Whilst the company has a contractual duty to pay interest on debentures, there is no duty on it to pay dividends on shares. B is therefore incorrect.

2   B. A mortgage is an example of a fixed charge. It can extend to, for instance, plant and machinery as well as land.

3   True. A register of charges must be kept, a register of debentureholders is not required to be kept by the Act.

4   A, C and D are true. As the charge does not attach to the asset until crystallisation, B is untrue.

5   False. Certain charges such as charges securing a debenture issue and floating charges need to be registered within 21 days.

Now try the questions below from the Practice Question Bank

Number
35, 36

17

Capital maintenance and dividend law

Topic list	Syllabus reference
1 Capital maintenance	E3(a)
2 Reduction of share capital	E3(a)
3 Distributing dividends	E3(b)

Introduction

The capital which a limited company obtains from its members as consideration for their shares is sometimes called **'the creditors' buffer'**. No one can prevent an unsuccessful company from losing its capital by trading at a loss. However, whatever capital the company does have must be held for the payment of the company's debts and may not be returned to members except under procedures which safeguard the interest of creditors. That is the price which members of a limited company are required to pay for the protection of limited liability. This principle has been developed in a number of detailed applications.

- Capital may only be distributed to members under the formal procedure of a **reduction** of **share capital** or a **winding up** of the company.
- **Dividends** may only be paid out of distributable profits.

Study guide

		Intellectual level
E	Capital and the financing of companies	
3	Capital maintenance and dividend law	
(a)	Explain the doctrine of capital maintenance and capital reduction	2
(b)	Explain the rules governing the distribution of dividends in both private and public companies	2

Exam guide

Capital maintenance can be a difficult area. The different components could all be examined separately in multiple choice questions, or as part of a scenario question.

1 Capital maintenance

FAST FORWARD

> The rules which dictate how a company is to manage and maintain its capital exist to maintain the delicate balance between the **members' enjoyment of limited liability** and the **creditors' requirements that the company shall remain able to pay its debts**.

Key term

> **Capital maintenance** is a fundamental principle of company law: that limited companies should not be allowed to make payments out of capital to the detriment of company creditors. Therefore the Companies Act contains many examples of control upon capital payments. These include provisions restricting dividend payments, and capital reduction schemes.

Exam focus point

> The rules affecting the possible threats to capital are complicated in certain areas. However, provided you know the rules, questions on capital maintenance tend to be straightforward.

2 Reduction of share capital

FAST FORWARD

> Reduction of capital can be achieved by: **extinguishing/reducing liability on partly paid shares**; **cancelling paid-up share capital**; or **paying off part of paid-up share capital**. Court confirmation is required for public companies. The court considers the interests of creditors and different classes of shareholder. There must be power in the articles and a special resolution.

Under the Companies Act 2006 (TSO, 2006) a limited company is permitted without restriction to cancel **unissued shares** as that change does not alter its financial position.

If a limited company with a share capital wishes to **reduce** its **issued share capital** it may do if:

* The **power to do so has not been restricted by the company's articles** (if it does not have power in the articles, these may be amended by a **special resolution**).
* It passes a **special resolution**. (If the articles have been amended, this is another special resolution.)
* It obtains **confirmation** of the reduction **from the court**.

A company's **share premium account** and **capital redemption reserve** are treated as share capital and can therefore be reduced using the above procedure. This allows the company to clean up its capital by removing old balances.

2.1 Solvency statement

A private company need not apply to the court if it supports its special resolution with a solvency statement.

> A **solvency statement** is a declaration by the directors, provided 15 days in advance of the meeting where the special resolution is to be voted on. It states there is no ground to suspect the company is currently unable or will be unlikely to be able to pay its debts for the next 12 months. All possible liabilities must be taken into account and the statement should be in the prescribed form, naming all the directors.

It is an **offence** for directors to deliver to the Registrar a solvency statement without having **reasonable grounds** for the opinions expressed in it.

The **benefits** to a private company of using a solvency statement, rather than going to court, to reduce its share capital include the **faster speed of** the procedure and the **lower cost** of filing documents, rather than involving expensive legal representation in court.

2.2 Why reduce share capital?

A company may wish to **reduce its capital** for one or more of the **following reasons**.

- The company has suffered a **loss** in the **value** of its **assets** and it reduces its capital to reflect that fact.

- The company wishes to **extinguish** the **interests** of some members entirely.

- The capital reduction is part of a **complicated arrangement** of capital which may involve, for instance, replacing share capital with loan capital.

There are **three basic methods of reducing share capital** specified in the Companies Act.

Method	What happens	Effects
Extinguish or reduce liability on partly paid shares	Eg Company has nominal value £1 shares 75p paid up. Either (a) reduce nominal value to 75p; or (b) reduce nominal value to a figure between 75p and £1	Company gives up claim for amount not paid up (nothing is **returned** to shareholders)
Pay off part of paid-up share capital out of surplus assets	Eg Company reduces nominal value of fully paid shares from £1 to 70p and repays this amount to shareholders	Assets of company are reduced by 30p in £
Cancel paid-up share capital which has been lost or which is no longer represented by available assets	Eg Company has £1 nominal fully paid shares but net assets only worth 50p per share. Difference is a debit balance on reserves. Company reduces nominal value to 50p, and applies amount to write off debit balance	Company can resume dividend payments out of future profits without having to make good past losses

2.3 Role of the court in reduction of share capital

When the court receives an application for reduction of capital, its **first concern** is the effect of the reduction on the company's ability to pay its debts, that is, that the creditors are protected.

If the reduction is by extinguishing liability or paying off part of paid-up share capital, the court requires that **creditors** shall be **invited** by advertisement to state their objections (if any) to the reduction. Where paid-up share capital is cancelled, the court **may** require an invitation to creditors.

Normally the company persuades the court to dispense with **advertising for creditors' objections** (which can be commercially damaging to the company).

Two possible approaches are:

- To **pay off** all **creditors** before application is made to the court; or, if that is not practicable.

- To produce to the court a **guarantee**, say from the company's bank, that its existing debts will be paid in full.

The **second** concern of the court, where there is more than one class of share, is whether the reduction is fair in its effect on different classes of shareholder.

If the reduction is, **in the circumstances**, a **variation of class rights** the **consent** of the class must be obtained under the variation of class rights procedure.

Within each class of share it is usual to make a uniform reduction of every share by the same amount per share, though this is **not** obligatory.

The court may also be concerned that the **reduction should not confuse or mislead people who may deal with the company in future**. It may insist that the company add 'and reduced' to its name or publish explanations of the reduction.

2.3.1 Confirmation by the court

If the court is satisfied that the reduction is in order, it confirms the reduction by making an order to that effect. A **copy of the court order** and a **statement of capital**, approved by the court, to show the altered share capital is delivered to the Registrar who issues a certificate of registration.

3 Distributing dividends

FAST FORWARD

Various rules have been created to ensure that dividends are only paid out of **available profits**.

Key term

A **dividend** is an amount payable to shareholders from profits or other distributable reserves.

3.1 Power to declare dividends

Under the Companies Act 2006 (TSO, 2006) a company may only pay dividends out of **profits available for the purpose**. The power to declare a dividend is given by the articles which often include the following rules.

Rules related to the power to declare a dividend
The **company** in **general meeting** may declare dividends.
No dividend may exceed the **amount recommended** by the directors who have an implied power in their discretion to set aside profits as reserves.
The directors may declare such **interim dividends** as they consider justified.
Dividends are normally declared payable on the **paid-up amount** of **share capital**. For example a £1 share which is fully paid will carry entitlement to twice as much dividend as a £1 share 50p paid.
A dividend may be paid **otherwise than in cash**.
Dividends may be paid by **cheque** or **warrant** sent through the post to the shareholder at their registered address. If shares are held jointly, payment of dividend is made to the first-named joint holder on the register.

Listed companies generally pay two dividends a year; an **interim dividend** based on interim profit figures, and a **final dividend** based on the annual accounts and approved at the AGM.

A **dividend becomes a debt** when it is **declared** and **due for payment**. A shareholder is not entitled to a dividend unless it is declared in accordance with the procedure prescribed by the articles and the declared date for payment has arrived. This is so even if the member holds **preference shares** carrying a priority entitlement to receive a specified amount of dividend on a specified date in the year. The directors may decide to withhold profits and cannot be compelled to recommend a dividend.

If the articles refer to 'payment' of dividends this means **payment in cash**. A power to pay dividends **in specie** (otherwise than in cash) is not implied but may be expressly created. **Scrip dividends** are dividends paid by the issue of additional shares. Any provision of the articles for the declaration and payment of dividends is subject to the overriding rule that **no dividend may be paid except out of profits distributable by law**.

3.2 Distributable profit

Distributable profits may be defined as 'accumulated realised profits ... less accumulated realised losses'. **'Accumulated'** means that any losses of previous years must be included in reckoning the current distributable surplus. **'Realised'** profits are determined in accordance with generally accepted accounting principles.

Key term

> **Profits available for distribution** are accumulated realised profits (which have not been distributed or capitalised) less accumulated realised losses (which have not been previously written off in a reduction or reorganisation of capital).

The word **'accumulated'** requires that any **losses** of **previous years** must be included in reckoning the current distributable surplus. A profit or loss is deemed to be **realised** if it is treated as realised in accordance with generally accepted accounting principles. Hence, financial reporting and accounting standards in issue, plus generally accepted accounting principles (GAAP), should be taken into account when determining realised profits and losses.

Depreciation must be treated as a **realised loss**, and debited against profit, in determining the amount of distributable profit remaining.

However, a **revalued asset** will have deprecation charged on its historical cost and the increase in the value in the asset. The Companies Act allows the depreciation provision on the valuation increase to be treated also as a realised profit. Effectively there is a cancelling out, and at the end **only depreciation that relates to historical cost will affect dividends**.

 Illustration

Suppose that an asset purchased for £20,000 has a 10-year life. Provision is made for depreciation on a straight line basis. This means an annual depreciation charge of £2,000 (£20,000/10 years) must be deducted in reckoning the company's realised profit less realised loss.

After five years the asset is written-down value is £10,000 (£20,000 less £2,000 × 5 years). Suppose that the asset is then revalued to £50,000. The increase in the value of the asset (£40,000) is credited to the revaluation reserve.

The consequences of this revaluation are that the annual depreciation charge is raised to £10,000 (£50,000/5 remaining years of the asset's life) and £8,000 (£40,000/5 years) is transferred from the revaluation reserve to realised profit each year for the remaining life of the asset.

The net effect is that each year realised profits are still reduced by £2,000 (£10,000 – £8,000) in respect of depreciation.

If, on a **general revaluation** of all fixed assets, it appears that there is a diminution in value of any one or more assets, then any related provision(s) need **not** be treated as a realised loss. The Act states that if a company shows **development expenditure** as an asset in its accounts it must usually be treated as a realised loss in the year it occurs. However, it can be carried forward in special circumstances (generally taken to mean in accordance with accounting standards).

3.3 Dividends of public companies

A public company may only make a distribution if its **net assets** are, at the time, **not less than the aggregate of its called-up share capital and undistributable reserves**. It may only pay a dividend which will leave its net assets at not less than that aggregate amount.

A public company may only make a distribution if its **net assets are**, at the time, **not less than the aggregate of its called-up share capital and undistributable reserves**. The dividend which it may pay is limited to such amount as will leave its net assets at not less than that aggregate amount.

Undistributable reserves are defined as:

(a)   **Share premium account**

(b)   **Capital redemption reserve**

(c)   Any **surplus** of **accumulated unrealised profits** over **accumulated unrealised losses** (known as a revaluation reserve). However a deficit of accumulated unrealised profits compared with accumulated unrealised losses must be treated as a realised loss

(d)   Any **reserve** which the company is **prohibited** from **distributing** by **statute**, its **constitution** or **law**

Illustration

Suppose that a public company has an issued share capital (fully paid) of £800,000 and £200,000 on share premium account (which is an undistributable reserve). If its assets less liabilities are less than £1 million it may not pay a dividend. If, however, its net assets are, say, £1,250,000 it may pay a dividend but only of such amount as will leave net assets of £1 million or more: so its maximum permissible dividend is £250,000.

The **dividend rules apply** to every form of **distribution of assets, except** the following:

- The **issue of bonus shares** whether fully or partly paid
- The **redemption** or **purchase** of the company's **shares** out of **capital** or **profits**
- A **reduction** of **share capital**
- A **distribution** of **assets** to members in a **winding up**

Exam focus point

> You must appreciate how the rules relating to public companies in this area are more stringent than the rules for private companies.

3.4 Relevant accounts

The profits available for distribution are generally determined from the **last annual accounts** to be prepared.

Whether a company has profits from which to pay a dividend is determined by reference to its **'relevant accounts'**, which are generally the last annual accounts to be prepared.

If the auditor has qualified their report on the accounts they must also state in writing whether, in their opinion, the subject matter of their qualification is **material** in determining whether the dividend may be paid. This statement must have been circulated to the members (for a private company) or considered at a general meeting (for a public company).

A company may produce **interim accounts** if the latest annual accounts do not disclose a sufficient distributable profit to cover the proposed dividend. It may also produce **initial accounts** if it proposes to pay a dividend during its first accounting reference period or before its first accounts are laid before the company in general meeting. These accounts may be unaudited, but they must suffice to permit a proper judgement to be made of amounts of any of the relevant items.

If a **public** company produces initial or interim accounts they must be full accounts such as the company is required to produce as final accounts at the end of the year. They need not be audited. However, the auditors must, in the case of initial accounts, satisfy themselves that the accounts have been 'properly prepared' to comply with the Act. A copy of any such accounts of a public company (with any auditors' statement) must be delivered to the Registrar for filing.

3.5 Infringement of dividend rules

In certain situations the **directors** and **members** may be liable to make good to the company the amount of an **unlawful dividend**.

If a dividend is paid otherwise than out of distributable profits the company, the **directors and** the **shareholders** may be involved in making good the unlawful distribution.

The directors are held **responsible** since they either recommend to members in general meeting that a dividend should be declared or they declare interim dividends.

(a)   **The directors are liable if they declare a dividend which they know is paid out of capital.**

(b)   **The directors are liable if, without preparing any accounts, they declare or recommend a dividend which proves to be paid out of capital.** It is their duty to satisfy themselves that profits are available.

(c)   **The directors are liable if they make some mistake of law or interpretation of the constitution which leads them to recommend or declare an unlawful dividend.** However in such cases the directors may well be entitled to relief as their acts were performed 'honestly and reasonably'.

The directors may, however, **honestly** rely on proper accounts which disclose an apparent distributable profit out of which the dividend can properly be paid. They are not liable if it later appears that the assumptions or estimates used in preparing the accounts, although reasonable at the time, were in fact unsound.

The **position of members** is as follows.

•   A member may obtain an **injunction** to restrain a company from paying an unlawful dividend.

•   Members voting in general meeting **cannot authorise** the payment of an unlawful dividend nor release the directors from their liability to pay it back.

•   The company can **recover from members** an **unlawful dividend** if the **members knew** or had **reasonable grounds** to believe that it was unlawful.

•   If the directors have to make good to the company an unlawful dividend, they may claim **indemnity from members** who at the time of receipt knew of the irregularity.

•   Members knowingly receiving an unlawful dividend may **not bring an action** against the directors.

If an unlawful dividend is paid by **reason of error** in the **accounts** the company may be unable to claim against either the directors or the members. The company might then have a claim against its **auditors** if the undiscovered mistake was due to negligence on their part.

Chapter Roundup

- The rules which dictate how a company is to manage and maintain its capital exist to maintain the delicate balance between the **members' enjoyment of limited liability** and the **creditors' requirements that the company shall remain able to pay its debts**.

- Reduction of capital can be achieved by: **extinguishing/reducing liability on partly paid shares; cancelling paid-up share capital;** or **paying off part of paid-up share capital**. Court confirmation is required for public companies. The court considers the interests of creditors and different classes of shareholder. There must be power in the articles and a special resolution.

- Various rules have been created to ensure that dividends are only paid out of **available profits**.

- Distributable profits may be defined as 'accumulated realised profits ... less accumulated realised losses'. **'Accumulated'** means that any losses of previous years must be included in reckoning the current distributable surplus. **'Realised'** profits are determined in accordance with generally accepted accounting principles.

- A public company may only make a distribution if its **net assets** are, at the time, **not less than the aggregate of its called-up share capital and undistributable reserves**. It may only pay a dividend which will leave its net assets at not less than that aggregate amount.

- The profits available for distribution are generally determined from the **last annual accounts** to be prepared.

- In certain situations the **directors** and **members** may be liable to make good to the company the amount of an **unlawful dividend**.

1   Where application is made to the court for confirmation of a reduction in capital, the court may require that creditors should be invited by advertisement to state their objections. In which of the following ways can the need to advertise be avoided?

Select all that apply.

A   Paying off all creditors before application to the court
B   Producing a document signed by the directors stating the company's ability to pay its debts
C   Producing a guarantee from the company's bank that its existing debts will be paid in full
D   Renouncement by existing shareholders of their limited liability in relation to existing debts

2   **Fill in the blanks** in the statements below.

Distributable profits may be defined as ……………….. ……..….. profits less ……………….. ………….. losses.

3   If a company makes an unlawful dividend, who may be involved in making good the distribution?

A   The company only
B   The directors only
C   The shareholders only
D   The company, the directors and the shareholders

4   Give four examples of undistributable reserves.

5   **Fill in the blanks** in the statements below.

A private company does not need to apply to the court to reduce its share capital if it supports its ……………….. ……..….. with a ……………….. ………….. .

Answers to Quick Quiz

1 A and C. The only guarantee that the courts will accept is from the company's bank.

2 Distributable profits may be defined as **accumulated realised** profits less **accumulated realised** losses.

3 D. All three may be liable.

4 Share premium account

Capital redemption reserve

A surplus of accumulated unrealised profits over accumulated unrealised losses (revaluation reserve)

Any reserve which the company is prohibited from distributing by statute or by its constitution or any law.

5 A private company does not need to apply to the court to reduce its share capital if it supports its **special resolution** with a **solvency statement**.

Now try the questions below from the Practice Question Bank

Number
37, 38, 39

PART

F

Management, administration and the regulation of companies

BPP
LEARNING MEDIA

18

Company directors

Topic list	Syllabus reference
1 The role of directors	F1(a)
2 Appointment of directors	F1(b)
3 Remuneration of directors	F1(b)
4 Vacation of office	F1(b)
5 Disqualification of directors	F1(b)
6 Powers of directors	F1(c)
7 Powers of the Chief Executive Officer (Managing Director)	F1(c)
8 Powers of an individual director	F1(c)
9 Duties of directors	F1(d)

Introduction

In this chapter we turn our attention to the **appointment** and **removal**, and the **powers and duties, of company directors**.

The important principle to grasp is that the **extent of directors' powers is defined by the articles**.

If **shareholders** do not approve of the directors' acts they must either **remove them** or **alter the articles** to regulate their future conduct. However, they **cannot** simply **take over** the functions of the directors.

In essence, the directors act as **agents of the company**. This ties in with the **agency** part of your law studies. The different types of authority a director can have (implied and actual) are important in this area.

We also consider the **duties** of directors under statute and **remedies for the breach of such duties**.

Statute also imposes some duties on directors, specifically concerning openness when transacting with the company.

Finally we look at the duties and powers of the **company secretary** and **auditor**.

Study guide

		Intellectual level
F	**Management, administration and the regulation of companies**	
1	**Company directors**	
(a)	Explain the role of directors in the operation of a company, and the different types of directors, such as executive/non-executive directors or de jure and de facto directors, and shadow directors	2
(b)	Discuss the ways in which directors are appointed, can lose their office and the disqualification of directors	2
(c)	Distinguish between the powers of the board of directors, the managing director/chief executive and individual directors to bind their company	2
(d)	Explain the duties that directors owe to their companies, and the controls imposed by statute over dealings between directors and their companies, including loans	2

Exam guide

The relationship between members of a company and their directors could easily be examined. The detailed rules regarding directors and other company officers are all highly examinable.

1 The role of directors

FAST FORWARD

Any person who occupies the position of director is treated as such, the test being one of **function**.

Key term

> A **director** is a person who is responsible for the overall direction of the company's affairs. In company law, director means any person occupying the position of director, by whatever name called.

Under the Companies Act 2006 (TSO, 2006) any person who occupies the position of director is treated as such. The test is one of **function**. The directors' function is to take part in **making decisions** by **attending meetings** of the board of directors. Anyone who does that is a director whatever they may be called.

A person who is given the title of director, such as 'sales director' or 'director of research', to give them status in the company structure, is not a director in company law. This is unless by virtue of their appointment they are a **member** of the **board** of **directors**, or they carry out functions that would be properly discharged only by a director.

1.1 De jure and de facto directors

Most directors are **expressly appointed** by a company and are known as **de jure** directors. A **de facto** director is **anyone** who is **held out by a company** as a director, **performs the functions** of a director and is **treated by the board** as a director, although they have **never been validly appointed**.

1.2 Shadow directors

A person might seek to **avoid the legal responsibilities of being a director** by avoiding appointment as such but using their power, say as a major shareholder, to manipulate the acknowledged board of directors. In other words they seek the **power** and **influence** that come with the position of director, but **without the legal obligations** it entails.

Company law seeks to prevent this abuse by extending several statutory rules to **shadow directors**. Shadow directors are directors for legal purposes if the board of directors are accustomed to act in accordance with their directions and instructions. This rule does not apply to professional advisers merely acting in that capacity.

1.2.1 Shadow directors and de facto directors

Shadow directors differ from de facto directors because the public (and the authorities) are rarely aware of their existence. Whereas a de facto director performs the everyday tasks that a director would (dealing with suppliers and customers and being present at general meetings), the shadow director exerts their influence away from the day-to-day running of the business.

1.3 Alternate directors

A director may, if the articles permit, appoint an alternate director to attend and vote for them at board meetings which they are unable to attend. Such an alternate may be another director, in which case they have the vote of the absentee as well as their own. More usually they are an outsider. Company articles could make specific provisions for this situation.

1.4 Executive directors

Key term

> An executive director is a director who performs a specific role in a company under a service contract which requires a regular, possibly daily, involvement in management.

A director may also be an employee of their company. Since the company is also their employer there is a potential conflict of interest which, in principle, a director is required to avoid. To allow an individual to be both a director and employee the articles usually make express provision for it, but prohibit the director from voting at a board meeting on the terms of their own employment.

Directors who have additional management duties as employees may be distinguished by special titles, such as 'Finance Director'. However, any such title does not affect their personal legal position. They have two distinct positions as:

- A member of the board of directors; and
- A manager with management responsibilities as an employee.

1.5 Non-executive directors (NED)

Key term

> A non-executive director does not have a function to perform in a company's management but is involved in its governance.

In listed companies, the UK Corporate Governance guidelines state that boards of directors are more likely to be fully effective if they comprise both executive directors and strong, independent non-executive directors. The main tasks of the NEDs are as follows:

- Contribute an independent view to the board's deliberations
- Help the board provide the company with effective leadership
- Ensure the continuing effectiveness of the executive directors and management
- Ensure high standards of financial probity on the part of the company

Non-executive and shadow directors are subject to the same duties as executive directors.

1.6 The Chief Executive Officer (Managing Director)

Key term

> A Chief Executive Officer (also commonly known as a Managing Director) is one of the directors of the company appointed to carry out overall day-to-day management functions.

Boards of directors usually appoint one director to be **Chief Executive Officer** (this position is also commonly known as **Managing Director**). A Chief Executive Officer (CEO) or Managing Director (MD) has a special position and has wider apparent powers than any director who is not appointed to that position.

1.7 Number of directors

Every company must have at least **one** director; for a **public** company the minimum is **two**. There is no statutory maximum in the UK, but the articles usually impose a limit. All directors must be a **natural person**, not a body corporate.

1.8 The board of directors

Companies are run by the directors collectively, in a **board of directors**.

> The **board of directors** is the elected representative of the shareholders acting collectively in the management of a company's affairs.

One of the basic principles of company law is that the **powers** which are delegated to the directors under the articles are given to them as a **collective body**. The **board meeting** is the **proper place for the exercise of the powers,** unless they have been validly passed on, or 'sub-delegated', to committees or individual directors.

1.9 The Chair

According to the **UK Corporate Governance Code**, a company's Chair (or Chairman) is responsible for leading the board and ensuring its effectiveness. This is a very distinct role from that of the CEO/MD, who is responsible for leading the company's operations. The Chair's **power** may be contained within the company's **articles of association** and they should be **independent** of the company when they are appointed.

2 Appointment of directors

> The method of appointing directors, along with their rotation and co-option, is **controlled** by the **articles**.

As we saw earlier, a director may be **appointed expressly**, in which case they are known as a **de jure** director. Where a person acts as a director without actually being appointed as such (a **de facto** or **shadow director**) they incur the obligations and have some of the powers of a proper director. In addition, a shadow director is subject to many of the duties imposed on directors.

2.1 Appointment of first directors

Under the Companies Act 2006 (TSO, 2006) the application for registration delivered to the Registrar to form a company **includes particulars of the first directors**, with their consents. On the formation of the company those persons become the first directors.

2.2 Appointment of subsequent directors

Once a company has been formed further directors can be appointed, either to **replace** existing directors or as **additional** directors.

Appointment of further directors is carried out **as the articles provide**. Most company articles allow for the appointment of directors:

- By **ordinary resolution** of the shareholders, and
- By a **decision** of the directors.

However the articles do not have to follow these provisions and may impose **different methods** on the company.

When the appointment of directors is proposed at a general meeting of a public company a **separate** resolution should be proposed for the election of **each director**. However, the rule may be waived if a resolution to that effect is first carried without any vote being given against it.

2.3 Publicity

In addition to giving notice of the first directors, every company must within **14 days** give **notice** to the **Registrar** of any change among its directors. This includes any changes to the register of directors' residential addresses.

2.4 Age limit

The **minimum age** limit for a director is **16** and, unless the articles provide otherwise, there is no upper limit.

3 Remuneration of directors

Directors are entitled to **fees** and **expenses** as directors as per the articles, and **emoluments** (and compensation for loss of office) as per their service contracts (which can be inspected by members). Some details are published in the directors' remuneration report along with the accounts.

Details of **directors' remuneration are** usually contained within their service **contract**. This is a contract where the director agrees to personally perform services for the company.

3.1 Directors' expenses

Most articles state that directors are entitled to **reimbursement** of **reasonable expenses** incurred whilst carrying out their duties or functions as directors.

In addition, most directors have **written service contracts** setting out their entitlement to emoluments and expenses. Where service contracts **guarantee employment** for longer than **two years** then an **ordinary resolution** must be passed by the members of the company that the contract is with.

3.2 Compensation for loss of office

Any director may receive **non-contractual** compensation for loss of office, paid to them voluntarily. Any such compensation is lawful **only if** approved by members of the company in general meeting after proper disclosure has been made to all members, whether voting or not.

This only applies to **uncovenanted payments**; approval is not required where the company is contractually bound to make the payment.

Compensation paid to directors for loss of office is distinguished from any payments made to directors **as employees**. For example, to settle claims arising from the premature termination of the service agreements. These are contractual payments which do not require approval in general meeting.

3.3 Directors' remuneration report

Under the Companies Act 2006 (TSO, 2006) quoted companies are required to include a **directors' remuneration report** as part of their annual report, part of which is subject to audit. The report must cover:

- The details of each **individual director's remuneration package**
- The company's **remuneration policy**
- The **role** of the **board** and **remuneration committee** in deciding the **remuneration of directors**

It is the duty of the directors (including those who were a director in the preceding five years) to **provide any information about themselves** that is necessary to produce this report.

Quoted companies are required to allow a **vote by members on the directors' remuneration report**. The vote is purely advisory and does not mean the remuneration should change if the resolution is not passed. However, a negative vote would be a strong signal to the directors that the members are unhappy with remuneration levels.

Items not subject to audit

- Consideration by the directors (remuneration committee) of matters relating to directors' remuneration
- Statement of company's policy on directors' remuneration
- Performance graph (share performance)
- Directors' service contracts (dates, unexpired length, and compensation payable for early termination)

Items subject to audit

- Salary/fees payable to each director
- Bonuses paid/to be paid
- Expenses
- Compensation for loss of office paid
- Any benefits received
- Share options and long-term incentive schemes – performance criteria and conditions
- Pensions
- Excess retirement benefits
- Compensation to past directors
- Sums paid to third parties in respect of a director's services

3.4 Inspection of directors' service agreements

A company must make available for inspection by members a copy or particulars of **contracts of employment** between the company or a subsidiary with a director of the company. Such contracts must cover all services that a director may provide, including services outside the role of a director, and those made by a third party in respect of services that a director is contracted to perform.

Contracts must be **retained** for **one year** after expiry and must be available either at the **registered office**, or any other location permitted by the Secretary of State.

Prescribed particulars of **directors' emoluments** must be given in the accounts and also particulars of any **compensation for loss of office** and directors' **pensions**.

4 Vacation of office

FAST FORWARD

A director may vacate office as director due to: **resignation**; **not going** for **re-election**; **death**; **dissolution** of the company; **removal**; **disqualification**.

Under the Companies Act 2006 (TS, 2006) a **director may leave office** in the following ways.

- **Resignation**
- Not **offering themselves for re-election** when their term of office ends
- **Death**
- **Dissolution of the company**
- Being **removed** from office
- Being **disqualified**

A form should be filed with the **Registrar** whenever and however a director vacates office.

4.1 Retirement and re-election of directors

The **model articles** for **public companies** provide the following **rules** for the **retirement** and **re-election** of all directors ('rotation') at AGMs.

(a) At the **first AGM** of the company **all directors shall retire**.

(b) At every subsequent AGM any **directors appointed by the other directors** since the **last AGM** shall retire.

(c) Directors who were **not appointed** or **re-elected at one of the preceding two AGMs** shall retire.

Directors who are **retired by rotation** are eligible to offer themselves for **re-election**. This mandatory retirement of directors provides another **control over their performance**. Rather than having to go through the process of seeking a resolution to remove a director, members have the opportunity every three years to dispose of an under-performing director by **simply not electing** them.

4.2 Removal of directors

In addition to provisions in the articles for removal of directors, a director may be removed from office by **ordinary** resolution at a meeting of which **special notice** to the company has been given by the person proposing it.

On receipt of the special notice the company must send a copy to the director who may require that a **memorandum of reasonable length** shall be issued to members. They also have the **right to address the meeting** at which the resolution is considered.

The articles and the service contract of the director **cannot override the statutory power**. However, the articles can **permit dismissal without the statutory formalities** being observed, for example dismissal by a resolution of the board of directors.

The power to remove a director is **limited** in its effect in four ways.

Restrictions on power to remove directors	
Shareholding qualification to call a meeting	In order to propose a resolution to remove a director, the shareholder(s) involved must call a general meeting. To do this they must hold: • Either, 10% of the paid up share capital • Or, 10% of the voting rights where the company does not have shares
Shareholding to request a resolution	Where a meeting is already convened, 100 members holding an average £100 of share capital each may request a resolution to remove a director.
Weighted voting rights	A director who is also a member may have weighted voting rights given to them under the constitution for such an eventuality, so that they can automatically defeat any motion to remove them as a director.
Class right agreement	It is possible to draft a shareholder agreement stating that a member holding each class of share must be present at a general meeting to constitute quorum. If so, a member holding shares of a certain class could prevent a director being removed by not attending the meeting.

Exam focus point

The courts have stressed that the power of members to remove directors is an important right, but you should remember the ways in which members' intentions might be frustrated.

The dismissal of a director may also entail payment of a **substantial sum** to settle their claim for breach of contract if they have a service contract. Under the Act no resolution may deprive a removed director of any compensation or damages related to their termination to which they are entitled to.

5 Disqualification of directors

FAST FORWARD

Directors may be required to vacate office because they have been disqualified on grounds dictated by the articles. Directors **may** be disqualified from a wider range of company involvements under the Company Directors Disqualification Act 1986 (CDDA).

A person cannot be appointed as a director or continue in office if they are or become **disqualified** under the articles or statutory rules.

5.1 Disqualification under model articles

Model articles include a number of grounds for disqualification. These include where:

- A person **ceases to be a director** by virtue of any **provision of the Companies Act 2006**, or is prohibited from being a director by law;

- A **bankruptcy order** is made against that person;

- A composition is made with that **person's creditors** generally in satisfaction of that person's debts;

- A **registered medical practitioner**, who is treating that person, gives a written opinion to the company stating that that person has become physically or mentally incapable of acting as a director and may remain so for more than three months;

- Notification is received by the company from the director that the **director is resigning from office**, and such resignation has taken effect in accordance with its terms.

Unless the court approves it, an **undischarged bankrupt** cannot act as a director nor be concerned directly or indirectly in the management of a company. If they do continue to act, they become personally liable for the company's relevant debts.

In addition to the main grounds of disqualification, the articles may provide that **a director shall automatically vacate office** if they are **absent** from **board meetings** (without obtaining the leave of the board) for a **specified period** (say six months). The effect of this disqualification depends on the words used.

- If the articles refer merely to 'absence' this includes involuntary absence due to illness.
- The words 'if they shall absent himself' restrict the disqualification to periods of voluntary absence.

The **specified period** is reckoned to begin from the **last meeting** which the absent director did attend. The normal procedure is that a director who foresees a period of absence, applies for leave of absence at the last board meeting which they attend; the leave granted is duly minuted. They are not then absent 'without leave' during the period.

If they fail to obtain leave but later offer a reasonable explanation the other directors may let the matter drop by simply not resolving that they shall vacate office. The general intention of the rule is to **impose a sanction against slackness**; a director has a duty to attend board meetings when they are able to do so.

5.2 Disqualification under statute

The **Company Directors Disqualification Act 1986** (HMSO, 1986) (CDDA 1986) provides that a **court may** formally **disqualify a person from being a director** or in any way directly or indirectly being concerned or taking part in the promotion, formation or management of a company.

The terms of the disqualification order are very wide, and include acting as a consultant to a company. The Act, despite its title, is not limited to the disqualification of people who have been directors. **Any person** may be disqualified if they fall within the appropriate grounds.

5.3 Grounds for disqualification of directors

Directors may be **disqualified** from acting as directors or being involved in the management of companies in a number of circumstances. They must be disqualified if the company is insolvent, and the director is found to be unfit to be concerned with management of a company.

Under the CDDA 1986 the court **may** make a disqualification order on any of the following grounds.

(a) **Where a person is convicted of an indictable offence (either in the UK or overseas) in connection with the promotion, formation, management or liquidation of a company or with the receivership or management of a company's property**.

 An indictable offence is an offence which may be tried at a Crown Court; it is therefore a serious offence. It need not actually have been tried on indictment, but if it was the maximum period for which the court can disqualify is 15 years, compared with only five years if the offence was dealt with summarily (at the magistrate's court).

(b) **Where it appears that a person has been persistently in default in relation to provisions of company legislation.**

 This legislation requires any return, account or other document to be filed with, delivered or sent or notice of any matter to be given to the Registrar. Three defaults in five years are conclusive evidence of persistent default.

 The maximum period of disqualification is five years.

(c) **Where it appears that a person has been guilty of fraudulent trading**. This means carrying on business with intent to defraud creditors or for any fraudulent purpose whether or not the company has been, or is in the course of being, wound-up.

 The person does not actually have to have been convicted of fraudulent trading. The legislation also applies to anyone who has otherwise been guilty of any fraud in relation to the company or of any breach of their duty as an officer.

 The maximum period of disqualification is 15 years.

(d) **Where the Secretary of State, acting on a report made by the inspectors or from information or documents obtained under the Companies Act, applies to the court for an order believing it to be expedient in the public interest.**

 If the court is satisfied that the person's conduct in relation to the company makes that person unfit to be concerned in the management of a company, then it may make a disqualification order. Again the maximum is 15 years.

(e) **Where a director was involved in certain competition violations**. Maximum – 15 years.

(f) **Where a director of an insolvent company has participated in wrongful trading**. Maximum – 15 years.

The court **must** make an order where it is satisfied that the following apply:

(a) A person has been a director of a company which has at any time become **insolvent** (whether while they were a director or subsequently) and

(b) Their conduct as a director of that company makes them **unfit** to be **concerned** in the **management** of a company. The courts may also take into account their conduct as a director of other companies, whether or not these other companies are insolvent. Directors can be disqualified under this section even if they take no active part in the running of the business.

 When determining **unfitness**, the following factors should be taken into account (the company concerned may be based in the UK or overseas):

 • The extent to which the person was responsible for the company breaking the law

 • The extent to which the person was responsible for causing the company to become insolvent

 • The nature and extent of the loss or damage caused by the person's conduct

In such cases the **minimum** period of disqualification is two years.

Offences for which directors have been disqualified include the following.

(a) **Insider dealing**

(b) **Failure** to **keep proper accounting records**

(c) **Failure to read the company's accounts**

(d) **Loans** to another company for the purposes of purchasing its own shares with **no grounds for believing the money would be repaid**

(e) **Loans** to associated companies on **uncommercial terms** to the detriment of creditors

5.4 Disqualification periods

In *Re Sevenoaks Stationers (Retail) Ltd 1991* the Court of Appeal laid down certain 'disqualification brackets'. The appropriate period of disqualification which should be imposed was a **minimum of two to five years** if the conduct was not very serious, **six to ten years** if the conduct was serious but did not merit the maximum penalty, and **over ten years** only in particularly serious cases.

Disqualification as a director need not mean disqualification from all involvement in management, so a disqualified director may continue to act as an **unpaid director** but only if the court gives leave to act.

5.4.1 Mitigation of disqualification

Examples of **circumstances** which have led the court to imposing a **lower period of disqualification** include the following.

* **Lack of dishonesty**
* **Loss of director's own money** in the company
* **Absence of personal gain**, for example excessive remuneration
* **Efforts to mitigate** the situation
* **Likelihood of reoffending**
* **Proceedings hanging over director** for a long time

5.5 Procedures for disqualification

Company **administrators**, **receivers** and **liquidators** all have a **statutory duty to report directors** to the Government where they believe the conditions for a disqualification order have been satisfied. The **Secretary of State** then decides whether to apply to the court for an order, but if they do decide to apply they must do so within two years of the date on which the company became insolvent.

5.6 Acting as a director whilst disqualified

Acting as a director whilst disqualified is a **serious offence** and, where it is committed, **directors are personally liable for the debts of the company**.

5.7 Disqualification for commercial misjudgement

The courts' approach has been to view **'ordinary commercial misjudgement'** as insufficient to justify disqualification.

Re Uno, Secretary of State for Trade and Industry v Gill 2004

The facts: A group consisting of two furniture companies carried on trading while in serious financial difficulties, while the directors tried to find a way out of the situation. Uno continued to take deposits from customers for furniture to fund its working capital requirements.

Decision: The directors were not disqualified for acting in this way as their behaviour was not dishonest or lacking in commercial probity and did not make them unfit to manage a company. They had been trying to explore realistic opportunities to save the businesses and were not to blame for the eventual collapse of the businesses and the subsequent loss of customers.

A **lack of commercial probity**, or gross negligence or total incompetence, however, might render disqualification appropriate.

Secretary of State for Trade and Industry v Thornbury 2008

The facts: A director failed to carry out any further investigation after receiving verbal assurances from other directors regarding the financial status of the company. The company was in breach of its statutory obligations to pay HMRC.

Decision: Although the director had not been dishonest, it had not been reasonable for him to leave matters in the other directors' hands to such a degree. He was held to be unfit to be concerned in the management of a company and disqualified for two years.

Exam focus point

An article titled 'Company Directors Disqualification Act 1986' appeared in *Student Accountant* and is available on the ACCA website.

6 Powers of directors

The **powers** of the directors are **defined** by the **articles**.

The powers of the directors are **defined by the articles**. The directors are usually authorised 'to manage the company's business' and 'to exercise all the powers of the company for any purpose connected with the company's business'.

Therefore they may take **any decision which is within the capacity** of the company **unless** either **the Act** or **the articles** themselves **require** that the **decision shall be taken by the members in general meeting**.

6.1 Restrictions on directors' powers

Directors' powers may be restricted by statute or by the articles. The directors have a duty to exercise their powers in what they honestly believe to be the **best interests** of the company and for the **purposes** for which the powers are given.

6.1.1 Statutory restrictions

Many transactions, such as an alteration of the articles or a reduction of capital, must by law be effected by passing a **special resolution**. If the directors propose such changes they must secure the passing of the appropriate resolution by shareholders in a general meeting.

6.1.2 Restrictions imposed by articles

As an example, the articles often set a maximum amount which the directors may borrow. If the directors wish to exceed that limit, they should **seek authority** from a **general meeting**.

When the directors clearly have the necessary power, their decision may be challenged if they exercise the power in the wrong way.

They must exercise their powers:

- In what they **honestly believe to be the interests of the company**
- For a **proper purpose**, being the purpose for which the power is given

6.1.3 Members' control of directors

There is a **division of power** between the board of directors who manage the business and the members who as owners take the major policy decisions at general meetings. How, then, do the owners seek to 'control' the people in charge of their property?

- The members **appoint** the directors and may **remove** them from office.

- The members can, by **altering the articles** (special resolution needed), reallocate powers between the board and the general meeting.

- Articles may allow the members to pass a **special resolution ordering** the **directors to act** (or **refrain from acting**) in a **particular way**. Such special resolutions cannot invalidate anything the directors have already done.

Remember that **directors are not agents of the members.** They cannot be instructed by the members in general meeting as to how they should exercise their powers. **The directors' powers are derived from the company as a whole** and are to be exercised by the directors as they think best in the **interests of the company**.

6.1.4 Control by the law

Certain powers must be exercised **'for the proper purpose'** and all powers must be exercised *bona fide* **for the benefit of the company**. Failure by the directors to comply with these rules will result in the **court setting aside their powers** unless the shareholders **ratify** the directors' actions by **ordinary resolution** (simple majority).

7 Powers of the Chief Executive Officer (Managing Director)

FAST FORWARD

> The CEO or MD has **apparent authority** to make **business contracts** on behalf of the company. Their **actual authority** is whatever the **board gives** them.

In their dealings with outsiders the CEO or MD has **apparent authority** as agent of the company to **make business contracts**. No other director, even if they work full time, has that **apparent** authority as a director, though if they are employed as a manager they may have apparent authority at a slightly lower level. The CEO or MD's **actual authority** is whatever the board gives them.

Although appointment as CEO or MD has special status, it may be **terminated** just like that of any other director (or employee); they then revert to the position of an ordinary director. Alternatively the company in general meeting may **remove them from their office of director** and they immediately cease to be CEO or MD since being a director is a necessary qualification for holding the post.

7.1 Agency and the CEO/MD

The directors are **agents of the company, not the members**. Where they have **actual or usual** authority they can **bind the company**. In addition a director may have **apparent authority** by virtue of **holding out**.

Holding out is a basic rule of the law of agency. This means, if the principal (the company) holds out a person as its authorised agent they are estopped from denying that they are its **authorised agent**. They are bound by a contract entered into by them on the company's behalf.

Apparent authority is the authority which an agent appears to have to a third party. A contract made within the scope of such authority will bind the principal even though the agent was not following their instructions.

Therefore if the board of directors **permits a director** to behave as if they are a **CEO** or **MD** duly appointed when in fact they are not, the company may be bound by their actions.

A CEO or MD has, by virtue of their position, **apparent authority** to make commercial contracts for the company. Moreover, if the board allows a director to enter into contracts, being aware of their dealings and taking no steps to disown them, the company will usually be bound.

Freeman & Lockyer v Buckhurst Park Properties (Mangal) Ltd 1964

The facts: A company carried on a business as property developers. The articles contained a power to appoint a Managing Director but this was never done. One of the directors of the company, to the knowledge of, but without the express authority of, the remainder of the board, acted as if he were Managing Director. He found a purchaser for an estate and also engaged a firm of architects to make a planning application. The company later refused to pay the architect's fees on the grounds that the director had no actual or apparent authority.

Decision: The company was liable since by its acquiescence it had represented that the director was a Managing Director with the authority to enter into contracts that were normal commercial arrangements, and which the board itself would have been able to enter.

In the *Freeman & Lockyer* case, the judge laid down **four conditions** which must be satisfied in claiming under the principle of **holding out**. The claimant must show that:

(a) A **representation** was made to them that the **agent had** the **authority** to enter on behalf of the company into the contract of the kind sought to be enforced.

(b) Such **representation** was **made by a person** who had 'actual' authority to **manage** the **business** of the company.

   The board of directors would certainly have actual authority to manage the company. Some commentators have also argued that the CEO/MD has actual or apparent authority to make representations about the extent of the actual authority of other company agents. (However, a third party cannot rely on the representations a CEO/MD makes about their own actual authority.)

(c) They were **induced** by the **representation** to enter into the contract; they had in fact relied on it.

(d) There must be **nothing** in the **articles** which would prevent the company from giving valid authority to its agent to enter into the contract.

8 Powers of an individual director

The position of any **other individual director** (not an MD) who is also an employee is that:

(a) They **do not have the apparent authority to make general contracts** which attaches to the position of MD, but they have **whatever apparent authority attaches** to their **management position**.

(b) **Removal** from the office of director may be a **breach** of their **service contract** if that agreement stipulates that they are to have the status of director as part of the conditions of employment.

9 Duties of directors

FAST FORWARD

The Companies Act 2006 sets out the **seven principal duties** of **directors**.

The Companies Act 2006 (TSO, 2006) sets out the **principal duties** that directors owe to their company. Many of these duties developed over time through the operation of **common law** and **equity**, or are **fiduciary duties** which have now been codified to make the law clearer and more accessible.

When deciding whether a duty has been broken, the courts will consider the Companies Act primarily. All case law explained in this section applied before the 2006 Act and is included here to help you understand the types of situation that arise and how the law will be interpreted and applied by the courts in the future.

In the text below on directors' statutory duties we have included references to sections of the Companies Act 2006. They have been provided purely for reference. Exam questions will focus on the content of the duties.

Fiduciary duty is a duty imposed upon certain persons because of the position of trust and confidence in which they stand in relation to another. The duty is more onerous than generally arises under a contractual or tort relationship. It requires full disclosure of information held by the fiduciary, a strict duty to account for any profits received as a result of the relationship, and a duty to avoid conflict of interest.

Broadly speaking directors must be **honest** and **not allow their personal interests to conflict with their duties as directors**. The directors are said to hold a **fiduciary position** since they make contracts as **agents** of the company and have control of its property.

The duties included in the Companies Act 2006 form a **code of conduct** for directors. They do not tell them what to do but rather create a framework that sets out how they are expected to **behave** generally. This code is important as it addresses situations where:

- A director may put their **own interests** ahead of the company's; and
- A director may be **negligent** and liable to an action in tort.

9.1 Who are the duties owed to?

Section 170 of the Companies Act makes it clear that directors owe their duties to the company, **not** the members. This means that **only the company itself can take action against a director** who breaches them. However, it is possible for a member to bring a derivative claim against the director on behalf of the company.

The effect of the **duties are cumulative**; in other words, a director owes **every duty** to the company that could apply in any given situation. The Act provides guidance for this. Where a director is offered a bribe, for instance, they will be breaking the duty not to accept a benefit from a third party and they will also not be promoting the company for the benefit of the members.

When deciding whether or not a director has breached a duty, the court should consider their actions in the context of **each individual duty** in turn.

9.2 Who are the duties owed by?

Every person who is **classed as a director** under the Act owes the company a number of duties. Certain aspects of the duties regarding conflicts of interest and accepting benefits from third parties also apply to **past directors**. This is to prevent directors from exploiting a situation for their own benefit by simply resigning. The courts are directed to apply duties to **shadow directors** where they are capable of applying.

Directors must at all times continue to **act in accordance with all other laws**; no authorisation is given by the duties for a director to breach any other law or regulation.

9.3 The duties and the articles

The **articles** may provide **more onerous regulations** than the Act, but they may not reduce the level of duty expected unless it is in the following circumstances:

- If a director has **acted in accordance with the articles** they cannot be in breach of the duty to exercise independent judgement.

- Some **conflicts of interest by independent directors** are permissible by the articles.

- Directors will not be in breach of duty concerning **conflicts of interest** if they follow any **provisions in the articles for dealing with them** as long as the provisions are lawful.

- The company may **authorise anything** that would otherwise be a breach of duty.

9.4 The duties of directors

FAST FORWARD

The **statutory duties** owed by directors are to:

- Act within their powers
- Promote the success of the company
- Exercise independent judgement
- Exercise reasonable skill, care and diligence
- Avoid conflicts of interest
- Not accept benefits from third parties
- Declare an interest in a proposed transaction or arrangement

We shall now consider the duties placed on directors by the Act. Where cases are mentioned it is to **demonstrate** the previous common law or equitable principle that courts will follow when interpreting and applying the Act.

9.4.1 Duty to act within powers (s 171)

The directors owe a duty to act in accordance with the company's constitution, and only to exercise powers for the purposes for which they were conferred. They have a **fiduciary duty to the company to exercise their powers bona fide in what they honestly consider to be the interests of the company.** This 'honest belief' is effective even if, in fact, the interests of the company were not served.

This duty is owed **to the company** and **not generally to individual shareholders**. The directors will not generally be liable to the members if, for instance, they purchase shares without disclosing information affecting the share price.

In exercising the powers given to them by the articles the directors have a fiduciary duty not only to act *bona fide* **but also only to use their powers for a proper purpose.**

The powers are restricted to the **purposes** for **which they were given**. If the directors infringe this rule by exercising their powers for a collateral purpose the transaction will be invalid **unless** the **company** in **general meeting authorises it, or subsequently ratifies it**.

Most of the directors' powers are found in the **articles,** so this duty means that the directors must not act outside their power or the capacity of the company (in other words, *ultra vires*).

If the irregular use of directors' powers is in the **allotment of shares** the votes attached to the new shares may not be used in reaching a decision in general meeting to sanction it.

> **Howard Smith Ltd v Ampol Petroleum Ltd 1974**
>
> *The facts:* Shareholders who held 55% of the issued shares intended to reject a takeover bid for the company. The directors honestly believed that it was in the company's interest that the bid should succeed. The directors allotted new shares to a prospective bidder so that the shareholders opposed to the bid would then have less than 50% of the enlarged capital and the bid would succeed.
>
> *Decision:* The allotment was invalid. 'It must be unconstitutional for directors to use their fiduciary powers over the shares in the company purely for the purpose of destroying an existing majority or creating a new majority which did not previously exist'.

Any **shareholder** may **apply to the court** to declare that a transaction in breach of s 171 should be set aside. However, the practice of the courts is generally to **remit the issue** to the **members in general meeting** to see if the members wish to confirm the transaction. If the majority approve what has been done (or have authorised it in advance) that decision is treated as a proper case of **majority control** to which the minority must normally submit.

> **Hogg v Cramphorn 1966**
>
> *The facts:* The directors of a company issued shares to trustees of a pension fund for employees to prevent a takeover bid which they honestly thought would be bad for the company. The shares were paid for with money belonging to the company, provided from an employees' benevolent and pension fund account. The shares carried ten votes each and, as a result, the trustees and directors together had control of the company. The directors had power to issue shares but not to attach more than one vote to each. A minority shareholder brought the action on behalf of all the other shareholders.
>
> *Decision:* If the directors act honestly in the best interests of the company, the company in general meeting can ratify the use of their powers for an improper purpose, so the allotment of the shares would be valid. But only one vote could be attached to each of the shares because that is what the articles provided.

> **Bamford v Bamford 1969**
>
> *The facts:* The directors of Bamford Ltd allotted 500,000 unissued shares to a third party to thwart a takeover bid. A month after the allotment a general meeting was called and an ordinary resolution was passed ratifying the allotment. The holders of the newly-issued shares did not vote. The claimants (minority shareholders) alleged that the allotment was not made for a proper purpose.
>
> *Decision:* The ratification was valid and the allotment was good. There had been a breach of fiduciary duty but the act had been validated by an ordinary resolution passed in general meeting.

These cases can be **distinguished** from the *Howard Smith* case (where the allotment was invalid) in that in the *Howard Smith* case the original majority would not have sanctioned the use of directors' powers. In the *Bamford* case the decision could have been sanctioned by a vote which excluded the new shareholders.

Ratification is not effective when it attempts to validate a transaction when

- It constitutes **fraud on a minority**.
- It involves **misappropriation of assets**.
- The transaction **prejudices creditors' interests** at a time when the company is insolvent.

Under the Companies Act, any resolution which proposes to **ratify the acts** of a director which are **negligent, in default** or in **breach of duty** or **trust** regarding the company must exclude the director or any members connected with them from the vote.

Much of the case law in this area concerns the **duty of directors** to exercise their power to allot shares.

This is only one of the powers given to directors that are subject to this **fiduciary duty**. Others include:

- Power to borrow
- Power to give security
- Power to refuse to register a transfer of shares
- Power to call general meetings
- Power to circulate information to shareholders

9.4.2 Duty to promote the success of the company (s 172)

An overriding theme of the Companies Act 2006 is the principle that the **purpose of the legal framework** surrounding companies should be **to help companies do business**. Their main purpose is to create wealth for the shareholders.

This theme is evident in the **duty of directors to promote the success of a company**. During the development of the Act, the independent Company Law Review recommended that company law should consider the interests of those for whom companies are run. It decided that the new Act should embrace the principle of **'enlightened shareholder value'**.

In essence, this principle means that the law should encourage **long-termism** and **regard for all stakeholders** by directors and that **stakeholder interests** should be **pursued** in an **enlightened** and **inclusive** way.

To achieve this, a duty of directors to act in a way, which, in **good faith**, promotes the success of the company for the benefit of the members as a whole, was created.

The requirements of this duty are difficult to define and possibly problematic to apply, so the Act provides directors with a **non-exhaustive list** of issues to keep in mind.

When exercising this duty directors should consider:

- The **consequences of decisions** in the long term
- The **interests of** their **employees**
- The need to **develop good relationships** with **customers** and **suppliers**
- The **impact of the company** on the **local community** and the **environment**
- The desirability of **maintaining high standards of business conduct** and a **good reputation**
- The need to **act fairly as between all members** of the company

The list identifies areas of **particular importance** and **modern-day expectations** of **responsible business behaviour**. For example, the interests of the company's employees and the impact of the company's operations on the community and the environment.

The **Act does not define** what should be regarded as the **success of a company**. This is down to a director's judgement in good faith. This is important, as it ensures that business decisions are for the directors rather than the courts.

No guidance is given for what the **correct course of action** would be where the various s 172 **duties** are in **conflict**. For example, a decision to shut down an office may be in the long-term best interests of the company but it is certainly not in the interests of the employees affected, nor the local community in which they live. Conflicts such as this are inevitable and could potentially leave directors open to breach of duty claims by a wide range of stakeholders if they do not deal with them carefully.

9.4.3 Duty to exercise independent judgement (s 173)

This is a simple duty that states directors must **exercise independent judgement**. They should **not delegate** their powers of decision making or be **swayed by the influence of others**. Directors may delegate their functions to others, but they must continue to make independent decisions.

This duty is not infringed by acting in accordance with any agreement by the company that restricts the exercise of discretion by directors, or by acting in a way authorised by the company's constitution.

9.4.4 Duty to exercise reasonable skill, care and diligence (s 174)

Directors have a **duty of care** to show **reasonable skill, care and diligence**.

Section 174 provides that a director owes a duty to their company to exercise the same standard of care, **skill** and **diligence** that would be exercised by a reasonably diligent person with:

(a)   The general knowledge, skill and experience that may **reasonably be expected of a person carrying out the functions carried out by the director** in relation to the company; and

(b)   The general knowledge, skill and experience that the **director has**.

There is, therefore, a **reasonableness test** consisting of two parts:

(a)   An **objective test**

Did the director act in a manner reasonably expected of a person performing the same role?

A director, when carrying out their functions, must show such **care** as could **reasonably** be expected from a **competent person** in that role. If a 'reasonable' director could be expected to act in a certain way, it is no defence for a director to claim, for example, lack of expertise.

(b)   A **subjective test**

Did the director act in accordance with the skill, knowledge and experience that they actually have?

In the case of *Re City Equitable Fire and Insurance Co Ltd 1925* it was held that a director is expected to show the **degree of skill** which may **reasonably be expected** from a person of their knowledge and experience. The standard set is personal to the person in each case. An accountant who is a director of a mining company is not required to have the expertise of a mining engineer, but they should show the expertise of an accountant.

The duty to be competent extends to **non-executive directors**, who may be liable if they fail in their duty.

Dorchester Finance Co Ltd v Stebbing 1989

The facts: Of all the company's three directors S, P and H, only S worked full-time. P and H signed blank cheques at S's request who used them to make loans which became irrecoverable. The company sued all three; P and H, who were experienced accountants, claimed that as non-executive directors they had no liability.

Decision: All three were liable; P's and H's acts in signing blank cheques were negligent and did not show the necessary objective or subjective skill and care.

In other words, the **standard of care** is an objective 'competent' standard, plus a higher 'personal' standard of application. If the director actually had particular expertise, that leads to a higher standard of competence being reasonably expected.

The company may recover damages from its directors for loss caused by their negligence. However, something more than imprudence or want of care must be shown. It must be shown to be a case of **gross negligence**. This was defined in *Overend, Gurney & Co v Gibb 1872* as conduct such that 'no men with any degree of prudence, acting on their own behalf, would have entered into such a transaction as they entered into'.

Therefore, in the absence of fraud it was difficult to control careless directors effectively. The statutory provisions on **disqualification** of directors of insolvent companies and on **liability** for wrongful trading therefore both set out how to judge a director's competence, and provide more effective enforcement.

The company by decision of its members in general meeting decides whether to sue the directors for their negligence. Even if it is a case in which they could be liable **the court has discretion under the Act to relieve directors of liability** if it appears to the court that:

•   The directors acted **honestly** and **reasonably**.
•   They **ought**, having regard to the circumstances of the case, **fairly to be excused**.

> *Re D'Jan of London Ltd 1993*
>
> *The facts:* D, a director of the company, signed an insurance proposal form without reading it. The form was filled in by D's broker. An answer given to one of the questions on the form was incorrect and the insurance company rightly repudiated liability for a fire at the company's premises in which stock worth some £174,000 was lost. The company became insolvent and the liquidator brought this action under s 212 of the Insolvency Act 1986, alleging D was negligent.
>
> *Decision:* In failing to read the form D was negligent. However, he had acted honestly and reasonably and ought therefore to be partly relieved from liability by the court.

The following is one of the **first cases on directors' statutory duties** and indicates how the law may be applied in the future.

> *Lexi Holdings plc (in administration) v Luqman 2009*
>
> *The facts:* Two sisters and their brother were directors of a company. The brother had convictions for offences of dishonesty in the past. The sisters knew this but played no part in the company, demanded no explanations from their brother of his business dealings and did not advise the other directors, auditors or the bank of his convictions. The brother took nearly £60m in fictitious loans, false facility letters and by misappropriation of company funds.
>
> *Decision:* It was held that the sisters were, or ought to have been, aware of various matters in relation to the fraud perpetrated on the company by their brother. As a result, they were liable as they were in breach of their fiduciary and common law duties of care owed to the company.

9.4.5 Duty to avoid conflicts of interest (s 175)

Directors have a **duty to avoid circumstances** where their **personal interests conflict**, or may possibly conflict, **with the company's interests**. It may occur when a director makes personal use of information, property or opportunities belonging to the company, whether or not the company was able to take advantage of them at the time. Therefore directors must be careful not to breach this duty when they **enter into a contract** with their company or if they **make a profit in the course of being a director**.

This duty does not apply to a **conflict of interest** in relation to a **transaction** or **arrangement** with the company, **provided the director declared an interest**.

As **agents**, directors have a **duty to avoid a conflict of interest**. In particular:

- The directors must **retain their freedom of action** and **not fetter their discretion** by agreeing to vote as some other person may direct.

- The directors owe a fiduciary duty to **avoid a conflict of duty and personal interest**.

- The directors **must not obtain any personal advantage** from their position as directors **without the consent of the company** for whatever gain or profit they have obtained.

The following **cases** are important in the area of **conflict of interest**.

Regal (Hastings) Ltd v Gulliver 1942

The facts: The company owned a cinema. It had the opportunity of acquiring two more cinemas through a subsidiary to be formed with an issued capital of £5,000. However the company could not proceed with this scheme since it only had £2,000 available for investment in the subsidiary.

The directors and their friends therefore subscribed £3,000 for shares of the new company to make up the required £5,000. The chairman acquired his shares not for himself but as nominee of other persons. The company's solicitor also subscribed for shares. The share capital of the two companies (which then owned three cinemas) was sold at a price which yielded a profit of £2.80 per share of the new company in which the directors had invested. The new controlling shareholder of the company caused it to sue the directors to recover the profit which they had made.

Decision:

(a) The directors were **accountable** to the company for their profit since they had obtained it from an opportunity which came to them as directors.

(b) It was **immaterial** that the **company** had **lost nothing** since it had been unable to make the investment itself.

(c) The directors might have kept their profit if the company had **agreed** by resolution passed in general meeting that they should do so. The directors might have used their votes to approve their action since it was not fraudulent (there was no misappropriation of the company's property).

(d) The chairman was not accountable for the profit on his shares since he did not obtain it for himself. The solicitor was not accountable for his profit since he was **not a director** and so was not subject to the rule of accountability as a director for personal profits obtained in that capacity.

Industrial Development Consultants Ltd v Cooley 1972

The facts: C was Managing Director of the company which provided consultancy services to gas companies. A gas company was unlikely to award a particular contract to the company but C realised that, acting personally, he might be able to obtain it. He told the board of his company that he was ill and persuaded them to release him from his service agreement. On ceasing to be a director of the company, C obtained the contract on his own behalf. The company sued him to recover the profits of the contract.

Decision: C was accountable to his old company for his profit.

Directors will **not be liable** for a breach of this duty if:

- The **members** of the company **authorised** their actions.

- The **situation cannot reasonably be regarded** as likely to give rise to a conflict of interest.

- The **actions have been authorised by the other directors**. This only applies if they are genuinely independent from the transaction and:

  - If the company is private: the articles do not restrict such authorisation; or
  - If it is public: the articles expressly permit it.

- The **company explicitly rejected the opportunity they took up**: *Peso Silver Mines v Cropper 1966*.

The following case was one of the first to apply the new statutory s 175 duty.

> *Towers v Premier Waste Management Ltd 2012*
>
> *The facts*: A company director accepted a personal loan of equipment from a customer without charge and without disclosing the transaction or seeking approval of it. The customer then invoiced the company, which sued the director for breach of duty.
>
> *Decision*: It was held that the director had gained an advantage from a potential conflict and had disloyally deprived the company of the opportunity to object to an opportunity being diverted from the company to the director personally. It was irrelevant that the company had suffered no loss or that the director had no corrupt motive.

PO1 requires you to protect yourself against threats to your professional independence and this means avoiding conflicts of interest. Whilst you may not be a director, the rules in s 175 give you a good idea of what is expected by others who have the same duty.

9.4.6 Duty not to accept benefits from third parties (s 176)

This duty **prohibits the acceptance of benefits** (including bribes) from third parties conferred by reason of them being director, or doing (or omitting to do) something as a director. Where a director accepts a benefit that may also create or potentially create a conflict of interest, they will also be in breach of their s 175 duty.

Unlike s 175, an act which would potentially be in breach of this duty **cannot be authorised** by the **directors**, but **members do have the right to authorise it**.

Directors will not be in breach of this duty if the acceptance of the benefit **cannot reasonably** be regarded as likely to give rise to a conflict of interest.

9.4.7 Duty to declare interest in proposed transaction or arrangement (s 177)

Directors are required to disclose to the other directors the nature and extent of any interest, direct or indirect, that they have in relation to a **proposed transaction** or **arrangement** with the **company**. Even if the director is not a party to the transaction, the duty may apply if they are aware, or ought reasonably to be aware, of the interest. For example, the interest of another person in a contract with the company may require disclosure under this duty if that other person's interest is a direct or indirect interest on the part of the director.

Directors are required to disclose their interest in any transaction **before** the company enters into the transaction. Disclosure can be made:

- By written notice
- By general notice
- Verbally at a board meeting

Disclosure to the **members** is **not** sufficient to discharge the duty. Directors must declare the **nature** and **extent** of their interest to the **other directors** as well. If the declaration becomes **void** or **inaccurate**, a **further declaration** should be made. No declaration of interest is required if the director's interest in the transaction **cannot reasonably** be regarded as likely to give rise to a conflict of interest.

9.5 Consequences of breach of duty

Breach of duty comes under the **civil law** rather than criminal law and, as mentioned earlier, the company itself must take up the action. This usually means the other directors starting proceedings. **Consequences for breach** include:

- **Damages** payable to the company where it has suffered loss
- **Restoration** of company property
- **Repayment of any profits** made by the director
- **Rescission of contract** (where the director did not disclose an interest)

9.6 Declaration of an interest in an existing transaction or arrangement (s 182)

Directors have a **statutory obligation** to **declare any direct** or **indirect interest** in an **existing transaction** entered into by the company. This obligation is almost identical to the duty to disclose an interest in a proposed transaction or arrangement under s 177. However, this section is relevant to transactions or arrangements that have already occurred. A declaration under s 182 is **not** required if:

- It has **already been disclosed** as a proposed transaction under s 177.

- The director is **not aware** of either:

    - **The interest** they have in the transaction, or
    - **The transaction** itself

- The director's interest in the transaction **cannot reasonably** be regarded as likely to give rise to a conflict of interest.

- The **other directors are aware** (or reasonably should be aware) of the situation.

- It concerns the **director's service contract** and it has been considered by a board meeting or special board committee.

Where a declaration is required it should be made as soon as **reasonably practicable** either by written notice, by general notice or verbally at a board meeting. If the declaration becomes **void** or **inaccurate**, a **further declaration** should be made.

9.7 Other controls over directors

The table below summarises other statutory controls over directors included in the Companies Act 2006.

CA06 Ref	Control
188	Directors' service contracts lasting more than two years must be approved by the members.
190	Directors or any person connected to them may not acquire a non-cash asset from the company without approval of the members. This does not apply where the asset's value is less than £5,000, or less than 10% of the company's asset value. All sales of assets with a value exceeding £100,000 must be approved.
197	Any loans given to directors, or guarantees provided as security for loans provided to directors, must be approved by members if over £10,000 in value.
198	Expands section 197 to prevent unapproved quasi-loans to directors of over £10,000 in value (PLCs only).
201	Expands section 197 to prevent unapproved credit transactions by the company for the benefit of a director of over £15,000 in value (PLCs only).
204	Directors must seek approval of the members where the company loans them over £50,000 to meet expenditure required in the course of business.
217	Non-contractual payments to directors for loss of office must be approved by the members.

9.8 Examples of remedies against directors

Remedies against directors for breach of duties include accounting to the company for a **personal gain**, **indemnifying the company**, and **rescission of contracts** made with the company.

The **type of remedy** varies with the breach of duty.

(a)   The director may have to **account for a personal gain**.

(b)   They may have to **indemnify the company** against loss caused by their negligence, such as an unlawful transaction which they approved.

(c)   If they contract with the company in a conflict of interest the **contract may be rescinded by the company**. However, under common law rules the company cannot both affirm the contract and recover the director's profit.

(d)   The court may declare that a transaction is *ultra vires* or unlawful.

A company may, either by its **articles** or by **passing a resolution** in general meeting, **authorise or ratify** the conduct of directors in breach of duty. There are some limits on the power of members in general meeting to **sanction a breach of duty** by directors or to release them from their strict obligations.

(a)   If the directors **defraud** the company and vote in general meeting to approve their own fraud, their votes are invalid.

(b)   If the directors **allot shares** to alter the balance of votes in a general meeting, the votes attached to those shares may not be cast to support a resolution approving the issue.

9.9 Directors' liability for acts of other directors

A director is **not liable** for acts of fellow directors. However, if they become aware of serious breaches of duty by other directors, they may have a duty to inform members of them or to take control of assets of the company without having proper delegated authority to do so.

In such cases the director is **liable for their own negligence** in what they allow to happen and not directly for the misconduct of the other directors.

9.10 Directors' personal liability

As a **general rule** a **director** has **no personal liability for the debts of the company**. But there are certain exceptions.

*   Personal liability **may arise** by **lifting the veil** of incorporation.

*   A **limited company** may by its articles or by **special resolution** provide that its directors shall have unlimited liability for its debts.

*   A director may be **liable** to the **company's creditors** in certain circumstances.

*   In cases of **fraudulent** or **wrongful trading** liquidators can apply to the court for an order that those responsible (usually the directors) are liable to repay all or some specified part of the company's debts.

Can a director be held personally liable for **negligent advice** given by their company? The case below shows that they can, but only when they assume responsibility in a personal capacity for advice given, rather than simply giving advice in their capacity as a director.

Williams and Another v Natural Life Health Foods Ltd 1998

The facts: The director was sued personally by claimants who claimed they were misled by the company's brochure. The director helped prepare the brochure, and the brochure described him as the source of the company's expertise. The claimants did not, however, deal with the director but with other employees.

Decision: The House of Lords overruled the Court of Appeal, and ruled that the director was not personally liable. In order to have been liable, there would have had to have been evidence that the director had assumed personal responsibility. Merely acting as a director and advertising his earlier experience did not amount to assumption of personal liability.

Chapter Roundup

- Any person who occupies the position of director is treated as such, the test being one of **function**.

- The method of appointing directors, along with their rotation and co-option, is **controlled** by the **articles**.

- Directors are entitled to **fees** and **expenses** as directors as per the articles, and **emoluments** (and compensation for loss of office) as per their service contracts (which can be inspected by members). Some details are published in the directors' remuneration report along with the accounts.

- A director may vacate office as director due to: **resignation**; **not going** for **re-election**; **death**; **dissolution** of the company; **removal**; **disqualification**.

- Directors may be required to vacate office because they have been disqualified on grounds dictated by the articles. Directors **may** be disqualified from a wider range of company involvements under the Company Directors Disqualification Act 1986 (CDDA).

- Directors may be **disqualified** from acting as directors or being involved in the management of companies in a number of circumstances. They must be disqualified if the company is insolvent, and the director is found to be unfit to be concerned with management of a company.

- The **powers** of the directors are **defined** by the **articles**.

- Directors' powers may be restricted by statute or by the articles. The directors have a duty to exercise their powers in what they honestly believe to be the **best interests** of the company and for the **purposes** for which the powers are given.

- The CEO or MD has **apparent authority** to make **business contracts** on behalf of the company. Their **actual authority** is whatever the **board gives** them.

- The Companies Act 2006 sets out the **seven principal duties** of **directors**.

- The **statutory duties** owed by directors are to:

    - Act within their powers
    - Promote the success of the company
    - Exercise independent judgement
    - Exercise reasonable skill, care and diligence
    - Avoid conflicts of interest
    - Not accept benefits from third parties
    - Declare an interest in a proposed transaction or arrangement

1   A person who is held out by a company as a director and performs the duties of a director without actually being validly appointed is a:

   A   Shadow director
   B   De facto director
   C   Non-executive director
   D   Executive director

2   **Fill in the blanks** in the statements below.

   Under model articles directors are authorised to m……………….. the b……………….. of the company, and e……………….. the p……………….of the company.

3   Under which of the following grounds may a director be disqualified if they are guilty, and under which must a director be disqualified?

   A   Conviction of an indictable offence in connection with a company
   B   Persistent default with the provisions of company legislation
   C   Wrongful trading
   D   Director of an insolvent company whose conduct makes them unfit to be concerned in the management of the company

4   What are the two principal ways by which members can control the activities of directors?

5   A public company must have two directors, a private company only needs one.

   True   ☐

   False ☐

Answers to Quick Quiz

1 B. The description is of a de facto director.

2 Under model articles directors are authorised to **manage** the **business** of the company, and **exercise all** the **powers** of the company.

3 A to C are grounds under which a director may be disqualified; D is grounds under which a director must be disqualified.

4 Appointing and removing directors in general meeting

   Reallocating powers by altering the articles

5 True. Private companies only need one director.

Now try the questions below from the Practice Question Bank

Number
40, 41

BPP
LEARNING MEDIA

19

Other company officers

Topic list	Syllabus reference
1 The company secretary	F2(a)
2 The company auditor	F2(b)

Introduction

In this short chapter we shall consider two other important company roles. That of **company secretary** and **auditor**. In each case we shall consider their appointment, duties and powers.

An important distinction to make is that a company secretary is a role performed by an individual **internal** to the company. An auditor is an **independent** third party.

Study guide

		Intellectual level
F	**Management, administration and the regulation of companies**	
2	**Other company officers**	
(a)	Discuss the appointment procedure relating to, and the duties and powers of, a company secretary	2
(b)	Discuss the appointment procedure relating to, and the duties and rights of a company auditor and their subsequent removal or resignation	2

Exam guide

Exam questions on company secretaries may hinge on an application of agency law so it is important to revise this area if you are not certain about it. Questions on auditors may focus on their role and rights, duties and removal.

1 The company secretary

FAST FORWARD

Every public company must have a **company secretary**, who is one of the officers of a company and may be a director. Private companies are not required to have a secretary.

Under the Companies Act 2006 (TSO, 2006) every public company must have a **company secretary**, who is one of the officers of a company and may be a director. Private companies are not required to have a secretary. In this case the roles normally done by the company secretary may be done by one of the directors, or an approved person. The secretary of state may require a public company to appoint a secretary where it has failed to do so.

1.1 Appointment of a company secretary

To be appointed as a **company secretary** to a plc, the directors must ensure that the candidate should be **qualified** by virtue of:

- **Employment** as a plc's secretary for **three out of the five years** preceding appointment
- **Membership** of one of a list of **qualifying bodies**: the ACCA, CIMA, ICAEW, ICAS, ICAI or CIPFA
- **Qualification** as a **solicitor**, **barrister** or **advocate** within the UK
- **Employment** in a position or **membership** of a professional body that, in the opinion of the directors, **appears to qualify that person** to act as company secretary

They should also have the **'necessary knowledge and experience'** as deemed by the directors.

A **sole director** of a private company cannot also be the company secretary, but a company can have **two** or more joint secretaries. A **corporation** can fulfil the role of company secretary. A register of secretaries must be kept. Under **UK Corporate Governance guidelines** the appointment of the company secretary is a matter for the board as a whole.

1.2 Duties of a company secretary

The specific **duties** of each company secretary are **determined by the directors** of the company. As a company officer, the company secretary is responsible for ensuring that the company complies with its statutory obligations.

In particular, this means:

- **Establishing** and **maintaining** the company's **statutory registers**
- **Filing accurate returns** with the Registrar on time
- **Organising** and **minuting** company and **board meetings**
- **Ensuring** that **accounting records** meet **statutory requirements**
- **Ensuring** that **annual accounts** are **prepared** and **filed** in accordance with **statutory requirements**
- **Monitoring statutory requirements** of the company
- **Signing company documents** as may be required by law

Under **UK Corporate Governance guidelines** the company secretary should:

- **Ensure good information flows** within the board and its committees
- **Facilitate induction of board members** and assist with professional development
- **Advise** the **chairman** and the **board** on all **governance issues**

1.3 Powers and authority of a company secretary

The powers of the company secretary have historically been very limited. However, the common law increasingly recognises that they may be able to act as agents to exercise apparent or **ostensible authority**, therefore, they may enter the company into contracts connected with the administrative side of the company.

Panorama Developments (Guildford) Ltd v Fidelis Furnishing Fabrics Ltd 1971

The facts: B, the secretary of a company, ordered cars from a car hire firm, representing that they were required to meet the company's customers at London Airport. Instead he used the cars for his own purposes. The bill was not paid, so the car hire firm claimed payment from B's company.

Decision: B's company was liable, for he had apparent authority to make contracts such as the present one, which were concerned with the administrative side of its business. The decision recognises the general nature of a company secretary's duties.

---

2 The company auditor

FAST FORWARD

Every company (apart from certain small companies) must appoint appropriately qualified **auditors**. An audit is a check on the stewardship of the directors.

Under the **Companies Act 2006** (TSO, 2006) **every company** (except a dormant private company and certain small companies) must **appoint auditors** for each financial year.

2.1 Appointment

The **first auditors** may be appointed by the directors, to hold office until the **first general meeting** at which their appointment is considered. **Subsequent auditors** may not take office until the previous auditor has ceased to hold office. They will hold office until the end of the next financial period (private companies) or the next accounts meeting (public companies) unless reappointed.

Appointment of auditors	
Members	• Usually appoint an auditor in general meeting by ordinary resolution.
	• Auditors hold office from 28 days after the meeting in which the accounts are laid until the end of the corresponding period the next year. This is the case even if the auditors are appointed at the meeting where the accounts are laid.
	• May appoint in general meeting to fill a casual vacancy.
Directors	• Appoint the first-ever auditors. They hold office until the end of the first meeting at which the accounts are considered.
	• May appoint to fill a casual vacancy.

Appointment of auditors	
Secretary of State	• May appoint auditors if members fail to. • Company must notify Secretary of State within 28 days of the general meeting where the accounts were laid.

2.1.1 Eligibility as auditor

Membership of a **recognised supervisory body** is the main prerequisite for eligibility as an auditor. An audit firm may be either a body corporate, a partnership or a sole practitioner.

The Act requires an auditor to hold an **'appropriate qualification'**. A person holds an 'appropriate qualification' if they:

- Have satisfied **existing criteria** for appointment as an auditor
- Hold a **recognised qualification** obtained in the UK
- Hold an **approved overseas qualification**

2.1.2 Ineligibility as auditor

Under the Companies Act 2006, a person may be ineligible on the grounds of **'lack of independence'**.

A person is **ineligible** for appointment as a **company auditor** if they are:

- An **officer** or **employee** of the company being audited

- A **partner** or **employee** of such a person

- A **partnership** in which such a person is a partner

- **Ineligible** by virtue of the above for appointment as auditor of any parent or subsidiary undertaking where there exists a **connection** of any description as may be specified in regulations laid down by Secretary of State

2.1.3 Effect of lack of independence or ineligibility

No person may act as auditor if they lack independence or become ineligible. If, during their term of office, an auditor loses their independence or eligibility they must **resign** with immediate effect, and **notify** their client of their resignation giving the reason.

A person continuing to act as auditor despite losing their independence or becoming ineligible is **liable to a fine**. However, it is a defence if they can prove they were not aware that they lost independence or became ineligible.

The legislation does **not** disqualify the following from being an auditor of a limited company:

- A shareholder of the company
- A debtor or creditor of the company
- A close relative of an officer or employee of the company

However, the **regulations** of the **accountancy bodies** applying to their own members are **stricter than statute in this respect**.

2.2 Reappointing an auditor of a private company

The rules on appointment make reference to a **meeting** where the accounts are laid. This is not always relevant for private companies as under the Act they are not required to hold an AGM or lay the accounts before the members.

Therefore **auditors of private companies are deemed automatically reappointed** unless one of the following circumstances apply.

- The auditor was **appointed by the directors** (most likely when the first auditor was appointed).
- The **articles require formal reappointment**.
- **Members holding 5% of the voting rights** serve notice that the auditor should not be reappointed.
- A **resolution** (written or otherwise) has been passed that prevents reappointment.
- The **directors have resolved that auditors should not be appointed** for the forthcoming year as the company is likely to be exempt from audit.

2.3 Auditor remuneration

Whoever appoints the auditors has power to **fix their remuneration** for the period of their appointment. It is usual when the auditors are appointed by the general meeting to leave it to the directors to fix their remuneration (by agreement at a later stage). The auditors' remuneration must be **disclosed** in a **note to the accounts**.

2.4 Exemption from audit

Certain **companies** are exempt from audit, provided the following conditions are fulfilled.

(a)   A company is exempt from the annual audit requirement in a financial year if it meets the criteria for being a small company (two from, turnover being less than **£10.2 million**, **balance sheet total not more than £5.1 million** and having **50 or fewer employees**).

(b)   The exemptions do not apply to **public companies**, **banking** or **insurance companies** or those subject to a **statute-based regulatory regime**.

(c)   The company is a **non-commercial**, **non-profit-making public sector body,** which is subject to audit by a **public sector auditor**.

(d)   **Members** holding **10%** or more of the capital of any company can veto the exemption.

(e)   **Dormant companies** which qualify for exemption from an audit as a dormant company.

2.5 Duties of auditors

The **statutory duty** of auditors is to report to the members whether the accounts give a **true and fair view** and have been properly prepared in accordance with the Companies Act. They must also:

- **State** whether or not the **directors' report** is **consistent** with the **accounts**.
- For **quoted companies**, **report** to the members on the **auditable** part of the **directors' remuneration report** including whether or not it has been properly prepared in accordance with the Act.
- Be **signed** by the **auditor**, stating their **name**, and **date**. Where the auditor is a firm, the **senior auditor** must sign in their **own name** for, and on behalf, of the auditor.

To fulfil their statutory duties, the auditors **must carry out such investigations as are necessary** to form an opinion as to whether:

(a)   **Proper accounting records** have been kept and proper returns adequate for the audit have been received from branches.

(b)   The **accounts** are in **agreement** with the **accounting records**.

(c)   The **information** in the **directors' remuneration report** is consistent with the **accounts**.

The auditors' report must be **read** before any general meeting at which the accounts are considered and must be open to inspection by members. Auditors have to make disclosure of other services rendered to the company and the remuneration received.

Where an auditor **knowingly** or **recklessly** causes their report to be **materially misleading**, **false** or **deceptive**, they commit a criminal offence and may be liable to a **fine**.

2.6 Rights of auditors

The Companies Act provides **statutory rights** for auditors to enable them to carry out their duties.

The **principal rights** of auditors, excepting those dealing with resignation or removal, are set out in the table below, and the following are notes on more detailed points.

Access to records	A right of access at all times to the books, accounts and vouchers of the company.
Information and explanations	A right to require from the company's officers, employees or any other relevant person, such information and explanations as they think necessary for the performance of their duties as auditors.
Attendance at/notices of general meetings	A right to attend any general meetings of the company and to receive all notices of and communications relating to such meetings which any member of the company is entitled to receive.
Right to speak at general meetings	A right to be heard at general meetings which they attend on any part of the business that concerns them as auditors.
Rights in relation to written resolutions	A right to receive a copy of any written resolution proposed.

If auditors have **not received** all the information and explanations they consider necessary, they should state this fact in their audit report.

The Act makes it an **offence** for a company's officer knowingly or recklessly to make a statement in any form to an auditor which:

- Conveys or purports to convey any information or explanation required by the auditor; and
- Is materially misleading, false or deceptive.

The **penalty** is a maximum of two years' imprisonment, a fine or both.

2.7 Auditors' liability

Under the Companies Act any **agreement** between an auditor and a company that seeks to **indemnify the auditor** for their own negligence, default, or breach of duty or trust is **void**. However, an agreement can be made which **limits the auditor's liability** to the company.

Such **liability limitation agreements** can only stand for **one financial year** and must therefore be replaced annually.

Liability can only be **limited** to what is **fair and reasonable** having regard to the auditor's responsibilities, their contractual obligations and the professional standards expected of them.

Such agreements must be approved by the members and **publicly disclosed** in the **accounts** or **directors' report**.

2.8 Termination of auditors' appointment

Auditors may leave office in the following ways: **resignation**; **removal from office** by an ordinary resolution with special notice passed before the end of their term; **failing** to **offer themselves** for **re-election**; and **not being re-elected** at the general meeting at which their term expires.

Departure of auditors from office can occur in the following ways.

(a) Auditors may **resign** their appointment by giving notice in writing to the company delivered to the registered office.

(b) Auditors may **decline reappointment**.

(c) Auditors may be **removed** from office before the expiry of their appointment by the passing of an ordinary resolution in general meeting. Special notice is required and members and auditors must be notified. **Private companies cannot remove an auditor by written resolution;** a meeting must be held.

(d) Auditors **do not have to be reappointed** when their term of office expires, although in most cases they are. Special notice must be given of any resolution to appoint auditors who were not appointed on the last occasion of the resolution, and the members and auditor must be notified.

Where a private company resolves to **appoint** a replacement auditor by **written resolution**, copies of the resolution must be sent to the proposed and outgoing auditor. The outgoing auditor may circulate a **statement of reasonable length** to the members if they notify the company within 14 days of receiving the copy of the written resolution.

2.8.1 Resignation of auditors

FAST FORWARD

However auditors leave office they must either: state there are **no circumstances** which should be brought to **members' and creditors' attention**; or list **those circumstances**. Auditors who are resigning can also: **circulate a statement** about their resignation to members; **requisition a general meeting**; **or speak** at a general meeting.

Procedures for resignation of auditors	
Statement of circumstances	Auditors must deposit a statement at the registered office with their resignation stating: • For quoted companies – the circumstances around their departure. • For non-quoted public companies and all private companies – there are no circumstances that the auditor believes should be brought to the attention of the members or creditors. • If there are such circumstances the statement should describe them. • Statements should also be submitted to the appropriate audit authority.
Company action	• The company must send notice of the resignation to the Registrar. • The company must **send** a copy of the statement of circumstances to **every person entitled to receive a copy of the accounts**.
Auditor rights	If the auditors have deposited a statement of circumstances, they may: • Circulate a statement of reasonable length to the members. • Requisition a general meeting to explain their reasons. • Attend and speak at any meeting where appointment of successors is to be discussed.

If the auditors decline to seek reappointment at an AGM, they must nevertheless fulfil the requirements of a **statement of the circumstances** just as if they had resigned. The reason for this provision is to prevent auditors who are unhappy with the company's affairs keeping their suspicions secret. The statement must be deposited not less than **14 days** before the time allowed for next appointing auditors.

2.8.2 Removal of the auditor from office

Procedures for removal from office	
Auditor representations	If a resolution is proposed either to: • Remove the auditors before their term of office expires or • Change the auditors when their term of office is complete, the auditors have the right to make representations of reasonable length to the company
Company action	The company must: • Notify members in the notice of the meeting of the representations • Send a copy of the representations in the notice • If it is not sent out, the auditors can require it is read at the meeting
Attendance at meeting	Auditors removed before expiry of their office may: • Attend the meeting at which their office would have expired • Attend any meeting at which the appointment of their successors is discussed
Statement of circumstances	If auditors are removed at a general meeting they must: • Make a statement of circumstances for members and creditors

Exam focus point

Remember: A statement of circumstances/no circumstances must be deposited **however** the auditors leave office.

BPP
LEARNING MEDIA

Chapter Roundup

- Every public company must have a **company secretary**, who is one of the officers of a company and may be a director. Private companies are not required to have a secretary.

- Every company (apart from certain small companies) must appoint appropriately qualified **auditors**. An audit is a check on the stewardship of the directors.

- The Companies Act provides **statutory rights** for auditors to enable them to carry out their duties.

- Auditors may leave office in the following ways: **resignation**; **removal from office** by an ordinary resolution with special notice passed before the end of their term; **failing** to **offer themselves** for **re-election**; and **not being re-elected** at the general meeting at which their term expires.

- However auditors leave office they must either: state there are **no circumstances** which should be brought to **members' and creditors' attention**; or list **those circumstances**. Auditors who are resigning can also: **circulate a statement** about their resignation to members; **requisition a general meeting**; **or speak** at a general meeting.

Quick Quiz

1   A private company with a sole director is not legally required to have a company secretary, but if it does, the sole director cannot also be the company secretary.

   True ☐

   False ☐

2   State two reasons why a person would be ineligible to be an auditor under Companies Act 2006.

   (1)   ....

   (2)   ....

3   Which of the following is **not** a recognised qualification that allows an individual to act as a company secretary?

   A   ACCA
   B   Solicitor
   C   Business Studies degree
   D   Employment as a company secretary for three of the five preceding years

4   Zee plc is a retailer of sportswear. Last year its turnover was £3 million and its balance sheet total was £1.5 million.

   Zee plc is exempt from audit.

   True ☐

   False ☐

5   Which of the following resolutions is required to remove an auditor of a private company?

   A   Ordinary resolution with usual notice
   B   Ordinary resolution with special notice
   C   Special resolution with usual notice
   D   Special resolution with special notice

Answers to Quick Quiz

1   True. Sole directors cannot be company secretaries. Private companies are not legally required to have a company secretary.

2   Any of:

   (1)   Is an officer/employee of the company being audited
   (2)   A partner or employee of a person in (1)
   (3)   A partnership in which (1) is a partner
   (4)   Ineligible by (1), (2) and (3) to be auditor of any of the entity's subsidiaries

3   C. A degree is not a recognised qualification for acting as a company secretary.

4   False. Although its turnover and balance sheet total suggest the company is small and exempt from audit, the company is a plc and therefore the exemption does not apply. Zee plc must have an audit.

5   B. An ordinary resolution with special notice is required to remove an auditor of any company.

Now try the questions below from the Practice Question Bank

Number
42, 43

Company meetings and resolutions

Topic list	Syllabus reference
1 The importance of meetings	F3(a)
2 General meetings	F3(a)
3 Types of resolution	F3(b)
4 Calling a meeting	F3(c)
5 Proceedings at meetings	F3(c)
6 Class meetings	F3(a)
7 Single member private companies	F3(a–c)

Introduction

In this chapter we consider the **procedures** by which companies are controlled by the shareholders, namely general meetings and resolutions. These afford members a measure of protection of their investment in the company. There are many transactions which, under the Act, cannot be entered into without a **resolution** of the company.

Moreover, a general meeting at which the annual accounts and the auditors' and directors' reports will be laid must normally be held annually by public companies. This affords the members an opportunity of questioning the directors on their **stewardship**.

Study guide

			Intellectual level
F	**Management, administration and the regulation of companies**		
3	**Company meetings and resolutions**		
(a)	Distinguish between types of meetings: general meetings and annual general meetings		1
(b)	Distinguish between types of resolutions: ordinary, special and written		2
(c)	Explain the procedure for calling and conducting company meetings		2

Exam guide

For the exam you must be quite clear about the different types of resolution, when each type is used, and the percentage vote needed for each type to be passed. This topic lends itself to multiple choice questions. However, resolutions in particular are important in many areas of the corporate part of the syllabus and meetings of members are an important control on the acts of the directors. Therefore, this topic could easily be incorporated into a scenario question.

1 The importance of meetings

FAST FORWARD

> Although the management of a company is in the hands of the directors, the **decisions which affect the existence of the company**, its structure and scope are **reserved to the members** in general meeting.

The decision of a general meeting is only valid and binding if the meeting is **properly convened** by notice and if the **business** of the meeting is **fairly** and **properly conducted**. Most of the rules on company meetings are concerned with the issue of notices and the casting of votes at meetings to carry resolutions of specified types.

1.1 Control over directors

The members in general meeting can exercise control over the directors, though only to a limited extent.

(a) Under normal procedure **one-third** of the **directors retire** at each annual general meeting, though they may offer themselves for re-election.

(b) Member approval, in general meeting, is required if the directors wish to:

    (i)   **Exceed their delegated power** or to use it for other than its given purpose
    (ii)   **Allot shares** (unless private company with one class of shares)
    (iii)   **Make a substantial contract** of sale or purchase with a director
    (iv)   Grant a director a **long-service agreement**

(c) The **appointment and removal of auditors** is normally done in general meeting.

1.2 Resolution of differences

In addition, general meetings are the means by which **members resolve differences** between themselves by voting on resolutions.

2 General meetings

FAST FORWARD

There are two kinds of general meeting of members of a company:

- **Annual general meeting (AGM)**
- **General meetings at other times**

2.1 Annual general meeting (AGM)

Under the Companies Act 2006 (TSO, 2006) the **AGM** plays a major role in the life of a public company, although often the business carried out seems fairly routine. It is a statutorily protected way for members to have a regular assessment and discussion of their company and its management.

Private companies are **not required** to have an **AGM** each year and therefore their business is usually conducted through **written resolutions**. However, members holding sufficient shares or votes can request a general meeting or written resolution.

Rules for directors calling an AGM
• Public companies must hold an AGM within **six months** of their year end
• Must be in **writing** and in **accordance** with the **articles**
• May be in **hard** or **electronic form** and also by means of a **website**
• At least **21 days' notice** should be given; a longer period may be specified in the articles
• **Shorter notice** is only valid if **all members** agree
• The notice must specify the **time**, **date** and **place** of the meeting and that the meeting is an AGM
• Where notice is given on a **website** it must be available from the **date of notification** until the **conclusion of the meeting**

The business of an annual general meeting usually includes:

- Considering the accounts
- Receiving the directors' report, the directors' remuneration report and the auditors' report
- Dividends
- Electing directors
- Appointing auditors

2.2 General meetings at other times

2.2.1 Directors

The **directors** may have power under the articles to convene a general meeting whenever they see fit.

2.2.2 Members

The directors of **public and private** companies may be required to convene a general meeting by **requisition of the members**.

Rules for members requisitioning a general meeting	
Shareholding	• The requisitioning members must hold at least **5%** of the **paid up share capital** holding **voting rights**.
Requisition	• They must deposit a **signed requisition** at the registered office or make the request in electronic form.
	• This must state the 'objects of the meeting': the **resolutions proposed**.

Rules for members requisitioning a general meeting	
Date	• A notice conveying the meeting must be sent out within **21 days** of the requisition. • It must be held within **28 days** of the notice calling to a meeting being sent out. • If the directors have not called the meeting within 21 days of the requisition, the **members may convene** the meeting for a date within 3 months of the deposit of the requisition.
Quorum	• If **no quorum** is present, the meeting is **adjourned**.

2.2.3 Court order

The court, on the application of a director or a member entitled to vote, may order that a meeting shall be held and may give instructions for that purpose, including fixing a quorum of one. This is a method of last resort to resolve a deadlock such as the refusal of one member out of two to attend (and provide a quorum) at a general meeting.

2.2.4 Auditor requisition

An auditor who gives a statement of circumstances for their resignation or other loss of office in their written notice may also requisition a meeting to receive and consider their explanation.

2.2.5 Loss of capital by public company

The directors of a public company must convene a general meeting if the net assets fall to half or less of the amount of its called-up share capital.

3 Types of resolution

FAST FORWARD

A meeting can pass two types of resolution. **Ordinary resolutions** are carried by a simple majority (more than 50%) of votes cast and requiring 14 days' notice. **Special resolutions** require a 75% majority of votes cast and also 14 days' notice.

A meeting reaches a decision by passing a resolution (either by a show of hands or a poll). Under the Companies Act 2006 (TSO, 2006) there are **two major kinds** of resolution, and an additional one for **private** companies.

Types of resolution	
Ordinary	For most business Requires simple (50%+) majority of the votes cast 14 days' notice
Special	For major changes Requires 75% majority of the votes cast 14 days' notice
Written (for private companies)	Can be used for all general meeting resolutions except for removing a director or auditor before their term of office expires. Either a simple (50%+) or 75% majority is required, depending on the business being passed.

3.1 Differences between ordinary and special resolutions

Apart from the required size of the majority and period of notice, the main differences between the types of resolution are as follows.

(a)　The **text** of **special resolutions** must be **set out** in **full** in the notice convening the meeting, and it must be described as a special resolution. This is not necessary for an ordinary resolution if it is routine business.

(b)   A **signed copy** of every **special resolution** must be **delivered** to the **Registrar** for filing. **Some ordinary resolutions**, particularly those relating to share capital, have to be **delivered** for filing but many do not.

3.2 Special resolutions

A special resolution is required for **major changes** in the company, such as the following.

*   A change of name
*   Restriction of the objects or other alteration of the articles
*   Reduction of share capital
*   Winding up the company
*   Presenting a petition by the company for an order for a compulsory winding up

3.3 Written resolutions

FAST FORWARD

A private company can pass any decision needed by a **written resolution**, except for removing a director or auditor before their term of office has expired.

As we saw earlier, a private company is **not** required to hold an **AGM**. Therefore the Act provides a mechanism for directors and members to conduct business solely by **written resolution**.

3.3.1 Written resolutions proposed by directors

Copies of the resolution proposed by directors must be sent to **each member** eligible to vote by hard copy, electronically or by a website. Alternatively, the same copy may be sent to each member in turn.

The resolution should be accompanied by a statement informing the member:

*   How to **signify their agreement** to the resolution
*   The **date** the resolution must be passed by

3.3.2 Written resolutions proposed by members

Members holding 5% (or lower if authorised by the articles) of the **voting rights** may request a written resolution, providing it:

*   **Would be effective** (not prevented by the articles or law)
*   Is **not defamatory, frivolous** or **vexatious**

A **statement** containing no more than **1,000 words** on the subject of the resolution may accompany it.

Copies of the resolution, and statements containing information on the subject matter, how to agree to it and the date of the resolution, must be sent to each member within **21 days** of the request for resolution.

Expenses for circulating the resolution **should be met by the members** who requested it unless the company resolves otherwise.

The company may **appeal to the court** not to circulate the 1,000 word statement by the members if the rights provided to the members are being abused by them.

3.3.3 Agreement

The members may indicate their agreement to the resolution in **hard copy** or **electronically**.

If no **period for agreement** is specified by the articles, then the default period is **28 days** from the date the resolution was circulated. Agreement after this period is ineffective. Once agreed, a member **may not revoke** their decision. Either a **simple** (50% plus one) or **75% majority** is required to pass a written resolution depending on the nature of the business being decided. Three further points should be noted concerning written resolutions.

(a)   Written resolutions can be used **notwithstanding any provisions** in the company's **articles**.

(b)   A written resolution **cannot** be **used to remove a director or auditor** from office, since such persons have a right to **speak** at a **meeting**.

(c)   **Copies of written resolutions** should be **sent to auditors** at or before the time they are sent to shareholders. Auditors do not have the right to object to written resolutions. If the auditors are not sent a copy, the resolution remains valid; however the directors and secretary will be liable to a fine. The purpose of this provision is to ensure auditors are kept informed about what is happening in the company.

4 Calling a meeting

FAST FORWARD

A meeting cannot make valid and binding decisions until it has been properly convened. Notice of general meetings must be given **14 days** in advance of the meeting. The notice should contain **adequate information** about the meeting.

Meetings must be called by a **competent person** or authority.

A meeting cannot make valid and binding decisions until it has been properly convened according to the company's articles, though there are also statutory rules under the Companies Act 2006 (TSO, 2006).

(a)   The meeting must generally be **called by** the **board of directors** or other competent person or authority.

(b)   The notice must be issued to members in advance of the meeting so as to give them **14 days'** clear notice of the meeting. The members may agree to waive this requirement.

(c)   The **notice** must be sent to every member (or other person) entitled to receive the notice.

(d)   The notice must include any information **reasonably necessary** to enable shareholders to know in advance what is to be done.

(e)   As we saw earlier, members may require the directors to call a meeting if:

(i)   They hold at least **5% of the voting rights**

(ii)   They provide a **statement of the general business** to be conducted and the text of any proposed resolution

The directors must within **21 days call a meeting** to be held no later than **28 days from the date of the notice** they send calling the meeting.

In most cases the notice need **not** be sent to a member whose only shares do not give them a right to attend and vote (as is often the position of **preference shareholders**).

4.1 Electronic communication

We have already seen that **notice** may be given by means of a **website** and in **electronic form**. Also, where a company gives an **electronic address** in a notice calling a meeting, any information or document relating to the meeting may be sent to that address.

4.2 Timing of notices

FAST FORWARD

Clear notice must be given to members. **Notice** must be **sent to all members** entitled to receive it.

Members may – and in small private companies often do – waive the required notice. For **short notice** to be effective:

(a)   All **members** of a public company must consent in respect of an **AGM**.

(b)   In respect of a **general meeting**, members holding 90% of the issued shares of a private company and 95% of the issued shares of a public company may agree to shorter notice.

The following specific rules by way of exception should be remembered.

- When **special notice** of a resolution is given to the company it must be given **28 days** in advance of the meeting.

- In a **creditors' voluntary winding up** there must be at least **seven days notice** of the **creditors' meeting** (to protect the interests of creditors). The members may shorten the period of notice down to seven days but that is all.

The **clear days rule** in the Act provides that the day of the meeting and the day the notice was given are **excluded** from the required notice period.

4.3 Special notice of a resolution

FAST FORWARD

Special notice of 28 days of intention to propose certain resolutions (removal of directors/auditors) must be given.

Key term

> **Special notice** is notice of 28 days which must be given to a company of the intention to put certain types of resolution at a company meeting.

Special notice must be given **to the company** of the intention to propose a resolution for any of the following purposes.

- To **remove** an **auditor** or to **appoint** an **auditor other** than the **auditor** who was **appointed** at the **previous year's meeting**

- To **remove a director from office** or to appoint a substitute in their place after removal

A member may request a resolution to be passed at a particular meeting. In this case, the **member must give special notice** of their intention **to the company** at **least 28 days** before the date of the meeting. If, however, the company calls the meeting for a date less than 28 days after receiving the special notice, that notice is deemed to have been **properly given**.

On receiving special notice a **public company may be obliged** to **include the resolution** in the **AGM notice** which it issues.

If the company gives notice to members of the resolution it does so by a **21-day notice** to them that special notice has been received and what it contains. If it is not practicable to include the matter in the notice of meeting, the company may give notice to members by newspaper advertisement or any other means permitted by the articles.

Where special notice is received of intention to propose a resolution for the removal of a director or to change the auditor, the company must send a copy to the **director** or **auditor**. This is to allow them to exercise their statutory right to defend themself by issuing a memorandum and/or addressing the meeting in person.

The essential point is that a **special notice is given to the company**; it is **not a notice from the company to members** although it will be followed (usually) by such notice.

4.4 Members requisitioning a resolution

FAST FORWARD

Members rather than directors may be able to requisition resolutions. This may be achieved by requesting the directors call a meeting, or proposing a resolution to be voted on at a meeting already arranged.

The directors normally have the **right to decide** what resolutions shall be included in the notice of a meeting. However, apart from the requisition to call a general meeting, members can also take the initiative to requisition certain resolutions be considered at the AGM.

Rules for members requisitioning a resolution at the AGM	
Qualifying holding	• The members must represent 5% of the voting rights, or • Be at least 100 members holding shares with an average paid up of £100, per member
Request	• Must be in hard copy or electronic form, identify the resolution and be delivered at least six weeks in advance of an AGM or other general meeting
Statement	• Members may request a statement (<1,000 words) be circulated to all members by delivering a **requisition**. Members with a qualifying holding may request a statement regarding their own resolution or any resolution proposed at the meeting • The company must send the statement with the notice of the meeting or as soon as practicable after

In either instance, the **requisitionists** must bear the incidental costs unless the company resolves otherwise.

The right of members to have resolutions included on the agenda of AGM or other meetings could easily be the subject of a question in your exam. It is an **important consideration if some of the members disagree with the directors**.

4.5 Content of notices

FAST FORWARD

The **notice** convening the meeting must give certain details: **date**, **time** and **place** of the meeting, and identification of AGM and special resolutions. Sufficient information about the business to be discussed at the meeting should be provided, to enable shareholders to know what is to be done.

The notice of a general meeting must contain adequate information on the following points.

(a)   The **date**, **time** and **place** of the meeting must be given.

(b)   An **AGM** or a **special resolution** must be described as such.

(c)   Information must be given of the business of the meeting **sufficient** to enable members (in deciding whether to attend or to appoint proxies) to **understand what will be done** at the meeting.

4.5.1 Routine business

In issuing the notice of an AGM it is standard practice merely to list the **items of ordinary or routine business** to be transacted, such as the following.

• Declaration of dividends (if any)
• Election of directors
• Appointment of auditors and fixing of their remuneration

The articles usually include a requirement that members shall be informed of any intention to **propose** the **election** of a director, other than an existing director who retires by rotation and merely stands for re-election.

5 Proceedings at meetings

5.1 How a meeting proceeds

FAST FORWARD

Company meetings need to be properly run if they are to be **effective** and within the **law**.

A meeting can only reach binding decisions if:

- It has been properly **convened** by notice
- A **quorum is present**
- A **chairman presides**
- The **business** is **properly transacted** and **resolutions** are **put to the vote**

There is no obligation to allow a member to be present if their shares do not carry the right to attend and vote. However, **full general meetings** and **class meetings** can be held when shareholders not entitled to vote are present.

Each **item of business** included in the notice should be taken separately, discussed and **put to the vote**.

Members may propose **amendments** to any resolutions proposed. The chairman should reject any amendment which is outside the limits set by the notice convening the meeting.

If the relevant business is an **ordinary resolution** it may be possible to amend the resolution's wording so as to **reduce its effect** to something less (provided that the change does not entirely alter its character). For example, an ordinary resolution authorising the directors to borrow £100,000 might be amended to substitute a limit of £50,000 (but not to increase it to £150,000 as £100,000 would have been stated in the notice).

5.2 The Chair (chairman)

FAST FORWARD

The meeting should usually be chaired by the **chairman** of the board of directors. They do not necessarily have a casting vote.

The articles usually provide that the **Chair (chairman)** of the board of directors **is to preside** at general meetings; in their absence another director chosen by the directors shall preside instead. As a last resort a member chosen by the members present can preside.

The chairman derives their authority from the articles and they have **no casting vote unless** the **articles give them one**. Their duties are to **maintain order** and to **deal** with the **agenda** in a methodical way so that the business of the meeting may be properly transacted.

The chairman:

- **May dissolve** or **adjourn** the **meeting** if it has become disorderly or if the members present agree
- Must **adjourn** if the meeting **instructs** them to do so

5.3 Quorum

FAST FORWARD

The **quorum** for meetings may be two or more (except for single member private companies). **Proxies** can attend, speak and vote on behalf of members.

Key term

A **quorum** is the minimum number of persons required to be present at a particular type of (company) meeting. In the case of shareholders' meetings, the figure is usually two, in person or by proxy, but the articles may make other provisions.

There is a legal principle that a 'meeting means a coming together of more than one person'. Hence it follows that as a matter of law **one person generally cannot be a meeting**.

The rule that at least two persons must be present to constitute a 'meeting' does not require that both persons must be members. Every member has a **statutory right to appoint a proxy** to attend as their representative.

5.3.1 Proxies

> A **proxy** is a person appointed by a shareholder to vote on behalf of that shareholder at company meetings.

Under the Companies Act 2006 (TSO, 2006) any member of a company which has a share capital, provided they are entitled to attend and vote at a general or class meeting of the company, has a statutory right to appoint an **agent**, called a **'proxy'**, to attend and vote for them.

Rules for appointing proxies	
Basic rule	<ul><li>Any **member** may appoint a proxy</li><li>The proxy **does not** have to be a member</li><li>Proxies **may speak** at the meeting</li><li>A member may **appoint more than one proxy** provided each proxy is appointed in respect of a different class of share held by the member</li></ul>
Voting	<ul><li>Proxies **may vote** on a **poll** and on a **show of hands**</li><li>Proxies may **demand a poll** at a meeting</li><li>Most companies provide **two-way proxy cards** that the member can use to instruct a proxy how to vote, either for or against a resolution</li></ul>
Notice	<ul><li>Every notice of a meeting must **state** the member's right to a proxy</li><li>**Notice** of a proxy appointment should be given to the company at least 48 hours before the meeting (excluding weekends and bank holidays)</li></ul>

Hence one member and another member's proxy may together provide the quorum (if it is fixed, as is usual, at 'two members present in person or by proxy'). However, one member who is also the proxy appointed by another member cannot by themself be a meeting, since a **minimum of two individuals** present is required.

There may, however, be a meeting attended by one person only, if:

(a)   It is a **class meeting** and all the **shares** of that class are **held** by **one member**.

(b)   The **court**, in exercising a power to order a general meeting to be held, **fixes** the **quorum** at one. This means that in a two-member company, a meeting can be held with one person if the other deliberately absents themself to frustrate business.

(c)   The company is a **single member private company**.

The articles usually fix a **quorum** for general meetings which may be as low as two (the minimum for a meeting) but may be more – though this is unusual.

If the articles do fix a quorum of two or more persons present, the meeting lacks a quorum (it is said to be an 'inquorate' meeting) if either:

- The **required number** is **not present** within a **stipulated time** (usually half an hour) of the appointed time for commencing a meeting.

- The **meeting begins** with a **quorum** but the **number present dwindles** to less than the quorum – unless the articles provide for this possibility.

The articles usually provide for automatic and compulsory **adjournment of an inquorate meeting**.

The articles can provide that a meeting which begins with a quorum may continue despite a reduction in numbers present to less than the quorum level. However, there must still be **two or more persons present**.

5.4 Voting and polls

Voting at general meetings may be on a **show of hands** or a **poll**.

The **rights of members** to **vote** and the **number of votes** to which they are entitled in respect of their shares are fixed by the **articles**.

One vote per share is normal but some shares, for instance preference shares, may carry no voting rights in normal circumstances. To shorten the proceedings at meetings the procedure is as follows.

5.4.1 Voting on a show of hands

Key term

> A **show of hands** is a method of voting for or against a resolution by raising hands. Under this method each member has one vote irrespective of the number of shares held, in contrast to a poll vote.

On putting a resolution to the vote the chairman calls for a show of hands. One vote may be given by each member present in person, including proxies.

Unless a poll is then demanded, the chairman's declaration of the result is **conclusive**. However, it is still possible to challenge the chairman's declaration on the grounds that it was fraudulent or manifestly wrong.

5.4.2 Voting on a poll

Key term

> A **poll** is a method of voting at company meetings which allows a member to use as many votes as their shareholding grants them.

If a **real test of voting strength** is required a poll may be demanded. The result of the previous show of hands is then disregarded. On a poll every member and also proxies representing absent members may cast the full number of votes to which they are entitled. A poll need not be held at the time but may be postponed so that arrangements to hold it can be made.

A poll may be **demanded** by:

- Not **less than five members**
- Member(s) **representing** not less than **one-tenth** of the **total voting rights**
- Member(s) **holding shares** which **represent** not less than **one-tenth** of the **paid-up capital**

Any provision in the articles is **void** if it seeks to prevent such members demanding a poll or to exclude the right to demand a poll on any question other than the election of a chairman by the meeting or an adjournment.

When a poll is held it is usual to appoint **'scrutineers'** and to ask members and proxies to sign voting cards or lists. The votes cast are checked against the register of members and the chairman declares the result.

Members of a quoted company may require the directors to obtain an **independent report** in respect of a poll taken, or to be taken, at a general meeting if:

- They represent at least 5% of the voting rights; or
- Are at least 100 in number holding at least £100 of paid up capital.

5.4.3 Result of a vote

In voting, either by show of hands or on a poll, the **number of votes cast determines the result**. Votes which are not cast, whether the member who does not use them is present or absent, are simply disregarded. Hence the majority vote may be much less than half (or three-quarters) of the total votes which could be cast.

Results of quoted company polls must be made available on a **website**. The following information should be made available as soon as **reasonably practicable**, and should remain on the website for at least **two years**.

- Meeting date
- Text of the resolution or description of the poll's subject matter
- Number of votes for and against the resolution

5.5 Minutes of company meetings

Minutes must be kept of all **general, directors'** and **management meetings**, and members can inspect those of general meetings.

Minutes are a record of the proceedings of meetings. Company law requires minutes to be kept of all company meetings including general, directors' and managers' meetings.

Every company is **required to keep minutes** which are a formal written record of the proceedings of its general meetings for ten years. These minutes are usually kept in **book form**. If a loose leaf book is used to facilitate typing there should be safeguards against falsification, such as sequential prenumbering.

The chairman **normally signs** the minutes. If they do so, the signed minutes are admissible evidence of the proceedings, though evidence may be given to contradict or supplement the minutes or to show that no meeting at all took place.

Members of the company have the **right to inspect** minutes of general meetings. The minutes of general meetings must be held at the registered office (or the single alternative inspection location (SAIL)) and be available for inspection by members, who are also entitled to demand copies.

5.6 The assent principle

A unanimous decision of the members is often treated as a substitute for a formal decision in general meeting properly convened and held, and is equally binding.

6 Class meetings

Class meetings are held where the interests of different groups of shareholders may be affected in different ways.

6.1 Types of class meeting

Class meetings are of two kinds.

(a) If the company has more than one class of share, for example if it has 'preference' and 'ordinary' shares, it may be necessary to call a meeting of the holders of one class, to approve a proposed **variation** of the **rights** attached to their shares.

(b) Under a **compromise** or **arrangements with creditors** the holders of shares of the same class may nonetheless be divided into **separate** classes if the scheme proposed will affect each group differently.

When separate meetings of a class of members are held, the same procedural rules as for general meetings apply (but there is a different rule on quorum).

6.2 Quorum for a class meeting

The standard general meeting rules, on issuing notices and on voting, apply to a class meeting.

However the **quorum** for a class meeting is fixed at two persons who hold, or represent by proxy, at least **one-third** in nominal value of the issued shares of the class (unless the class only consists of a single member).

If no quorum is present, the meeting is **adjourned** (under the standard adjournment procedure for general meetings). When the meeting resumes, the quorum is **one** person (who must still hold at least one-third of the shares).

7 Single-member private companies

FAST FORWARD

There are **special rules** for **private companies** with only **one shareholder**.

Under the Companies Act 2006 (TSO, 2006) if the sole member takes any decision that could have been taken in general meeting, that member shall (unless it is a written resolution) provide the company with a **written record** of it. This allows the sole member to conduct members' business informally without notice or minutes.

Filing requirements still apply, for example, in the case of alteration of articles.

Written resolutions **cannot** be used to remove a director or auditor from office, as these resolutions require special notice.

Chapter Roundup

- Although the management of a company is in the hands of the directors, the **decisions which affect the existence of the company**, its structure and scope are **reserved to the members** in general meeting.

- There are two kinds of general meeting of members of a company:
    - **Annual general meeting (AGM)**
    - **General meetings at other times**

- A meeting can pass two types of resolution. **Ordinary resolutions** are carried by a simple majority (more than 50%) of votes cast and requiring 14 days' notice. **Special resolutions** require a 75% majority of votes cast and also 14 days' notice.

- A private company can pass any decision needed by a **written resolution**, except for removing a director or auditor before their term of office has expired.

- A meeting cannot make valid and binding decisions until it has been properly convened. Notice of general meetings must be given **14 days** in advance of the meeting. The notice should contain **adequate information** about the meeting.

- Meetings must be called by a **competent person** or authority.

- **Clear notice** must be given to members. **Notice** must be **sent to all members** entitled to receive it.

- **Special notice of 28 days** of intention to propose certain resolutions (removal of directors/auditors) must be given.

- **Members** rather than directors may be able to requisition resolutions. This may be achieved by requesting the directors call a meeting, or proposing a resolution to be voted on at a meeting already arranged.

- The **notice** convening the meeting must give certain details: **date**, **time** and **place** of the meeting, and identification of AGM and special resolutions. Sufficient information about the business to be discussed at the meeting should be provided, to enable shareholders to know what is to be done.

- Company meetings need to be properly run if they are to be **effective** and within the **law**.

- The meeting should usually be chaired by the **chairman** of the board of directors. They do not necessarily have a casting vote.

- The **quorum** for meetings may be two or more (except for single-member private companies). **Proxies** can attend, speak and vote on behalf of members.

- Voting at general meetings may be on a **show of hands** or a **poll**.

- **Minutes** must be kept of all **general, directors'** and **management meetings**, and members can inspect those of general meetings.

- **Class meetings** are held where the interests of different groups of shareholders may be affected in different ways.

- There are **special rules** for **private companies** with only **one shareholder**.

1   Which of the following decisions can only be taken by the members in general meeting?

Select all that apply.

A   Alteration of articles
B   Change of name
C   Reduction of capital
D   Appointment of a managing director

2   Before a private company can hold a general meeting on short notice, members holding a certain percentage of the company's shares must agree. Which one of the following percentages is correct?

51%	90%
75%	95%

3   A plc must hold its AGM within six months of its year end.

True   ☐

False   ☐

4   Minutes of company meetings must be kept for:

A   1 year
B   5 years
C   10 years
D   15 years

5   A member of a public company may only appoint one proxy, but the proxy has a statutory right to speak at the meeting.

True   ☐

False   ☐

1   A, B and C. The board can appoint someone to be managing director, so D is incorrect.

2   90%

3   True. A plc must hold its AGM within six months of its year end.

4   C. Under the Companies Act, minutes must be kept for ten years.

5   False. Public company members can appoint more than one proxy. They have a statutory right to speak.

Now try the questions below from the Practice Question Bank

Number
44, 45, 46

P
A
R
T

G

Insolvency law

21

Insolvency and administration

Topic list	Syllabus reference
1 What is liquidation?	G1(a), G1(b)
2 Voluntary liquidation	G1(a)
3 Compulsory liquidation	G1(b), G1(c)
4 Differences between compulsory and voluntary liquidation	G1(a), G1(b)
5 Saving a company: administration	G1(d), G1(e)

Introduction

A **company in difficulty** or **in crisis** (an **insolvent** company) basically has a choice of two alternatives:

(1)   To carry on with the business, using statutory methods to help remedy the situation

(2)   To stop

A company which is heading towards insolvency can often be **saved**, using a variety of **legal protections** from creditors until the problem is sorted out.

Alternative 1 does not have to mean carrying on as if everything is normal. It can mean **seeking help** from the **court** or a **qualified insolvency practitioner** to put a plan together to **save the company** and get it out of its bad financial position.

Unfortunately, many companies cannot be saved, and the members and directors are forced to take alternative 2, **to stop** operating the business through the company. Liquidation, sometimes called 'winding up', is **when a company is formally dissolved** and ceases to exist.

The Insolvency Act 1986 (HMSO, 1986) applies to this chapter unless otherwise stated.

Study guide

		Intellectual level
G	**Insolvency law**	
1	**Insolvency and administration**	
(a)	Explain the meaning of and procedure involved in voluntary liquidation, including members' and creditors' voluntary liquidation	2
(b)	Explain the meaning of, the grounds for, and the procedure involved in compulsory liquidation	2
(c)	Explain the order in which company debts will be paid off on liquidation	2
(d)	Explain administration as a general alternative to liquidation	2
(e)	Explain the way in which an administrator may be appointed, the effects of such appointment, and the powers and duties of an administrator	2

Exam guide

As well as being examined in questions in its own right, you may find that elements of insolvency creep into scenario questions on company finances and directors.

1 What is liquidation?

> **FAST FORWARD**
>
> **Liquidation** is the **dissolution** or **'winding up'** of a company.

Key terms

> **Liquidation** means that the company must be dissolved and its affairs 'wound up', or brought to an end.
>
> The assets are realised, debts are paid out of the proceeds, and any surplus amounts are returned to members. Liquidation leads on to **dissolution** of the company. It is sometimes referred to as **winding up**.

1.1 Who decides to liquidate?

> **FAST FORWARD**
>
> There are three different methods of **liquidation: compulsory, members' voluntary** and **creditors' voluntary**. Compulsory liquidation and creditors' voluntary liquidation are proceedings for insolvent companies, and members' voluntary liquidation is for solvent companies.

The **parties** most likely to be involved in the **decision to liquidate** are:

- The directors
- The creditors
- The members

The **directors** are best placed to know the financial position and difficulty that the company is in. The **creditors** may become aware that the company is in financial difficulty when their invoices do not get paid on a timely basis, or at all.

The **members** are likely to be the last people to know that the company is in financial difficulty, as they rely on the directors to tell them. In public companies, there is a rule that the directors must call a general meeting of members if the net assets of the company fall to half or less of the amount of its called-up share capital. There is no such rule for private companies.

As we shall see, there are three methods of winding up. They depend on **who has instigated the proceedings**. Directors cannot formally instigate proceedings for winding up, they can only make recommendations to the members.

However, if the **members refuse** to put the company in liquidation and the directors feel that to continue to trade will prejudice creditors, they could resign their posts in order to avoid committing **fraudulent** or **wrongful trading**.

In any case, if the company was in such serious financial difficulty for this to be an issue, it is likely that a **creditor** would have commenced proceedings against it.

1.1.1 Creditors

If a creditor has sufficient grounds they may **apply to the court** for the **compulsory winding up** of the company.

Creditors may also be closely involved in a **voluntary winding up**, if the company is **insolvent** when the **members** decide to wind the company up.

1.1.2 Members

The members may decide to wind the company up (probably on the advice of the directors). If they do so, the company is **voluntarily wound up**. This can lead to two different types of members' winding up:

- Members' voluntary winding up (if the company is solvent)
- Creditors' voluntary winding up (if the company is insolvent)

1.2 Role of the liquidator

FAST FORWARD

A **liquidator** must be an authorised, qualified insolvency practitioner.

Once the decision to liquidate has been taken, the company goes under the **control of a liquidator** who must be a **qualified** and **authorised** insolvency practitioner.

Although the liquidator's main role is to wind up the company, they also have a statutory duty to **report** to the Secretary of State where they feel that any **director** of the insolvent company is **unfit** to be involved in the management of a company.

1.3 Common features of liquidations

FAST FORWARD

Once **insolvency procedures** have commenced, share trading must cease, the company documents must state that the company is in liquidation and the directors' power to manage ceases.

Regardless of what method of liquidation is used, similar **legal problems** may arise in each of them. In addition, the following factors are true at the start of any liquidation:

- **No share dealings** or **changes in members** are allowed
- All company documents (eg invoices, letters, emails) and the website must **state the company is in liquidation**
- The **directors' power to manage ceases**

2 Voluntary liquidation

FAST FORWARD

A **winding up** is **voluntary** where the decision to wind up is taken by the company's members, although if the company is insolvent, the creditors will be heavily involved in the proceedings.

As we saw earlier there are two types of voluntary liquidation:

- A **members' voluntary winding up**, where the company is **solvent** and the members merely decide to 'kill it off'
- A **creditors' voluntary winding up**, where the company is **insolvent** and the members resolve to wind up in consultation with creditors

The **main differences** between a members' and a creditors' voluntary winding up are set out below.

Function	Winding up	
	Members' voluntary	**Creditors' voluntary**
(1) **Appointment of liquidator**	By members	Nominated by members, subject to approval by creditors
(2) **Approval for liquidator's actions**	General meeting of members	Liquidation committee
(3) **Liquidation committee**	None	Up to five representatives of creditors

The effect of the voluntary winding up being a creditors' one is that the **creditors** have a **decisive influence** on the conduct of the liquidation.

In both kinds of voluntary winding up, the **court has the power to appoint a liquidator** (if for some reason there is none acting) or to remove one liquidator and appoint another.

2.1 Members' voluntary liquidation

In order to be a members' winding up, the directors must make a **declaration of solvency**. It is a criminal offence to make a declaration of solvency without reasonable grounds.

Type of resolution to be passed	
Ordinary	This is **rare, but** if the **articles** specify liquidation at a certain point, only an ordinary resolution is required
Special	A company may resolve to be **wound up** by special resolution

Under the Insolvency Act 1986 (HMSO, 1986) the winding up **commences** on the passing of the resolution. A signed copy of the resolution must be delivered to the Registrar within 15 days. A **liquidator** is usually appointed by the same resolution (or a second resolution passed at the same time).

2.1.1 Declaration of solvency

A voluntary winding up is a members' voluntary winding up **only** if the directors make and deliver to the Registrar a **declaration of solvency**.

This is a **statutory declaration** that the directors have made full enquiry into the affairs of the company and are of the opinion that it will be able to pay its debts, within a specified period not exceeding 12 months.

(a) The **declaration is made by all the directors** or, if there are more than two directors, by a **majority** of them.

(b) The declaration includes a **statement of the company's assets and liabilities** as at the latest practicable date before the declaration is made.

(c) The **declaration must** be:

(i) Made not more than **five weeks** before the resolution to wind up is passed; and

(ii) Delivered to the Registrar within **15 days** after the meeting.

Exam focus point

It is a **criminal offence** punishable by fine or imprisonment for a director to make a declaration of solvency without having **reasonable grounds** for it. If the company proves to be insolvent they will have to justify their previous declaration or be punished.

In a members' voluntary winding up the **creditors play no part** since the assumption is that their debts will be paid in full. The liquidator calls special and annual general meetings of contributories (members), to whom they report:

(a)   Within **three months** after each anniversary of the commencement of the winding up, the liquidator must call a meeting and lay before it an account of their transactions during the year.

(b)   When the liquidation is complete the liquidator, calls a meeting to lay before it their **final accounts**.

After holding the final meeting the liquidator sends a **copy of their accounts** to the Registrar who dissolves the company three months later by removing its name from the register.

2.2 Creditors' voluntary liquidation

FAST FORWARD

When there is no declaration of solvency there is a **creditors' voluntary winding** up.

If no declaration of solvency is made and delivered to the Registrar the liquidation proceeds as a creditors' voluntary winding up **even if**, in the end, the company pays its debts in full.

To commence a creditors' voluntary winding up the directors convene a general meeting of members to pass a **special resolution** (private companies may pass a written resolution with a 75% majority), **nominate a liquidator** and establish a **liquidation committee**.

Creditor approval for the choice of liquidator is then sought. This is obtained either through the deemed consent procedure (where less than 10% of creditors object to the nominee) or by a hosting a virtual (online) meeting for a vote. However, creditors are entitled to request a meeting if this wish.

The decision of the creditors on the nomination of the liquidator must be received after 3 working days following delivery of the notice, but within 14 working days of the resolution to wind up the company.

2.2.1 Centrebinding

In the past, the members' nominee for liquidator has been exploited for the purpose known as **'centrebinding'**.

Re Centrebind Ltd 1966

The facts: The directors convened a general meeting, without making a statutory declaration of solvency, but failed to call a creditors' meeting for the same or the next day. The penalty for this was merely a small default fine. The liquidator chosen by the members had disposed of the assets before the creditors could appoint a liquidator. The creditors' liquidator challenged the sale of the assets (at a low price) as invalid.

Decision: The first liquidator had been in office when he made the sale and so it was a valid exercise of the normal power of sale.

In a 'centrebinding' transaction the assets are sold by an **obliging liquidator** to a new company formed by the members of the insolvent company. The purpose is to defeat the claims of the creditors at minimum cost and enable the same people to continue in business until the next insolvency supervenes.

The Government has sought to limit the abuses during the period between the members' and creditors' meetings. The **powers of the members' nominee as liquidator are now restricted** to:

•   Taking control of the company's property,

•   Disposing of perishable or other goods which might diminish in value if not disposed of immediately; and

•   Doing all other things necessary for the protection of the company's assets.

If the members' liquidator wishes to perform any act other than those listed above, they will have to **apply to the court for leave**.

3 Compulsory liquidation

> There are **seven statutory reasons** for the compulsory liquidation of a company, which can all be found in the Insolvency Act 1986.

There are **seven statutory reasons** for the compulsory liquidation of a company, which can all be found in the Insolvency Act 1986 (HMSO, 1986). We shall consider the two most important here.

Statutory reasons for compulsory liquidation
Company is unable to pay its debts
It is just and equitable to wind up the company

The **parties** who can apply for the **compulsory liquidation** of a company will depend on the reason being cited.

In cases where the company is **unable to pay its debts**, it is a **creditor** who applies for the liquidation as a last resort when the company has not settled a debt.

In **just and equitable** cases, it is usually the **company itself**, the **members** or **directors** that decide the company should be wound-up.

The **Government** may petition for the compulsory winding up of a company:

- If a public company has not obtained a, **trading certificate** within one year of incorporation

- Following a report by government inspectors that it is in the **public interest** and **just and equitable** for the company to be wound up

An **administrator** of a company may also apply for the company's compulsory liquidation, on behalf of the company, as a means of ending an **administration process**.

3.1 Company unable to pay its debts

> A creditor may apply to the court to wind up the company if the company is **unable to pay its debts**. There are statutory tests to prove that a company is unable to pay its debts.

A creditor who petitions on the grounds of the company's insolvency must show that the company is **unable to pay its debts**. There are three permitted ways to do that.

(a) A **creditor owed more than £750 serves** the company at its registered office a **written demand** for payment and the **company fails** to **pay the debt** or to offer security for it within **21 days**.

  If the company denies it owes the amount demanded on apparently **reasonable grounds**, the court will dismiss the petition and leave the creditor to take legal proceedings for debt.

(b) A creditor obtains **judgement** against the company for debt, and attempts to enforce the judgement. However, they are **unable to obtain payment** because no assets of the company have been found and seized.

(c) A creditor satisfies the court that, taking into account the contingent and prospective liabilities of the company, it is **unable to pay its debts**. The creditor may show this in one of two ways:

  (i) By proof that the company is not able to pay its debts as they fall due – the **commercial insolvency test**

  (ii) By proof that the company's assets are less than its liabilities – the **balance sheet test**

  This is a **residual category**. Any evidence of actual or prospective insolvency may be produced.

Exam focus point

A secured creditor might appoint a receiver to control the secured asset for the purpose of realising the creditors' loan. If the receiver cannot find an asset to realise, the creditor might file a petition for compulsory liquidation under (b).

3.2 The just and equitable ground

FAST FORWARD

A **dissatisfied member** may get the court to wind the company up on the **just and equitable ground**.

A member who is dissatisfied with the directors or controlling shareholders over the management of the company may petition the court for the company to be wound up on the **just and equitable ground**. For such a petition to be successful, the member must show that **no** other remedy is available. It is not enough for a member to be **dissatisfied** to make it just and equitable that the company should be wound up, since winding up what may be an otherwise healthy company is a **drastic step**.

3.2.1 Examples: When companies have been wound up

(a) **The substratum of the company has gone – the only or main object(s) of the company (its underlying basis or substratum) cannot be or can no longer be achieved.**

> *Re German Date Coffee Co 1882*
>
> *The facts:* The objects clause specified very pointedly that the sole object was to manufacture coffee from dates under a German patent. The German government refused to grant a patent. The company manufactured coffee under a Swedish patent for sale in Germany. A member petitioned for compulsory winding up.
>
> *Decision:* The company existed only to 'work a particular patent' and as it could not do so it should be wound up.

(b) **The company was formed for an illegal or fraudulent purpose or there is a complete deadlock in the management of its affairs.**

> *Re Yenidje Tobacco Co Ltd 1916*
>
> *The facts:* Two sole traders merged their businesses in a company of which they were the only directors and shareholders. They quarrelled bitterly and one sued the other for fraud. Meanwhile they refused to speak to each other and conducted board meetings by passing notes through the hands of the secretary. The defendant in the fraud action petitioned for compulsory winding up.
>
> *Decision:* 'In substance these two people are really partners' and by analogy with the law of partnership (which permits dissolution if the partners are really unable to work together) it was just and equitable to order liquidation.

(c) **The understandings between members or directors which were the basis of the association have been unfairly breached by lawful action.**

> *Ebrahimi v Westbourne Galleries Ltd 1973*
>
> *The facts:* E and N carried on business together for 25 years, originally as partners and for the last 10 years through a company in which each originally had 500 shares. E and N were the first directors and shared the profits as directors' remuneration; no dividends were paid. When N's son joined the business he became a third director and E and N each transferred 100 shares to N's son. Eventually there were disputes. N and his son used their voting control in general meeting (600 votes against 400) to remove E from his directorship.
>
> *Decision:* The company should be wound up. N and his son were within their legal rights in removing E from his directorship, but the past relationship made it 'unjust or inequitable' to insist on legal rights and the court could intervene on equitable principles to order liquidation.

> *Re A company 1983*
>
> *The facts:* The facts were similar in essentials to those in *Ebrahimi's* case but the majority offered and the petitioner agreed that they would settle the dispute by a sale of his shares to the majority. This settlement broke down, however, because they could not agree on the price. The petitioner then petitioned on the just and equitable ground.
>
> *Decision:* An order for liquidation on this ground may only be made 'in the absence of any other remedy'. As the parties had agreed in principle that there was an alternative to liquidation the petition must be dismissed.

3.3 Other circumstances for compulsory liquidation

As mentioned previously, there are a **number of other circumstances** where compulsory liquidation may be commenced. These are:

- The **company passed a special resolution** that it should be wound up by the court

- The company registered as a **public limited company** more than a year previously but has not yet been issued with a **trading certificate**

- The company is an **'old' public company** (a PLC that existed on or before 22nd December 1980 and has remained as a PLC since)

- The company has **not begun trading within a year** of its incorporation or **has suspended its trading** for a whole year

- A **moratorium for a voluntary arrangement** for the company has passed and no voluntary arrangement is in place

3.4 Proceedings for compulsory liquidation

When a petition is presented to the **court** a copy is delivered to the **company** in case it objects. It is advertised so that other creditors may intervene if they wish.

The petition **may** be presented by a member. If the petition is presented by **a member** they **must show** that:

(a) The company is **insolvent** or alternatively refuses to supply information of its financial position; and

(b) They have been a **registered shareholder** for at least 6 of the 18 months up to the date of their petition. However this rule is not applied if the petitioner acquired their shares by allotment direct from the company or by inheritance from a deceased member or if the petition is based on the number of members having fallen below two.

Attention!

> The court will not order compulsory liquidation on a member's petition if they have nothing to gain from it. If the company is insolvent they would receive nothing since the creditors will take all the assets.

Once the court has been petitioned, a **provisional liquidator** may be appointed by the **court**. The **official receiver** is usually appointed, and their powers are conferred, by the court. These powers usually extend to taking control of the company's property and applying for a special manager to be appointed.

Key term

> The **official receiver** is an officer of the court. They are appointed as liquidator of any company ordered to be wound up by the court, although an insolvency practitioner may replace them.

3.5 Effects of an order for compulsory liquidation

The effects of an **order** for compulsory liquidation are:

(a) The **official receiver becomes liquidator**.

(b) The liquidation is **deemed to have commenced at the time when the petition was first presented**.

(c) Any **disposition** of the **company's property** and any transfer of its shares subsequent to the commencement of liquidation is **void** unless the court orders otherwise.

(d) Any **legal proceedings** in progress against the company are halted (and none may thereafter begin) unless the court gives leave. Any seizure of the company's assets after commencement of liquidation is void.

(e) The **employees** of the company are **automatically dismissed**. The liquidator assumes the powers of management previously held by the directors.

(f) Any **floating charge crystallises**.

The assets of the company may remain the company's legal property but **under the liquidator's control** unless the court by order **vests** the assets in the liquidator. The business of the company may continue but it is the liquidator's duty to continue it with a view only to realisation, for instance by sale as a going concern.

Within 21 days of the making of the order for winding up a **statement of affairs** must be delivered to the liquidator verified by one or more directors and by the secretary (and possibly by other persons). The statement shows the assets and liabilities of the company and includes a list of creditors with particulars of any security.

The liquidator may require that any **officers or employees** concerned in the recent management of the company shall join in submitting the statement of affairs.

3.5.1 Investigations by the official receiver

The official receiver **must investigate**:

- The **causes of the failure** of the company; and
- Generally the **promotion**, **formation**, **business dealings** and **affairs** of the company.

The official receiver **may report** to the court on the results.

(a) The official receiver may require the **public examination,** in open court, of those believed to be implicated (a much-feared sanction).

(b) The official receiver may apply to the court for public examination where half the **creditors** or three-quarters of the **shareholders** (in value in either case) so request. Failure to attend, or reasonable suspicion that the examinees will abscond, may lead to arrest and detention in custody for contempt of court.

3.5.2 Meetings of contributories and creditors

Key term

> **Contributories** are **members** of a company.
>
> At winding up, members may have to make payments to the company in respect of any unpaid share capital or guarantees.

The official receiver has 12 weeks to decide whether or not to convene **separate meetings** of creditors and contributories. The meetings provide the creditors and contributories with the opportunity to appoint their own nominee as permanent liquidator to replace the official receiver, and a **liquidation committee** to work with the liquidator.

If the official receiver believes there is little interest and that the creditors will be unlikely to appoint a liquidator they can **dispense with a meeting**, informing the court, the creditors and the contributories of

the decision. They can always be required to call a meeting, if at least 25% in value of the creditors require them to do so.

If no meeting is held, or one is held but no liquidator is appointed, the official receiver continues to act as liquidator. If the creditors do hold a meeting and **appoint their own nominee** this person automatically becomes liquidator, subject to a right of objection to the court. Any person appointed to act as liquidator must be a qualified insolvency practitioner.

At any time after a winding up order is made, **the official receiver may ask the Secretary of State to appoint a liquidator**. Similarly, they may request an appointment if the creditors and members fail to appoint a liquidator.

If separate meetings of creditors and contributories are held and different persons are nominated as liquidators, it is the **creditors' nominee** who **takes precedence**. Notice of the order for compulsory liquidation and of the appointment of a liquidator is given to the Registrar and in the *London Gazette*.

If, while the liquidation is in progress, the liquidator decides to call meetings of contributories or creditors they may arrange to do so under powers vested in the court.

3.6 Order of payments on liquidation

In a compulsory liquidation (and often in a voluntary one) the liquidator follows a **prescribed order** for distributing the company's assets:

	Order	Explanation
1	Costs	These include the costs of selling the assets, the liquidator's remuneration and all costs incidental to the liquidation procedure
2	Preferential debts	<ul><li>Employees' wages (subject to a statutory maximum)</li><li>Accrued holiday pay</li><li>Contributions to an occupational pension fund</li></ul>
3	Debts secured by floating charges	Subject to the 'prescribed part' (see below)
4	Debts owed to unsecured ordinary creditors	A proportion of assets (known as the 'prescribed part') is 'ring-fenced' for unsecured creditors. This proportion (which is subject to a statutory maximum) is calculated as 50% of the first £10,000 of realisations of debts secured by floating charge and 20% of the floating charge realisations thereafter (subject to a prescribed maximum)
5	Deferred debts	These include dividends declared but not paid and interest accrued on debts since liquidation
6	Members	Any surplus (unlikely in compulsory and creditors' voluntary liquidations) is distributed to members according to their rights under the articles or the terms of issue of their shares.

It is important to remember that **creditors with fixed and floating charges may appoint a receiver** to sell the charged asset – any surplus is passed onto to the liquidator. In the event of a shortfall they become unsecured creditors for the balance.

3.7 Completion of compulsory liquidation

When the liquidator completes their task they report to the Government, which **examines their accounts**. They may apply to the court for an order for dissolution of the company.

An official receiver may also apply to the Registrar for an **early dissolution** of the company if its realisable assets will not cover their expenses and further investigation is not required.

4 Differences between compulsory and voluntary liquidation

FAST FORWARD

The differences between compulsory and voluntary liquidation are associated with **timing**, the **role** of the **official receiver**, **stay of legal proceedings** and the **dismissal of employees**.

The main differences in **legal consequences** between a compulsory and a voluntary liquidation are as follows.

	Differences
Control	Under a members' voluntary liquidation the members control the liquidation process. Under a creditors' voluntary liquidation the creditors control the process. The court controls the process under a compulsory liquidation.
Timing	A voluntary winding up commences on the day when the **resolution to wind up is passed**. It is not retrospective. A compulsory winding up, once agreed to by the court, commences on the day the **petition was presented**.
Liquidator	The **official receiver** plays **no role** in a **voluntary winding up**. The members or creditors select and appoint the liquidator and they are not an officer of the court.
Legal proceedings	In a voluntary winding up there is no automatic **stay of legal proceedings** against the company, nor are previous dispositions or seizure of its assets void. However, the liquidator has a general right to apply to the court to make any order which the court can make in a compulsory liquidation. They would do so, for instance, to prevent any creditor obtaining an unfair advantage over the other creditors.
Management and staff	In any **liquidation the liquidator replaces the directors** in the management of the company (unless the liquidator decides to retain them). However, the employees are **not automatically dismissed by commencement of voluntary liquidation**. Insolvent liquidation may amount to repudiation of their employment contracts (provisions of the statutory employment protection code apply).

5 Saving a company: administration

Administration is a method of **'saving' a company from liquidation**, under the Enterprise Act 2002 (TSO, 2002).

5.1 What is administration?

FAST FORWARD

An **administrator** is appointed primarily to try to rescue the company as a going concern. A company may go into administration to carry out an established plan to save the company.

Key term

> **Administration** puts an **insolvency practitioner** in **control** of the company with a defined programme for **rescuing the company** from insolvency as a going concern.

Its purpose is to **insulate** the company **from its creditors while it seeks:**
- To save itself as a going concern, or failing that
- To achieve a better result for creditors than an immediate winding up would secure, or failing that
- To realise property so as to make a distribution to creditors

Administration orders and liquidations are **mutually exclusive**. Once an administration order has been passed by the court, it is **no longer possible to petition the court** for a **winding up** order against the company. Similarly, however, once an order for winding up has been made, an administration order cannot be granted (except when appointed by a floating chargeholder).

Administration can be initiated **with** or **without a court order**.

5.2 Appointment without a court order

FAST FORWARD

Some parties – **secured creditors** and **directors** and the **members** by resolution – can appoint an administrator without a court order.

It is possible to appoint an administrator **without reference to the court**. There are three sets of people who might be able to do this:

- Floating chargeholders
- Directors
- Company

5.2.1 Floating chargeholders

Floating chargeholders have the right to appoint an administrator without reference to the court, even if there is no actual or impending insolvency. They may also **appoint an administrator even if the company is in compulsory liquidation**. This enables steps to be taken to save the company before its financial situation becomes irreversible.

In order to qualify for this right, the **floating charge must entitle the holder to appoint an administrator**. This would be in the terms of the charge. It must also be over all, or substantially all, the company's property.

Point to note

In practice, such a floating chargeholder with a charge over all or substantially all the company's property is likely to be a **bank**.

However, the **floating chargeholder may only appoint an administrator** if:

- They have given **two days'** written notice to the holder of any prior floating charge where that person has the right to appoint an administrator.
- Their floating charge is **enforceable**.

After any relevant two-day notice period the floating chargeholder will file the following **documents** at court:

- A **notice of appointment** in the prescribed form identifying the administrator
- A **statement by the administrator** that they **consent to the appointment**
- A **statement by the administrator** that, in their **opinion**, the **purpose of the administration** is likely to be **achieved**
- A **statutory declaration** that they **qualify** to make the appointment

Once these documents have been filed, the **appointment is valid**. The appointer must notify the administrator, and other people prescribed by regulations of the appointment, as soon as is reasonably practicable.

5.2.2 Company and directors

The process by which a company commences appointing an administrator will depend upon its **articles of association**. A company or its directors may appoint an administrator if:

- The company has not done so in the last 12 months or been subject to a **moratorium** as a result of a voluntary arrangement with its creditors in the last 12 months.
- The company is, or is likely to be, **unable to pay its debts**.

- **No petition for winding up** nor any **administration order** in respect of the company has been presented to the court and is outstanding.
- The company is **not in liquidation**.
- **No administrator** or **receiver** is already in office.

The company or its directors must give notice to any floating chargeholders entitled to appoint an administrator. This means that the **floating chargeholders may** appoint their own administrator within this time period, and so **block the company's choice of administrator**.

5.3 Appointment with a court order

FAST FORWARD

Various parties can apply for **administration** through the court.

There are **four sets of parties** that may **apply to the court** for an administration order:

- The **company** (that is, a majority of the members by (ordinary) resolution)
- The **directors** of the company
- One or more **creditors** of the company
- Another **court** following non-payment of a fine imposed on the company (just like any other creditor)

The court will grant the **administration order** if it is satisfied that the company is, or is likely to be, **unable to pay its debts**, and the administration order is reasonably likely to **achieve the purpose of administration**. The application will name the person whom the applicants want to be the **administrator**. Unless certain interested parties object, this person is appointed as administrator.

5.4 The effects of appointing an administrator

FAST FORWARD

The **effects** of administration depend on whether it is affected by the **court** or by a **floating chargeholder**, to some degree.

Effects of an administrator appointment
A **moratorium** over the company's debts commences (that is, no creditor can enforce their debt during the administration period without the court's permission). This is the advantageous aspect of being in administration.
The court must give its permission for: • **Security** over company property to be **enforced** • Goods held under hire purchase to be **repossessed** • A landlord to conduct **forfeiture** by peaceable entry • Commencement/continuation of any **legal process** against the company
The **powers of management** are subjugated to the authority of the administrator and managers can only act with their consent.
All outstanding **petitions for winding-up** of the company are **dismissed**.
Any **administrative receiver** in place must **vacate office**. No appointments to this position can be made.

5.5 Duties of the administrator

FAST FORWARD

The administrator has **fiduciary duties** to the company as its agent, plus some legal duties.

The administrator is an **agent of the company** and the **creditors as a whole**. They therefore owe fiduciary duties to them and have the following legal duties.

Legal duties of the administrator
As soon as **reasonably practicable** after appointment they must:
• **Send notice** of appointment to the company.
• **Publish notice** of appointment.
• Obtain a list of **company creditors** and send a notice of appointment to each.
• Within seven days of appointment, send notice of appointment to **Registrar**.
• Require certain relevant people to provide a **statement of affairs** of the company.
• Ensure that every **business document** of the company **bears the identity** of the administrator and a statement that the affairs, business and property of the company are being managed by them.
• Consider the **statements of affairs** submitted to them and set out their **proposals** for achieving the aim of administration. The proposals must be **sent to the Registrar** and the company's **creditors,** and be made available to **every member of the company** as soon as is reasonably practicable, and **within eight weeks**.
• Whilst preparing their proposals, the administrator must **manage the affairs** of the company.

The **statement of affairs** must be provided by the people from whom it is requested within 11 days of it being requested. It is in a prescribed form, and contains:

- Details of the **company's property**
- The company's **debts** and **liabilities**
- The **names** and **addresses** of the **company's creditors**
- Details of any **security** held by any **creditor**

Failing to provide a statement of affairs, or providing a statement in which the writer has no reasonable belief of truth, is a **criminal offence** punishable by fine.

5.6 Administrator's proposals

> The administrator must either **propose a rescue plan**, or state that the **company cannot be rescued**.

Having considered all information the administrator must, within eight **weeks** (subject to possible extension):

- Set out their proposals for achieving the aim of the administration; or
- Set out why it is not reasonable and practicable that the company be rescued. In this case they will also set out why the creditors as a whole would benefit from winding up.

The **proposal** must **be sent to all members** and **creditors** they are aware of. It must not:

- Affect the right of a **secured creditor** to enforce their security
- Result in a non-preferential debt being paid in priority to a preferential debt
- Result in one preferential creditor being paid a smaller proportion of their debt than another

5.6.1 Creditors' meeting

The administrator must call a **meeting of creditors** within **ten weeks** of their appointment to approve the proposals. The creditors may either accept or reject them. Once the proposals have been agreed, the administrator cannot make any substantial amendment without first gaining the creditors' consent.

5.7 Administrator's powers

> The administrator takes on the **powers** of the directors.

An **administrator** of a company may do **anything necessarily expedient** for the management of the affairs, business and property of the company.

Administrators have **the same powers as those granted to directors** and the following **specific powers** to:

- Remove or appoint a **director**
- Call a **meeting of members or creditors**
- **Apply to court for directions** regarding the carrying out of their functions
- Make payments to **secured or preferential creditors**
- With the permission of the court, **make payments to unsecured creditors**

The administrator usually requires the permission of the court to make payments to unsecured creditors. However, this is not the case if the administrator feels that paying the unsecured creditors will assist the **achievement of the administration**. For example, paying a major supplier to enable trading to continue.

5.8 End of administration

FAST FORWARD

Administration can last up to **12 months**.

The **administration period ends** when:

- The administration has been successful
- Twelve months have elapsed from the date of the appointment of administrator
- The administrator or a creditor applies to the court to end the appointment
- An improper motive of the applicant for applying for the administration is discovered

The administrator automatically vacates office after **12 months of their appointment**. However, this time period can be extended by court order or by consent from the appropriate creditors.

Alternatively, the administrator may **apply to the court** when they think:

- The purpose of administration cannot be achieved
- The company should not have entered into administration
- The administration has been successful (if appointed by the court)

They must also apply to the court if required to by the **creditors' meeting**. Where the administrator was appointed by a chargeholder or the company/its directors, and they feel that the purposes of administration have been achieved, they must file a **notice** with the court and the Registrar.

5.9 Advantages of administration

FAST FORWARD

Administration has many advantages for the **company**, the **members** and the **creditors**.

Advantages of administration	
To the company	The company does not necessarily cease to exist at the end of the process, whereas liquidation will always result in the company being wound up.
	It provides a temporary breathing space from creditors to formulate rescue plans.
	It prevents any creditor applying for compulsory liquidation.
	It provides for past transactions to be challenged.
To the members	They will continue to have shares in the company which has not been wound up. If the administration is successful, regenerating the business should enhance share value and will restore any income from the business.
To the creditors	Creditors should obtain a return in relation to their past debts from an administration.
	Unsecured creditors will benefit from asset realisations.
	Any creditor may apply to the court for an administration order, while only certain creditors may apply for other forms of relief from debt. For example, the use of receivers or an application for winding up.
	Floating chargeholders may appoint an administrator without reference to the court.
	It may also be in the interests of the creditors to have a continued business relationship with the company once the business has been turned around.

Chapter Roundup

- **Liquidation** is the **dissolution** or 'winding up' of a company.

- There are three different methods of **liquidation: compulsory**, **members' voluntary** and **creditors' voluntary**. Compulsory liquidation and creditors' voluntary liquidation are proceedings for insolvent companies, and members' voluntary liquidation is for solvent companies.

- A **liquidator** must be an authorised, qualified insolvency practitioner.

- Once **insolvency procedures** have commenced, share trading must cease, the company documents must state that the company is in liquidation and the directors' power to manage ceases.

- A **winding** up is **voluntary** where the decision to wind up is taken by the company members, although if the company is insolvent, the creditors will be heavily involved in the proceedings.

- In order to be a members' winding up, the directors must make a **declaration of solvency**. It is a criminal offence to make a declaration of solvency without reasonable grounds.

- When there is no declaration of solvency there is a **creditors' voluntary winding** up.

- There are **seven statutory reasons** for the compulsory liquidation of a company, which can all be found in Section 122 of the Insolvency Act 1986.

- A creditor may apply to the court to wind up the company if the company is **unable to pay its debts**. There are statutory tests to prove that a company is unable to pay its debts.

- A **dissatisfied member** may get the court to wind the company up on the **just and equitable ground**.

- The differences between compulsory and voluntary liquidation are associated with **timing**, the **role** of the **official receiver**, **stay of legal proceedings** and the **dismissal of employees**.

- An **administrator** is appointed primarily to try to rescue the company as a going concern. A company may go into administration to carry out an established plan to save the company.

- Some parties – **secured creditors** and **directors** and the **members** by resolution – can appoint an administrator without a court order.

- Various parties can apply for **administration** through the court.

- The **effects** of administration depend on whether it is affected by the **court** or by a **floating chargeholder**, to some degree.

- The administrator has **fiduciary duties** to the company as its agent, plus some legal duties.

- The administrator must either **propose a rescue plan**, or state that the **company cannot be rescued**.

- The administrator takes on the **powers** of the directors.

- Administration can last up to **12 months**.

- Administration has many advantages for the **company**, the **members** and the **creditors**.

Quick Quiz

1   Complete the following definition:

Liquidation means that a company must be .... and its affairs wound up.

2   Name three common effects of liquidations.

(1)   ....

(2)   ....

(3)   ....

3   What are the two most important grounds for compulsory liquidation?

(1)   ....

(2)   ....

4   A members' voluntary winding up is where the members decide to dissolve a healthy company.

True   ☐

False   ☐

5   Name two advantages of administration.

(1)   ....

(2)   ....

Answers to Quick Quiz

1   Dissolved

2   (1)   No further changes in membership permitted
    (2)   All documents must state prominently that company is in liquidation
    (3)   Directors' power to manage ceases

3   (1)   Company is unable to pay its debts
    (2)   It is just and equitable to wind up the company

4   True. Members can decide to wind up a healthy company.

5   (1)   It does not necessarily result in the dissolution of the company
    (2)   It prevents creditors applying for compulsory liquidation

    Subsidiary advantages are

    (3)   All creditors can apply for an administration order
    (4)   The administrator may challenge past transactions of the company

Now try the questions below from the Practice Question Bank

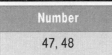

Number
47, 48

Corporate fraudulent
and criminal behaviour

22

Fraudulent and criminal behaviour

Topic list	Syllabus reference
1 Financial crime	H1 (a–f)
2 Insider dealing	H1(a)
3 Market abuse	H1(b)
4 Money laundering	H1(c)
5 Bribery	H1(d)
6 Criminal activity relating to companies	H1(e), H1(f)

Introduction

In this chapter, we shall look specifically at some **financial crimes** and the **measures** that have been put into place to combat them.

Insider dealing is a statutory offence relating to the trading of shares or other securities. It has proved difficult to convict people of the crime of insider dealing, hence the introduction of the civil wrong of market abuse.

The issue of **money laundering** is a highly topical issue. Money laundering is the process of 'legalising' funds raised through crime. Money laundering crosses national boundaries and it can be difficult to enforce the related laws.

Finally we shall look at some **other offences** in relation to companies.

Study guide

		Intellectual level
H	**Corporate fraudulent and criminal behaviour**	
1	**Fraudulent and criminal behaviour**	
(a)	Recognise the nature and legal control over insider dealing	2
(b)	Recognise the nature and legal control over market abuse	2
(c)	Recognise the nature and legal control over money laundering	2
(d)	Recognise the nature and legal control over bribery	2
(e)	Discuss potential criminal activity in the operation, management and liquidation of companies	2
(f)	Recognise the nature and legal control over fraudulent and wrongful trading	2

Exam guide

Financial crime is highly examinable, in both types of question. Expect to be asked to identify whether or not a crime has been committed, or explain the opportunities that exist for perpetrating such crimes.

1 Financial crime

FAST FORWARD

Crime is **conduct prohibited by the law**. Financial crime can be international in nature, and there is a need for international co-operation to prevent it.

Law tends to be organised on a **national basis**. However, as we shall see later, some crime, particularly money laundering, is perpetrated **across national borders**. Indeed, the international element of the crime contributes to its success.

Particularly with regard to money laundering, international bodies are having to **co-operate** with one another in order to control financial crimes, which spreads across national boundaries.

1.1 Example: international financial crime

Money laundering is a crime in Country A but not in Country B. Money laundering can be effected legally in Country B and the proceeds returned to Country A. Hence Country A cannot prosecute for the crime of money laundering, which has not been committed within its national boundaries.

PO1 requires you to apply professional ethics, values and judgement. Prevention of financial crime is an important part of this.

2 Insider dealing

FAST FORWARD

Insider dealing is the statutory offence of **dealing** in securities while in **possession** of **inside information** as an insider, the securities being price-affected by the information.

The **Criminal Justice Act 1993** (HMSO, 1993) (CJA) contains the rules on **insider dealing**. It was regarded and treated as a crime since a few people are enriched at the expense of the reputation of the stock market and the interests of all involved in it.

2.1 What is insider dealing?

Insider dealing is dealing in securities while in possession of inside information as an insider, the securities being **price-affected** by the information.

To prove **insider dealing**, the prosecution must prove that the possessor of inside information:

- **Dealt** in **price-affected securities** on a regulated market

- **Encouraged another** to **deal** in them on a regulated market

- **Disclosed** the **information** other than in the proper performance of their employment, office; or profession.

2.1.1 Dealing

Dealing is **acquiring or disposing** of, or **agreeing** to **acquire** or **dispose** of, relevant securities whether **directly** or **through an agent** or nominee or a person acting according to direction.

2.1.2 Encouraging another to deal

An offence is also committed if an individual, having information as an insider, **encourages another person** to deal in price-affected securities in relation to that information. They must **know** or have reasonable cause to believe that **dealing** would **take place**.

It is irrelevant whether:

- The person encouraged realises that the securities are **price-affected** securities

- The **inside information is given** to that person. For example, a simple recommendation to the effect that 'I cannot tell you why but now would be a good time to buy shares in Bloggs plc' would infringe the law

- **Any dealing takes place**, the offence being committed at the time of encouragement

2.2 Securities covered by the Act

Securities include **shares** and **associated derivatives**, **debt securities** and **warranties**.

2.3 Inside information

Inside information is **'price-sensitive information'** relating to a **particular issuer** of **securities** that are price-affected and not to securities generally.

Inside information must, if made public, be likely to have a **significant effect on price** and it must be **specific or precise**. Specific would, for example, mean information that a takeover bid would be made for a specific company; precise information would be details of how much would be offered for shares.

2.4 Insiders

Under the CJA a person has information as an **insider** if it is (**and** they **know** it is) inside information, and if they have it (**and know** they have) from an inside source:

- Through being a **director**, **employee** or **shareholder** of an issuer of securities
- Through access because of **employment**, **office** or **profession**

A person does not have to actually be one of the above to be an insider. They will also be an insider if they are given the **inside information** by someone who is an **inside source** – for example, a friend or family member.

2.5 General defences

An individual has a **defence** regarding **dealing and encouraging others to deal** if they prove that:

- They did **not expect** there to be a **profit** or avoidance of loss.
- They had **reasonable grounds** to **believe** that the information had been **disclosed widely** enough to ensure that those taking part in the dealing would be prejudiced by having the information.
- They would have **done** what they did **even** if they did not have the **information**, for example, where securities are sold to pay a pressing debt.

Defences to **disclosure of information** by an individual are that:

- They **did not expect** any person to deal.
- Although dealing was expected, **profit** or **avoidance of loss** was **not expected.**

2.6 'Made public'

Information is made public if:

- It is **published** under the rules of the regulated market, such as the stock exchange.
- It is in **public records**, for example, notices in the *London Gazette.*
- It can **readily be acquired** by those likely to deal.
- It is **derived** from **public information**.

Information **may** be treated as made public, even though:

- It can **only** be **acquired** by **exercising diligence** or expertise (helping analysts to avoid liability).
- It is **communicated only** to a **section** of the **public** (thus protecting the 'brokers' lunch' where a company informs only selected City sources of important information).
- It can be **acquired** only by **observation**.
- It is **communicated** only on a **payment of a fee** or is published outside the UK.

2.7 Penalties

Maximum penalties given by the statute are **seven years' imprisonment** and/or an **unlimited fine**. Contracts remain valid and enforceable at civil law.

2.8 Territorial scope

The offender or any professional intermediary must be **in the UK** at the time of the offence or the market must be a UK regulated market.

2.9 Problems with the laws on insider dealing

> The law on insider dealing has had some **limitations**, and new offences, such as market abuse, have been brought in to reduce security-related crime.

The courts may have problems deciding whether information is **specific** or **precise**. The statute states that information shall be treated as relating to an issuer of securities not only when it is **about the company** but also where it may **affect the business prospects** of the company.

The requirement that price-sensitive information has a **significant effect on price** limits the application of the legislation to fundamental matters. These include an impending takeover, or profit or dividend levels which would be out of line with market expectations. As a result, the concept of **'market abuse'** was introduced in the UK in 2000. This was partly in response to the perceived ineffectiveness of the insider dealing provisions in the Criminal Justice Act 1993.

Exam focus point

> Exam questions may be set on insider dealing and market abuse. If this is the case, remember that insider dealing is a criminal offence, market abuse is a civil matter.

3 Market abuse

FAST FORWARD

Market abuse relates to behaviour which amounts to abuse of a person's position regarding the stock market.

Key term

> **Market abuse** is behaviour which satisfies one or more of the prescribed conditions likely to be regarded as a failure on the part of the person or persons concerned to **observe the standard of behaviour reasonably expected of a person in their position in relation to the market**.

The offence of **market abuse** under the Financial Services and Markets Act 2000 (TSO, 2000) complements legislation covering insider dealing, by providing a civil law alternative. The FCA has issued a **Code of Market Conduct**, which applies to any person dealing in certain investments on recognised exchanges and which does not require proof of intent to abuse a market.

The FCA has statutory civil powers to impose unlimited fines for the offence of **market abuse**. **It also has statutory** powers to require information, and requires anyone to co-operate with investigations into market abuse.

Market abuse is often connected with activities such as **recklessly making a statement** or **forecast** that is **misleading, false or deceptive**, or engaging in a **misleading course of conduct** for the purpose of inducing another person to exercise, or refrain from exercising, rights in relation to investments.

3.1 Examples of market abuse

The following are other examples of behaviour that would constitute **market abuse**.

3.1.1 Misuse of information

This is any behaviour by an individual that is based on information that is **not publicly available**, but if it was, it would **influence an investor's decision**. For example, a person who buys shares in a company that they know is a takeover target of their employer, before a general disclosure of the proposed takeover is made.

3.1.2 Manipulating transactions

This behaviour involves **interfering with the normal process of share prices** moving up and down in accordance with supply and demand for the shares. For example, an individual who trades, or places orders to trade, who creates a misleading impression of the supply or demand of securities and that has the effect of raising the price of the investment to an abnormal or artificial level.

3.1.3 Manipulating devices

This behaviour is the same as manipulating transactions except that the trading is followed by the **creation of false statements** so that other investors make incorrect trading decisions. For example, an individual buys a large number of shares to artificially raise the share price and then makes false statements to the market that encourage other investors to buy the shares, driving the price up further.

3.1.4 Market distortion

This is any behaviour that **interferes with the normal process of market prices** moving up and down in accordance with supply and demand, such as a Chief Executive Officer who increases the activities of their business in order to make the company appear busier than it actually is. This improves the image and prospects of the business and suggests that a share price increase is imminent, encouraging investors to buy shares.

3.1.5 Dissemination of information

This behaviour involves the creation of **false or misleading information** about supply and demand, or prices and values of investments, and then leaking it into the public domain. For example, a person who posts an inaccurate story about a company's future plans on an internet bulletin board.

Remarks made by the judge when sentencing in *R v Bailey 2005* suggested that **directors will be held personally responsible for public announcements** in order to ensure the integrity of the market is preserved and the public protected.

4 Money laundering

4.1 What is money laundering?

Money laundering is the attempt to **make money from criminal activity appear legitimate**, by disguising its original source.

Key term

> **Money laundering** is the term given to attempts to make the proceeds of crime appear respectable.
>
> It covers any activity by which the apparent source and ownership of money representing the proceeds of income are changed so that the money appears to have been obtained legitimately.

Money laundering is a **crime** that is **against the interests of the state**, and it is associated with drug and people trafficking in particular, and with organised crime in general.

Money laundering legislation has been influenced on a number of different Acts of Parliament:

*   Drug Trafficking Offences Act 1986
*   Criminal Justice Act 1993
*   Terrorism Act 2000
*   Anti-terrorism Crime and Security Act 2001
*   Proceeds of Crime Act 2002
*   Money Laundering Regulations 2007

4.2 Categories of criminal offence

In the UK, there are various offences relating to **money laundering**, including tipping off a money launderer (or suspected money launderer) and failing to report reasonable suspicions.

There are **three categories of criminal offences** in the Proceeds of Crime Act 2002 (TSO, 2002).

*   **Laundering**: acquisition, possession or use of the proceeds of criminal conduct, or assisting another to retain the proceeds of criminal conduct and concealing, disguising, converting, transferring or removing criminal property. This relates to its nature, source, location, disposition, movement or ownership of the property. Money laundering includes possession of the proceeds of one's own crime, and facilitating any handling or possession of criminal property, which may take any form, including in money or money's worth, securities, tangible property and intangible property. There is no *de minimis* limit, so an offence may be committed in respect only of £1.

*   **Failure to report** by an individual: failure to disclose knowledge or suspicion of money laundering ('suspicion' is more than mere speculation, but falls short of proof or knowledge).

*   **Tipping off**: disclosing information to any person if disclosure may prejudice an investigation into drug trafficking, drug money laundering, terrorist-related activities, or laundering the proceeds of criminal conduct.

For the purposes of laundering, '**criminal property**' is defined by the CJA as a property which the alleged offender knows (or suspects) constitutes or represents being related to any criminal conduct.

This is any conduct that constitutes or would constitute an offence in the UK. In relation to **laundering**, a person may have a **defence** if they make disclosure to the authorities:

- As soon as possible after the transaction
- Before the transaction takes place

Alternatively, they may have a defence if they can show there was a **reasonable excuse** for not making a disclosure.

In relation to **failure to report**, the person who suspects money laundering must disclose this to a nominated **Money Laundering Reporting Officer** (MLRO) within their organisation if it has one, or alternatively directly to the **National Crime Agency** (NCA) in the form of a Suspicious Activity Report (SAR). The NCA has responsibility in the UK for collecting and disseminating information related to money laundering and related activities. The nominated MLRO in an organisation acts as a filter and notifies NCA too.

In relation to **tipping off**, this covers the situation when a person making a disclosure to the NCA also tells the person at the centre of their suspicions about the disclosure. There is a **defence** to the effect that the person did not know that tipping off would prejudice an investigation.

4.3 Penalties

The law sets out the following penalties in relation to money laundering:

(a)   14 years' imprisonment and/or a fine, for **knowingly assisting** in the **laundering** of criminal funds

(b)   5 years' imprisonment and/or a fine, for **failure to report knowledge** or the **suspicion** of money laundering

(c)   5 years' imprisonment and/or a fine for **tipping off** a suspected launderer.

The **money laundering process** usually involves three phases:

- **Placement** – this is the initial disposal of the proceeds of the initial illegal activity into apparently legitimate business activity or property

- **Layering** – this involves the transfer of monies from business to business, or place to place, to conceal the original source

- **Integration** – having been layered, the money has the appearance of legitimate funds

For accountants, the most worrying aspect of the law on money laundering relates to the offence of '**failing to disclose**'. It is relatively straightforward to identify actual 'knowledge' of money laundering, and therefore of the need to disclose it, but the term 'suspicion' of money laundering is not defined. The nearest there is to a definition is that suspicion is more than mere speculation but falls short of proof or knowledge. It is a question of judgement.

To fulfill PO4 you should comply with all money laundering regulations and contact the relevant person in your organisation if you have any suspicions that it may be occuring.

4.4 The Money Laundering Regulations 2017

The **Money Laundering Regulations 2017** (TSO, 2017) require **organisations** to **establish internal systems** and **procedures** which are designed to deter criminals from using the organisation to launder money or finance terrorism. Such systems also assist in detecting the crime and prosecuting the perpetrators.

These regulations apply to all **'relevant persons'**, a term which covers a wide range of organisations, including banking and investment businesses, accountants and auditors, tax advisers, lawyers, estate agents and casinos. They set out a prescriptive approach in the form of a firm-wide written risk assessment that includes a number of factors that must be taken into account.

As each organisation is different, **systems** should be designed which are **appropriate and tailored to each business**.

These include:

(a) **Internal reporting procedures**
These should include appointing a Money Laundering Reporting Officer (MLRO) to receive internal reports of suspected money laundering and, where appropriate, to report them to the NCA.

(b) **Customer due diligence measures**
These should include identifying and verifying customers and monitoring the business relationship according to the level of risk of money laundering.

(c) **Record-keeping procedures**
Such procedures may include, for example, retaining copies of customer identity details such as passports. These procedures are important in proving compliance with the regulations.

(d) **Ensuring that employees are educated**
Employees should receive appropriate training concerning the law relating to money laundering and the business's policies and procedures in dealing with it.

Should a business fail to implement these measures a criminal offence, punishable with a maximum sentence of **two years' imprisonment and/or an unlimited fine**, is committed irrespective of whether money laundering has taken place.

Exam focus point

> You must be clear how these rules seek to prevent or minimise money laundering.

5 Bribery

 FAST FORWARD

> **Bribery** is a serious offence which often relates to the **offering** and **receiving** of **gifts** or **hospitality**.

The **Bribery Act 2010** (TSO, 2010) brought together, and is intended to simplify, the previous law on bribery and corruption which was contained in both common law and statute.

5.1 Bribery offences

The **Bribery Act** created **four main offences,** the first three of which are committed by **individuals** while the fourth is a **corporate** offence. The offences are:

- Bribing another person
- Being bribed
- Bribing a foreign public official
- Corporate failure to prevent bribery

5.1.1 Bribing another person

This offence is committed where a person **offers, promises or gives financial** or **other advantages** to another person with the intention of inducing that person to **perform improperly** a **relevant function** or **activity**, or to **reward** them for such **improper performance**.

It does not matter whether or not the person being bribed is the **same person** as the one who would **usually perform** the function or whether the offer is made **directly** or via a **third party**. This offence can also be committed where **acceptance of an advantage** itself **constitutes improper performance** of a function or activity.

5.1.2 Being bribed

This offence is committed where a person **requests** or **accepts** a **financial** or **other advantage improperly**, or as a **reward** for **improper performance** of a **relevant function** or **activity**, or intending **that improper performance should result**. It does not matter whether the advantage is received **direct** or through a **third party**. The offence also applies if a person **receives** a benefit on **behalf of another person**.

5.1.3 Relevant function or activity

Both of the above offences make reference to a **'relevant function or activity'** and it is important to be aware of what this means. In terms of the Act, a relevant function or activity includes any function of **a public nature** or any **activity connected with business** or **carried out in the course of employment**. It applies to individuals who perform that function or activity from a **position of trust** or are otherwise expected to perform it in **good faith** or **impartially**.

It is irrelevant whether the **function** or **activity** has a **connection with the UK** – for example if it is performed outside the UK. 'Improper' performance means performance which does not meet the **standard** that a **reasonable person** in the UK would expect.

5.1.4 Bribing a foreign public official

This offence is similar to that of **bribing another person**, but is committed where the bribe is offered to a **foreign public official** (FPO). It is committed where a person offers financial or other advantages to an **FPO** or a **third party** with the intention of influencing the FPO in that capacity and to obtain or retain business or an advantage in the conduct of business, where that official is not permitted or required by the written law applicable to them to be so influenced.

An **FPO** is any individual who holds a **legislative**, **administrative** or **judicial position** of any kind outside the UK, or who exercises a **public function** outside the UK, or who is an **official** or **agent** of a **public international organisation**.

5.1.5 Defences and penalties for individual offences

It is a **defence** for an individual charged with a bribery offence if they can prove that their **conduct was necessary for the proper exercise of any function of an intelligence service** or the **proper exercise of any function of the armed forces when engaged on active service**.

The maximum **penalty** for bribery under the Act is **ten years' imprisonment** and/or an **unlimited fine**.

5.1.6 Corporate failure to prevent bribery

The offence of corporate failure to prevent bribery is **committed by an organisation** that **fails to prevent** a **bribery offence** being committed by a **person who performs services** for it in any capacity – such as an agent, employee or subsidiary. Under the Act, an **organisation** includes **companies** and **partnerships** based in the UK or doing business in the UK.

5.1.7 Defence and penalties for corporate offences

An organisation has a **defence** to this offence if it can prove that it had in place '**adequate procedures**' designed to prevent persons associated with it from committing bribery.

'Adequate procedures' are not defined by the Act, but the Secretary of State's non-prescriptive published guidance on adequate procedures is based around six principles:

(a)   **Proportionate procedures** – organisations should have procedures in place aimed at preventing bribery. The scale and complexity of the procedures should be proportionate to the size of the organisation. The procedures expected of a small organisation will differ from that of a large one.

(b)   **Top-level commitment** – an organisation's senior management should be committed to preventing bribery and should foster a culture in the organisation that sees bribery as unacceptable.

(c) **Risk assessment** – organisations should assess the nature and extent of their exposure to bribery from both inside and outside the organisation. Some industries and some overseas markets are seen as, by their nature, more susceptible to bribery and therefore risk assessments in these areas should be even more stringent.

(d) **Due diligence** – organisations should perform due diligence procedures in respect of those who perform services for the organisation or on its behalf, to mitigate the risk of bribery.

(e) **Communication** – anti-bribery policies and procedures should be embedded in the fabric of the organisation and communicated both internally and externally. This is likely to include relevant training if proportionate to the risk.

(f) **Monitoring and review** – the anti-bribery policies and procedures should be regularly monitored and reviewed. Amendments and improvements must be made as appropriate. This is because the risks an organisation faces will change, so adaptation is necessary.

Whether an organisation had **adequate procedures is a matter for the courts** that will look at the particular circumstances an organisation is faced with. However, the onus is on the organisation to prove that its procedures were adequate. **Reasonable** and **proportionate hospitality** is **not prohibited,** although what is reasonable and proportionate will be determined in future cases.

The **maximum penalty** that may be imposed on a guilty organisation is an **unlimited fine**. However, it is likely that its **business will suffer** too, as a consequence of **loss of reputation** and **compensation payable** for civil claims against the directors for failure to maintain adequate procedures.

Bribery cases are mainly heard in magistrates' and Crown Courts and go largely unreported. Examples of cases that have resulted in convictions include: a court clerk who accepted £500 for not adding motoring offences to the court record, a person taking a driving test to become a taxi driver who offered £300 to their examiner to turn a failure into a pass, and a university student who offered his tutors £5,000 for remarking an essay from a 37% fail to a pass at 40%.

Exam focus point

An article titled 'Bribery Act 2010' was the subject of a technical article in *Student Accountant* and is available on the ACCA website.

6 Criminal activity relating to companies

We have already seen a number of potential **crimes** in relation to the operation and management of companies, and the way in which these can be investigated.

With regard to the **operation and management of companies**, a company as a legal person may be prosecuted for many different types of crime. However, this is nearly always in conjunction with the directors and/or managers of the company. Companies have been prosecuted for manslaughter (unsuccessfully), fraud, and breaches of numerous laws for which fines are stated as being punishment, such as health and safety laws.

Where there is evidence that a company or partnership has committed certain offences, such as fraud, money laundering, bribery or forgery, it is possible for the prosecution and the organisation to make a **deferred prosecution agreement** (DPA) under the **Crime and Courts Act 2013** (TSO, 2013).

Such agreements mean that the **organisation admits wrongdoing** but stops short of pleading guilty to the offence. In return, a judge awards a fine against the business but **no criminal prosecution takes place**. This saves the prosecution time and money in bringing the case to court and, in return, the organisation is saved the reputational damage that a court case would bring.

It is up to the **prosecution** to determine whether a DPA should be offered. Offering it should be in the interests of justice and its terms must be fair, reasonable and proportionate. No individual should benefit from the offer of a DPA, which is why they are only offered to business organisations.

6.1 Criminal offences in relation to winding up

FAST FORWARD

Criminal offences in relation to **winding up** include: making a declaration of solvency without reasonable grounds and fraudulent trading.

Prosecutions are often brought against directors of **insolvent** companies for **fraudulent** trading and **wrongful trading**.

The law seeks to **protect creditors** who may be disadvantaged by the company being liquidated. **Directors** can be found guilty of various criminal offences if they try to **deceive** creditors and, in some cases, even if they do not attempt to deceive creditors, but the effect is the same as if they had.

6.2 Declaration of solvency

A winding up can only be a members' voluntary winding up if the company is solvent. If the company is not solvent, the creditors are far more involved in the winding up process. In order to carry out a members' voluntary winding up, the directors have to file a **declaration of solvency**.

It is a **criminal offence** punishable by fine or imprisonment for a director to make a **declaration of solvency without** having **reasonable grounds** for it. If the company proves to be insolvent, they will have to justify their previous decision, or be punished.

6.3 Fraudulent trading

This **criminal offence** occurs under the **Companies Act 2006** (TSO, 2006) where a company has traded with **intent to defraud creditors** or for any fraudulent purpose. For example, a director obtaining credit when there is no good reason to expect that the company will be able to repay the debt; *R v Grantham 1984*. Offenders are liable to imprisonment for up to ten years or a fine.

There is also a **civil offence** of the same name under the Insolvency Act 1986 (HMSO, 1986) that applies to companies which are in liquidation or administration. Under this offence courts may declare that **any persons** who were knowingly parties to carrying on the business in this fashion shall be liable for the debts of the company.

Various rules have been established to determine **what is fraudulent trading**:

(a) Only persons who **take the decision** to carry on the company's business in this way or play some active part are liable.

(b) **'Carrying on business'** can include a single transaction and also the mere payment of debts as distinct from making trading contracts.

(c) It relates not only to **defrauding creditors**, but also to carrying on a business for the purpose of any kind of fraud.

Under the civil offence, if the liquidator considers that there has been fraudulent trading they should apply to the court for an order that those responsible are liable to make good to the company all or some specified part of the **company's debts**.

6.4 Wrongful trading

The problem which faced the creditors of an insolvent company before the introduction of 'wrongful trading' was that it was exceptionally difficult to prove the necessary fraud. Therefore a further civil liability for 'wrongful trading' was introduced, which means that the director will have to make such contribution to the company's assets as the court sees fit.

Directors will be liable if the liquidator or administrator proves the following.

(a) The director(s) of the insolvent company **knew**, or **should have known**, that there was **no reasonable prospect** that the **company** could **have avoided insolvency**. This means that directors cannot claim they lacked knowledge if their lack of knowledge was a result of failing to comply with Companies Act requirements, for example preparation of accounts.

(b) The director(s) did not take **sufficient steps** to minimise the potential loss to the creditors.

Directors will be deemed to know that the company could not avoid insolvency if that would have been the conclusion of a **reasonably diligent person** with the **general knowledge, skill and experience** that might reasonably be expected of a person carrying out that particular director's duties. If the director has greater than usual skill then they will be judged with reference to their own capacity.

6.5 Other offences in relation to winding up

Other **offences** which may be committed just before or during a liquidation include the following.

6.5.1 Acting as a director whilst disqualified

The **Company Directors Disqualification Act 1986** (HMSO, 1986) makes a person who **acts as a director whilst disqualified** personally liable for the company's debts. Directors of insolvent companies may be disqualified under the Act if the court deems they are unfit to be involved in the management of a company.

6.5.2 Phoenix companies

Phoenix companies are created by directors of insolvent companies as a **method of continuing their business**. Very often they have similar names as (or similar enough to suggest an association with) the insolvent company. The Insolvency Act 1986 (HMSO, 1986) makes it a **criminal offence** where a director **creates such a company within five years of the original company being liquidated**. The person is liable to a fine or imprisonment.

6.5.3 Fraud and deception

The Insolvency Act 1986 makes it a criminal offence to **conceal** or **fraudulently remove company assets** or **debt** – including falsifying records. It is also an offence to **dispose of property** that was **acquired on credit** that has **not been paid** for.

6.5.4 Defrauding creditors

Once a winding up commences, the Insolvency Act 1986 makes it an offence to make a **gift** of, or **transfer**, **company property**, unless it can be proved there was no intent to defraud creditors.

6.5.5 Misconduct during a liquidation

A **company officer** may be **liable** for a number of offences due to their **misconduct**. These include:

- Not identifying company property to the liquidator
- Not delivering requested books and papers to the liquidator
- Not informing the liquidator if identified debts do not turn out to be debts

6.5.6 Falsification of company books

The **destruction, mutilation, alteration** or **falsification of company books** is an offence under the Insolvency Act 1986.

6.5.7 Omissions

It is an offence under the Insolvency Act 1986 to **omit material information** when making statements concerning a company's affairs.

6.6 Examples: offences in relation to winding up

The standard expected of a listed company director would be **higher** than for the director of a small owner-managed private company.

Halls v David and Another 1989

The facts: The directors sought to obtain relief from liability for wrongful trading by the application of the Companies Act 2006. This stated that in proceedings for negligence, default, breach of duty or breach of trust against a director, if it appears that he has acted honestly and reasonably the court may relieve him wholly or partly from liability on such terms as it sees fit.

Decision: The Companies Act 2006 is not available to excuse a director from liability.

Re Produce Marketing Consortium Ltd 1989

The facts: Two months after the case above, the same liquidator sought an order against the same directors – this time, that they should contribute to the company assets (which were in the hands of the liquidator) since they had been found liable for wrongful trading.

Decision: The directors were jointly and severally liable for the sum of £75,000 plus interest, along with the costs of the case. The judge stated that the fact that wrongful trading was not based on fraud was not a reason for giving a nominal or low figure of contribution. The figure should, however, be assessed in the light of all the circumstances of the case.

This case was significant for creditors, since the assets available for distribution in a winding up will (potentially) be much increased by a **large directors' contribution**. It serves as a warning to directors to take professional advice sooner rather than later.

6.7 Companies Act 2006 offences

The Companies Act 2006 (TSO, 2006) includes provision for a **number of offences** in relation to the **management** and **operation** of a company.

6.7.1 Company records

Company records and **registers**, such as the register of members and record of resolutions **must be kept adequately for future reference**. Officers in default are liable to a fine. **Falsification** of **information**, **hiding falsification**, or **failing to prevent falsification** are also offences and the wrongdoer is liable to a fine.

6.7.2 Accounting records

Where a company fails to **keep adequate accounting records**, every officer who defaults is subject to a fine. However, they have a **defence** if they **acted honestly** and the **circumstances** surrounding the company's business makes the default **excusable**.

6.7.3 Trading disclosures

Companies are required to disclose **certain information** (such as its name) in **specific locations**. If these disclosures are not made then defaulting officers are criminally liable for a fine and may also be liable for losses under the civil law.

6.7.4 Filing accounts

If a company fails to **file its accounts within the time limit following its year end** then any defaulting officer is liable to a fine. However, they will have a **defence** if they took **reasonable steps** to **ensure the requirements** were **complied with**.

6.7.5 False information

Company officers are liable for making **false disclosures** in relation to the **directors' report**, **directors' remuneration report** and **summary financial statements** based on those reports. An officer is also liable for **providing false** or **misleading information to an auditor**. Punishment is either imprisonment or a fine.

6.8 The Fraud Act 2006

The **Fraud Act 2006** (TSO 2006), to which directors and secretaries are subject, created a **single offence of fraud**, which a person can commit in three different ways by:

- **False representation**: dishonestly making a false representation of fact or law, intending thereby to make a gain for themselves or another, or to cause another party loss, or to expose that party to the risk of making a loss

- **Failure to disclose information when there is a legal duty to do so**: dishonestly failing to disclose to another person information which they are under a legal duty to disclose, thereby intending to make a gain for themselves or another, or to cause another party loss or expose that party to the risk of making a loss

- **Abuse of position**: occupying a position in which they are expected to safeguard, or not to act against, the financial interest of another person, and dishonestly abusing that position, thereby intending to make a gain for themselves or another, or to cause another party loss or expose that party to the risk of suffering loss.

6.9 The Criminal Finances Act 2017

The **Criminal Finances Act 2017** (TSO 2017) potentially makes companies and partnerships criminally liable if their staff or agents are involved in tax evasion. It applies even if the organisation was not involved in the act or had no knowledge of it.

The business will be liable if:

- **There is criminal tax evasion**: by a taxpayer or business,

- **A member of staff or agent facilitated the tax evasion**: by aiding or abetting the taxpayer or business in the evasion of tax, and

- **The business failed to prevent the member of staff or agent from committing the offence**: a business has a defence if it had reasonable prevention procedures in place, or in the circumstances it was unreasonable or unrealistic to have such procedures in place.

The maximum penalty under the Act is a conviction and unlimited fine.

Chapter Roundup

- Crime is **conduct prohibited by the law**. Financial crime can be international in nature, and there is a need for international co-operation to prevent it.

- Insider dealing is the statutory offence of **dealing** in securities while in **possession** of **inside information** as an insider, the securities being price-affected by the information.

- The law on insider dealing has had some **limitations**, and new offences, such as market abuse, have been brought in to reduce security-related crime.

- **Market abuse** relates to behaviour which amounts to abuse of a person's position regarding the stock market.

- Money laundering is the attempt to **make money from criminal activity appear legitimate**, by disguising its original source.

- In the UK, there are various offences relating to **money laundering**, including tipping off a money launderer (or suspected money launderer) and failing to report reasonable suspicions.

- **Bribery** is a serious offence which often relates to the **offering** and **receiving** of **gifts** or **hospitality**.

- **Criminal offences** in relation to **winding up** include: making a declaration of solvency without reasonable grounds and fraudulent trading.

Quick Quiz

1   Insider dealing is a criminal offence.

   True ☐

   False ☐

2   Fill in the blanks:

   Inside information is '....... ....' relating to a .... of **securities** that are price-affected and not to securities generally.

3   Define money laundering.

4   Which one of the following is **not** a UK offence relating to money laundering?

   A   Concealing the proceeds of criminal activity
   B   Tipping off
   C   Dealing in price affected securities
   D   Failing to report suspicion of money laundering

5   A business will be criminally liable where an employee assists in tax evasion.

   True ☐

   False ☐

Answers to Quick Quiz

1   True. Insider dealing is a criminal offence.

2   **Inside information** is '**price sensitive information**' relating to a **particular issuer** of **securities** that are price-affected and not to securities generally.

3   **Money laundering** is the term given to attempts to make the proceeds of crime appear respectable.

   It covers any activity by which the apparent source and ownership of money representing the proceeds of income are changed so that the money appears to have been obtained legitimately.

4   C. This could be insider dealing, if the person dealing was an insider and was using inside information.

5   False. Under the Criminal Finances Act 2017, a business is only liable if it failed to prevent the facilitation of tax evasion. It has a defence if it had reasonable prevention procedures in place or if it was unreasonable or unrealistic for it to have such procedures.

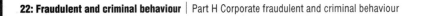

Now try the questions below from the Practice Question Bank

Number
49, 50, 51

BPP
LEARNING MEDIA

Practice question and answer bank

Question 1

In the English system of courts, which of the following offences would only be heard at a magistrates' court?

A   Summary offences
B   'Triable either way' offences
C   Indictable offences   **(1 mark)**

Question 2

In the English criminal law system, which court would hear an appeal regarding a decision by a magistrates' court?

A   The Supreme Court
B   The County Court
C   The Crown Court
D   The Court of Appeal   **(2 marks)**

Question 3

In the English civil law system, which **two** of the following are the parties involved in a case?

(1)   Prosecution
(2)   Accused
(3)   Defendant
(4)   Claimant

A   1 and 4
B   1 and 2
C   2 and 3
D   3 and 4   **(2 marks)**

Question 4

In the context of English law, which of the following is **not** an advantage of binding precedent?

A   General legal principles are established
B   The law is based on actual, rather than theoretical, cases
C   Mistakes by judges are eliminated
D   The law is flexible and can develop with changing circumstances   **(2 marks)**

Question 5

In the English legal system, one role of a judge is to interpret statute law.

Which rule of statutory interpretation considers what the legislation is trying to achieve?

A   Golden rule
B   Purposive approach
C   Literal rule
D   Contextual rule   **(2 marks)**

Question 6

Which of the following is an example of a standard form contract?

A A contract between a mobile phone company and a private individual
B A contract of employment between a private individual and a small local shop
C A verbal agreement between two private individuals
D A contract for the sale of a house between two private individuals **(2 marks)**

Question 7

In the law of contract, which of the following would be regarded as valid, binding acceptance?

A A tender to perform one task
B Posting a letter of acceptance
C A counter-offer
D Acceptance 'subject to contract' **(2 marks)**

Question 8

Which of the following statements regarding the adequacy and sufficiency of consideration is correct?

A Consideration does not need to be sufficient but must be adequate
B Consideration does not need to have a value to be sufficient
C Consideration is sufficient if it has an identifiable value **(1 mark)**

Question 9

Which of the following statements regarding consideration is correct?

A Consideration can be in the form of any act, even if that act is impossible to perform
B Performance of an illegal act is valid consideration
C Past consideration is sufficient to create liability on a bill of exchange
D Suffering some loss or detriment is not valid consideration **(2 marks)**

Question 10

Which of the following statements concerning the incorporation of terms into contracts is correct?

A A history of consistent dealings between the parties is not sufficient to incorporate terms into a contract
B Particularly unusual or onerous terms in a contract must be sufficiently highlighted
C A person is not bound by a contract they have signed if they have not read it **(1 mark)**

Question 11

A term may be implied into a contract by

(i) Statute

(ii) Trade practice, unless an express term overrides it

(iii) The court, to provide for events not contemplated by the parties

(iv) The court, to give effect to a term which the parties had agreed upon but failed to express because it was obvious

(v) The court, to override an express term which is contrary to normal custom

A (ii) and (iii) only
B (i), (ii) and (iv) only
C (i), (iv) and (v) only
D (i), (ii), (iv) and (v) only   (2 marks)

Question 12

Which of the following describes liquidated damages?

A A specific sum payable in the event of a breach of contract
B A genuine pre-estimate of losses payable in the event of breach of contract
C A sum equal to the amount of work done plus an element of profit that is payable in the event of a breach of contract   (1 mark)

Question 13

Which of the following statements in relation to damages for breach of contract is correct?

A In order to claim damages an innocent party is required to take reasonable steps to mitigate their losses

B Damages are not payable in relation to mental distress

C Damages to rectify a defect are still payable even if they are wholly disproportionate to the size of the breach

D Damages in the form of a penalty clause are valid and enforceable   (2 marks)

Question 14

In January Elle offered to buy Jane's boat for £3,000. Jane immediately wrote a letter to Elle saying 'For a quick sale I would accept £3,500. If you are not interested please let me know as soon as possible.' Elle did not see the letter until March when she returned from a business trip but then replied. 'I accept your offer. I trust that if I pay £3,000 now, you can wait until June for the remaining £500.' On receiving the letter, Jane attached a 'sold' sign to the boat but forgot to reply to Elle

(a)   Which of the following correctly describes the content of Jane's letter to Elle?

      O   An acceptance

      Ø   A counter-offer

      O   A revocation

      O   An offer   **(2 marks)**

(b)   Which of the following statements concerning the content of Jane's letter to Elle is correct?

      O   The content is valid indefinitely

      O   The content expired the day after the letter was delivered

      Ø   The content is valid for a reasonable time

      O   The content was never valid   **(2 marks)**

(c)   Which of the following statements concerning the situation between Jane and Elle is correct?

      O   There is an open offer from Elle but no acceptance from Jane

      Ø   There is a valid contract between them

      O   There is a valid offer and acceptance but no consideration

      O   There is no contract due to lack of intention between Elle and Jane   **(2 marks)**

                                                   (Total = 6 marks)

Question 15

In the context of the tort of negligence, what is the legal effect of *res ipsa loquitur*?

A   The claimant must prove that they acted reasonably
B   The claimant must prove that the defendant was negligent
C   The defendant must prove that they were not negligent   **(1 mark)**

Question 16

To establish a case of 'passing-off', what must the claimant prove?

A   There is some similarity between the name of the defendant's business and that of the claimant
B   The defendant is using a similar business model to the claimant
C   The consumer purchased fake goods
D   The name of the defendant's business is similar enough to the claimant's to mislead the consumer

                                                  (2 marks)

BPP
LEARNING MEDIA

Question 17

In employment law, which of the following statements concerning employment contracts is correct?

A   Consideration is not required in an employment contract

B   Employment contracts may include terms implied by custom and practice of the industry

C   Employment contracts must be in writing   **(1 mark)**

Question 18

In the context of employment law and statutory protection for the self-employed, which of the following statements is correct?

A   The self-employed are entitled to a minimum wage

B   The self-employed are entitled to a minimum notice period

C   The self-employed are entitled to protection from unfair dismissal

D   There is no statutory employment protection available to the self-employed   **(2 marks)**

Question 19

In employment law, which of the following types of dismissal occurs when no notice is given to the employee?

A   Unfair dismissal

B   Constructive dismissal

C   Summary dismissal   **(1 mark)**

Question 20

Where an employee has been wrongfully dismissed, which of the following remedies are available to them?

A   Statutory compensation

B   Damages

C   Re-engagement

D   Re-instatement   **(2 marks)**

Question 21

Charles saw a sign advertising vacancies at a local building site. He contacted the foreman and was told *self-emp* that he would be required but that, because work depended on the weather conditions, he would not be given an employment contract – he would be accountable for his own income tax and National Insurance. The foreman added that he would be provided with tools and that at the beginning of each day he would be told which site he would work on that day. Lateness or theft of materials would lead to his dismissal.

Nick commences employment under a three-year contract with Equis Ltd on 1 August 20X6. On 10 July 20X9 he is given notice that the contract is not to be renewed. On dismissal, all employees of Equis Ltd are entitled only to the statutory minimum notice period.

(a) Which of the following statements about Charles is correct?

O   Charles is an independent contractor because he does not have an employment contract

☑   Charles is an independent contractor because he is required to pay his own income tax and national insurance

O   Charles is an employee because he is given work tools and told which site he must work at

O   Charles is an employee because under the terms of the agreement he can be dismissed for lateness or theft of materials   **(2 marks)**

(b) Has Nick been given sufficient notice in regards to the termination of his employment contract and why?

O   Yes, because the contract was for a fixed term and therefore no notice is necessary

☒   Yes, even though the contract was for a fixed term, Equis Ltd was required to give Nick at least two week's notice which it did

O   No, Nick was entitled to three months' notice which he was not given

☒   No, Nick was entitled to a month's notice which he was not given   **(2 marks)**

(c) Which **TWO** of the following compensation claims can Nick make?

☑   Wrongful dismissal

☐   Unfair dismissal

☐   Redundancy

☑   Loss of earnings   **(2 marks)**

                                                                          (Total = 6 marks)

Question 22

'Holding out' is a key element of which form of agency?

A   Agency by estoppel
B   Agency by necessity
Ⓒ   Agency by implied agreement   **(1 mark)**

Question 23

What is the extent of an agent's ostensible authority?

A   What is usual in the circumstances only

B   What is implied from the agency relationship only

C   What the principal gives the agent expressly only

D   What is usual in the circumstances and what the principal gives them expressly or impliedly

(2 marks)

Question 24

In the context of partnership law, a partner's actual authority to bind the partnership in a contract is determined by which of the following?

A   What is agreed between the partners

B   The perception third parties have of the purpose of the partnership

C   The actual purpose of the partnership

(1 mark)

Question 25

To wind up a Limited Liability Partnership (LLP), which of the following is required?

A   An order from the Registrar of Companies

B   It must be formally wound up

C   A deed signed by the partners

D   A court order

(2 marks)

Question 26

Which of the following companies does not have share capital?

A   A public company

B   A company limited by guarantee

C   An unlimited liability company

(1 mark)

Question 27

Which of the following is a company that has its shares traded on a public stock exchange?

A   Unlimited company

B   Listed company

C   Public company

D   Private company

(2 marks)

Question 28

Before it can trade, which of the following criteria must a public company meet?

A   Its shares must be listed on a stock exchange

B   It must have appointed an auditor

C   It must obtain a trading certificate from the Registrar of Companies

(1 mark)

Question 29

Which of the following statements concerning promoters is correct?

A   A promoter may not make a profit as a result of their position

B   An accountant who acts in a professional capacity in the formation of a company is a promoter

C   A promoter may not own shares in the company that they are forming

D   A promoter that acts as an agent for others must not put themselves into a position where their own interests clash with that of the company they are forming   **(2 marks)**

Question 30

In regards to a company changing its articles of association, which of the following statements is correct?

A   A company must send copies of the amended articles to the Registrar of Companies within 28 days of the amendment taking place

B   A company may only change its articles once in a financial year

C   A company requires a special or written resolution with a 75% majority to change its articles

     (1 mark)

Question 31

Under the Companies Act 2006, which of the following parties is contractually bound by a company's constitution?

A   Members in a capacity other than as a member

B   The company

C   Third parties with a business relationship with the company

D   Company directors   **(2 marks)**

Question 32

National Hair Brushes plc was incorporated in June 20X6. The directors have received a letter from another company, Lancashire Hair Brushes plc, stating that it was incorporated in 20X5, that its business is being adversely affected by the use of the new company name and demanding that National Hair Brushes plc changes the company name.

(a) Which **TWO** of the following are means that companies can use to change their name?

- [✓] Ordinary resolution
- [ ] Special resolution
- [ ] Extra-ordinary resolution
- [✓] Any means provided in its articles **(2 marks)**

(b) Which **THREE** of the following would Lancashire Hair Brushes plc need to prove in order to establish that it is a victim of 'passing-off'

- [✓] Confusion has arisen because of National Hair Brushes' use of its registered name
- [✓] The company has incurred losses due to National Hair Brushes' use of its registered name
- [✓] The company lays claim to something exclusive and distinctive
- [ ] The company lays claim to something that is not in general use **(2 marks)**

(c) Which of the following could Lancashire Hair Brushes plc ask to compel National Hair Brushes Inc to change its name?

- O The Registrar of Companies
- ⊘ The Company Names Adjudicator
- O The *London Gazette*
- O The Official Receiver **(2 marks)**

(Total = 6 marks)

Question 33

Which of the following statements correctly describes a rights issue?
A An offer to debentureholders to purchase shares in the company
B An offer to existing shareholders to purchase further shares in the company
C The allotment of additional shares to existing shareholders in proportion to their holdings
(1 mark)

Question 34

Which of the following statements correctly describes a company's called up share capital?

A The type, class, number and amount of shares issued and allotted to shareholders
B The maximum amount of share capital that a company can have in issue
C The amount the company has required shareholders to pay on existing shares
D The amount shareholders have paid on existing shares **(2 marks)**

Question 35

A floating charge will crystallise on the occurrence of which of the following events?

A   Sale of the assets subject to the charge
B   Resignation of the finance director
C   The chargee appointing a receiver   **(1 mark)**

Question 36

In the context of debentures, which of the following **must** be created using a debenture trust deed?

A   Debenture stock
B   A single debenture
C   Register of debenture holders
D   Series debentures   **(2 marks)**

Question 37

Which type of dividend is paid by the issue of additional shares?

A   Scrip dividends
B   Equity dividends
C   Capital dividends   **(1 mark)**

Question 38

Dividends that are paid part of the way through a company's financial year are known by which of the following names?

A   Interim dividends
B   Semi-dividends
C   Dividends paid in specie
D   Preference dividends   **(2 marks)**

Question 39

Reginald owns 100 shares of Linsey Ltd. Each share has a nominal value of £2.50 and Reginald paid £1.00 per share on issue.

Linsey Ltd also issued some debentures which are secured as follows. A fixed charge over a property in favour of Margaret on 1 May 20X7. It then created a floating charge in favour of Chris over the same property on 13 May 20X7. The company has Chris's charge registered on 25 May 20X7, and Margaret's charge on 29 May 20X7.

(a) What is the extent of Reginald's liability in the event of Linsey Ltd's liquidation?

- O £250, being the nominal value of the shares he owns (£2.50 × 100)
- O £100, being the amount he paid on the shares on issue (£1.00 × 100)
- Ø £150, being the amount unpaid on the shares that he owns (£1.50 × 100)
- O Zero liability   **(2 marks)**

(b) Which of the following statements concerning debentureholders is correct?

- O Debentureholders have a right to share in the profits of the company
- Ø Debentureholders are creditors of the company
- O Debentureholders have a right to vote at company meetings
- O Debentureholders have a right to buy debentures at a discount to their nominal value
                                                                               (2 marks)

(c) Which of the following statements concerning the priority of Margaret and Chris' debentures is correct?

- O Margaret's charge has priority because it was created first
- Ø Margaret's charge has priority because it is a fixed charge
- O Chris' charge has priority because it is a floating charge
- O Chris' charge has priority because Margaret's charge was not registered correctly
                                                                               (2 marks)

                                                                      (Total = 6 marks)

Question 40

Which of the following statements correctly describes a Chief Executive Officer's (Managing Director's) actual authority?

A   The authority that the Chief Executive Officer says to others they have
B   The authority that the board expressly gives to them
C   The authority that is usual for a Chief Executive Officer   **(1 mark)**

Question 41

Which of the following is a director who has not been validly appointed but is held out by the company to be a director?

A   De facto director
B   De jure director
C   Alternate director
D   Shadow director   **(2 marks)**

Question 42

A company secretary is a company officer that **must** be appointed by which of the following companies?

A   Public limited company
B   Private limited company
C   Unlimited liability company

(1 mark)

Question 43

A company auditor has which of the following rights?

A   To vote in the company's general meetings
B   To attend board meetings
C   To appoint non-executive directors
D   To access, at all times, the books, accounts and vouchers of the company

(2 marks)

Question 44

What is the notice period for a meeting at which a special resolution is to be voted on?

A   14 days
B   21 days
C   28 days

(1 mark)

Question 45

The ordinary business of an annual general meeting includes which of the following?

A   Reducing the company's share capital
B   Changing the company's name
C   Appointing an administrator
D   Approving the payment of dividends

(2 marks)

Question 46

The Chief Executive Officer of KL Ltd is Jeremy. Jeremy also runs his own business, FD Ltd, in his spare time. KL Ltd recently contracted to buy a significant amount of commercial goods from FD Ltd. Jeremy attended the KL Ltd board meeting that approved the contract and voted in favour of it, without revealing his association with FD Ltd.

(a) Which of the following statements concerning a director's fiduciary duties is correct?

- O   Fiduciary duties are based on criminal law principles
- O   Fiduciary duties are less onerous than a director's contractual obligations
- ☑   Under fiduciary duties, directors must account for any profits they make in their role as director
- ☒   Fiduciary duties require directors to disclose information that they feel is relevant

(2 marks)

(b) Which **TWO** of the following director's statutory duties did Jeremy breach?

- [ ] Duty to exercise reasonable skill, care and diligence
- [✓] Duty to exercise independent judgement
- [ ] Duty to declare interest in proposed transaction or arrangement
- [✓] Duty to declare interest in an existing transaction or arrangement   **(2 marks)**

(c) Which **TWO** of the following consequences might Jeremy face for his breach of statutory duty?

- [✓] Imprisonment
- [ ] Rescission of the contract between KL Ltd and FD Ltd
- [ ] Repayment profit earned on the contract between KL Ltd and FD Ltd
- [✓] Disqualification as a director   **(2 marks)**

(Total = 6 marks)

Question 47

There are various grounds for the compulsory winding-up of a company. In which of the following situations will a court order the winding-up of a company on the 'just and equitable' ground?

A   Where 50% of the members disagree with the actions of the directors
B   Where the company has failed to pay its creditors for three months
C   When the main object of the company cannot be achieved   **(1 mark)**

Question 48

What is the name given to the person in charge of a voluntary winding-up of a company?

A   Administrator
B   Receiver
C   Chargee
D   Liquidator   **(2 marks)**

Question 49

In the offence of money laundering, what is the name given to the initial disposal of the proceeds of criminal activity?

A   Placement
B   Layering
C   Integration   **(1 mark)**

Question 50

Which of the following is a defence to a charge of insider dealing?

A   The individual had reasonable grounds to believe that the information was about to be published
B   The individual had no expectation of profit
C   The individual was not seeking to profit from the transaction personally
D   The individual had reasonable grounds to believe their action was in the public interest   **(2 marks)**

Question 51

Vlad generates a substantial income from illegal tax evasion and sought advice from Gloria (his personal accountant) on how to dispose of his illegal earnings. Gloria suggested that to disguise the source of the funds, Vlad should purchase a chain of restaurants and pass his gains from the illegal operation through the restaurants' accounts. Vlad agreed with Gloria's proposal and appointed her as the restaurant chain's finance director and together they passed the illegal money through the operation.

(a)   Which of the following describes the money laundering process known as layering?

        ○   Transferring funds from an illegal activity from business to business, or place to place, to conceal the original source

        ○   Giving funds obtained from an illegal activity the appearance of legitimate funds

        ○   Depositing funds from an illegal activity directly into an apparently legitimate business activity

        ○   Avoiding customer due diligence procedures to conceal a deposit of funds from an illegal activity   **(2 marks)**

(b)   Identify which of the following offences Gloria and Vlad have committed.

	Money laundering	Failure to report	Both offences
Gloria	○	○	○
Vlad	○	○	○

                                                                    (4 marks)

                                                                        (Total = 6 marks)

Answer 1

A Summary offences are minor offences that would only be heard at a magistrates' court. Indictable offences are serious offences that would only be heard at a Crown Court. A 'triable either way' offence is one where the accused has the choice of which court will hear the case.

Syllabus area A1(b)

Answer 2

C In the English criminal law system, an appeal regarding a decision by a magistrates' court would be heard by the Crown Court.

Syllabus area A1(b)

Answer 3

D A civil law case is between the claimant and defendant. A criminal law case is between the prosecution and accused.

Syllabus area A1(a)

Answer 4

C Mistakes by judges can never be eliminated. The other statements are advantages of binding precedent.

Syllabus area A2(a)

Answer 5

B Under the purposive approach to statutory interpretation, the purpose, or what the legislation is trying to achieve, is considered.

Syllabus area A2(c)

Answer 6

A A standard form contract is a document set out by large organisations that states the terms on which its customers will do business with it. There is no negotiation, either the customer accepts the terms or goes elsewhere. The contracts in the other options include scope for negotiation.

Syllabus area B1(a)

Answer 7

B The postal rule states that acceptance is valid when a letter of acceptance is posted. The other options are not regarded as acceptance – a counter-offer is, in effect, a new offer; acceptance 'subject to contract' means the offeree is agreeable to the terms but the parties should negotiate a valid contract; and a tender to perform a task is an offer.

Syllabus area B1(d)

Answer 8

C   Consideration must be sufficient but not necessarily adequate. It must have some identifiable value to be sufficient.

Syllabus area B1(f)

Answer 9

C   Past consideration is sufficient to create liability on a bill of exchange – this is one of the few exceptions to the rule on past consideration. Suffering loss or detriment is valid consideration. Impossible or illegal acts are not valid consideration.

Syllabus area B1(e)

Answer 10

B   Particularly unusual or onerous terms must be highlighted. Previous consistent dealings can be enough to incorporate terms into a contract. A person is deemed to have read a contract if they have signed it.

Syllabus area B2(c)

Answer 11

B   Courts will not imply factors outside the contemplation of the parties or override an express term.

Syllabus area B2(b)

Answer 12

B   Liquidated damages is a genuine pre-estimate of losses payable in the event of a breach of contract. A penalty clause is a fixed amount payable on breach of contract.

Syllabus area B3(c)

Answer 13

A   Innocent parties are required to mitigate their losses. Damages are payable in respect of mental distress – although the scope of such payments is limited. Damages that are wholly disproportionate to the breach are not payable (*Ruxley Electronics and Construction Ltd v Forsyth 1995*). Penalty clauses are void and not enforceable.

Syllabus area B3(c)

Answer 14

(a)   A counter-offer. Elle's offer of £3,000 is an offer so therefore Jane's letter, which changes the terms of the offer, forms a counter-offer.

(b)   The content is valid for a reasonable time. There is nothing to indicate that Jane's (counter) offer is not still open in March. An offer may be expressed to last for a specified time. It then expires at the end of that time. If, however, there is no express time limit set, it expires after a reasonable time.

(c)   There is a valid contract between them. Following *Butler Machine Tool Co v Ex-Cell-O Corp (England) 1979*, a counter-offer introduces new terms (price). The price is therefore £3,500. As to date of payment, it would appear that the attachment of a 'sold' sign to the boat is confirmation that the revised terms proposed by Jane are acceptable.

Answer 15

C   Where *res ipsa loquitur* applies, the burden of proof is reversed and the defendant must prove that they were not negligent.

Syllabus area B4(c)

Answer 16

D   'Passing-off' involves the use of a business name, trademark or description that is similar enough to another business so that the consumer is misled into believing that one business is that of another.

Syllabus area B4(b)

Answer 17

B   Employment contracts may be oral or in writing. As with all contracts, consideration is required. Terms can be implied from trade custom and practice.

Syllabus area C1(b)

Answer 18

D   There is no statutory employment protection for the self-employed.

Syllabus area C1(a)

Answer 19

C   Dismissal without notice is known as summary dismissal.

Syllabus area C2(b)

Answer 20

B   Wrongful dismissal involves a breach of contract and damages are payable for the loss of notice period only. The other remedies are for unfair dismissal.

Syllabus area C2(c)

Answer 21

(a)   Charles is an employee because he is given work tools and told which site he must work at. Even though he does not receive an employment contract the facts indicate a contract of service because of the degree of control the employer has over him (in that the employer provides tools and tells him where to work). The right of the employer to dismiss Charles does not in itself make Charles an employee. The fact that Charles must pay his own income tax and national insurance does not in itself make him an independent contractor.

(b)   Yes, even though the contract was for a fixed term, Equis Ltd was required to give Nick at least two weeks' notice which it did. Dismissal occurs when a fixed-term contract is not renewed even though such an eventuality is implicit in the fact that the agreement has a fixed term. At the point Nick was dismissed he had only completed two full years of employment and therefore he was entitled to a minimum of two weeks' notice. Equis Ltd gave more than this and therefore Nick was granted sufficient notice of dismissal.

(c)   Unfair dismissal and redundancy. Nick's dismissal entitles him to claim for redundancy pay and/or compensation for unfair dismissal if he can prove the requisite facts. However, non-renewal cannot give rise to a claim for wrongful dismissal, which is only possible when there has been summary dismissal or dismissal with less than the required period of notice. Loss of earnings is not a recognised claim for dismissal.

Answer 22

A   Agency by estoppel occurs where one party 'holds out' to another that a person is acting as their agent.

Syllabus area D1(b)

Answer 23

D   Ostensible authority is wide ranging and includes whatever is usual in the circumstances plus whatever the principal gives the agent either expressly or impliedly.

Syllabus area D1(c)

Answer 24

A   Partnership authority is based on agency law. Actual authority is determined by what the partners agree.

Syllabus area D2(c)

Answer 25

B   To dissolve an LLP, it needs to be wound up, in a similar way to a company.

Syllabus area D2(e)

Answer 26

B   Companies limited by guarantee do not have share capital.

Syllabus area D3(c)

Answer 27

B   A public company does not have to have its shares traded on a public stock exchange. If it does so, then it becomes known as a listed (or quoted) company.

Syllabus area D3(c)

Answer 28

C   Before it can trade, a public company must be issued with a trading certificate from the Registrar of Companies. None of the other options are criteria for obtaining a trading certificate.

Syllabus area D4(c)

Answer 29

D   Where a promoter acts as an agent for others, they must not put themselves into a position where their own interests clash with those of the company. Accountants acting in a professional capacity are not promoters. A promoter may make a legitimate profit as a result of their position. There is nothing to stop a promoter from owning shares in the company that they form.

Syllabus area D4(a)

Answer 30

C   A special or written resolution with a 75% majority is sufficient to change a company's articles. There is no restriction on the number of times a year the articles may be changed. Copies of the amended articles must be submitted to the Registrar within 15 days of the amendment taking effect.

Syllabus area D4(g)

Answer 31

B   A company's constitution contractually binds the company and members in their capacity as members.

Syllabus area D4(e)

Answer 32

(a)   Special resolution, any means provided in its articles. A company must usually pass a special resolution to change its name. However, if its articles provide a different means then that could be used as well. Extra-ordinary resolutions do not exist under the Companies Act 2006.

(b)   Confusion has arisen because of National Hair Brushes' use of its registered name, the company lays claim to something exclusive and distinctive, the company lays claim to something that is not in general use. In order to be successful in a passing-off claim, Lancashire Hair Brushes plc will need to satisfy the court that confusion has arisen because of National Hair Brushes' use of its registered name and it lays claim to something exclusive and distinctive and not something in general use.

(c)   The Company Names Adjudicator. Lancashire Hair Brushes plc could object to the Company Names Adjudicator that the name National Hair Brushes is too like its own name and is causing confusion. They would be appealing for the Adjudicator to exercise their power under the Companies Act to compel a change of name. The other parties do not have the power to compel a change of company name.

Answer 33

B   A rights issue is an offer to existing shareholders to buy further shares in the company. A bonus issue is the allotment of additional shares to shareholders in proportion to their holdings.

Syllabus area E1(c)

Answer 34

C   Called-up share capital is the amount the company has required shareholders to pay on existing shares. A company's issued share capital is the type, class, number and amount of shares issued to shareholders. The amount existing shareholders have paid on existing shares is the paid-up share capital.

Syllabus area E1(a)

Answer 35

C   Active intervention by the chargee, such as appointing a receiver, will cause the charge to crystallise. The other options will not cause the charge to crystallise.

Syllabus area E2(d)

Answer 36

A   Out of the options, only debenture stock must be created using a debenture trust deed. Single and series debentures may use a debenture trust deed but this is not compulsory.

Syllabus area E2(b)

Answer 37

A   Scrip dividends are paid by issuing additional shares.

Syllabus area E3(b)

Answer 38

A   Dividends paid part of the way through a company's financial year are known as interim dividends. Dividends paid in specie are paid using a method other than cash.

Syllabus area E3(b)

Answer 39

(a)   £150, being the amount unpaid on the shares that he owns (£1.50 × 100). Reginald is liable to pay the unpaid capital on his shares. This is £150 (100 × £1.50).

(b)   Debentureholders are creditors of the company. Unlike shareholders, they are creditors of the company and may not vote at company meetings. They are paid interest on their loan rather than sharing in profits. Some debentures are offered for sale at a discount to their nominal value, but debentureholders have no right to such a discount.

(c)   Chris' charge has priority because Margaret's charge was not registered correctly. Margaret's charge would have taken precedence because it was created first and because it is a fixed charge, had it been registered within the allowed period of 21 days, up to 22 May. However, it was not registered until 29 May, and Chris's charge was legitimately registered in the period between 22 and 29 May when Margaret's charge was void. The court would probably have allowed late registration of Margaret's charge but not at the expense of Chris's rights.

Answer 40

B   A CEO's actual authority is whatever the board gives to them.

Syllabus area F1(c)

Answer 41

A   A de jure director is expressly appointed. A de facto director is held out by the company to be a director. A shadow director is neither, they are a person whose instructions the actual directors are accustomed to follow. An alternate director is appointed by a director of a company to attend and vote for them at board meetings they are unable to attend.

Syllabus area F1(a)

Answer 42

A   Only a public limited company must have a company secretary.

Syllabus area F2(a)

Answer 43

D   A company auditor has the right, at all times, to access the books, accounts and vouchers of the company.

Syllabus area F2(b)

Answer 44

A   14 days' notice is required for a special resolution.

Syllabus area F3(b)

Answer 45

D   Approving dividends is included in the ordinary business of an AGM.

Syllabus area F3(a)

Answer 46

(a)   Under fiduciary duties, directors must account for any profits they make in their role as director. A fiduciary duty is one based on common (not criminal) law principles of trust and honesty. Such a duty requires directors to make full disclosure of information and includes a strict duty to account for any profits received as a result of being a director. Fiduciary duties are more onerous than generally arises under a contractual or tort relationship.

(b)   Duty to declare interest in proposed transaction or arrangement, duty to declare interest in an existing transaction or arrangement. Jeremy has not disclosed either his interest in FD Ltd or his interest in this particular contract. Under s 177 of the Companies Act the interest should have been stated at the board meeting that Jeremy attended which approved the contract. It was not. It should also have been declared under s 182 of the Companies Act once it had occurred – but it was not either.

(c)   Rescission of the contract between KL Ltd and FD Ltd, repayment profit earned on the contract between KL Ltd and FD Ltd.

Breach of statutory duties comes under the civil law rather than criminal law. Consequences for breach of duty are:

- Damages payable to the company where it has suffered loss
- Restoration of company property
- Repayment of any profits made by the director
- Rescission of contract (where the director did not disclose an interest)

Therefore imprisonment and disqualification are not consequences that Jeremy will face.

Answer 47

C   The 'just and equitable' ground will be applied where the object of the company cannot be achieved, such as, for example, where the company only existed to 'work a particular patent' *Re German Date Coffee Co 1882*. The other options are not grounds for the just and equitable winding-up of a company.

Syllabus area G1(b)

Answer 48

D   A liquidator is in charge of a voluntary winding-up. The official receiver is in charge of a compulsory winding-up. An administrator is in charge of an administration.

Syllabus area G1(a)

Answer 49

A   The initial disposal of the proceeds of a crime is known as placement.

Syllabus area H1(c)

Answer 50

B   'No expectation of profit' is a valid defence to a charge of insider dealing. The other options are not valid defences.

Syllabus area H1(a)

Answer 51

(a)   Transferring funds from an illegal activity from business to business, or place to place, to conceal the original source.

The three stages of the money laundering process are:

- Placement – the initial disposal of the proceeds of the initial illegal activity into apparently legitimate business activity or property

- Layering – transferring monies from business to business, or place to place, to conceal the original source

- Integration – laundered money now has the appearance of legitimate funds

(b)   Gloria has assisted in Vlad's money laundering, so may be convicted of money laundering under the Proceeds of Crime Act. She may also be found guilty of failure to report under the Proceeds of Crime Act.

Vlad is guilty of the main offence of money laundering under the Proceeds of Crime Act.

Bibliography

BPP
LEARNING MEDIA

Bribery Act 2010. (2010). London, TSO.

Civil Liability (Contribution) Act 1978. (1890). London, HMSO.

Companies (Audit, Investigation and Community Enterprise) Act 2004. (2004). London, TSO.

Companies Act 2006 (Strategic Report and Directors' Report) Regulations 2013. (2013) SI 2013/1970. London, TSO.

Companies Act 2006. (2006). London, TSO.

Company Directors Disqualification Act 1986. (1986). London, HMSO.

Constitutional Reform Act 2005. (2005). London, TSO.

Consumer Rights Act 2015. (2015). London, TSO.

Contracts (Rights of Third Parties) Act 1999. (1999). London, TSO.

Crime and Courts Act 2013. (2013). London, TSO.

Criminal Finances Act 2017. (2017). London, TSO.

Criminal Justice Act 1993. (1993). London, HMSO.

Employment Act 2002. (2002). London, TSO.

Employment Relations Act 1999. (1999). London, TSO.

Employment Rights Act 1996. (1996). London, TSO.

Employment Tribunals (Constitution and Rules of Procedure) Regulations 2013. (2013) SI 2013/1237. London, TSO.

Enterprise Act 2002. (2002). London, TSO.

Enterprise and Regulatory Reform Act 2013. (2013). London, TSO.

Equality Act 2010. (2010). London, TSO.

Financial Services and Markets Act 2000. (2000). London, TSO.

Fraud Act 2006. (2006). London, TSO.

Health and Safety at Work Act 1974. (1974). London, HMSO.

Human Rights Act 1998. (1998). London, TSO.

Insolvency Act 1986. (1986). London, HMSO.

Interpretation Act 1978. (1978). London, HMSO.

Limited Liability Partnership Act 2000. (2000). London, TSO.

Limited Partnership Act 1907. (1907). London, TSO.

Management of Health and Safety at Work Regulations 1999. (1999) SI 1999/3242. London, TSO.

Money Laundering Regulations 2017. (2017) SI 2017/692. London, TSO.

National Minimum Wage Act 1998. (1998). London, TSO.

Partnership Act 1890. (1890). London, HMSO.

Proceeds of Crime Act 2002. (2002). London, TSO.

Road Traffic Act 1972. (1972). London, HMSO.

Small Business, Enterprise and Employment Act 2015. (2015). London, TSO.

The Civil Procedure Rules 1998. (1998) SI 1998/3132. London, TSO.

Trade Union and Labour Relations (Consolidation) Act 1992. (1992). London, HMSO.

Unfair Contract Terms Act 1977. (1977). London, HMSO.

Unfair Dismissal and Statement of Reasons for Dismissal (Variation of Qualifying Period) Order 2012. (2012) SI 2012/0000. London, TSO.

Unsolicited Goods and Services Act 1971. (1978). London, HMSO.

Working Time Regulations 1998. (1998) SI 1998/1833. London, TSO.

http://www.nationalarchives.gov.uk/doc/open-government-licence/version/3/

Contains public sector information licensed under the Open Government Licence v3.

Case bibliography

A Company, Re 1983 ....[1983] 1 BCC 98937

Adams v Cape Industries plc 1990 .... [1990] 2 WLR 657

ADT Ltd v BDO Binder Hamlyn 1995 ....[1996] BCC 808

Airfix Footwear Ltd v Cope 1978 .... [1978] ICR 1210

Alderslade v Hendon Laundry 1945 .... [1945] 1 KB 189

Alexander v Rolls Royce Motor Cars Ltd 1995.. [1996] RTR 95

Anglia Television Ltd v Reed 1972 ....[1972] 1 QB 60

Anns v Merton London Borough Council 1977 .... [1977] 2 WLR 1024

Autoclenz v Belcher 2011 .... [2011] ICR 1157

Azimut-Benetti SpA v Darrell Marcus Healey 2010...........................[2010] EWHC 2234 (Comm)

Balfour v Balfour 1919 ....[1919] 2 KB 571

Barclays Bank plc v Grant Thornton UK LLP 2015 .... [2015] EWHC 320 (Comm)

Barings plc v Coopers & Lybrand 1997... [1997] 1 BCLC 427

Barnett v Chealsea and Kensington HMC 1969 ....[1969] 1 QB 428

BCCI (Overseas) Ltd v Ernst & Whinney 1997 .... [1997] 3 WLR 849

Beard v London General Omnibus Co 1900 ....[1900] 2 QB 530

Bellinger v Bellinger 2003 ....[2003] 2 AC 467

Beswick v Beswick 1968 ....[1968] 1 AC 58

Bettini v Gye 1876 ....1 QBD 183

Bigg v Boyd Gibbons 1971 .... [1971] 1 WLR 913

Bolton v Stone 1951..[1951] 1 AC 850

Boston Deep Sea Fishing and Ice Co v Ansell 1888 .... 39 ChD 339

Branca v Cobarro 1947 ....[1947] 1 KB 854

Bridge v Campbell Discount Co 1962.. [1962] 2 WLR 439

British Broadcasting Corporation v Farnworth 1998 .... [1998] ICR 1116

British Steel Corpn v Cleveland Bridge and Engineering Co Ltd 1984 ....[1984] 1 All ER 504

Brogden v Metropolitan Railway Co 1877 ....2 App Cas 666

Brown v British Abrasive Wheel Co 1919..[1919] 1 CH 290

Bunge Corporation v Tradax SA 1981 .... [1981] 1 WLR 711

Butler Machine Tool Co v Ex-cell-O Corp (England) 1979.................................. [1979] 1 WLR 401

Byrne v Van Tienhoven 1880..5 CPD 344

C & P Haulage v Middleton 1983 .... [1983] 1 WLR 1461

Candler v Crane, Christmas & Co 1951 ....[1951] 2 KB 164

Caparo Industries plc v Dickman and Others 1990 ....[1990] 2 AC 605

Carlill v Carbolic Smoke Ball Company 1893...[1893] 1 QB 256

Carslogie Steamship Co Ltd v Royal Norwegian Government 1952 ....[1952] 1 AC 292

Casey's Patents 1892, Re...[1892] 1 CH 104

Cassidy v Ministry of Health 1951 ....[1951] 2 KB 343

Cehave v Bremer 1975 .... [1975] 3 WLR 447

Central London Property Trust v High Trees House 1947....................................[1947] 1 KB 130

Centrebind Ltd 1966, Re .... [1967] 1 WLR 377

Chapelton v Barry UDC 1940..[1940] 1 KB 532

Chappell & Co v Nestle Co 1960...[1960] AC 87

Charter v Sullivan 1957 .... [1957] 2 WLR 528

Cimex Tissues Ltd 1994, Re...[1995] 1 BCLC 409

City Equitable Fire and Insurance Co Ltd 1925, Re...[1925] 1 CH 407

Corkery v Carpenter 1950 ....[1951] 1 KB 102

Currie v Misa 1875 ....10 LR Exch 153

Curtis v Chemical Cleaning Co 1951 ....[1951] 1 KB 805

D and C Builders v Rees 1966 .... [1966] 2 WLR 288

D' Jan of London Ltd 1993, Re .... [1993] BCLC 646

Dafen Tinplate Co Ltd v Llanelly Steel Co (1907) Ltd 1920 .... [1920] 2 CH 124

Daimler Co Ltd v Continental Tyre and Rubber Co (GB) Ltd 1916........................... [1916] 2 AC 307

Dann v Hamilton 1939.. [1939] 1 KB 509

DHN Food Distributors v Tower Hamlets LBC 1976 .... [1976] 1 WLR 852

Dick Bentley Productions v Arnold Smith Motors 1965 .... [1965] 1 WLR 623

Dickinson v Dodds 1876 .... 2 ChD 463

Donoghue v Stevenson 1932 .... [1932] 1 AC 562

Dorchester Finance Co Ltd v Stebbing 1989 .... [1989] BCLC 498

DPP v Bull 1995.. [1995] QB 88

Dubai Aluminium Co Ltd v Salaam and ors 2002 .... [2002] 3 WLR 1913

Dunlop Pneumatic Tyre Co Ltd v New Garage & Motor Co Ltd 1915 .... [1915] 1 AC 847

Ebrahimi v Westbourne Galleries Ltd 1973.. [1973] 1 AC 360

Edwards v Skyways Ltd 1964... [1964] 1 WLR 349

Eley v Positive Government Security Life Assurance Co 1876 .... 1 ExD 88

Entores v Miles Far Eastern Corporation 1955 .... [1955] 3 WLR 48

Erlanger v New Sombrero Phosphate Co 1878 .... 3 App Cas 1218

Ewing v Buttercup Margarine Co Ltd 1917... [1917] 2 CH 1

F G Films Ltd 1953, Re .... [1953] 1 WLR 483

Faccenda Chicken Ltd v Fowler 1986 .... [1986] ICR 297

Fairchild v Glenhaven Funeral Services Ltd & Others 2002................................... [2002] 3 WLR 89

Ferguson v John Dawson & Partners 1976... [1976] 1 WLR 1213

Financings Ltd v Stimson 1962... [1962] 1 WLR 1184 2

Fisher v Bell 1961... [1961] 1 QB 394

Fitzgerald v Lane & Patel 1989... [1989] 1 AC 328

Foakes v Beer 1884 .... 9 App Cas 605

Ford Motor Co (England) Ltd v Armstrong 1915... [1915] 31 TLR 267

Fox-Davis v Burberry 2017 .... [2017] EWCA Civ 1129

Franks v Reuters Ltd 2003 .... [2003] ICR 1166

Freeman & Lockyer v Buckhurst Park Properties (Mangal) Ltd 1964 .... [1964] 2 QB 480

Gardiner v Sevenoaks RDC 1950 .... [1950] 66 TLR 1091

GE Tunbridge Ltd 1995, Re .... [1995] 1 BCLC 409

German Date Coffee Co 1882, Re... 20 ChD 169

GHSP Inc v A B Electronic Ltd 2010... [2010] CILL 2915

Gilford Motor Co Ltd v Home 1933 .... [1933] 1 CH 935

Glasbrook Bros v Glamorgan CC 1925 .... [1925] 1 AC 270

Glasgow Corporation v Taylor 1922.. [1922] 1 AC 44

Great Northern Railways v Witham 1873 .... 9 LR CP 16

Greenhalgh v Arderne Cinemas Ltd 1946.. [1946] 1 All ER 512

Greenhalgh v Arderne Cinemas Ltd 1950.. [1951] Ch 286

H and Others 1996, Re .... [1996] 1 AC 563

H Parsons (Livestock) v Uttley Ingham 1978 .... [1978] 1 QB 791

Halls v David and Another 1989 .... [1989] 1 WLR 745

Harris v Sheffield United F.C. Ltd 1988 .... [1988] 1 QB 77

Harvey v Facey 1893 .... [1893] 1 AC 552

Hedley Byrne & Co Ltd v Heller and Partners Ltd 1963....................................... [1964] 1 AC 465

Hely-Hutchinson v Brayhead Ltd 1968 ....[1968] 1 QB 549

Henry v London General Transport Services Ltd 2001 .... [2002] ICR 910

HFC Bank v Midland Bank 2000 ....[2000] FSR 176

Hickman v Kent or Romney Marsh Sheepbreeders Association 1915...............[1915] 1 CH 881

High Table Ltd v Horst and Others 1997 .... [1998] ICR 409

Hivac Ltd v Park Royal Scientific Instruments Ltd 1946 ....[1946] 1 CH 169

Hogg v Cramphorn 1966..[1966] 3 WLR 995

Hollier v Rambler Motors 1972 ....[1972] 2 QB 71

Holwell Securities v Hughes 1974 .... [1974] 1 WLR 155

Hong Kong Fir Shipping Co Ltd v Kawasaki Kisa Kaisha Ltd 1961 ....[1961] EWCA Civ 7

Horton v Horton 1961 ....[1961] 1 QB 215

Houghton v Trafalgar Insurance 1954 ....[1954] 1 QB 247

Household Fire and Carriage Accident Insurance Co v Grant 1879 ....4 ExD 216

Howard Smith Ltd v Ampol Petroleum Ltd 1974 ....[1974] 1 AC 821

ICI v Shatwell 1965...[1965] 1 AC 656

Industrial Development Consultants Ltd v Cooley 1972 .... [1972] 1 WLR 443 2

Interfoto Picture Library Ltd v Stiletto Visual Programmes Ltd 1988....................... [1988] 2 WLR 615

International Sports Ltd v Thomson 1980..[1980] IRLR 340

Isle of Wight Tourist Board v Coombes 1976... [1976] IRLR 413

J Spurling Ltd v Bradshaw 1956 .... [1956] 1 WLR 461

Jarvis v Swans Tours 1973 ....[1973] 1 QB 233

JEB Fasteners Ltd v Marks, Bloom & Co 1981 ....[1981] 3 All ER 289

Jolley v London Borough of Sutton 2000.. [2000] 1 WLR 1082

Jones v Padavatton 1969 .... [1969] 1 WLR 328

Jones v Vernons Pools 1938...[1938] 2 All ER 626

Jubilee Cotton Mills Ltd v Lewes 1924 ....[1924] 1 AC 958

Kleinwort Benson Ltd v Malaysia Mining Corpn Bhd 1989 .... [1989] 1 WLR 379

Knightley v Johns 1982... [1982] 1 WLR 349

Lamb v Camden LBC 1981.. [1981] 2 WLR 1038

Latimer v AEC Ltd 1952 ....[1952] 2 QB 701

Law Society v KPMG Peat Marwick 2000.. [2000] 1 WLR 1921

Lee v Lee's Air Farming Ltd 1960.. [1960] 3 WLR 758

Les Affreteurs v Walford 1919 ....[1919] AC 801

L'Estrange v Graucob 1934..[1934] 2 KB 394

Lewis Shops Group Ltd v Wiggins 1973 .... [1973] ICR 335

Lexi Holdings plc (in administration) v Luqman 2009..[2009] EWCA Civ 117

Linden Gardens Trust Ltd v Lenesta Sludge Disposals Ltd 1994 ....[1994] 1 AC 85

Lister and ors v Hesley Hall Ltd 2001...[2002] 1 AC 215

Liverpool City Council v Irwin 1977...[1977] 1 AC 239

MacDonald v Costello 2011..[2012] 1 QB 244

MacNaughton (James) Papers Group Ltd v Hicks Anderson & Co 1991 ....[1991] 1 All ER 134

Mahon v Osborne 1939...[1939] 2 KB 14

Mareva Compania Naviera SA v International Bulkcarriers SA 1975.....................[1975] 2 Lloyd's Rep 509

Massey v Crown Life Assurance 1978.. [1978] ICR 590

McArdle 1951, Re...[1951] 1 CH 669

McKew v Holland, Hannen and Cubbitts (Scotland) Ltd 1969....................................[1969] 3 All ER 1621

Merritt v Merritt 1970 .... [1970] 1 WLR 1211

Mersey Docks & Harbour Board v Coggins & Griffiths (Liverpool) 1947 .... [1947] 1 AC 1

Preston (formerly Moore) v President of the Methodist Conference 2013 .... [2013] 2 AC 163

Mihalis Angelos, The 1971 .... [1970] 3 WLR 601

Moorcock, The 1889 .... 14 PD 64

Morgan Crucible Co plc v Hill Samuel Bank Ltd and others 1990 .... [1991] 2 WLR 655

Motorola v Davidson and Melville Craig 2001 .... [2001] IRLR 4, EAT

Neale v Merrett 1930 .... [1930] WN 189 M

Nicolene v Simmonds 1953 .... [1953] 2 WLR 717

North Riding Garages v Butterwick 1967 .... [1967] 2 QB 56

NRG v Bacon and Woodrow and Ernst & Young 1995 .... [1995] 1 All ER 976

O'Kelly v Trusthouse Forte Plc 1983 .... [1983] ICR 728

Olley v Marlborough Court 1949 .... [1949] 1 KB 532

Ooregum Gold Mining Co of India v Roper 1892 .... [1892] 1 AC 125

Oscar Chess v Williams 1957 .... [1957] 1 WLR 370

Overend Gurney & Co v Gibb 1872 .... 5 LR HL 480

Panorama Developments (Guildford) Ltd v Fidelis Furnishing Fabrics Ltd 1971 .... [1971] 3 WLR 440

Paris v Stepney Borough Council 1951 .... [1951] 1 AC 367

Partridge v Crittenden 1968 .... [1968] 1 WLR 1204

Payzu Ltd v Saunders 1919 .... [1919] 2 KB 581

Pender v Lushington 1877 .... 6 ChD 70

Pepper v Hart 1992 .... [1993] 1 AC 593

Pepper v Webb 1969 .... [1969] 1 WLR 514

Peso Silver Mines v Cropper 1966 .... [1966] SCR 673

Pharmaceutical Society of Great Britain v Boots Cash Chemists (Southern) 1952 .... [1953] 2 WLR 427

Photo Productions v Securicor Transport 1980 .... [1980] UKHL 2

Pilkington v Wood 1953 .... [1953] 3 WLR 522

Poussard v Spiers 1876 .... 1 QBD 410

Powell v Kempton Park Racecourse 1899 .... [1899] 1 AC 143

Powell v Lee 1908 .... [1908] 99 LT 284

Produce Marketing Consortium Ltd 1989, Re .... [1989] 1 WLR 745

R & B Customs Brokers Ltd v United Dominions Trust Ltd 1988 .... [1988] 1 WLR 321

R in Right of British Columbia v Federal Business Development Bank 1988 .... [1988] 1 WWR1 (B.C.C)

R v Bailey 2005 .... [2005] EWCA Crim 3487

R v Clarke 1927 .... [1927] 40 CLR 227

R v Grantham 1984 .... [1984] QB 675

R v OLL Ltd 1994 .... Unreported

Ramsgate Victoria Hotel Co v Montefiore 1866 .... 1 LR Exch 109

Rayfield v Hands 1958 .... [1958] 2 WLR 851

Ready Mixed Concrete (South East) v Ministry of Pensions & National Insurance 1968 ...... [1968] 2 QB 497

Regal (Hastings) Ltd v Gulliver 1942 .... [1942] UKHL 1

Richley v Faull 1965 .... [1965] 1 WLR 1454

Rose and Frank v Crompton 1923 .... [1923] 2 KB 261

Routledge v McKay 1954 .... [1954] 1 WLR 615

Royal Bank of Scotland v Bannerman Johnstone Maclay 2005 .... [2005] 1 SC 579

RTS Flexible Systems Ltd v Molkerei Alois Müller GmbH 2010 .... [2010] UKSC 14

Ruxley Electronics and Construction Ltd v Forsyth 1995 .... [1996] 1 AC 344

Salomon v Salomon & Co Ltd 1897 ....[1897] 1 AC 22

Sanders v Neale 1974 ....[1974] ICR 565

Sayers v Harlow UDC 1958 ....[1958] 1 WLR 623

Scammell v Ouston 1941 ....[1941] 1 AC 251

Secretary of State for Trade and Industry v Thornbury 2008 ....[2008] 1 BCLC 139

Selectmove 1994, Re ....[1995] 1 WLR 474

Sevenoaks Stationers (Retail) Ltd 1991, Re ....[1991] 1 CH 164

Shanklin Pier Ltd v Detel Products Ltd 1951 ....[1951] 2 KB 854

Sidebottom v Kershaw, Leese & Co Ltd 1920 ....[1920] 1 CH 154

Siebe Gorman & Co Ltd v Barclays Bank Ltd 1979 ....[1979] 2 Lloyd's Rep 142

Sigsworth 1935, Re ....1935] 1 CH 89

Simpkins v Pays 1955 ....[1955] 1 WLR 975 2

Smith v Leech Brain & Co 1962 ....[1962] 2 WLR 148

Spartan Steel and Alloys Ltd v Martin & Co Ltd 1973 ....[1973] 1 QB 27

Spectrum Plus 2005, Re ....[2005] 2 AC 680

St Albans City and District Council v International Computers Ltd 1994 ....[1995] 21 FSR 686

Stevenson v McLean 1880 ....5 QBD 346

Stevenson v Teeside Bridge & Engineering Co Ltd 1971 ....[1971] 1 ALL ER 296

Stringfellow v McCain Foods GB 1984 ....[1984] RPC 450

The Heron II 1969 ....[1967] UKHL 4

The Wagon Mound 1961 ....[1961] AC 388

Thompson Ltd v Robinson (Gunmakers) Ltd 1955 ....[1955] 1 CH 177

Thompson v LMS Railway 1930 ....[1930] 1 KB 41

Thornton v Shoe Lane Parking Ltd 1971 ....[1971] 2 WLR 585

Tiffin v Lester Aldridge LLP 2012 ....[2012] ICR 647

Towers v Premier Waste Management Ltd 2012 ....[2012] IRLR 73 (CA)

Troutbeck SA v White and Todd 2013 ....[2013] EWCA Civ 1171

Unit Construction Co Ltd v Bullock 1960 ....[1960] 1 AC 351

Uno, Secretary of State for Trade and Industry v Gill 2004, Re ....[2004] All ER (D) 345

Vaux and Associated Breweries v Ward 1969 ....[1969] 113 Sd. J. 920 (Div'l Ct.)

Victoria Laundry (Windsor) v Newman Industries 1949 ....[1949] 2 K.B 528

Walker v Crystal Palace FC 1910 ....[1910] 1 KB 87

Warner Bros Pictures Inc v Nelson 1937 ....[1937] 1 KB 209

Watteau v Fenwick 1893 ....[1893] 1 QB 346

White & Carter (Councils) v McGregor 1961 ....[1962] 1 AC 413

White v Bristol Aeroplane Co Ltd 1953 ....[1953] 2 WLR 144

Whitely v Chappel 1868 ....(1868) LR 4 QB 147

Williams and Another v Natural Life Health Foods Ltd 1998 ....[1998] UKHL 17

Williams v Compair Maxam Ltd 1982 ....[1982] ICR 156

Williams v Roffey Bros & Nicholls (Contractors) Ltd 1990 ....[1990] 2 WLR 1153

Wilsher v Essex AHA 1988 ....[1988] 1 AC 1074

Wilson v Racher 1974 ....[1974] ICR 428

Wright v North Ayrshire Council 2013 ....[2014] ICR 77

Yates Building Co v R J Pulleyn & Sons (York) 1975 ....[1975] 237 EG 183

Yenidje Tobacco Co Ltd 1916, Re ....[1916] 2 CH 426

List of cases and index

A company 1983, Re 338
Adams v Cape Industries plc 1990 194
Adams v Lindsell 1818 49
ADT Ltd v BDO Binder Hamlyn 1995 117
Airfix Footwear Ltd v Cope 1978 129
Alderslade v Hendon Laundry 1945 82
Alexander v Rolls Royce Motor Cars Ltd 1995 96
Anglia Television Ltd v Reed 1972 95
Anns v Merton London Borough Council 1977 108
Anon 1495 62
Autoclenz v Belcher 2011 130
Azimut-Benetti SpA v Darrell Marcus Healey 2010 98

B alfour v Balfour 1919 63
Bannerman v White 1861 74
Barclays Bank plc v Grant Thornton UK LLP 2015 119
Barings plc v Coopers & Lybrand 1997 118
Barnett v Chealsea and Kensington HMC 1969 110
BCCI (Overseas) Ltd v Ernst & Whinney 1997 118
Beard v London General Omnibus Co 1900 114
Bellinger v Bellinger 2003 31
Beswick v Beswick 1968 .... 22, 67
Bettini v Gye 1876 78
Bigg v Boyd Gibbons 1971 42
Blyth v Birmingham Water Works 1856 108
Bolton v Stone 1951 108
Boston Deep Sea Fishing and Ice Co v Ansell 1888 133
Bracebridge Engineering v Darby 1990 133
Bradbury v Morgan 1862 46
Branca v Cobarro 1947 47
Bridge v Campbell Discount Co 1962 98
British Broadcasting Corporation v Farnworth 1998 155
British Steel Corpn v Cleveland Bridge and Engineering Co Ltd 1984 47
Brogden v Metropolitan Railway Co 1877 46
Brown v British Abrasive Wheel Co 1919 221
Bunge Corporation v Tradax SA 1981 78
Butler Machine Tool Co v Ex-cell-O Corp (England) 1979 44
Byrne v Van Tienhoven 1880 45

C & P Haulage v Middleton 1983 95
Candler v Crane, Christmas & Co 1951 115
Caparo Industries plc v Dickman and Others 1990 .... 108, 116
Carlill v Carbolic Smoke Ball Company 1893 .... 41, 48, 50
Carslogie Steamship Co Ltd v Royal Norwegian Government 1952 112
Casey's Patents 1892, Re 58
Cassidy v Ministry of Health 1951 128
Cavendish Square Holding BV v Talal El Makdessi 2015 98
Cehave v Bremer 1975 78
Central London Property Trust v High Trees House 1947 62
Centrebind Ltd 1966, Re 335
Chapelton v Barry UDC 1940 80
Chappell & Co v Nestle Co 1960 59

Charter v Sullivan 1957 95
Cimex Tissues Ltd 1994, Re 257
City Equitable Fire and Insurance Co Ltd 1925, Re 294
Collins v Godefroy 1831 59
Corkery v Carpenter 1950 26
Curtis v Chemical Cleaning Co 1951 81

D and C Builders v Rees 1966 62
D' Jan of London Ltd 1993, Re 295
Dafen Tinplate Co Ltd v Llanelly Steel Co (1907) Ltd 1920 221
Daimler Co Ltd v Continental Tyre and Rubber Co (GB) Ltd 1916 193
Dann v Hamilton 1939 113
De Barnardy v Harding 1853 99
DHN Food Distributors v Tower Hamlets LBC 1976 194
Dick Bentley Productions v Arnold Smith Motors 1965 75
Dickinson v Dodds 1876 45
Donoghue v Stevenson 1932 108
Dorchester Finance Co Ltd v Stebbing 1977 294
DPP v Bull 1995 26
Dubai Aluminium Co Ltd v Salaam and ors 2002 114
Dunlop Pneumatic Tyre Co Ltd v New Garage & Motor Co Ltd 1915 97

Ebrahimi v Westbourne Galleries Ltd 1973 .... 194, 337
Edwards v Skyways Ltd 1964 64
Eley v Positive Government Security Life Assurance Co 1876 224
Entores v Miles Far Eastern Corporation 1955 49
Erlanger v New Sombrero Phosphate Co 1878 203
Ewing v Buttercup Margarine Co Ltd 1917 227

F G Films Ltd 1953, Re 193
Faccenda Chicken Ltd v Fowler 1986 133
Factortame 13
Fairchild v Glenhaven Funeral Services Ltd & Others 2002 111
Felthouse v Bindley 1862 47
Ferguson v John Dawson & Partners 1976 127
Financings Ltd v Stimson 1962 46
Fisher v Bell 1961 43
Fitzgerald v Lane & Patel 1989 113
Foakes v Beer 1884 61
Ford Motor Co (England) Ltd v Armstrong 1915 97
Fox-Davis v Burberry (2017), ... 210
Franks v Reuters Ltd 2003 128
Freeman & Lockyer v Buckhurst Park Properties (Mangal) Ltd 1964 .... 166, 289

Gardiner v Sevenoaks RDC 1950 27
GE Tunbridge Ltd 1995, Re 257
German Date Coffee Co 1882, Re 337
GHSP Inc v A B Electronic Ltd 2010 39
Gilford Motor Co Ltd v Home 1933 193
Glasbrook Bros v Glamorgan CC 1925 60
Glasgow Corporation v Taylor 1922 108

Great Northern Railways v Witham 1873 48
Greenhalgh v Arderne Cinemas Ltd 1946 242
Greenhalgh v Arderne Cinemas Ltd 1950 220
Gregory and Parker v Williams 1817 67
Gunthing v Lynn 1831 41

H and Others 1996, Re 193
H Parsons (Livestock) v Uttley Ingham 1978 94
Hadley v Baxendale 1854 93
Halls v David and Another 1989 363
Harris v Sheffield United F.C. Ltd 1988 60
Hartley v Ponsonby 1857 60
Harvey v Facey 1893 42
Hedley Byrne & Co Ltd v Heller and Partners Ltd 1963 115
Hely-Hutchinson v Brayhead Ltd 1968 165
Henry v London General Transport Services Ltd 2001 132
HFC Bank v Midland Bank 2000 107
Hickman v Kent or Romney Marsh Sheepbreeders Association 1915 224
High Table Ltd v Horst and Others 1997 155
Hivac Ltd v Park Royal Scientific Instruments Ltd 1946 133
Hochster v De La Tour 1853 91
Hogg v Cramphorn 1966 292
Hollier v Rambler Motors 1972 82
Holwell Securities v Hughes 1974 49
Hong Kong Fir Shipping Co Ltd v Kawasaki Kisa Kaisha Ltd 1961 79
Horton v Horton 1961 59
Houghton v Trafalgar Insurance 1954 79
Household Fire and Carriage Accident Insurance Co v Grant 1879 49
Howard Smith Ltd v Ampol Petroleum Ltd 1974 292
Hutton v Warren 1836 76
Hyde v Wrench 1840 44

ICI v Shatwell 1965 113
Industrial Development Consultants Ltd v Cooley 1972 296
Interfoto Picture Library Ltd v Stiletto Visual Programmes Ltd 1988 82
International Sports Ltd v Thomson 1980 152
Isle of Wight Tourist Board v Coombes 1976 133

J Spurling Ltd v Bradshaw 1956 81
Jarvis v Swans Tours 1973 96
JEB Fasteners Ltd v Marks, Bloom & Co 1981 116
Jolley v London Borough of Sutton 2000 112
Jones v Padavatton 1969 64
Jones v Vernons Pools 1938 65
Jubilee Cotton Mills Ltd v Lewes 1924 205

Kleinwort Benson Ltd v Malaysia Mining Corpn Bhd 1989 65
Knightley v Johns 1982 111

Lamb v Camden LBC 1981 112
Lampleigh v Braithwaite 1615 58

Latimer v AEC Ltd 1952 109
Law Society v KPMG Peat Marwick 2000 118
Lee v Lee's Air Farming Ltd 1960 191
Les Affreteurs v Walford 1919 76
L'Estrange v Graucob 1934 80
Lewis Shops Group Ltd v Wiggins 1973 151
Lexi Holdings plc (in administration) v Luqman 2009 295
Limpus v London General Omnibus Co 1862 114
Linden Gardens Trust Ltd v Lenesta Sludge Disposals Ltd 1994 67
Lister and ors v Hesley Hall Ltd 2001 114
Liverpool City Council v Irwin 1977 77

MacDonald v Costello 2011 191
MacNaughton (James) Papers Group Ltd v Hicks Anderson & Co 1991 117
Mahon v Osborne 1939 110
Mareva Compania Naviera SA v International Bulkcarriers SA 1975 100
Massey v Crown Life Assurance 1978 127
McArdle 1951, Re 57
McKew v Holland, Hannen and Cubbitts (Scotland) Ltd 1969 111
Merritt v Merritt 1970 63
Mersey Docks & Harbour Board v Coggins & Griffiths (Liverpool) 1947 127
Mihalis Angelos, The 1971 78
Moorcock, The 1889 77
Morgan Crucible Co plc v Hill Samuel Bank Ltd and others 1990 117
Motorola v Davidson and Melville Craig 2001 129

Neale v Merrett 1930 48
Nicolene v Simmonds 1953 76
North Riding Garages v Butterwick 1967 155
NRG v Bacon and Woodrow and Ernst & Young 1995 118

O'Kelly v Trusthouse Forte Plc 1983 129
Olley v Marlborough Court 1949 81
Ooregum Gold Mining Co of India v Roper 1892 245
Oscar Chess v Williams 1957 75
Overend Gurney & Co v Gibb 1872 294

Panorama Developments (Guildford) Ltd v Fidelis Furnishing Fabrics Ltd 1971 305
Paris v Stepney Borough Council 1951 109
ParkingEye Limited v Beavis 2015 98
Partridge v Crittenden 1968 43
Payzu Ltd v Saunders 1919 96
Pender v Lushington 1877 224
Pepper v Hart 1992 29
Pepper v Webb 1969 .... 133, 146
Peso Silver Mines v Cropper 1966 296
Pharmaceutical Society of Great Britain v Boots Cash Chemists (Southern) 1952 43
Photo Productions v Securicor Transport 1980 83
Pilkington v Wood 1953 97
Pinnel's Case 1602 62
Poussard v Spiers 1876 78

Powell v Kempton Park Racecourse 1899 27
Powell v Lee 1908 50
Preston (formerly Moore) v President of the Methodist Conference 2013 131
Produce Marketing Consortium Ltd 1989, Re 363

R & B Customs Brokers Ltd v United Dominions Trust Ltd 1988 85
R in Right of British Columbia v Federal Business Development Bank 1988 257
R v Bailey 2005 356
R v Clarke 1927 50
R v Grantham 1984 361
R v OLL Ltd 1994 191
Ramsgate Victoria Hotel Co v Montefiore 1866 45
Rayfield v Hands 1958 224
Ready Mixed Concrete (South East) v Ministry of Pensions & National Insurance 1968 128
Regal (Hastings) Ltd v Gulliver 1942 296
Richley v Faull 1965 110
Roscorla v Thomas 1842 58
Rose and Frank v Crompton 1923 64
Routledge v Grant 1828 45
Routledge v McKay 1954 75
Royal Bank of Scotland v Bannerman Johnstone Maclay 2005 118
RTS Flexible Systems Ltd v Molkerei Alois Muller GmbH 2010 65
Ruxley Electronics and Construction Ltd v Forsyth 1995 96

Salomon v Salomon & Co Ltd 1897 190
Sanders v Neale 1974 156
Sayers v Harlow UDC 1958 113
Scammell v Ouston 1941 75
Secretary of State for Trade and Industry v Thornbury 2008 287
Selectmove 1994, Re 61
Sevenoaks Stationers (Retail) Ltd 1991, Re 286
Shadwell v Shadwell 1860 61
Shanklin Pier Ltd v Detel Products Ltd 1951 ....51, 67
Sidebottom v Kershaw, Leese & Co Ltd 1920 221
Siebe Gorman & Co Ltd v Barclays Bank Ltd 1979 257
Sigsworth 1935, Re 26
Simpkins v Pays 1955 64
Smith v Leech Brain & Co 1962 109
Spartan Steel and Alloys Ltd v Martin & Co Ltd 1973 110
Spectrum Plus 2005, Re 257
St Albans City and District Council v International Computers Ltd 1994 84
Stevenson v McLean 1880 44
Stevenson v Teeside Bridge & Engineering Co Ltd 1971 138
Stilk v Myrick 1809 60
Stringfellow v McCain Foods GB 1984 107

The Heron II 1969 94
The Wagon Mound 1961 112
Thomas v Thomas 1842 59
Thompson Ltd v Robinson (Gunmakers) Ltd 1955 95
Thompson v LMS Railway 1930 80
Thornton v Shoe Lane Parking Ltd 1971 81

Tiffin v Lester Aldridge LLP 2012 130
Towers v Premier Waste Management Ltd 2012 297
Troutbeck SA v White and Todd 2013 127
Tulk v Moxhay 1848 68
Tweddle v Atkinson 1861 66

Unit Construction Co Ltd v Bullock 1960 193
Uno, Secretary of State for Trade and Industry v Gill 2004, Re 287

Vaux and Associated Breweries v Ward 1969 155
Victoria Laundry (Windsor) v Newman Industries 1949 94

Walker v Crystal Palace FC 1910 127
Warner Bros Pictures Inc v Nelson 1937 100
Watteau v Fenwick 1893 165
Welby v Drake 1825 62
White & Carter (Councils) v McGregor 1961 92
White v Bristol Aeroplane Co Ltd 1953 241
Whitely v Chappel 1868 26
Williams and Another v Natural Life Health Foods Ltd 1998 299
Williams v Carwardine 1833 50
Williams v Compair Maxam Ltd 1982 152
Williams v Roffey Bros & Nicholls (Contractors) Ltd 1990 60
Wilsher v Essex AHA 1988 111
Wilson v Racher 1974 146
Woods v Robarts 1818 62
Wright v North Ayrshire Council 2013 146

Yates Building Co v R J Pulleyn & Sons (York) 1975 48
Yenidje Tobacco Co Ltd 1916, Re 337

Acceptance, 46
Acceptance of a tender, 48
Acceptance 'subject to contract', 47
Accounting records, 211
Action for the price, 99
Actual authority, 166
Adequacy of consideration, 59
Administration, 341
Administrators, 344
Administrators' power, 345
Administrators' proposals, 345
Adoption leave and pay, 137
Advertisements, 43
Agency, 162
Agency formation, 163
Agency termination, 167
Agency workers, 128
Agent authority, 164
Agent by estoppel, 164
Agent by necessity, 164
Agent liability, 168
Agreement, 90
Allotment of shares, 243
Allotted share capital, 238
Alternate directors, 279
Annual accounts, 212
Annual general meeting (AGM), 315
Ante-natal care, 136
Anticipatory breach, 91
Apparent authority, 289
Apparent/ostensible authority, 166
Appeal court, 12
Articles of association, 219
Auction sales, 42
Auctioneers, 163
Authorised share capital, 238
Automatically fair reasons for dismissal, 152
Automatically unfair reasons for dismissal, 153

Basic award, 154
Battle of the forms, 39
Becoming a member, 236
Bill of exchange, 58
Board of directors, 280
Bonus issue, 245
Borrowing, 252
Breach of an innominate term, 91
Breach of condition, 91
Breach of contract, 90
Breach of duty of care, 108
Bribery, 358

Bribery Act 2010, 358
Brokers, 163
Business name, 227
'But for' test, 110
Bye-laws, 25

Called up share capital, 238
Capacity, 40
Capital maintenance, 266
Case management, 10
Causality, 110
Centrebinding, 335
Certificate of incorporation, 205
Chancery Division, 11
Charge, 256
Chartered corporations, 185
Chief Executive Officer, 279
Civil court structure, 7
Civil Division, 12
Civil law, 6
Civil Liability (Contribution) Act 1978, 176
Civil Procedure Rules Act 1998, 9
Class meetings, 324
Class rights, 239
Collateral contract, 51
Commercial agents, 163
Common law, 5, 18
Communication of acceptance, 48
Community Interest Companies (CICs), 185
Companies Act 2006, 181
Companies Act 2006 (Strategic Report and
   Directors' Report) Regulations 2013, 212
Company, 183
Company auditor, 305
Company auditor appointment, 305
Company auditor duties, 307
Company auditor liability, 308
Company auditor removal, 308
Company auditor remuneration, 307
Company auditor resignation, 309
Company auditor rights, 308
Company constitution, 218
Company constitution as a contract, 224
Company Directors Disqualification Act 1986,
   284
Company meeting convening, 318
Company meetings, 314
Company meetings minutes, 324
Company meetings notice, 320
Company meetings polls, 323
Company meetings proceedings, 320

Company meetings voting, 323
Company name, 225
Company Names Adjudicators, 227
Company objects, 222
Company registered office, 228
Company registration, 204
Company re-registration, 206
Company resolutions, 316
Company resolutions requisitioning, 319
Company secretary, 304
Company secretary appointment, 304
Company secretary duties, 304
Company secretary powers and authority, 305
Compensatory award, 154
Compulsory liquidation, 336
Condition, 78
Confirmation statement, 213
Consideration, 56
Constitutional Reform Act 2005, 12
Constructive dismissal, 145, 146
Consumer Rights Act 2015, 84
Content, 40
Contextual rule, 27
Continous employment, 138
Contra proferentem rule, 82
Contract, 38
Contract by deed, 41
Contract of employment, 126
Contract terms, 74
Contracts (Rights of Third Parties) Act 1999, 68
Contributories, 339
Contributory negligence, 113
Control test, 127
Corporate personality, 184
Corporations sole, 185
Cost of cure, 96
Counter-offer, 44, 48
County Court, 9
Court of Appeal, 12
Court of first instance, 12
Creditors' meeting, 345
Creditors' voluntary liquidation, 335
Crime, 6
Crime and Courts Act 2013, 360
Criminal court structure, 8
Criminal Division, 12
Criminal Finances Act 2017, 364
Criminal Justice Act 1993, 352
Criminal law, 6
Cross-offers, 50
Crown Court, 10
Crystallisation, 257

Damages, 93
De facto directors, 278

De jure directors, 278
Debenture, 253
Debenture trust deed, 254
Declaration of incompatibility, 31
Declaration of solvency, 334, 361
Defences to negligence, 113
Deferred prosecution agreement, 360
Delegated legislation, 24
Director, 278
Directors' appointment, 280
Directors' disqualification, 284
Directors' disqualification for commercial
    misjudgement, 286
Directors' disqualification under model articles,
    284
Directors' disqualification under statute, 284
Directors' duties, 289
Directors' personal liability, 299
Directors' powers, 287
Directors' removal, 283
Directors' remuneration, 281
Directors' rotation, 283
Directors' service agreements, 282
Directors' vacation of office, 282
Discharge of contract, 90
Disciplinary procedure, 150
Dissemination of information, 356
Distinguishing the facts, 20
Distributable profit, 269
Dividend, 268
Duty not to accept benefits from third parties,
    297
Duty of care, 107
Duty to act within powers, 291
Duty to avoid conflicts of interest, 295
Duty to declare interest in proposed transaction
    or arrangement, 297
Duty to exercise independent judgement, 293
Duty to exercise reasonable skill, care and
    diligence, 294
Duty to promote the success of the company,
    293

Ejusdem generis, 27
Electronic contract, 39, 68
Employee, 126
Employee's duties, 133
Employer's duties, 133
Employment Act 2002, 132
Employment contract, 131
Employment Rights Act 1996, 125, 143
Employment Tribunals (Constitution and Rules
    of Procedure) Regulations 2013, 147
Enabling legislation, 24
Enterprise Act 2002, 342

Enterprise and Regulatory Reform Act 2013, 137, 147
Equality Act 2010, 135
Equitable remedies, 99
Equity, 18, 239
Equity (law), 5, 18
Equity (share), 239
Equity share capital, 239
European Convention for the Protection of Human Rights and Fundamental Freedoms, 29
European Court of Human Rights, 13
European Court of Justice, 13
Exclusion clause, 79
Executed consideration, 57
Executive director, 279
Executory consideration, 57
Exemption clauses, 79
Exhibition of goods for sale, 43
Expectation interest, 94
Express authority, 165
Express term, 75
Expressio unius est exclusio alterius, 28
Extrinsic aids, 28

Factors, 163
Failing to disclose, 357
Failure of a condition, 46
Failure to report, 356
Fair dismissal, 145
Family Division, 11
Fast track, 10
Fiduciary duty, 203, 290
Financial (economic) loss, 110
Financial crime, 352
Financial Services and Markets Act 2000, 355
Fixed charge, 256
Flexible working, 137
Floating charge, 256
Form, 40
Fraud Act 2006, 364
Fraudulent trading, 192, 361
Freedom of contract, 38
Freezing injunctions, 100
Frustration, 90
Fundamental breach, 83

General meetings, 315
General rules of interpretation, 27
Genuine consent, 40
Golden rule, 26

Health and safety, 137

Health and Safety at Work Act 1974, 137
High Court, 11
Holding out, 166
Human Rights Act 1998, 29

Implied authority, 165
Implied term, 76
In pari materia, 28
Incapacitation, 91
Indictable offences, 8
Initial accounts, 271
Injunction, 18, 100
Innominate terms, 78
Inside information, 353
Insider dealing, 353
Insolvency Act 1986, 331
Integration, 357
Integration test, 127
Intention to create legal relations, 63
Interim accounts, 271
Intrinsic aids, 28
Invitation for tenders, 43
Invitation to treat, 42
Issued share capital, 238
Issuing shares at a premium, 247
Issuing shares at a premium and at a discount, 245

Judicial precedent, 19
Just and equitable ground for winding up, 337

Lapse of time, 45
Laundering, 356
Law, 4
Law reports, 19
Layering, 357
Legal personality, 183, 190
Legality, 40
Legislation, 23
Letters of comfort, 65
Letters of intent, 47
Liability limited by guarantee, 185
Liability limited by shares, 185
Limited by guarantee, 185
Limited by shares, 185
Limited companies, 185
Limited liability, 184
Limited liability partnership (LLP), 177
Limited Liability Partnership Act 2000, 119, 177
Limited Partnership Act 1907, 178
Liquidated damages, 97
Liquidation, 332
Liquidation – order of payments, 340

Liquidator, 333
Literal rule, 26
Loan capital, 238, 253
London Gazette, 209

Magistrates' Court, 8
Main purpose rule, 82
Managing Director, 279
Manipulating devices, 355
Manipulating transactions, 355
Market abuse, 355
Market distortion, 355
Market price rule, 95
Maternity leave and pay, 136
Maternity rights, 136
Measure of damages (Contract law), 94
Member, 236, 340
Members' voluntary liquidation, 334
Memorandum of association, 218
Micro-entities regime, 190
Minors, 40
Minutes, 324
Mischief rule, 26
Misuse of information, 355
Mitigation of loss, 96
Mobility clauses, 146
Model Articles of Association, 219
Money laundering, 356
Money Laundering Regulations 2017, 357
Multinational company, 190
Multiple (economic reality) test, 128
Multi-track, 10

National Minimum Wage Act 1998, 134
Negative pledge clauses, 259
Negligence, 107
Nominal value, 237
Non-executive director, 279
Noscitur a sociis, 28
Notice period, 144
Novus actus interveniens, 111

Obiter dicta, 20
Off the shelf companies, 206
Offer, 41
Offer for sale, 243
Official receiver, 338
Onerous terms, 82
Option contract, 45
Orders in council, 25
Ordinary shares, 239
Overrule, 22

Paid up share capital, 238
Par, 245
Parent company, 188
Parental leave, 137
Parliamentary procedure, 24
Parliamentary sovereignty, 23
Partly paid shares, 245
Partners' authority, 175
Partners' liability, 176
Partnership, 172
Partnership Act 1890, 172
Partnership agreement, 174
Partnership formation, 174
Partnership termination, 174
Passing-off, 106
Passing-off action, 226
Past consideration, 57
Paternity leave and pay, 136
Penalty clause, 98
Per incuriam, 21
Performance, 90
Personal guarantees, 252
Persuasive precedents, 21
Placement, 357
Placing, 243
Poll, 323
Postal rule, 49
Potentially fair reasons for dismissal, 151
Powers of an individual director, 289
Powers of the Chief Executive Officer (Managing Director), 288
Precedent, 19
Pre-emption rights, 244
Preference shares, 239
Pre-incorporation contract, 203
Presumptions of statutory interpretation, 28
Priority of charges, 259
Private Acts, 24
Private company, 186, 187
Private law, 5
Privity of contract, 66
Privy Council, 13
Proceeds of Crime Act 2002, 356
Professional advice, 114
Professional Regulations, 25
Profits available for distribution, 269
Promissory estoppel, 62
Promoter, 202
Promoters' duties, 202
Proxy, 322
Public Acts, 24
Public company, 186
Public law, 5
Public offer, 243
Purposive approach, 27

Quantum meruit, 99
Quasi-partnership, 194
Queen's Bench Division, 11
Quorum, 321
Quoted companies, 189

Ratio decidendi, 20
Rectification, 18
Redeemable shares, 241
Redundancy, 154
Redundancy pay, 155
Re-engagement, 154
Register of charges, 261
Register of debentureholders, 211, 254
Register of directors, 210
Register of members, 210
Register of people with significant control, 210
Registered companies, 185
Registrar of Companies, 209
Registration of charges, 260
Reinstatement, 153
Rejection, 44
Reliance interest, 94
Remedies for unfair dismissal, 153
Remoteness of damage, 110
Remoteness of damage (Contract law), 93
Remoteness of damage (Tort), 112
Renunciation, 91
Representation, 74
Repudiation, 90
Repudiatory breach, 91
Request for information, 44
Res ipsa loquitur, 110
Rescission, 18, 101
Reverse, 22
Revocation of an offer, 45
Rights issue, 244
Road Traffic Act 1972, 68
Romalpa clause, 258
Rules of Court, 25
Rules of statutory interpretation, 26

Secured debentureholders' rights, 261
Service contract, 211
Settlement agreements, 147
Shadow directors, 278
Share, 237
Share capital, 238
Share capital reduction, 266
Share premium, 247
Share premium account, 247
Shared parental leave, 136

Shareholder agreements, 225
Show of hands, 323
Silence, 47
Simple contract, 41
Single alternative inspection location (SAIL), 209
Single member private companies, 325
Small Business, Enterprise and Employment Act 2015, 147, 206
Small claims track, 10
Small companies regime, 189
Sole traders, 182
Solvency statement, 267
Special notice, 319
Special resolutions, 317
Specific performance, 18, 100
Standard form contract, 38, 79
Stare decisis, 19
Statement of intention, 42
Statute law, 5
Statutory books, 209
Statutory corporations, 185
Statutory duties, 134
Statutory instruments, 25
Statutory interpretation, 26
Statutory shared parental pay, 136
Strategic report, 212
Subscriber shares, 236
Sufficiency of consideration, 59
Summary dismissal, 145, 146
Summary offences, 8
Supply of information, 41, 42
Supreme Court, 12

Termination by death, 46
Termination of offer, 44
Terms implied by custom, 76
Terms implied by statute, 77
Terms implied by the courts, 77
The Management of Health and Safety at Work Regulations 1999, 137
Time off work, 136
Tipping off, 356
Tort, 106
Trade Union and Labour Relations (Consolidation) Act 1992, 65
Trading certificate, 208
Transfer of undertakings, 139
Treasury shares, 241
Triable either way, 8
Types of company, 185
Types of law, 4

Ultra vires, 223
Undistributable reserves, 270
Unenforceable contract, 40
Unfair Contract Terms Act 1977, 83
Unfair dismissal, 145, 148
Unfair Dismissal and Statement of Reasons for
    Dismissal (Variation of Qualifying Period)
    Order 2012, 149
Unilateral contracts, 50
Unlimited liability company, 185
Unsecured debentureholders' rights, 261
Unsolicited Goods and Services Act 1971, 47

Valid consideration, 56
Validity factors, 40
Variation of class rights, 241
Veil of incorporation, 191
Veil of incorporation – ignoring, 191
Vicarious liability, 114
Void contract, 40
Voidable contract, 40
Volenti non fit injuria, 113
Voluntary liquidation, 333

Warranty, 78
Worker, 126
Working Time Regulations 1998, 138
Work-life balance, 136
Written particulars, 132
Written resolutions, 317
Wrongful dismissal, 145, 147
Wrongful trading, 192, 361

Review Form – Corporate and Business Law (LW) (ENG) (01/18)

Please help us to ensure that the ACCA learning materials we produce remain as accurate and user-friendly as possible. We cannot promise to answer every submission we receive, but we do promise that it will be read and taken into account when we update this Study Text.

Name: _____   Address: _____

_____

_____

How have you used this Study Text?
(Tick one box only)

☐ On its own (book only)

☐ On a BPP in-centre course _____

☐ On a BPP online course

☐ On a course with another college

☐ Other _____

Why did you decide to purchase this Study Text? *(Tick one box only)*

☐ Have used BPP Study Texts in the past

☐ Recommendation by friend/colleague

☐ Recommendation by a lecturer at college

☐ Saw information on BPP website

☐ Saw advertising

☐ Other _____

During the past six months do you recall seeing/receiving any of the following?
(Tick as many boxes as are relevant)

☐ Our advertisement in *ACCA Student Accountant*

☐ Our advertisement in *Pass*

☐ Our advertisement in *PQ*

☐ Our brochure with a letter through the post

☐ Our website www.bpp.com

Which (if any) aspects of our advertising do you find useful?
(Tick as many boxes as are relevant)

☐ Prices and publication dates of new editions

☐ Information on Study Text content

☐ Facility to order books

☐ None of the above

Which BPP products have you used?

Study Text	☑	*Passcards*	☐	*Other*	☐
Kit	☐	*i-Pass*	☐		

Your ratings, comments and suggestions would be appreciated on the following areas.

	Very useful	Useful	Not useful
Introductory section	☐	☐	☐
Chapter introductions	☐	☐	☐
Key terms	☐	☐	☐
Quality of explanations	☐	☐	☐
Examples	☐	☐	☐
Exam focus points	☐	☐	☐
Questions and answers in each chapter	☐	☐	☐
Fast forwards and chapter roundups	☐	☐	☐
Quick quizzes	☐	☐	☐
Question Bank	☐	☐	☐
Answer Bank	☐	☐	☐
Index	☐	☐	☐

Overall opinion of this Study Text.	*Excellent* ☐	*Good* ☐	*Adequate* ☐	*Poor* ☐

Do you intend to continue using BPP products?   *Yes* ☐   *No* ☐

On the reverse of this page is space for you to write your comments about our Study Text. We welcome your feedback.

The author of this edition can be emailed at: accaqueries@bpp.com

TELL US WHAT YOU THINK

Please note any further comments and suggestions/errors below. For example, was the text accurate, readable, concise, user-friendly and comprehensive?